JUSTICE STEPHEN FIELD

Shaping Liberty from the Gold Rush to the Gilded Age

Paul Kens

University Press of Kansas

This book has been supported by grants from the National
Endowment for the Humanities, an independent federal agency.

Published by the University Press of Kansas (Lawrence, Kansas
66049), which was organized by the Kansas Board of Regents and is
operated and funded by Emporia State University, Fort Hays State
University, Kansas State University, Pittsburg State University, the
University of Kansas, and Wichita State University

Library of Congress Cataloging-in-Publication Data

Kens, Paul.
Justice Stephen Field : shaping liberty from the gold rush to the
gilded age / Paul Kens.
p.   cm.
Includes bibliographical references and index.
ISBN 0-7006-0817-6 (alk. paper)
1. Field, Stephen Johnson, 1816-1899.   2. United States. Supreme
Court—Biography.   3. Judges—United States—Biography.   I. Title.
KF8745.F5K46   1997
347.73′2634—dc20
[B]
[347.3073534]
[B]   96-46575

British Library Cataloguing in Publication Data is available.

Printed in the United States of America

10 9 8 7 6 5 4 3 2 1

The paper used in this publication meets the minimum requirements
of the American National Standard for Permanence of Paper for
Printed Library Materials Z39.48-1984.

CONTENTS

For Carla,
and in memory of my parents,
Eugene Kens and Betty Kens Dugan

ACKNOWLEDGMENTS

This project has spanned several years and taken me from the East Coast to the West in search of information. It is a pleasure to finally be able to thank the many people who have helped me along the way. My wife, Carla Underhill, was truly a partner in the project. She is a physician, not an academic or writer. But she is an avid reader and has a keen eye for vagueness and inconsistencies. I suspect she may have this book memorized. She read every draft, providing both the encouragement I needed and critique I trusted.

Friends and colleagues have been extremely generous in sharing their ideas and their time. Robert L. Clinton, James W. Ely Jr., and R. Hal Williams have provided helpful ideas and comments along the way. As the book began to take shape, they, along with Christian Fritz, Howard Gillman, Lewis Gould, Paul Lowengrub, Wallace Mendelson, and Bartholomew Sparrow, reviewed the entire manuscript. Their comments improved the work immeasurably. Harold Hyman and Edward Keynes got me off to a good start with their reviews of my prospectus. R. Ben Brown and Linda Przybyszewski provided valuable comments on an early version of chapter 6, and Paula Mitchell Marks graciously let me use her then unpublished manuscript on the gold rush. My friends Robert Clinton, Pat Conge, and Gwenn Okruhlik often forced me to clarify my thinking while explaining it to them.

I also owe a debt of gratitude to people who helped me find the time to complete this project. Jack Gravitt, Dean of Liberal Arts at Southwest Texas State University, has consistently displayed confidence in me and provided research time when I most needed it. The pace of my work was sped along when I received a National Endowment for the Humanities Fellowship. I also received a travel-to-collections grant and a summer stipend from the N.E.H. The enthusiasm of Carl Dolan, outreach officer for the N.E.H., encouraged me to apply for funding. When I did, the office of Research and Sponsored Programs at Southwest Texas State, under the leadership first of Paul Fonteyn and then of Marion Tangum, provided invaluable expertise and critique for each of my grant proposals.

Several people helped me with important details. Christian Axsiom undertook the difficult job of checking references. He and Rebecca Conway Axsiom also created the index. Jody Neal Post and Dean Curtis served as research assistants in the early stages. Mike Briggs, Editor-in-Chief at the University Press of Kansas, offered ideas as well as encouragement as he gently prodded this project along.

Much of my research was done at the Perry–Castaneda Library and the Tarlton Law Library–Joseph D. Jamail Center for Legal Research at the University of Texas, Austin. I also often turned to the Albert B. Alkek Library at Southwest Texas State University. Throughout the course of the project I was fortunate to have the help of many efficient and knowledgeable staff members at these libraries and the other university libraries, historical societies, and local libraries I visited.

My thanks to all these people who made this book better than it otherwise would have been.

INTRODUCTION

On the evening of December 28, 1849, the steamship *California* passed the Golden Gate on its fourth round-trip voyage between Panama City and San Francisco.[1] On board was a thirty-three-year-old attorney who was destined to become a prominent personality in early California history and one of the most significant figures in American law. He was Stephen J. Field, a New Yorker who, like his fellow passengers, was following the scent of gold.

The story that follows is not just about Stephen Field, nor is it intended to be a comprehensive survey of the constitutional doctrine of his time. It is a story about law, society, and politics during the last half of the nineteenth century. And it is a story about a generation's attempts to define the nature of liberty. Stephen Field, who served as a city judge, California Supreme Court justice, and justice of the United States Supreme Court, provides a clear link to the development of American legal doctrine during the era. But Field was more than a judge; he was an irascible, outspoken, and colorful character whose personality and politics made him a lightning rod for many of the important conflicts of his time.

Field's story begins with the gold rush not only because he had a significant impact on the development of California but also because the gold rush left an indelible imprint on him. Field's experiences in this great adventure forever affected his views about power, privilege, liberty, and the role of a judge. Moreover, the forty-niners' migration to the West raises in sharp relief the ideals and dreams many Americans shared in the decade before the Civil War.

In chapter 1 I describe the struggles of California's pioneers, most of whom faced their first ordeal before they even arrived in the West. The journey itself, whether over land or by sea, was fraught with hardship and danger. When they finally arrived, most pioneers found themselves deposited in a chaotic mass of humanity. These new Californians came into a country that had been under Mexican rule, bringing American political and social traditions along with them. Yet they were relatively isolated. To a great extent they faced the prospect of building a new social order. Field was part of that building process. Less than a year after arriving in the West he helped found a new town, called Marysville, where he was elected as the town's alcalde. This was a Mexican form of office that functioned as both mayor and judge. Field also later served as a member of the California legislature.

By the mid-1850s Field had landed a seat on the California Supreme Court and was in the thick of the battle over who would control the land and wealth of the new state. The struggle often pitted small farmers, ranchers, and miners against people who claimed to own vast estates under Mexican land grants. In chapters 2 and 3 I trace Field's record as a justice of the California Supreme Court. Whether he deserved it or not, during his six-year term on the state bench Field acquired a reputation as guardian of the interests of powerful elites. To some extent this was the result of the part he played in giving John C. Frémont control over the rich mining country in Mariposa County. In these two chapters I also introduce some of the themes that run throughout the book. Underlying the obvious self-interest inherent in land disputes was a conflict over the nature of rights, the sanctity of property, the desire for liberty, and the source of privilege.

The Civil War was at full pitch when Abraham Lincoln appointed Field to the Supreme Court of the United States in 1863. Thus his early years on the high court came in the wake of the war and at a time when the nation struggled to redefine the structure of federalism and the meaning of liberty. In chapter 4 the circumstances of Field's appointment and some of his Reconstruction-era opinions are described. Whatever may have been his reputation in California, Field demonstrated in these early cases that he had a genuine concern for liberty. In the *Test Oath Cases,* for example, he vigorously argued that state and national governments had no right to require loyalty oaths as a condition for holding influential jobs.[2] At the same time, however, Field began to sketch out one of the ideas that would make his definition of liberty controversial. This theory began with the benign proposition that individuals possessed a fundamental right to pursue a lawful trade or profession. He continued to press this idea after ratification of the Fourteenth Amendment and other postwar amendments to the Constitution. Eventually it would evolve into a doctrine—liberty of contract—and would become an important part of Field's legacy.

By the 1870s the railroads had come to symbolize the evolution of economic life in America, and attempts to regulate them epitomized the political, social, and economic conflicts of the time. Although the transcontinental railroad and most other lines were popular when they were being built, they soon became objects of suspicion. Opponents viewed the railroad as a prime example of special privilege, the beneficiary of government handouts in the form of land and money. They also regarded the industry as a "monopoly" that could squeeze the lifeblood out of a local economy. And they saw the railroads as a power that threatened liberty as they understood it. Consequently, they occasionally turned to government to help combat that power. For Stephen Field and others, however, government regulation posed the real threat to individual liberty. In chapter 5 I describe the building of the transcontinental railroad and then use the railroad to explore the relationships between liberty and economic growth, law and economic theory.

In the middle of his career on the Supreme Court, Field ventured into the realm of national politics with a bid to be the Democratic party's 1880 presidential nominee. Field's hope for winning the nomination may have been illusory, and his run for it is not extremely significant in the study of political history. What makes the episode interesting, however, is that Field did not resign from his seat on the high court in order to run for office; rather, he used his seat as an election platform. Thus his campaign presents an unusual opportunity to observe the link between law and politics. Field's bid for elective office is detailed in chapters 6 and 7.

Field's campaign strategy, which promised he could deliver the western vote and the southern vote, highlighted many of the conflicts that he had already addressed in judicial opinions. In the months before the Democratic convention several cases involving the rights of Chinese residents and black citizens came before the Court. Field's use of these cases for a platform provides a means for studying his ideas about civil rights and reveals an insight into his theories of liberty. It was a different aspect of liberty that mattered most to Field, however, an aspect moored to economics rather than to race. Ultimately, Field's future in presidential politics hinged on economic issues. He could not shake his reputation as a "friend of the railroads." Given the atmosphere of California politics in those years, that reputation weakened his support in his home state and consequently doomed his bid for the presidency. Field began a run for the nomination again in 1884, but his campaign came to a quick halt when the California Democratic Convention resolved not to support his candidacy.

Although ego may have continued to prod him into thinking he ought to lead the nation from the executive branch, Field abandoned his presidential aspirations and turned his attention to the Supreme Court. By 1884 he had been on the bench for more than two decades and had clearly demonstrated that he was a man of vision. His opinions, his theories, and his arguments tended to be forceful, bold, and often innovative. He had demonstrated a passionate devotion to liberty. But it was a devotion to liberty as he defined it, and by the mid-1880s it would become clearer than ever how he defined it. In chapter 8 I describe how Field's ideas about liberty manifested themselves in his opinions of the 1880s and 1890s. With their emphasis on corporate equal protection, entrepreneurial liberty, and property rights, these opinions envisioned an economic society free from government intrusion. Field and his admirers believed that liberty defined in this way was not only right in the abstract but would also have the beneficial effect of releasing forces for economic change.

Critics did not see Field's vision of entrepreneurial liberty as protecting individual liberty at all. Field's view of liberty emphasized freedom from restraint. Reformers viewed liberty as also involving freedom from oppression. In their minds the concentration of economic power had come to pose the greatest threat to liberty, and neither aspect of liberty would be secure without economic reform. They believed that, by raising the Constitution as a barrier to economic reform, the legal doctrine to which Field subscribed simply justified and perpetuated concentrations of economic power.

Critics might have found some comfort in realizing that most often Field labored in the minority on the Supreme Court. Yet he had also established himself as one of the Court's intellectual leaders. Although I have referred to them as "Field's theories," Field was not the originator of all the doctrine he championed. Many of the ideas he advocated were popular among legal scholars and members of the bar and had been adopted by lower courts. Field's importance is derived from his place on the bench of the Supreme Court. There he steadfastly tried to mold the doctrine of entrepreneurial liberty into constitutional law and often did so in a way that was bold and innovative. Field's perseverance paid off. Shortly before he resigned, a majority of the Supreme Court came to embrace many of the ideas he had been advocating for years. Those ideas would guide the Court for the next four decades.

ALTHOUGH MY PRIMARY PURPOSE is to tell a story of a generation's struggle to define liberty, Stephen Field's legacy does have a place in modern historical debate. Field is known as a champion of two theories of constitutional law that had a substantial impact on the direction of American legal history. Both theories grew out of the Fourteenth Amendment guarantee that no state shall deprive any person of life, liberty, or property without due process of law. One of these theories, "substantive due process," held that due process in the Fourteenth Amendment guaranteed more than correct judicial procedure; it also allowed the Court to review the substance of state legislation. The other theory, "liberty of contract," was an expansion of Field's "right to pursue a lawful trade or calling." Liberty of contract suggested that the Fourteenth Amendment's protection of liberty and property established a constitutional right to enter into virtually any contract one might desire.

The full impact of substantive due process and liberty of contract doctrine was not felt until about the time of Field's resignation in 1897. From that time until 1937, however, the Supreme Court used these theories as a rationale to overrule government economic regulations. It was a period of Supreme Court history often called the laissez-faire era, and it produced a body of legal doctrine often referred to as laissez-faire constitutionalism. The term laissez faire, of course, refers to an economic theory predicated on the free market and the idea that prosperity could best be achieved in a system where individuals were left free to pursue their own self-interest. It placed its faith in Adam Smith's *Wealth of Nations* and the idea that the "invisible hand of the market" would ensure that the economy would operate smoothly and efficiently.

To its proponents, laissez-faire theory was more than a preferred policy. It was a matter of natural law and of natural rights. Of these natural rights two stood out. First was the natural right of property. The other, called "the natural right of free exchange," was the natural, self-evident, and inalienable right of all people to employ their own efforts for the gratification of their own wants, either directly or through exchange.

Inspired by these beliefs, Adam Smith's American successors, the laissez-faire economists, polished and advanced the principle that government should not interfere in economic matters. Francis Wayland, an economist tied to the laissez-faire tradition, argued that "government's efforts to solve economic problems, no matter how sincere, had the opposite effect. They upset the economic balance, destroyed the incentive for labor, and sapped the spirit of enterprise and productive energies of the nation."[3] The ideas of these economists began to pervade economic thinking in the mid-1800s and were reinforced by the growth of the philosophy of Social Darwinism. Combined, they created a legacy that formed a theoretical basis for opposition to government regulation.

Under laissez-faire theory, property and free exchange were natural rights. But were they protected by or incorporated into the Constitution? Certainly the Constitution includes protections for property. The Article I, section 10 guarantee that no state shall pass any law impairing the obligation of contract provides some protection both for property and for free exchange. But that provision primarily protects the sanctity of existing contracts, not an inalienable right to be free from government interference. The Constitution also guarantees, in the Fifth and Fourteenth Amendments, that property shall not be taken without due process of law. And the Fifth

Amendment guarantees that property shall not be taken for public use without just compensation. These provisions give substantial protection to property, but they do not go so far as to prohibit regulation or to make any sweeping limitation on government involvement in economic matters.

Nevertheless, according to the traditional version of constitutional history, judges of the late nineteenth and early twentieth century did interpret the Constitution in a way that provided sweeping limitations on government involvement in economic matters. The Court's critics claimed that judges had constructed these theories from thin air, that liberty of contract and substantive due process were not based on the words of the Constitution but on an economic theory that a large part of the country did not share.[4] Frustrated Progressive Era reformers complained that the Court had given itself a veto over any attempt to reform the economy or to address the growing economic and social problems that came with industrialization. The Court, according to Theodore Roosevelt, had created an insurmountable barrier to economic reform.[5]

The Court's Progressive Era critics had a significant influence on historical thinking. Traditional legal history portrays Justice Stephen Field as laying the foundation for the conservative era. When he faced a tough question about the validity of economic regulation, the tradition sees him turning to Adam Smith's *Wealth of Nations* rather than to the Constitution. In this version of history, Field's nephew Justice David Brewer, along with Justice Rufus Peckham, carried his work into the twentieth century; and the Four Horsemen, Justices George Sutherland, James C. McReynolds, Pierce Butler, and Willis VanDevanter, extended it into the 1930s. Inspired by laissez-faire economics, these men pursued a policy emphasizing protection of property and freedom from government regulation. According to this traditional version of history, the legal doctrine that developed between the 1890s and 1937 was the product of a deliberate campaign to attach laissez-faire theory to the Constitution. And Stephen Field is cast as forebearer of this doctrine.

This traditional view remains quite alive in legal history. Bernard Schwartz, for example, captured it in his recent history of the Supreme Court. The Court of the late nineteenth and early twentieth centuries, he says, was driven by a belief in the danger of any governmental interference with the economy and any infringement upon the rights of private property. Propelled by this belief, he continues, the Court severely restricted government's ability to enact legislation limiting economic freedom and adopted instead the theory of laissez faire.[6]

A trend in today's scholarship, however, rejects the idea that either Stephen Field or the laissez-faire–era justices had simply reached into their pocket, pulled out Adam Smith's *Wealth of Nations,* and attached it as an addendum to the Constitution. The tendency today is to explain late nineteenth-century and early twentieth-century jurisprudence as an outgrowth of older American traditions of liberty. Charles McCurdy, who has written extensively about Stephen Field, maintains that Field's legal doctrine and the doctrine of the laissez-faire era were not the result of judges simply attaching an economic theory to the Constitution. They were, in his words, the product of habits of thought that were deeply imbedded in the American consciousness well before the liberty of contract doctrine entered American law.[7]

What were these habits of thought to which McCurdy refers? Some writers find the roots of laissez-faire–era constitutional doctrine in the ideals of Jacksonian Democracy.[8] Although recognizing that judges of the laissez-faire era frequently extolled the virtues of private property and market liberty, they emphasize that the cases of the era "demonstrated a superior judicial commitment to the familiar Jacksonian preoccupation with political equality or government neutrality, the belief that government power could not be used by particular groups to gain special privileges or impose burdens on competing groups."[9]

Some of today's scholars find the roots of laissez-faire–era constitutionalism in antebellum free-labor thinking. That connection is quite evident in Justice Stephen Field's idea that the Constitution guarantees the right to choose a lawful profession. A laborer's right to agree to the terms of employment appears linked to free-labor thinking in its rawest form—as a contrast to indentured servitude. Field's doctrine thus appears not as a reflection of laissez-faire thinking but as an instance of justices steeped in free-labor ideology resisting the very idea of unfree labor contracts.[10] Field was not a disciple of Adam Smith, revisionist scholars would say. He was a follower of Andrew Jackson. The theories that he advocated reflected a traditional American distrust of special-interest legislation found in Jacksonian Democracy as well as the ideals of the free-labor movement and early abolitionism.

This book takes it as a given that Stephen Field's ideas about liberty had roots in Jacksonian Democracy and antebellum free-labor theory. Field, like most people who came to California, was weaned on Jacksonian Democracy. Jacksonian ideals set the tone of political discourse and thinking about liberty. Everyone of that time, even people who counted themselves Whigs, was affected. Field's was also a generation absorbed in a debate over slavery and moving toward civil war. Consequently, free-labor theory had a similar effect on setting the tone of political and philosophical discourse.

The revisionist point does not mean, however, that everyone raised in this tradition continued to agree about what it meant, or that Field and other contemporaries who shared his views were the only heirs to the Jacksonian-free labor tradition. It does not mean that Field's theories about law and liberty provided the only, or even the best, route consistent with that tradition. Nor does it rule out the possibility that Field's views were ultimately driven by laissez-faire economics.

A main theme of this book begins with the proposition that, as the century progressed, people with the same Jacksonian and free-labor roots split over the meaning of liberty and the proper scope of government power. Before the Civil War the relationship between power and liberty was a relatively simple equation. As historian William Wiecek observed, at the time of the Revolution Americans tended to think of power as an attribute of government and liberty as an attribute of the people. They were two parts of a zero-sum game. The more power people yielded to government, the less liberty they retained for themselves.[11] The theories of Jacksonian Democracy added an element, but its equation for liberty remained roughly the same. For the Jacksonians, economic privilege undermined the workings of democracy and therefore constituted the greatest threat to individual liberty. The old Jacksonians concluded that the best way to protect liberty was to limit the power of government. Government was suspect because it dispensed privilege to a politically connected elite. Jacksonians were suspicious of government and despised privilege because they viewed the two as linked in a way that threatened individual liberty.

A streak of libertarianism, or individualism, underlay the antebellum Jacksonian tradition. Individualism was a common denominator that all of the heirs of that tradition inherited. As the nineteenth century progressed, however, a rift in the tradition developed. Some people who subscribed to Jacksonian and free-labor ideals emphasized one part of the antebellum formula—freedom from the excesses of privilege. These people came to believe that a business elite had replaced government as the dispenser of privilege. This "reformer" strain of the tradition thought that the railroads and other powerful industries stood independently as the threat to their liberty and as the barrier to achieving their expectations. Thus reformers turned to government to help combat that power. In contrast, the emphasis for another branch of the Jacksonian–free-labor tradition was on the other part of the formula—freedom from the excesses of government. This "radical individualist" strain downplayed the possibility that privilege could emanate from any source other than government. For these individualists, liberty was best achieved by limiting the power of government.

Free-labor theory underwent a similar evolution. In antebellum thinking, slavery and various forms of "unfree labor" represented legally imposed restraints on liberty. Free labor was initially a response to traditions that gave employers legal control over an employee's labor. Slavery and indentured servitude provide the obvious examples, but legal control existed even in situations where the laborer had entered into the employment agreement voluntarily. By the mid-nineteenth century most of these forms of legal compulsion had disappeared. But wage earners found that the repeal of legal compulsions did not ensure that their hopes for independence, choice, and opportunity would be achieved. Later, free-labor advocates realized that the force of private wealth could just as effectively restrain individual freedom. In a world where concentrated corporate power was becoming more predominant, economic compulsion could just as effectively threaten their liberty. Placed in this world, wage earners and reformers began to turn to government for help, and they did so in the name of free labor.[12]

One cause of confusion is that, for the most part, the language of liberty and individualism remained a constant. Reformers and radical individualists shared a common ground, but by stressing different sources of the perceived dangers to liberty, they reached very different conclusions about the nature of individualism and the role of government. Their battles during the latter part of the nineteenth century demonstrate that the concept of liberty is susceptible to a variety of meanings.

Over time, Stephen Field came to symbolize the radical individualist strain of the Jacksonian–free-labor tradition, which made him a magnet both for intense criticism and zealous acclaim. His opinions and the conflict that swirled around them thus provide a platform for understanding the schism between branches of the same general tradition. And his status as a U.S. Supreme Court justice illustrates how the schism was reflected in the development of constitutional law.

The development of constitutional law plays an important role in this book, but it is not my intention to provide a study of nineteenth-century legal doctrine. I have not attempted to trace any line of opinions thoroughly, and I have barely mentioned some important constitutional topics, such as the commerce clause and the contract clause. My interest is in the concept of liberty and in what it meant to people who thought they possessed it. My primary purpose is to inquire into the relation between law and the social order in the last half of the nineteenth century. The emphasis is on the political, social, and economic conflicts that occurred during that time. Law plays the supporting role. Stephen Field provides the link and sets some boundaries.

AT TIMES Stephen Field seemed not so much a judge as an advocate, and he appeared to be guided not so much by a philosophy as an agenda, which raises another theme that runs throughout this book. It has to do with the nature and power of the judicial branch. Although some people trace judicial activism to John Marshall, it is common today to think of judicial activism as a product of the Warren Court. Liberals such as William O. Douglas or William Brennan are usually presented as prime examples of activist judges. In many ways, however, Stephen Field was the prototype for the modern judicial activist. He was first to deliberately use written concurring and dissenting opinions to build a body of legal authority. His opinions from the high bench moved in and out of the Constitution. He relied on the Declaration of Independence or precepts of natural law to support his ideas. Finally, it is evident that personal philosophy played at least as much of a role as legal precedent in Field's decisionmaking and that he used the Court as a vehicle for expressing his own will. Throughout his career, Field aggressively tried to graft his idea of liberty onto the body of constitutional doctrine.

Rankings of Supreme Court justices usually place Stephen J. Field among the "near great," just below the likes of Marshall, Story, Holmes, and Brandeis. But in terms of impact on the direction of constitutional law and on the power of the Court, his stature easily rises to a place at the top. Length of tenure alone ensured that Field would have some influence. Appointed by Abraham Lincoln in 1863, he sat on the Court for thirty-four years, outlasting eight presidents and three chief justices before resigning in 1897. Stephen Field's time on the Court ran from the Civil War through the Gilded Age to within a breath of the twentieth century. And his story began on the day he first set foot on the shore of San Francisco.

1

A FORTY-NINER, NOT A MINER

"The Way They Go to California," N. Currier's 1849 lithograph lampooning the gold rush, shows scores of men, picks and shovels in hand, crowding a dock. Dozens of ships have already set sail without them. "I'm bound to go anyhow," yells one of the prospective gold miners as he dives into the water to swim after the last ship. Another, pick and shovel still in hand, dangles on the end of a parachute aimed roughly in the direction of a departed ship. Currier let his imagination run wild. He drew one group of forty-niners floating westward on a dirigible; one man was even riding a rocket to the West.

Lampooning aside, in 1849 the gold rush was on. The discovery of gold in California produced a level of excitement that shook the foundations of American society. Insanity is what Currier saw in the gold rush. Many other Americans, including Stephen Field, saw opportunity. Thousands sold their belongings and left their jobs or their farms to join the gold rush, many leaving their families behind. They sailed, they walked, and they rode through parts of the world they had never before seen. They knew little about the place to which they were going and less about the conditions they would find when they arrived. But they went anyway, and they became part of a great migration.

San Francisco was the destination for many of the travelers. In the mid-nineteenth century that city and California itself were relatively virgin country, totally unprepared for the deluge of adventurers who arrived in 1849 and 1850. Just a few years earlier the site that is now San Francisco was a cove made up of the village of Yerba Buena, the Mission of San Francisco, and a Mexican military base, the Presidio. In the mid-1840s the cove had some commercial significance for Mexico and some military significance during the Mexican-American War. Nevertheless, until the discovery of gold it was nothing more than a sleepy outpost. The combined population living in proximity of the cove in 1848 was less than 1,000; within two years it would increase one hundredfold, shooting up to an estimated 100,000. The new residents came from all directions. Many had traveled

"THE WAY THEY GO TO CALIFORNIA." A lithograph published in 1849 by Nathaniel Currier. (California Historical Society)

from South America, especially Chile. Others came from China. But most of the new Californians came from the East Coast and midwestern states.[1]

The adventurers who began to pour into San Francisco in 1849 quickly transformed the pastoral village into a place of utter chaos. Most travelers from the eastern states arrived by sea, and for them the chaos of the new city was evident even from a distance. As they stood on deck, straining to catch a first glimpse of their destination, the new arrivals thought they were sailing toward a forest rather than a harbor. It was an illusion created by masts of almost 1,000 ships that had been grounded and abandoned, when men who could not contain their excitement dashed off to the goldfields.

When the passengers reached their destination the apparent chaos became a real scene from bedlam. There was no welcome wagon to meet new arrivals. There was no visitors' bureau, money exchange, or tourist information, not even an immigrant processing center like Ellis Island. Most of the ships arriving in 1849 had to anchor some distance offshore. Once they were anchored, a horde of barges and shallow boats vied to ferry passengers and cargo ashore. The new arrivals and their possessions were then summarily deposited on a narrow beach, which quickly gave way to the hills that are the well-known symbols of today's San Francisco. There the forty-niners found themselves standing ankle-deep in water and sand and surrounded by nothing but litter. Astronomical prices caused the value of their money to plummet. Most of them knew they would be heading eastward toward the mountains, but they had no idea of how they would get there or where they would stay in the meantime.

This was the scene into which the thirty-three-year-old Stephen Field stepped in December 1849. The preacher's son from Stockbridge, a thriving town in the staid Berkshire Hills of western Massachusetts, could not have been fully prepared for what he found. It was true that he had spent the last several years in New York City, working in legal practice with his older brother David Dudley Field.[2] Still, the hustle-bustle of that great eastern city must have paled in comparison to the virtual anarchy of San Francisco.

Early California was made to order for independent and strong-willed individuals. Former status mattered little. Success in the new territory was more likely to be the result of inner strength, hard work, guile, and vision. Of course, luck played a role in many a success story. Nevertheless, the frontier created an atmosphere that allowed successful pioneers to believe that they had charted their own course, that they had carved their own path to greatness or wealth. And they could believe that in the bargain they had created a great state.[3]

Stephen Field was among this first group of pioneers. By the time he arrived in late 1849, entrepreneurs had built a few piers out into the cove. Field apparently had the good fortune to dock at one of these, thus avoiding some of the confusion on the beach. Still, his first day was a shock. Field recalled that he had brought along two trunks; unable to carry them by himself, he paid seven of his last ten dollars to have someone deliver his luggage to an old adobe building. There, he arranged to share a small one-bed room with two other passengers. "They took the bed, and I took the floor," Field said. "I do not think they had much the advantage on the score of comfort."[4]

Despite his apparent discomfort, Field was among the luckier of the arrivals. Housing was in desperately short supply in the early years, and it was not unusual to have to share a room in a makeshift building. Most forty-niners were happy to get a small room to share with five or more people; some could find no room at all. "Report says there are six thousand people here that have no shelter," one woman wrote to her daughter. Houses made of wood joists covered with cotton cloth and calico were going up on every corner. Another early arrival, Richard Hale, described the town as "a mass of wooden hovels and cloth tents, pitched without order on the sand banks and what few rocks were not sand covered." The shacks or tents were often

San Francisco Harbor circa 1851, showing abandoned ships being used for storage. (Courtesy Peabody Essex Museum, Salem, Mass.)

built or pitched wherever the occupants had a notion to light. Hale and his two partners, for example, "decided to build a shack on Telegraph Hill, overlooking the sand-bank that runs out to the bay."[5]

By 1851 a few brick buildings, along with some prefabricated buildings constructed of zinc and wood, adorned the business district. For the most part, however, the city was built of wood and canvas. There was a street layout but no specific plan for development. Commerce, one historian has noted, appeared to be the driving force. Because of the city's geography—its steep hills encroaching upon a narrow beach—flat land convenient for business was at a premium. Early settlers preferred the low ground near the docks and wharves, so much so that they soon began to fill in the bay. Some new arrivals even acquired water lots through public sale. Not to be mistaken for waterfront lots, these coveted pieces of property were *in* the water. The owners built homes and businesses on piles, or they filled in their shallow-water lots with trash. Some settlers used abandoned ships grounded on their property for storage and shops.

Still there was not enough room. Warehouses and shops began to spring

San Francisco Harbor circa 1851, showing the forest of masts. (Courtesy Peabody Essex Museum, Salem, Mass.)

up in the hills and away from the prime waterfront. Dirt streets that connected the burgeoning city commonly became ankle-deep in mud, making local transportation a nightmare.[6] Potholes were so deep that a young boy was said to have drowned one night after he fell into one.[7] Improvements were in the making, however. Laborers scraped down the hillsides and filled in the bay to create more flat land.[8] Private citizens and the city shared the cost of having streets graded, then covered with wooden planks. At least seven streets were completed by the end of 1850. The amazing aspect was how quickly this growth happened. In a short two years between 1849 and 1851 the quiet cove became a vibrant, if crude and disorganized, commercial center.

Speed, rather than long-range planning, characterized the city's early development. For some residents the disorganized growth caused a bit of inconvenience. In November 1850, the Megquier family built a two-story building that served as a store, boardinghouse, and residence. By April 1851, however, Mrs. Megquier complained to a daughter who had stayed in the East that they were going to have to raise the building: "When it was built, it was up to the skies," she wrote, "but filling up the street has made it quite under ground."[9] The image of unlucky San Franciscans climbing out of their homes on ladders may be humorous, but disorganized growth also had a tendency to produce a variety of more intense conflicts. Entrepreneurs who had built piers into the cove, for example, soon clashed with owners of water lots. When the lot owners filled in the bay, they made it impossible for ships to dock at some of the piers. The pier owners bitterly complained that these unregulated landfills deprived them of the just profits of their enterprise. In 1851 they prevailed upon the city to set a line beyond which the bay could not be filled, but the limit was largely ignored and the filling continued.[10]

The speed of construction and lack of organization also were factors in causing disaster. Fire was the greatest threat to early San Francisco. All but a few of the first permanent structures in the city were constructed of wood. Even the few brick buildings that existed had interiors partitioned with cloth. Wood-plank streets connected warehouses and homes. Shanties and wooden shacks were packed into the available flat and low land. Fire companies were not organized until after a devastating fire in May 1850, and cisterns were not filled until after another blaze in June 1851. As a result, from 1849 through 1852 fires wiped out much of the development that had been accomplished. Each time the city was rebuilt, however, it was better, with more masonry and stone.[11]

The system of supplying goods to the burgeoning city was characterized by the same disorganization. The forty-niners were not part of a planned expedition. They just took off. There was relatively little agricultural development in the region, and these pioneers were not interested in farming. They had come to California to get rich in the goldfields. As a consequence, food was imported from Oregon, southern California, and the East Coast or supplied by hunters and trappers. The new arrivals marveled at the expense of things. Reports of apples selling for eight dollars apiece or of paying five dollars for "a poor miserable turnip" were common.[12] Yet it was truly marvelous that any goods arrived at all.

Machinery, mercantile goods, and some food arrived from the East with regularity. Some of the merchandise was brought west by prospectors who planned to finance their expeditions by selling surplus goods for a huge profit. Most goods were shipped around the tip of South America, some by eastern merchants, some by hopeful entrepreneurs who came with their goods to California. Their success was not ensured, however, since the nature of the market could change quickly and drastically. Rather than responding to orders, merchants shipped whatever they thought, or were informed, might be in demand. They also had to take into consideration that perishables and breakables might not survive the long and rough voyage. As a result, "essentials" like tobacco and flour often glutted the market.[13] The only certainty in those early years was that labor, housing, and news from home were always in short supply. Adventure, enthusiasm, and hardship were plentiful.

Stephen Field published memoirs of his early days in California. They were written about three decades later and probably exaggerate the details. Nevertheless, his recollections of his state of mind in those first few days give a good sense of the atmosphere. His first days may have differed in some ways from the experience of other newcomers, but they were in many ways the same.

Once Field acquired a room, his next task was to find a bite to eat. "The next morning I started out early with three dollars in my pocket," he recalled. "I hunted up a restaurant and ordered the cheapest breakfast I could get. It cost me two dollars."[14] Despite his financial dilemma, however, Field remembers being neither alarmed nor dejected. As he strolled through the city he too was infected with the enthusiasm of the moment, and soon found himself saying to everybody he met the greeting he had heard all day: "Isn't it a glorious country?"

To the extent that he was impoverished, his poverty was accompanied by supreme confidence. This circumstance was not unusual since many of the newcomers had exhausted their financial resources by the time they arrived in San Francisco. But if food, shelter, and provisions were costly, they were matched by the going wages for labor. As earlier waves of forty-niners left for the goldfields, newcomers found themselves hiring out in order to earn the money they needed for their own expeditions. Generally, they considered their status as wage earner to be temporary.

For Field such employment turned out to be unnecessary. He had carried a bundle of New York papers with him on his voyage. In a city of people thirsty for news from the East, he was able to sell the bundle, making a handy profit of thirty-two dollars. Field had one other resource as well, a note demanding repayment of a loan that his brother David Dudley Field had made to a Col. Jonathan Stevenson. Having heard that Stevenson had grown rich in California, David Dudley gave the note to his younger brother and told him to collect whatever he could. Fortunately, Field found Colonel Stevenson in excellent financial health and convinced him to pay the amount of the loan, plus interest. He recalls it being $440 in Spanish doubloons or gold dust, enough for Field to rent a room and open a law office at the corner of Montgomery and Clay.[15]

Field's law practice in San Francisco was hardly a success. He remained in practice for less than a month, and about the only task he accomplished was to write a will for one of his fellow passengers from the trip to California. Like most early Californians, Field would move on, and he would continue to live by his wits. The only constant in those early days was chaos, change, and hardship. Society and government, as most people had known them, hardly existed. Yet these pioneers were supremely confident about their future. Besides, for many newcomers, the discomfort of their lives in this new land was a relief compared to the hardship of the journey to get there.

The Forty-niners

The forty-niners, or argonauts as they were sometimes called, poured into northern California via one of three routes. Some traveled by ship around the tip of South America. Others went overland by wagon train. A third group sailed to Panama, where they crossed the isthmus and then continued their journey on another ship up the West Coast.

Most of the ships lying abandoned in San Francisco Bay had traveled around South America laden with gold seekers, the vast majority of whom were men, most of them from the eastern states, and most of them young. In 1849 alone more than 6,000 argonauts sailed from the ports of New England and New York. Their trip down the Atlantic coast, around the Horn, and up the Pacific coast was more than 18,000 miles. These men had left wives, families, and friends behind. Many had spent all they owned, even taking loans, to pay for the expedition. Typically, they joined together in companies. On paper, these units were usually well organized; some, clad in flashy uniforms, even took on a paramilitary character. The companies usually elected leaders and wrote out a charter that set forth rules of conduct for the members as well as agreements regarding sharing costs and splitting profits. The members either pooled their resources or paid a fixed fee to buy the supplies and machinery needed for their expedition. They brought shovels, clothing, tents, and food, and some brought along goods to sell for profit in California. Others were talked into buying elaborate gold mining machines, most of which could later be found abandoned on the beaches of San Francisco. Some companies bought the ship on which they sailed, often a refitted vessel that had been rescued from salvage or dry dock; others hired both ship and crew for the voyage.

Storms, extremes of heat and cold, bad food, disease, and cramped quarters would test the adventurers. Passage through the Strait of Magellan was often harrowing. The journey could be dangerous, but tedium was the major hardship facing those who took this route to the goldfields. The adventurers could expect to be at sea for five to eight months before arriving in San Francisco. All the while, they were thinking that the best goldfields would be picked bare before they got there.

Even more people traveled overland to California. Hubert Howe Bancroft estimated that in April 1849 some 20,000 people were gathered in St. Joseph and Independence, Missouri, awaiting departure.[16] At first impression this route may have appeared to be the most comfortable because the means of travel was familiar. Most of the overland travelers rode their own horses. At least one man walked the entire way, carrying his belongings on his back. Many, traveling in wagons drawn by ox or mule, essentially brought their homes and families along. For most of the journey they traveled well-established routes—the Oregon-California Trail to the north or the Santa Fe Trail to the south. But even the most optimistic realized that the trip would be arduous. The typical journey covered thousands of miles and usually took months. Success hinged on both planning and luck. Some travelers learned too late that decisions such as when to start and what provisions to carry could ultimately mean the difference between life and death.

At least for those overland travelers who left early, the first miles were relatively peaceful. Travel across the Great Plains was smooth. Stock could feed on the tall grass and remain strong and healthy; equipment stayed intact and supplies were plentiful. But as the wagon trains continued west conditions began to deteriorate. On the northern route, for example, problems began when travelers emerged from the tall grass into the more desolate Black Hills country. Overloaded wagons began to break down and animals began to weaken. Supplies initially thought to be essential were found to be worthless and were abandoned along the trail. When oxen died or became too weak to go on, they were left behind as well. With their stock depleted, groups eventually had to abandon some of their wagons and many essentials. As this mass of humanity edged westward, it left behind rotting carcasses and polluted streams and water holes. To make matters worse, cholera struck the expeditions with a vengeance, with poor sanitation undoubtedly contributing to the extent of disease.

By the time the overland travelers reached the South Pass of the Rocky Mountains, many travelers had become dangerously low on supplies. Those who brought money or had something to barter were able to trade along the way—first at Fort Laramie and later at Salt Lake City. Sometimes groups with different needs joined in temporary partnerships.[17] But items of value, food, stock, and wagons were in short supply, and the most difficult part of the journey was still ahead. The northern route took them across the rugged, mountainous terrain of what is now Utah, past the Great Salt Lake Desert. The travelers skirted Death Valley but still were faced with alkali deserts before they could follow the Humbolt River to the rugged Sierra Nevada Mountains.

When the forty-niners reached the Sierra Nevada many were sick, starving, and destitute. The later travelers were in the worst shape. By the time they had set off, the grasses along the trail through the Great Plains had been depleted, and supplies at way stations had also been used up. After surviving most of the journey these later travelers found themselves stranded in the snow of the Sierra Nevada. The most famous of these, the Donner party, resorted to cannibalism to avoid starvation.

Although the wagon train provided a familiar means of travel, for many people it was the most harrowing route to the goldfields. Still, most travelers who set out from the Mississippi River eventually made it to the new territory. According to some estimates, in little more than a year more than 20,000 arrived in California via the overland routes.[18]

Stephen Field took the third route to the goldfields. On November 13, 1849, he boarded the steamer *Crescent City* bound from New York to the village of Chagres on the Isthmus of Panama. The *Crescent City* was one of a small fleet of steamers that the Pacific Mail Steamship Line operated under contract with the federal government to deliver mail between the East and West Coasts. The company planned to run a small fleet of steamers on the East Coast and to send another group of ships around the Horn to operate on the West Coast between Panama and San Francisco. When its plan was put into operation just before the gold rush, passenger traffic was not a key consideration. Consequently, the company was wholly unprepared to handle the demand for passage in the first few months after the news of gold hit. Ultimately, however, the trip across Panama provided the fastest and safest means to get to California; it was also the most expensive.

For most passengers the voyage from New York to Chagres was a pleasant beginning to a wondrous adventure. In balmy weather travelers sat on deck observing whales and flying fish or catching a glimpse of Cuba as they passed it. In a week or so they reached Chagres, a small village of thatched-roof houses nestled in a cove off the Caribbean Sea. From there they would boat and walk across the isthmus to Panama City, where they planned to board another steamer to San Francisco.

When Field arrived in Chagres eight months after the first groups of travelers there was still no comfortable means of crossing the isthmus. The first leg of the journey was by river for about forty miles to the villages of Gorgona or Cruces. A small steamer was able to navigate part way up the Chagres River, but Field and his companions, like many others, were transported in a small dugout canoe poled upriver by local boatmen. From there, the final twenty miles of the journey was overland by foot or mule to Panama City. The trails were, as one traveler put it, "rough in the extreme." From Gorgona the trail passed through tropical forest, knee-deep in mud and impassable during rain. Field took the trail from Cruces, which was only slightly better. Carved through the mountains, this part of the ancient Spanish Trail was passable even in the rainy season, but it was longer and rougher than the trail from Gorgona.

People arriving in Panama City found that many more people were waiting for steamers to take them up the Pacific coast to San Francisco than there was space available. Fifteen hundred people had amassed in the small city before the first of the Pacific Mail steamers made it around the Horn on January 30, 1849, and only about 400 were taken on board.[19] The backlog grew. One group of forty-niners who arrived in Panama City in March waited two months for transportation.[20] Meanwhile more people were pouring in from the East. The resale price of tickets soared, reaching $1,000 or more, and some of the less patient travelers sought alternative transportation. Small sailing vessels were pressed into service. At least one proved to be so unseaworthy that passengers were forced to abandon ship in lower California and walk the rest of the way to the goldfields.[21] There were even reports that an anxious group of adventurers started off in log canoes.[22] The stranded passengers in Panama City worried that their resources would dwindle away as they waited, but they soon discovered even greater problems.

The walled city of Panama, once a Spanish jewel in Central America, was simply not equipped to handle the influx of travelers. Although the Panamanians were apparently hospitable, living conditions soon became atrocious. If travelers could find lodging at all, they slept in hammocks, sometimes ten to a room. Others simply camped outside the city. Rats and insects swarmed throughout the burgeoning encampment. With sanitation almost nonexistent, dysentery and cholera spread rapidly. The heat and humidity of the tropics and swarms of mosquitoes added to the travelers' discomfort. Thousands of Yankees fell victim to malaria and yellow fever. Many of those who survived their stay in Panama took their diseases, which they called Panama Fever, with them on the vessels they boarded for San Francisco.

Stephen Field did not dally in Panama. He had booked passage on the steamer *California* and resisted any temptation to sell his ticket for a seemingly great profit. Yet he did not completely escape hardship. Like all ships bound for San Francisco in 1849, the *California* was dangerously overcrowded. The wooden side-wheel steamer was designed to accommodate 210 passengers, 60 in first class and the others in steerage and forward cabins. Yet Field estimated that on his voyage there were over 1,200 people on board. As Field recalled:

Unfortunately many of them carried with them the seeds of disease. The infection contracted under a tropical sun, being aggravated by hardships, insufficient food, and the crowded condition of the steamer, developed as the voyage proceeded. Panama fever in its worst form broke out; and it was not long before the main deck was literally covered with the sick. There was a physician attached to the ship; but unfortunately he was also prostrated.[23]

Field himself managed to avoid contracting disease. His primary recollection of the twenty-two-day journey was that he turned himself into a nurse and took care of two of his stricken fellow passengers.[24]

Thousands of travelers died on the sea routes and overland trails to the gold rush. Whatever the actual toll might have been, countless others barely survived starvation, accident, or wrenching disease. Gold lured them into taking this chance, but the allure of California gold explains only one side of the story. Circumstances on the opposite side of the continent must have been gnawing at these people as well. That so many were willing to leave their families and risk death in this quest for wealth and happiness implies that they were convinced that those pleasures were beyond their reach in the more comfortable surroundings back East.

For some people the gold rush was simply an adventure. "To see the elephant" was the phrase that meant they had experienced the unusual or faced the dangerous. And virtually every forty-niner saw the elephant somewhere along the journey. Some travelers, who were later successful, looked back upon their experience as one of personal growth. Lucius Fairchild, a seventeen-year-old store clerk, would later become governor of Wisconsin. "Fairchild considered his years in California a time of preparation and a way of making sure that he would never have to step back behind the dry-goods counter. When he returned to Madison—in high boots, spurs, a wide-brimmed hat, a money belt strapped around his waist—it was to play a man's part."[25]

Adventure and growth it surely was, but mixed into Fairchild's saga was a drive to break from constraints that bound him back home. So it was with

most of the forty-niners. The gold rush represented an emancipation. This
sense of liberation from social constraints was evident in the society Californians created in the 1850s. In manners of dress and social habits, the
pioneers were clearly independent. Gambling, one of the few forms of rec-
reation in the early years, was rampant. Church-going was occasional. One
woman who called herself "a worshiper at the shrine of liberty," observed
that churches were in abundance in San Francisco, but people could do as
they pleased about attending: "It is all the same whether you go to church
or play monte."[26] Even people who would seem to have had social advantages in the East were driven by this desire for independence. Charles A.
Kirkpatrick, a physician, explained that he joined the gold rush because
he wanted to break away from society's artificial constraints "and try for a
while the life of liberty and unrestrained indulgence."[27]

More significant, however, was the emancipation from economic constraints. Even while enduring hardship, forty-niners wrote of their relief
over being freed from dead-end jobs. One forty-niner observed that of the
several classes of people working the mines, "there are thousands who at
home would be obliged to work for a dollar a day and be under the eye
of an overseer, and who, consequently, are not disappointed at being their
own master."[28] "I wish you were here with me," another traveler wrote to
his brother. "It is far more pleasing to me, and I know it would be to you,
than to sit daily locked up in a dirty office."[29]

Women also enjoyed more freedom and opportunity than they had in
eastern society. Many women found financial independence doing laundry
or running a boardinghouse, enterprises that could be extremely profitable
in the predominantly male society. Other women ran gambling houses,
bars, and houses of prostitution. But still others took on less traditionally
female careers working the goldfields or as barbers, doctors, entrepreneurs,
or real estate speculators. Nevertheless, social barriers remained. A woman
named Charley Parkhurst, for example, still found it necessary to pose as
a man in order to drive stages for Wells Fargo.[30] Like women, minorities
could find more opportunity in 1849 in California than they would have in
the East. Yet racial and ethnic discrimination was evident from the earliest stages of the gold rush. Blacks, Mexicans, and foreigners, particularly
Chileans and Chinese, were the most frequent targets.

For white males, however, the circumstances of the gold rush had the
effect of leveling differences in social and economic status. Hubert Howe
Bancroft reported that in this era, "a laborer might gain the footing of
employer, . . . while former doctors, lawyers, and army officers could be
seen toiling for wages, even as waiters and shoeblacks."[31] This leveling

gave people who had come from working classes an invigorating sense of self-respect or even superiority. "This wonderful country seems to be a re-alization of the wild and extravagant fictions of the East," wrote one proud forty-niner. "Indeed, the poor workman, as one accustomed to manual la-bor, has a better chance of wealth than one who has hitherto been ashamed to dig. The carpet knights and silken striplings, who are perhaps, leaving their mothers' sides for the first time, are scarcely capable of sustaining the hardships, privations, and exposure—the digging, delving, and washing, by which the precious metal is obtained."[32]

For some, self-respect was also derived from the knowledge that they were not working for wages. Although wages were astronomical in the early years, one forty-niner observed that "[miners] would rather perform harder work in the mines and run chances of striking a lead and making a fortune than to accept a stated salary."[33] Even later when mining methods became more complicated and capital-intensive, gold seekers were reluctant to work for wages. To do so had little appeal for adventurers who were "psychologically unprepared for a return to the humdrum existence from which they had escaped when they left their eastern or European homes."[34]

An atmosphere of individualism flourished in the gold rush, and along with it, a sense of vitality, destiny, and liberty. Few people captured this spirit better than the forty-niner M. T. McClellan, who was having only modest success making a living in the goldfields. "I always believed I was born the child of destiny and that I never was to be subservient to the wealth, power, or dictation of man," he wrote, "and my belief is now real-ized."

The gold rush letters and journals that these people left behind do not reveal that they were spurred by a distinctive economic or political philoso-phy. Still, the evidence is overwhelming that forty-niners reveled in a ful-filling personal liberty. One obvious characteristic about their quest for lib-erty is that the forty-niners were not trying to escape from an oppressive system of government; they brought their form of government with them, both on the journey and when they arrived in California.[35] To the extent that the gold rush was an emancipation, it was an emancipation from op-pressive circumstances—circumstances created by private economic and so-cial forces.

There was yet another aspect of the sense of opportunity that drove the forty-niners. Most shared a sense that they were part of history in the mak-ing, and some were motivated by the belief that this was their chance to make history. This motive drew to California some of the most power-ful politicians of the state's early years, senators William Gwin and David

Broderick among them. Before leaving for California, Gwin predicted he would return as the state's senator. Broderick, a budding New York City politician who left for California after he was defeated for Congress, predicted the same for himself.[36] Greatness also lured Stephen Field; at least, that is how he later explained his decision to go to California. "There was the smack of adventure in it," Field recalled. He liked the idea of going to a country comparatively unknown and taking part in fashioning its institutions: " I always thought that the most desirable fame a man could acquire was that of being the founder of a state, or of exerting a powerful influence for good upon its destinies."[37]

Alcalde of Marysville

It did not take long for Field to realize that his opportunity to exert this powerful influence on the state's destinies might not lie in San Francisco. Although he had opened a law office, he had managed to attract only one client in three weeks. On the advice of a mercantile company that was interested in developing a town called Vernon, Field decided to move closer to the goldfields. On January 12, 1850, he left for Sacramento, where he boarded the steamer *Lawrence* and continued upriver. His plan to settle in Vernon changed quickly, however, because the entire Sacramento River Valley was flooded. When the *Lawrence* barely missed ramming an engulfed house, Field turned to the captain and asked, "What is this place?" "Vernon," said the Captain. "I believe I will not put my shingle at Vernon just yet," Field replied, "I would like to go farther on."[38]

Field, along with his fellow passengers, eventually disembarked at a place as far upstream as a steamer could travel. The settlement was then called Nye's Ranch or Yubaville but would soon become the town of Marysville. Cradled in the confluence of the Feather and Yuba rivers, it was an excellent jumping-off point for miners who worked the foothills of the Sierra Nevada along the Yuba and between the two rivers. In a very short time the town would become a thriving commercial center. Eventually, most supplies to the northern diggings would go to Marysville. Most miners would sleep overnight in its hotels and board the northbound stages in its plaza. One proud citizen later boasted that Marysville was the largest pack-mule center in California.[39] When Field arrived, however, there was nothing on the site other than an old adobe building and numerous tents. Field guessed that 500 to 1,000 people were gathered in the encampment, many of whom had been drawn there by an ad in the *Sacramento Placer Times* announcing the sale of lots.

Circumstances of the founding of Marysville were in many ways typical of the times. The site was located within the eleven square leagues of land that Mexican governor Juan Bautista Alvarado had granted to Capt. John Sutter in 1842. The rancho included Sutter's Mill, spot of the legendary discovery of California gold, as well as Sutter's home at Hock Farm. In 1842 Sutter gave Theodor Cordura a nine-year lease to farm and develop a rancho on that portion of his grant that lay north of the Yuba and east of the Feather rivers, which Cordura did for about six years. Then, after California became American territory and after gold was discovered, the situation changed rapidly and frequently. Cordura acquired a partner in October 1848, selling one-half of his interest to a French trapper and trader, Charles Covillaud. Within three months Cordura sold the rest of his interest to Covillaud's brothers-in-law Michael C. Nye and William Foster. On September 27, 1849, Nye and Foster sold their interest to Covillaud. On October 1, 1849, Covillaud sold part of what he owned to two Chileans, Jose Manuel Ramirez and John Sampson, and part to another Frenchman, Theodore Sicard. Although Charles Covillaud was involved in most of these transactions, interest in the property changed hands four times in less than a year.

The speed in which the interest in this property changed hands is even more amazing considering what exactly was being transferred. This was clearly stated in the deed from Cordura,

I [Theodor Cordura] . . . Have granted bargained sold and confirmed and by these presents Do bargain sell, and confirm unto said Michael C. Nye and William Foster the undivided one half of all the lands *leased* to me by Capt. Sutter upon the Jubo [*sic*] and Feather Rivers.[40]

All the Covillaud partnership owned was the rights under a lease! And it had only about two years to run. Yet the parties to these agreements treated the property as if it were theirs. In December 1849, the Covillaud partnership had the town surveyed and lots laid out. The *Placer Times* announcement of January 8, 1850, offering lots for sale was signed "Chas. Covillaud & Co. proprietors." When Field arrived on January 15, they were selling and delivering title to land they did not own. Field later took great delight in telling the story of his purchase:

I asked the price of the lots. He answered "Two hundred and fifty dollars each for lots 80 by 160 feet." I replied, "But, supposed a man puts his name down and afterwards don't want the lots." He rejoined, "Oh, you need not take them if you don't want them: put your names down gentlemen, you that want lots." I took him at his word and wrote my name down for sixty five lots, aggregating in all $16,250. This produced a great sensation. To the best of my recollection I had only about twenty dollars left of what Col. Stevenson had paid me; but it was immediately noised about that a great capitalist had come up from San Francisco to invest in lots in the rising town. The consequence was that the proprietors of the place waited upon me and showed me great attention.[41]

Whatever Field might have hoped to imply, it took no special business acumen to make his deal. Marysville was one of several cities furiously competing to become the commercial outlet to the mines. Spurred by the competition, the Covillaud partners may have decided to sell lots first, then worry about the title. Competition also made them willing to sell to anyone on almost any terms, for it was most important that they quickly establish the idea that they had a booming town. That image, they thought, would draw the suppliers and merchants as well as the miners to their site, in turn making the idea come true.

For almost a month, the Covillaud partners sold lots they did not own. On January 17, 1850, they finally convinced Captain Sutter to sell them the land upon which the city sat. The sale, though it did not clear up the title of lots previously sold, gave the Covillaud plan a more official character. January 18 was a banner day in the founding of Marysville. On that same day, Sutter signed the deed, the city elected its first official, and it acquired its name. Although he had arrived only three days earlier, Field was directly involved with the first two of these events. Fluent in French, he had quickly become friendly with Covillaud and Sicard. Consequently, when they learned he was a lawyer, they hired him to draw up the deed from Captain Sutter. A fortunate choice, it gave Field his first opportunity to influence the development of the new territory. Displaying both knowledge of the law and thoroughness, Field advised his clients that there was no mechanism in place to formalize the deed. Since there were more transactions to follow, he suggested, there should be an officer to take acknowledgments and to record the deeds and a magistrate to preserve order and to settle disputes. That was the evening of January 17, and Covillaud was in the mood to celebrate closing the deal with Sutter. He invited an undetermined number of people, to the prefabricated house he had just brought in by steamer. There, sitting on planks and sipping champagne, the revelers decided to call a meeting for the purpose of organizing a town.[42]

Government in California at that time was in a stage of awkward transition. Mexico had ceded sovereignty over the territory to the United States in 1846 as a result of the Mexican-American War, yet American governmental institutions had not yet been established. The Spanish model of government was therefore still in operation in most places, but Americans or recent immigrants occupied the offices. This pattern was followed in Marysville. Residents who attended the organizational meeting decided to form a government led by an ayuntamiento and an alcalde.[43] The former was the equivalent of a town council. But in the Mexican system most of the power of local government rested with the alcalde, a multifaceted officer who possessed some characteristics of mayor, some of judge, and perhaps some powers of a feudal lord.

When the election of officers took place the next afternoon Field was in the running for alcalde. As he tells the story, he won by a margin of six votes over an "old timer" who had been there all of six days. A longtime friend, W. H. Parks, liked to claim credit for Field's victory. In a letter to Field, Parks recalled that he and his friend, J. B. Clark, learned about the election when they returned from hauling a load of goods to the mountains. Despite having no knowledge about the candidates, they decided to wage dinner on the outcome of the election, with Parks betting on "the young New Yorker named Field." As they mingled with the crowd, Parks noticed that all nationalities were voting without any particular regard to citizenship. "It occurred to me that I had eleven Mexican packers working for me encamped but a few rods away," Parks recalled. "So I went to the camp and explained to them as well as I could that there was an election being held, and that I wanted them to vote. They consented, all came in with me and cast a 'straight' vote for Field of New York."[44]

Parks also remembered that "champayne was flowing freely" at the meeting and celebration that followed the election. It was there that the town settled on the name Marysville. Various names were suggested, Parks recalled, "but finally the Rev. Wm. Washburn proposed the name, Marysville, in honor of the handsomest lady in the place, Mrs. Mary Covillaud. She being the only lady then in the place of course there were none to take any exceptions and the name was adopted, all filling their glasses and drinking to Marysville."[45]

A few days later a higher-ranking judge in Sacramento swore in Field as the first alcalde of Marysville. Since Californians had just ratified a new constitution, officials in Sacramento believed that the judicial offices carried over from Mexican rule would soon be abolished. They therefore arranged to have Field appointed to the more American-style office of justice of the peace.[46] But Field operated the office as if he were an alcalde. Assuming mayoral functions, he had the banks of the river graded to facilitate commerce, and he replaced the elected marshal with a man of his own choosing.

As the town's judicial officer, he handled both civil and criminal cases, taking jurisdiction in every case brought before him.

The legal system existing in Marysville when Field took office was primitive to nonexistent. There was neither a courthouse nor a jail, and there were few formalities of law. Despite his ample legal skill, therefore, Field had to judge more by instinct than by law. This was apparently how he handled civil matters, for his favorite stories of those cases usually involve his getting people to compromise or to see the error of their complaints. The temper of the times, however, was best captured in the criminal arena. Field left a few colorful stories about the cases he handled as alcalde, but as a storyteller he was no match for William Schuyler Moses, a California pioneer who recalled his day in Field's court.

Moses had developed scurvy while mining a claim located about eighteen miles north of Marysville. In need of help, he left his claim and headed back to "the settlements." As he approached a place called Segar Bar he came across another miner who was even worse off than he. "His legs trembled—his skin the color of putty—hands swollen, and eyes of a dull leaden color, and I knew at once, that like myself—he was a Scurvy victim." The stranger, believing that he had either to quit his claim and live or stay and die, offered to sell the claim and equipment to Moses for twenty-five dollars. But Moses advised him that he did not need to give up the claim. "Leave your tools piled up in a corner of it—that will hold the claim from being jumped," Moses advised, "write some kind of notice, saying you are coming back when you get well." With that, Moses went on his way.

Sometime later Moses was working another claim when he was tapped to sit on a jury in a dispute over the ownership of a rich claim at Segar Bar. The trial took place in a saloon and gambling house, the Striped Tent. Moses recalled that the justice of the peace ordered the gambling to cease and opened court at a big gambling table in the center of the establishment. When the trial began, Moses immediately recognized the man claiming to be the first owner as the scurvy-ridden miner to whom he had given advice at Segar Bar. Each side presented its evidence, then the gambling resumed while the jury went to another room to deliberate. After only a short delay gambling stopped once again, the court opened, and the foreman announced the jury's decision in the once-sick miner's favor.

What followed, Moses tells, was "the most thrilling scene I ever witnessed in California." First the defeated lawyer denounced the jury, saying that "he should advise his Clients to resist that verdict at the point of the knife and the knife to the hilt." Then, pulling a revolver from its holster, the jury foreman asked whether the court intended to protect the jury or if the jury must protect itself. "In an instant there were at least twenty revolvers and other pistols of various kinds drawn and held muzzles up in the air," Moses recalled. But the judge's reaction impressed him most:

Then the Justice said: he would not allow such language by the Counsel— and would *Himself protect the Jury* and, doing what I never saw before— drew from his breast pocket an eight-inch Bowie knife, placed its back between his teeth, and from its Holster drew a Navy Colts revolver, cocked it, and placing its muzzle within six inches of the offending Counsels head— *Hissed at him, the command* "Eat those words, or Dam you, I'll send you to Hell." The Counsel meekly said "I eat," and the pistols were returned to their holsters. The Judge then said to the two [defendant] Miners, "Jumpers, you are dishonest men, this Bar don't want you on it. If you or your Counsel are here at sunrise tomorrow morning, you will never leave the Bar again—Court is closed."

That justice of the peace came up from Marysville, Moses tells us: "He was Stephen J. Field, late . . . Justice of the Supreme Court of the UNITED STATES."[47]

Tall though Moses's tale may be, it captures the moment. Field may not have been another Judge Roy Bean, but he was the only law northwest of the Yuba.[48] As alcalde he introduced American notions of procedural justice into his courtroom, calling juries and grand juries and appointing counsel. Yet he administered justice and discipline with impunity and with the flair common to gold-rush California. When a man named Gideon Nightingill was charged with stealing a cow, Field found "mitigating circumstances" because the man needed food and the cow was available. He ordered Nightingill to pay for the cow and court costs and dismissed the case.[49] Public whipping (and sometimes banishment) was the penalty Field ordered for thieves. He justified the punishment as the only way to save convicts from being lynched, but he also boasted that "there was something so degrading about a public whipping, that I have never known a man thus whipped to have stayed [in town] longer than he could help."[50] In one instance Field ordered that a man convicted of robbing a woman be given fifty lashes on two successive days unless he gave up the money, in which case he was to receive only the first fifty. After about twenty-two lashes, the thief agreed to give up his secret. He led the marshal to the cache and apologized to the woman. Although he probably thought his ordeal was over, the marshal disagreed. In Field's words, "He marched the wretch back to the tree and gave him the balance [twenty-eight lashes], which was his due."[51]

Field claimed that he was successful in keeping crime under control and arbitrating civil disputes in early Marysville, but the most important accomplishment of his tenure as alcalde was much less colorful. At the time of Marysville's founding he had suggested that the new city needed a system for recording deeds and registering transfers of property. The importance of filing deed records is that it provides evidence of a person's ownership and notice to any other person who might be interested in the land. Field displayed an innate understanding of the subtleties of law. He knew that the Covillaud partnership's claim to the property they were selling was weak. Furthermore, he probably knew that even Captain Sutter's claim was uncertain. In the Treaty of Guadalupe Hidalgo the United States promised to respect property rights acquired during Mexican rule, but no one was certain what that meant or how it would be applied, and the federal government had not yet given any direction. Nevertheless, Field knew that the recording system lends legal formality to the transfer of property, and he recognized that formal institutions lend legitimacy. With this in mind he and a clerk opened a deed records office and kept a registry of conveyances in the district, which was profitable to Field in two ways. First, he recalls that he received "a large sum" as fees for taking acknowledgments and affidavits and recording titles. Second, of course, any legitimacy the filing system bestowed on land transfers in general also applied to the sixty-five lots he had purchased from the partnership.

Despite Field's efforts to provide the town with deed records, Marysville quickly witnessed the kind of land dispute that was to become endemic in California. The town plat that the Covillaud partnership had commissioned set aside a large landing and plaza at the water's edge. The plaza, which was designed to be the commercial center of the town, was bordered by three adobe buildings that were used as trading posts and residences.[52] The Covillaud group owned at least one and possibly all the buildings. They, and others who owned land bordering the plaza, definitely had the best locations for business and trade. When squatters began to occupy the plaza the owners of the bordering lots petitioned Field to have them removed. Field reports that he called upon the squatters and threatened that if they did not leave by a certain time, he would be compelled to remove them by force. This was enough, Field proudly recalled; the squatters left the landing, and business continued smoothly.[53] The alcalde's response may have ended the incident, but it would become apparent within the year that it did not end the tension.

Field's reign as alcalde lasted only a couple of months. In April 1850 the county was reorganized and Marysville's original government disbanded.

Field might have continued to serve in a judicial capacity for some time, but if so, his status as a judge was somewhat uncertain. Beginning in February, the California legislature passed a series of laws abolishing the Mexican-style judicial offices and reorganizing the courts. In March it divided the state into nine judicial districts headed by district courts. Then in April, it set up county courts, with each county having one county judge and two justices of the peace.[54] Field, defeated in an election for county judge, was left out of the new government.[55] He remained a prominent and prosperous citizen, however. By Field's own estimation the value of his property increased tenfold, which would have made his lots worth more than $160,000. He sold a few lots, and according to one story, he may have gained others in good-natured poker games with his friend Judge Gordon N. Mott.[56] He also received $1,000 per month rent for frame and zinc houses he owned. In any case, Field obviously left office with a good financial basis upon which to begin a legal practice, and he remained friends with most of the town's early business and social elite.[57]

Even in his new status as private citizen, Field was not long removed from Marysville's limelight. In June 1850 the new district court judge, William R. Turner, replaced Field as the highest judicial authority in Marysville, and it was not long before the two men clashed. On June 7, while representing John Sutter in Turner's court, Field said something that obviously irritated the new judge. It irked him so much, in fact, that he held Field in contempt of court, ordered him to be confined for forty-eight hours, and fined him $500. There is no dependable record of the remarks that sparked the incident. Field claimed that Turner, a southerner, was prejudiced against him because he was from New York. For his part, Turner claimed that Field had been disrespectful in court, a charge that is not altogether unbelievable since Field at times displayed an ample capacity for arrogance. More than likely, however, the incident was a matter of personal animosity, a clash of egos that grew far out of proportion.

One aspect that makes the Turner-Field clash interesting, however, was the manner in which it tested the formal legal institutions that recently had been implanted in California. Claiming that he could not be confined without formal process, Field petitioned the county court for a writ of habeas corpus. Fellow attorneys, S. B. Mulford and Jessie O. Goodwin, testified that Turner's conduct had been outrageous. Technically, the county court's jurisdiction was inferior to that of Judge Turner's district court. Nevertheless, county court Judge H. P. Haun granted the petition and ordered Field released. That was on a Friday. Field celebrated by buying drinks and cigars for a crowd that had gathered to observe what was going on. That night a

crowd burned Judge Turner in effigy. Field claimed the crowd acted sponta-
neously after Turner had gone from saloon to saloon threatening Field
and his friends and calling them "perjured Scoundrels." Turner claimed
that Field incited the mob, exhorting them to throw the district judge into
the Yuba River. He also claimed that the mob fired gunshots into his office.

Whatever actually happened, the following Monday Turner responded
by holding Judge Haun in contempt and ordering Field, Goodwin, and
Mulford disbarred. When the sheriff and twenty armed men arrived in the
county court to carry out Turner's orders, Judge Haun expelled the posse
from the courtroom and fined the sheriff $200 for contempt. Later, Field
was locked up and Haun quietly paid his fine, but the matter of disbarment
remained. Acting for himself and the other two attorneys, Field appealed to
the state supreme court, which ruled in Field's favor, ordering that he, Mulford, and Goodwin be reinstated into the bar. Turner first complied with
the supreme court's order by reinstating Field and the others, but then he
disbarred Field once again. Field again appealed to the supreme court, and
again it ruled in his favor.[58]

The dispute between Field and Turner demonstrated that the administration of law in the new state had not yet been perfected. Confusion and
uncertainty reigned. The lower court judges tended to assume more power
than they would reasonably possess. Turner acted as a dictator, Haun tested
Turner by issuing a writ of habeas corpus, and Turner tested the supreme
court by circumventing its order to reinstate Field. The supreme court, on
the other hand, was cautious in its response to Turner. It never punished
him for ignoring its order or ruled that he had exceeded his authority by
disbarring Field. Rather, it simply reasoned that, by virtue of being a member of the bar of the state's highest court, Field must also be able to practice
in the lower courts. In the end, the somewhat slipshod legal process that
was in place in California did not at all hurt Field's chances to regain the
right to practice law. As he would often do again, Field proved to be superior at molding the forms of law to his own use.

The conflict between Field and Turner did not confine itself to the courts
of law; they attempted to affect the outcome of the dispute by appealing
to public sentiment. Each man published pamphlets and found newspapers willing to publicize his side of the story. They poured out charges,
countercharges, and epithets, written with a mix of erudition and crudity
that could only have come from the pen of frontier lawyers. Turner characterized Field's life as "a series of little-minded meanliness, of braggadocio
pusillanimity and contemptible vanity, which when known will sink him so
low in public estimation that the hand of the resurrectionist will never reach

him." Field described Turner as "a man of depraved tastes, of vulgar habits, of ungovernable temper, reckless of truth when his passion is excited, and grossly incompetent to discharge the duties of his office." "It is a sad thing," Field concluded, "that such a man should ever be clothed with the Judicial Ermine."[59] In keeping with their relationship, each man also reveled in calling the other a coward and providing examples. Field recalled that, after Turner made a threat on his life, he armed himself with a pair of revolvers and had a "slack-coat made with pockets from which the barrels could lie, and be discharged." After he practiced firing the pistols through his trick coat, Field was able to hit small objects across the street. He believed that this display of force and his courage in confronting Turner whenever they passed were the only reasons that violence was averted between them.[60]

Courage and tenacity are the traits Field emphasized in his recollections of the Turner incident, but other aspects of his personality became apparent during the half year that the rivalry continued. Vindictiveness was one. While the dispute was running, Field was elected to the state assembly, and he mounted an attempt to have Turner impeached. The impeachment was sidetracked in the legislative milieu, but it was not Field's only legislative weapon. He also introduced a bill to reorganize the judiciary. Field's bill created a new judicial district made up of still rugged and lightly populated Trinity and Klamath counties. When it passed, Turner became judge of the new district. Reveling in the success of his plan to get rid of a hated enemy, Field boasted that he had sent Turner "where there are only grizzly bears and Indians."[61]

Although vindictive, when seen in context Field's treatment of Turner was not necessarily outrageous. Field was fighting for his professional life in his new home. So long as he remained disbarred, he was unable to appear before the district court, in effect making it impossible for him to practice law in Marysville. Field later recalled that idleness forced him into speculations. When these went sour, he lost most of the property he had earlier gained. Expulsion from the bar thus deprived Field of his trade. In his appeal to the state supreme court, Field argued that he had a right to practice his profession. Further, he argued, he could not arbitrarily be deprived of that right without being given notice or a hearing.[62] Thirty years later, sitting on the U.S. Supreme Court, he heard a strikingly similar appeal from an attorney who had been disbarred. Field then reasoned that notice and hearing were a rule of natural justice, which "should be equally followed when proceedings are taken to deprive him of his right to practice his profession, as when they are taken to reach his real or personal property." Without observance of such a rule, Field warned, no one would be safe from oppression wherever power may be lodged.[63] By then, however, this concept of a right to practice a profession was more than a matter of running across a similar case. As we shall later see, it was becoming an integral part of a budding legal doctrine.

In late summer and fall 1850, while Field and Turner feuded, friends encouraged Field to run for the state legislature. He decided to enter the race, saying he wanted to reform the judiciary and to remove Turner from the district. That obviously was not the only issue on the voters' minds, but there is not much of an explicit record of Field's campaign platform or that of his opponent. Turner spread a rumor that Field was an abolitionist. It was true he had a brother living in New York who was a Free-Soiler, Field admitted, but he also had a brother who was a slaveholder in Tennessee.[64] The *Herald*, Marysville's only newspaper at the time, supported Field in the legislative race and joined in denying that he had abolitionist leanings: "Briefly, he believes that every state has the right to regulate the institution of slavery, or whether it shall or shall not exist in its own borders," wrote the *Herald*, "and he has often expressed to us the opinion that the abolition agitation can do no good, and that the General Government have no more right to meddle with slavery in the different States, than they have with slavery in Turkey."[65] This issue may have swayed a few voters, but the sectionalist rivalries that were important in national politics were subdued in the relative isolation of California. Other issues of more immediate personal interest to the new inhabitants probably held more sway.

In late September the *Herald*'s editor, R. H. Taylor, reported that Field had gone to the mountains to dig for gold with his own hands in order to defray the expenses of his campaign.[66] It seems highly unlikely that Field actually mined for gold; that would have been out of character. Perhaps Taylor meant that Field went to the mountains to mine for votes. Field's district included the mining regions as well as the city, and he claimed to have spoken in every precinct. He made a strong pitch to the miners' interest. Local magistrates should be given more authority, he said, so that miners could settle their disputes without going to the county seat. He also proposed legislation to protect miner's claims and to exempt their tools from forced sale. His appeal to the miners was a lucky move; as it turned out, he desperately needed their votes. The election of October 7, 1850, gave Field a seat in the state assembly. He won by an overall vote of 2,068 to 1,771, but the count revealed that he had been badly defeated in his hometown, Marysville, receiving only 42 percent of the vote to 58 percent for his opponent, John T. McCarty.[67]

Field later tried to explain away this embarrassment, maintaining that his defeat in Marysville was the fallout of an episode in which he defended an accused murderer from a lynch mob. Field, proud of his respect for the legal process, told how he had defended other intended victims of the lynch mob as well.[68] Sectionalism also may have played a part in his poor showing, and his dispute with Turner certainly lost the votes of Turner's friends. None of these explanations, however, is completely satisfying. The election demonstrated that, although Field made loyal friends and allies during the nine months he had lived in Marysville, he was not universally loved. It also showed that a majority of the community was not as impressed with his accomplishments as alcalde as was Field himself. The language of early California politics tended to be blunt, but the attacks on Field were especially vicious and personal. William T. Barbour, Turner's successor as district court judge, described Field with the plea, "May Heaven deliver us from the jaws of this monstrous reptile." John T. McCarty, his opponent, said Field was "a liar, a coward, and a villain" who was generally despised in the community. Field responded that McCarty was "a blustering miscreant."[69]

Squatters and Speculators

The fuel that fed these intense feelings probably was rivalry over the ownership of the land in and around Marysville. On August 6, 1850, the first issue of the *Herald* printed a notice signed by the five Covillaud partners claiming that they had legal title for most of the land surrounding the town and warning squatters who had settled in that area to leave and others to stay away. Many of the so-called squatters did not believe they were taking anyone's property. They thought of themselves as settlers who had as much, or more, right to the land as the Covillaud partners. They immediately formed an organization "for the purpose of taking some concerted action to guard against the monopoly of Landed Aristocracy whose pretended claims covered the whole country."[70] In a series of meetings held in August, they did little more than pass resolutions denying the validity of the partners' title to the rural lands and favoring what they viewed as a traditional right to homestead on 160 acres. The squatters also resolved to support only legislative candidates who favored repeal of the law called "forcible entry and detainer," which provided the legal procedure for removing trespassers from land.

This issue was not just local. By 1850 land disputes were erupting all over the state. Conflict over the ownership of land would dominate California politics and law for at least two decades to come. It would be a main topic of dispute when Field joined the state supreme court, and it would continue to be a problem during the first years that he sat on the U.S. Supreme Court. In both roles, Field would come to play a large part in determining how the dispute would be resolved. To some extent, at least, the decisions he would make when he became a judge grew from his experiences during his early years in Marysville.

Although the conflict in Marysville was peaceful, it coincided with a violent battle over ownership of the land in nearby Sacramento. Like Marysville, Sacramento was located in an area that was part of John Sutter's grant from the Mexican government. Sutter and his son laid out the city in January 1849, hoping that it would become the commercial center for the northern mining regions. Lots were put up for sale in January 1849, generally selling for $250. To encourage settlement the Sutters prohibited sales of more than four lots to one person, but they quickly lost control of the development of Sacramento. Early on, the Sutters' attorneys, Peter H. Burnett and Alexander Carey Peachy, acquired a substantial number of lots. Later, the Sutters gave favorable treatment to certain businesses. Priest, Lee, and Company and Sam Brannan, for example, received 500 lots as payment for not moving their businesses to the rival city of Sutterville. It was soon evident that there was a fortune to be made in land speculation. Within six months lots that had sold for $250 commanded as much as $3,000, and the escalation continued.

Despite bouts with cholera and floods, Sacramento, like San Francisco and Marysville, grew at a dizzying pace. Hubert Howe Bancroft estimated that within ten months it had grown to 10,000 inhabitants supporting 403 stores, including soda fountains, lemon syrup factories, and breweries as well as the usual clothing stores, livery stables, and blacksmith shops. Ninety physicians and seventy lawyers also called Sacramento home. During this growth spurt prices for lots reached as high as $30,000, and a building rented for as much as $5,000 per month. Yet many of the town lots remained vacant, which was the source of the problems that were to come.[71]

Newcomers, unable to afford land, settled on vacant lots, some of which speculators claimed under Sutter deeds. Maintaining that these people were driven in part by jealousy of those earlier arrivals who had invested in property, unfriendly newspapers of the day referred to them as squatters. The term carried a decidedly negative connotation. Yet these people could not be easily dismissed as merely thieves or deadbeats. Whether called squatter or settler, many were idealistic and hardworking. They thought that the land they had occupied was public land and therefore theirs for the taking. The law of nature, they believed, gave them the right to a parcel of land:

"The people who rushed to California took with them a view long held on the frontier that it was one of the fundamental rights of Americans to enter upon public lands, make improvements, create a farm, and eventually acquire ownership free or at a modest price."[72] Most believed that the practice of holding property for no other reason than to turn a profit from speculation was unfair, and they saw nothing wrong with settling on property that was not being used.

The speculators' greed, they thought, was spoiling their chance at the American dream. It was a dream that grew from the land policy that the American government applied in most other parts of the country. The government's goal was to encourage settlement of land in the public domain. The American approach had a distinctly democratic flair, in that it encouraged settlement from the bottom up, allowing individual homesteaders to claim a maximum of 160 acres. This policy was applied throughout much of the West, including California's neighboring territory, Oregon.

Homesteading was the tradition that American settlers were used to, but it was not the tradition under which Mexican California had been settled. The Mexican government's goal was the same as that of the American—to encourage settlement. Mexican policy, however, had an aristocratic tinge. It built from the top down, giving large holdings to leaders who would then guide the development of the region. It was under this policy that in 1841 Mexican governor Juan Bautista Alvarado had granted John Sutter the rights to eleven square leagues of land, roughly 50,000 acres covering an area that would include both Marysville and Sacramento.

Conflict between these two traditions arose from the treaty that ended the Mexican-American War and that gave California to the United States. As part of the Treaty of Guadalupe Hidalgo the United States guaranteed that the property rights of all residents should be inviolably respected. Nevertheless, settlers believed that the title claimed by people who had purchased property from Sutter was of questionable legality, and in any case, they thought it was immoral. Congress had not yet provided guidance for interpreting this provision of the treaty, but land seekers in California found it difficult to believe that some 700 individuals who had received grants under Mexican rule would be allowed to monopolize 13 to 14 million acres without appreciably improving or using them.[73]

In the settlers' minds, speculators were not only greedy, they also posed a serious threat to the homestead tradition. But, regardless of their motivations, the holders of paper title turned to another American tradition to justify their cause—an almost sacred respect for property. Titleholders emphasized that they possessed the legal title to the disputed property. They reasoned that the settlers' demand that land should be free to every settler implied that those property rights that had been vested under Mexican rule should be disregarded. This in turn implied that the Treaty of Guadalupe Hidalgo should be ignored.[74] Law and order thus became a key aspect of the titleholders' appeal. The law, at least in the formalities of law, appeared to be on their side. But any special claim that titleholders had in the property, whether legal or moral, depended entirely on the validity of Sutter's grant. Without that link they would be nothing other than squatters themselves.

On April 23, 1850, a Sacramento newspaper printed a purported "translation" of Sutter's grant, showing that it did not include Sacramento. This was all the settlers needed to justify their cause, for, if the report was true, the land on which the city sat would have been public domain. By June, squatters formed a settlers association and quickly seized on the moment. At the association's first meeting, Dr. Charles Robinson introduced a resolution claiming that land in California was presumed public and resolving that the association would protect any settler in the possession of land to the extent of one lot in the city or 160 acres in the country until valid title was proved.[75] Robinson quickly emerged as a leader of the Sacramento settler movement.

Hubert Howe Bancroft, the least sympathetic of contemporary observers, claimed that the squatters' movement was dominated by a criminal and lawless element. That was certainly the image the titleholders hoped to cultivate, but it was not entirely accurate.[76] There may have been a lawless aspect to the movement and there may have been a lawless element within it, but even critics admitted that Robinson was not a criminal. He was an idealist who later became a leader in the Free-Soil movement and the governor of Kansas. Josiah Royce, another unsympathetic contemporary observer, called Robinson a dangerous leader of a revolutionary movement but admitted he was a man whose motives seemed above any suspicion of personal greed.[77] Robinson's initial strategy was certainly not revolutionary. He hoped to bring the settlers' cause to federal courts, where he believed they would receive a fair hearing. Robinson also seemed to be aware of the possibility that settlers would be labeled criminals and that public sentiment would thus be turned against them. He therefore encouraged his followers not to be the instigators of violence.[78]

As the summer progressed, however, the settlers grew stronger and more assertive. The organization held regular meetings, at one point even voting that each member be assigned a city lot. Individual squabbles broke out over vacant lots. In response, the landowners of Sacramento formed a law-and-order association and organized a company of militia. When the vigilante group began to demolish squatters' houses and to tear down fences, the formula for violent confrontation was fully established. Even Robinson now thought the time for moderation had passed. He was ready to leave his corpse on his own bit of land rather than yield his rights. Declaring that every man had a sacred right to a homestead and a sacred right to defend it, Robinson announced that he would help rebuild the torn-down fences. "The land speculators' doctrine about land grants would certainly result in oppression of the poor man," he said; "the Southern slave is not worse treated." Others joined with him. If the landowners wanted to fight, let them fight, one settler warned, and the devil take the hindmost.[79]

Enraged settlers gathered on August 12 at a lot where the sheriff was to serve a warrant. Trouble was averted temporarily when Mayor Bigelow agreed to listen to the settlers' demands. Meanwhile, however, two settler leaders, James McClatchy and Michael Moran, were arrested and put in the prison barge. The next day thirty to forty armed settlers marched to the barge to release the prisoners. The scene that day would have been comic had it not turned out so tragically. One settler, James Maloney, rode on horseback with a sword drawn, leading his marching compatriots through the streets of Sacramento. They were followed by a crowd of unarmed citizens hooting and jeering and oblivious of any danger. But danger was present. The mayor and Sheriff Joseph McKinney, along with an armed force, caught up and ordered the settlers to lay down their arms and surrender. When one shouted, "Shoot the mayor!" gunfire erupted from both sides. The mayor fell from his horse wounded; Maloney fell dead. Two others were dead, and more, including Charles Robinson, were severely wounded. The settlers scattered, many of them fleeing town, but that was not the end of the matter. Skirmishes over the next few days resulted in more fatalities, including that of Sheriff McKinney.

Commentators have uniformly concluded that the Sacramento uprising was condemned throughout the state. It is curious, however, how little action was taken in prosecuting the people involved. At first, rumors that squatters would set the city afire swirled around Sacramento. Armed vigilante militia patrolled the streets. The settlers' attorney, threatened with hanging, left town, and Robinson was put in jail. But when the excitement settled down, even Josiah Royce noticed a tacit consent in the city to drop the subject.[80] Robinson was released after spending only a few weeks in prison. He founded the *Settlers' and Miners' Tribune* and continued to press the settlers' cause. Less than two months after the Sacramento squatters' uprising, Robinson was elected to the state assembly, where he joined Stephen Field.

The Sacramento uprising was not an isolated event. It was part of a spontaneous although disorganized movement that became the most pervasive and bitter issue in California politics in the 1850s.[81] Over the course of the decade, squatter unrest broke out at various places from Oakland in the north to Santa Barbara in the south. Nor was violence the only outlet for settlers; they also wielded considerable political power. In 1855 a settlers' convention threatened to establish its own political party, and at various times leaders such as Sen. William Gwin and Gov. John Bigler took up their cause. Settlers had some success in the passing of favorable legislation. Adverse possession laws, for example, gave settlers title to land that had been abandoned by the holders of legal title. Occupancy laws provided compensation to settlers who had improved land later found to be private property.[82]

The discontent of settlers also provides an explanation for Field's poor showing in his hometown when he ran for state assembly in 1850. Field's views on the question were not a mystery. In early confrontations over the ownership of land in Marysville, Field had made it plain that his sympathies were with the Covillaud partners and the people who had purchased land from them. Field was, after all, a speculator himself. As alcalde he had removed squatters from land near the river, threatening to call in the army if necessary. An article appearing in the *California Courier* shortly afterward lauded him for promoting local interests by overcoming squatters' intrusions.[83] Field did not deviate from his sympathy for titleholders. Even thirty years later he condemned "sharpers and squatters" who he thought had stripped Captain Sutter of everything he owned.[84]

Although land disputes were relatively quiet in Marysville, settlers undoubtedly considered Field an enemy. It is interesting that Charles Robinson's newspaper, the *Settlers' and Miners' Tribune,* supported Turner in his dispute with Field.[85] When settlers did organize in 1850 they chose as their leader John T. McCarty, a young lawyer from Indiana, who was to be Field's opponent in the upcoming election.[86] Field won election to the assembly, but it was obvious that he had not made friends of the people who were left out of the scramble for land.

The California Assembly

Field would serve only one term in the California assembly. His primary interest was on matters related to the judiciary and the legal process. The only standing committee to which he was appointed was the Committee on the Judiciary, and by using this position he was able to get even with Judge Turner. Other than that, the achievement of which Field was most proud was his sponsorship of new codes of criminal and civil procedure, which were adopted from model codes that his brother David Dudley Field had designed.[87]

Beyond these few bills, it is difficult to glean from the official record of the assembly how Field aligned himself politically. The few times he was matched against the settlers' champion, Charles Robinson, the two cast opposing votes. Yet in a choice that did not seem to fit with the reputation his opponents had given him, Field enthusiastically supported two debtor-relief statutes. One exempted certain items of personal property, such as basic provisions and tools of the trade, from forced sale to satisfy a debt. The other exempted a person's homestead up to a value of $5,000.[88]

Field did not forget the miners who had voted for him. As promised, he sponsored a bill that would have the effect of making customary mining law part of the state's statutes. He also served his constituents by passing laws to incorporate Marysville and the city of Nevada, to divide Yuba County, and to establish a new county called Medera.[89]

Field's own moral code was reflected in several other miscellaneous matters. He opposed legislation that would legalize lotteries. He proposed a bill that would provide new grounds for divorce for extreme cruelty, habitual intemperance, willful desertion of either the husband or the wife for two years, and failure of the husband to provide for the wife. And he voted against a resolution to prohibit smoking in the chambers while the assembly was in session.[90]

According to his own recollections, Field's days in the assembly were filled with frontier-style excitement. One such incident occurred during a hearing on the Turner impeachment. As Field relates the incident, he had just addressed the assembly, calling for Turner's impeachment, when another member, B. F. Moore, took his pistols out of his drawer, cocked them, and laid them on his desk. Moore, Field recalls, then launched into an offensive and personal attack against him. The *Marysville Herald* reported that during the course of his speech, Moore became so agitated that he cursed, swore, threw a book at Field, and slammed a cane on one of the desks as he advanced toward Field yelling, "God dam you, I'll beat your brains out." That evening, Field resolved to receive an apology or to "seek personal satisfaction." Since dueling was illegal, however, Field had some difficulty finding a second to deliver his demand, until he ran into David Broderick, then a state senator. When Broderick delivered the demand, Moore replied that he would not participate in an illegal duel, but he was willing to meet Field at any time or place. Field was unwilling to get into a street fight, Broderick told Drury Baldwin, Moore's second; he would ask for recognition in the assembly and accuse Moore of being a liar and a coward. "Then," said Baldwin, "Judge Field will get shot in his seat." It was a threat to be taken seriously. In those days it was not unusual for members of the assembly to be armed, Field recalled: "Of the thirty-six members of which the Assembly consisted, over two-thirds never made their appearance without having knives or pistols upon their persons, and frequently both." The following day, backed up by Broderick and "eight or nine of his personal friends, all armed to the teeth and ready for any emergency," Field prepared to make his accusations. Before he could speak, however, Moore apologized and that was the end of the matter.[91]

On a later occasion, while Broderick and Field were having a drink, Broderick noticed that Vicesimus Turner, "a brother of the Judge and man of desperate character," had drawn his revolver and leveled it at Field. Broderick abruptly shoved Field out of the barroom, apparently saving him once again. Later, Field recalled that Broderick's acts of friendship filled him with a profound sense of gratitude: "For years afterwards I thought and felt as if there was nothing I could do that would be a sufficient return for his kindness. On his account I took much greater interest in political matters than I otherwise should."[92]

When the legislative session ended on May 1, 1851, Field returned to Marysville to a private life practicing law, but he would not remain out of public office for long. Nor would he remain aloof from controversy. In 1857 Field would seek and win election to a seat on the California Supreme Court. Before turning to his record on the state bench, however, the next chapter will set the political stage in early California. In the process, it will examine the political ideals that inspired many of the new state's inhabitants and focus on disputes over mining rights and land ownership: the issues that dominated politics in the early years of statehood.

2

CALIFORNIA DREAMING

Tucked away among the baggage many new Californians brought west was their party affiliation. Although the constitutional convention of 1849 and the 1850 Marysville election in which Stephen Field won a seat in the assembly were not dominated by major political parties, it did not take long for the national parties to make their presence felt. Within a year of Field's election, Marysville's leading newspaper, the *Herald,* had declared itself a voice of the Whig party. The *Herald*'s announcement reflected a fast-moving trend. Political parties were taking hold throughout the state. Field quickly affiliated with the Democratic party. For the remainder of his life, even after joining the U.S. Supreme Court, he had one hand mired in party politics. Field's influence on state politics was insubstantial until late in the 1850s. Nevertheless, the events of the formative years were important in shaping his career and his outlook.

The Democrats and the Whigs both had a strong following in the state. But most of the political intrigue of the first decade of California politics centered not on rivalries between the parties but on rivalries among Democrats, who dominated the state from the early 1850s until the party collapsed in 1860 at the beginning of the Civil War. The split in the Democratic party has been attributed to a variety of intertwined factors. Local jealousies, individual ambitions, and personal loyalties explain much of the political maneuvering. National politics, with its competing sectional loyalties and its racial and ethnic animosities, played a role as well.[1]

Another factor contributing to the fray may have been the most important, however. Many of the people who ventured to California brought along a more abstract political identity, one that was broader, and perhaps deeper, than party ties. It was a distinctive blend of economic ideals and personal interest. These pioneers had come of age under the influence of Jacksonian Democracy. They lived in a time when the meaning of free labor was debated throughout the nation. They came to California in search of new opportunities, yet they could not completely discard the traditions of their past. Under these conditions Californians developed their own brand of political identity. It mixed equal parts of popular economic theory and political philosophy with the experience of the gold rush and the expectations of the people who migrated.

Gwin and Broderick

Struggle for control of the Democratic party centered on two individuals, William Gwin and David Broderick, who were as different in style, personality, and background as one could imagine. They had one thing in common, however; the overpowering ambition to be the United States senator from California. Their contest for that office, which culminated in the senatorial selection of 1857, overshadowed virtually every other political story in California's first five years of statehood.

William Gwin, leader of a wing of the party referred to as Chivalry Democrats, or Chivs, enjoyed a background of culture, education, and influential friends.[2] Born in Tennessee, he had a long association with Andrew Jackson, who was a neighbor of the Gwin family. Gwin's father had served with Old Hickory in the War of 1812. The younger Gwin continued the association, supporting Jackson politically and serving as confidential secretary to the president for a short time. Gwin was educated both in medicine and law. He practiced the former for a short time in Mississippi, but his attention soon turned to politics and business. His business speculations, though hugely profitable at first, collapsed during the panic of 1837. In 1840 Gwin was elected to Congress. Surprisingly, he became friends with Jackson's old nemesis, John C. Calhoun, who ignited the thought of California in Gwin's mind. After one term in Congress, Gwin was appointed to a lucrative patronage post as commissioner of Public Works in New Orleans. When his job there was jeopardized by the election of Whig president Zachary Taylor, Gwin decided it was time to head west.

In his early political and business life Gwin seemed to hover on the cusp of greatness. He had the connections and the intelligence, but he never seemed to make it over the edge. Perhaps that is why he left for California; certainly destiny was on his mind. An often-told story is that, while in Washington the day before his departure, Gwin happened to meet Sen. Stephen A. Douglas and remarked that he was leaving the next day for California. "One year from now I will return to Washington as a United States Senator from California," he told Douglas, "and I will ask you to present my credentials." Eleven months thereafter, the story goes, Gwin handed his credentials to Douglas, who presented them to the Senate.[3]

Almost as soon as he arrived in California, Gwin became a delegate to the constitutional convention of 1849. There he displayed Jacksonian roots by opposing the creation of a banking system and favoring restrictions of the privileges usually enjoyed by corporations. He also played a prominent role in the convention's efforts to set a state boundary. Gwin offered a proposal that would expand the state beyond the Sierra Nevada Mountains and cover most of the territory ceded to the United States in the treaty with Mexico, a plan that would have almost doubled the size of present-day California. At first glance it was a curious proposal for a southerner to make, since California was to be admitted as a free state. But Gwin may have been motivated more by personal ambition than by southern loyalties. He thought that his proposal would settle permanently the question of whether slavery should be extended into the western territories. Some observers claim that he was motivated by a belief that solving this problem, which had brought Congress to a standstill, would secure for him an exalted reputation when he arrived in the Senate.[4] Whatever his motives, the event certainly demonstrated that Gwin was not dogmatic regarding the slavery issue.

True to his prediction, William Gwin was selected as U.S. senator. On January 1, 1850, the California legislature chose him, along with John C. Frémont, as the state's first senators. California actually ratified its constitution and elected its congressional delegation before it was admitted as a state. When the delegation arrived in Washington, therefore, its first task was to get the state admitted to the Union. This priority was accomplished as part of the Compromise of 1850, by which Congress admitted California as a free state, abolished the slave trade in the District of Columbia, enacted the Fugitive Slave Act of 1850, and created the territories of New Mexico and Utah with instructions that each would be admitted as a state "with or without slavery, as their constitutions may prescribe at the time of admission." On September 9, 1850, Congress passed the act admitting California, and on September 11 Gwin and the other members of the delegation were sworn in.[5]

Gwin's chief rival in the Democratic party of the 1850s was a man whose early life was cut from a much rougher cloth.[6] The son of an Irish stonecutter, David Broderick was born in Washington, D.C., and spent most of his youth in New York where he took up his father's trade. His work as an apprentice stonecutter left little time for schooling, but the young Broderick was said to have been an avaricious reader. He also seemed to have a knack for the rough-and-tumble of city politics. His first move up the political ladder was to become foreman of one of the city's volunteer fire companies. In the Tammany Hall system of politics these companies did more than fight fires; they also served as gangs of political operatives who used intimidation and trickery to help the organization win elections. From foreman he moved up to ward boss and then to a federal patronage job. In 1846, when Broderick was just twenty-six years old, the Tammany Democrats nominated him for Congress, but he fell victim to a rift in the party and was defeated. Left with the impression that his political career was going nowhere in New York, Broderick decided to join the exodus to California. He left New York in 1849, telling a friend that if ever he returned to the East it would be as a U.S. senator.

Broderick did not reach that lofty post as quickly as did Gwin, but his political ascent within California was equally swift. Like Gwin, he was a member of the constitutional convention of 1849, but unlike Gwin, whose next step was to the federal Congress, Broderick's was to office within the state government. He was elected to the California Senate in 1850 and became lieutenant governor in 1851. Broderick's base of power was concentrated in San Francisco, where he applied the lessons he had learned in New York. He began by establishing a fire company, then quickly introduced the Tammany style of organization. Using ward organizations, Broderick was able to deliver votes to public servants who promised that he would control local patronage. Such control then enabled him to demand that government employees contribute a portion of their income to the organization. Controlling both money and appointments, he was able to instill significant party discipline in the city.

A system so successful was destined to produce a backlash, and in San Francisco it started with the vigilante committees of 1851 and 1856. Led by local merchants and businessmen, these committees were ostensibly a popular reaction to lawlessness in the city. The hanging and banishment of several supposed criminals left little doubt that the committees had some success on that front. The leaders of the vigilante movement had a political purpose as well, however. Underlying their campaign to eliminate crime was a deep opposition to Broderick's political organization.[7] While the vigilante movement was mixing and fanning anti-crime and anti-Broderick feelings, disaffected Democrats joined with Whigs and the Know-Nothing party to defeat Broderick's forces in the state elections of 1854. Nevertheless, Broderick was able to maintain control of a powerful vote-producing machine in San Francisco. Since a majority of the state's population lived in that city, he was later able to regroup and extend his power to the state Democratic committee.

The difference between Gwin and Broderick in terms of political philosophy is not as easy to determine as the differences in their background. Broderick is usually portrayed as a champion of the working class. Yet he was not above participating in money-making schemes and speculation in town lots. Gwin may have been more closely linked to the elites of American politics and society, but he often supported legislation favoring miners and settlers. It appears that political power and personal ambition, rather than ideology, fueled their rivalry. Yet that rivalry affected every California politician, including Stephen Field, who had connections with both men and played a small role when they confronted each other in the 1857 senatorial contest.

The issue of slavery dominated national politics in the late 1850s, and the names of the competing factions of the California Democratic party implies that it had some influence on California politics as well. One side, the Chivalry wing, was said to be of southern sentiment and thus, by association, proslavery. On the other side was the Tammany wing, which was northern more in its methods than in any attachment to abolitionism. Sectionalism would eventually have its day at the forefront of California politics; however, despite the names of these factions, the slavery question did not dominate California politics until the eve of the Civil War.[8] Without giving the subject any discussion at all, the delegates to the constitutional convention of 1849 voted to prohibit slavery in the state.[9]

Even though slavery itself was not the major issue in California politics of the early 1850s, racism was very much alive. The same convention that prohibited slavery refused to extend suffrage to nonwhites and proposed banning "free persons of color" from the state.[10] From the earliest years of statehood, racial and ethnic prejudice often entered California politics. Whether directed against blacks, Hispanics, Irish Catholics, or Chinese, it found its way into political rhetoric and legislation throughout the nineteenth century.

The new Californians were not unprejudiced. They just did not seem to be as preoccupied with slavery as were people in the East. Although the records of political conventions of the 1850s do contain debates on slavery, newspapers of the same time pay relatively little attention to the issue. While the slavery question appeared to be swimming in the undercurrent of political contests, matters of local concern dominated the attention of most people. The new Californians were more concerned with the distribution of the state's land, rules regarding mining, and building the transcontinental railroad.

In a way these issues and the slave controversy were flip sides of the same coin "in that they reflected a common concern with the shape of freedom."[11] The people who came to California were not idealists traveling to a new land to establish a society based on some unusual notion of freedom. Nor did they call a constitutional convention in 1849 in order to find a new meaning of freedom. They developed their ideas about liberty in the same way as did the people they left behind. Their ideas were driven by the changes taking place as America moved from a self-sufficient, agrarian-based economy to a market economy. The controversies that resulted and consequently the language of debate were dominated by two intertwined sets of ideals. One, which has been labeled Jacksonian Democracy, was a mix of idealism and a political movement. The other, free labor, was more akin to an economic or a political philosophy.

Jacksonian Democracy in California

Most of the people who went to California came of age in the "age of Jackson." Not all were loyal to Andrew Jackson's Democratic party, but they had a common heritage in the sense that they were weaned in a political environment in which Jacksonian ideals shaped the political and ideological debate. Historian Harry L. Watson probably best captured the mood of the era when he described the appeal of Jackson's veto of the Bank of the United States in 1832. In the public mind, Watson said, "the broadest promise of the American revolution was to make every white man his own master." Jackson's veto message restated that promise.[12]

In the hierarchy of Jacksonian ideals individual liberty sat at the very top. Jacksonians differed from their opponents, the Whig party, not primarily in their admiration of liberty but in what they viewed as the source of liberty and in what they considered a threat to its continued existence. Jackson's followers, according to Lawrence Frederick Kohl, tended to be people who were uncomfortable with America's movement to a market economy.[13] Liberty for them was grounded on a form of self-sufficiency, which they believed was most likely to be found in a society made up of independent farmers and tradesmen. Their opposition to the Bank of the United States stemmed in part from a belief that the credit system it symbolized was a direct threat to the independence such farmers and tradesmen should enjoy. No man who owes more than he can immediately pay is free, warned a Democratic newspaper: "The debtor is not his own master, and a nation of debtors, though it may boast of its freedom, is a nation of slaves."[14]

Second in the hierarchy of Jacksonian ideals was the opposition to special privilege, of which the Bank was a particularly odious form. Jacksonian disdain for privilege usually took the form of persistent attacks against "moneyed interests" or "monopolies." Although the Jacksonian philosophy thus displayed an egalitarian bent, wealth itself was not perceived to be the greatest evil. Wealth resulting from an individual's industry or ingenuity might be admired, but wealth acquired from influence, power, or oppression was not. Jacksonians considered the latter to be artificial wealth, sometimes referring to it as "law made wealth."[15]

The Jacksonian concern about artificial wealth led them to oppose corporations. It is understandable that they lumped corporations and special privilege into the same category. In the 1820s and 1830s corporations were a rare exclusive privilege that the government granted to a group of investors, usually to perform some public function such as building a bridge or canal. Yet Jacksonians also saw inherent danger in the more modern general corporation in that this new form of business tended to insulate individuals from accountability in decisionmaking. Leadership therefore tended to fall into the hands of speculators who were so interested in the pursuit of money that they lost sight of the public interest. More important, however, corporations tended to concentrate power.[16]

Jacksonians disliked privilege because it resulted in inequalities of wealth. They feared privilege because it tended to concentrate power. It created a vicious cycle that threatened their freedom. Inequalities in wealth gave the people with the most money the means with which to influence government, which in turn resulted in their receiving more special privilege. Thus special privilege in general, and more specifically the Bank of the United States, represented an indirect threat to the less wealthy, who tended to be rendered powerless by this very cycle. Jacksonians considered privilege an insidious, indirect threat to the individual liberty they so cherished.[17]

Third in the hierarchy of Jacksonian ideals was the belief in limited government. It is typically said that freedom to Jacksonians meant freedom from government authority; the government that governs least is best. In part their belief in limited government arose from their faith in natural law, the essence of which was freedom and equality. There was a difference between the inequality that existed in natural law and artificial inequality, which could result only from government interference. If government would leave the people alone, Jacksonians believed, nature's own leveling process would ensure equality and secure liberty.[18]

It is important, however, to understand that the Jacksonian distrust of government stemmed primarily from their fear of special privilege. Corporations and special privilege put too much power in the hands of too few individuals. The source of that power—the central agency of corruption—was government. The Bank of the United States, a private corporation created by Congress, was the most notable example of the danger, but Jacksonians saw government at all levels doling out public-works jobs and special charters, each contributing to the cycle of power. The rich and powerful, they believed, were able to bend government to their own purposes.

It is tempting to exaggerate the antigovernment theme in Jacksonian ideals. Later in the century, and even today, Jacksonian slogans about limited government are used to denounce business regulation. Jacksonians were not thinking of government as a source of economic regulations, however, but as a source of economic privilege. They wanted to limit government in order to limit the power of the moneyed interests. As one observer put it, they wanted to "starve the monster in its cradle."[19]

Given their desire for limited government and their concern about concentration of power, it is understandable that Jacksonians also feared what they called "centralized government." Liberty, they believed, could be protected only through majority rule. The transmission of majority will into public policy was best accomplished in smaller governmental units, with most power remaining closer to home. For the Jacksonians' comfort, the federal government was too powerful, too aloof, and too susceptible to the influence of the privileged.[20]

Perhaps Lawrence Kohl was right in hypothesizing that Jacksonians tended to be people who were uncomfortable with the changes taking place in the American economic and social order. Perhaps a disproportionate number of such people joined the exodus to California. Certainly many of the individuals who assumed political leadership in the new state thought the gold rush had created a genuine democracy of free individuals with potential to satisfy the Jacksonian ideal.[21] Whatever the reason, the Jacksonian tenets of individual liberty; opposition to privilege; desire for limited government; admiration for equality, democracy, and natural law; and most of all, fear of concentration of power tended to dominate debate early in the state's history. The Jacksonian presence was strong in the constitutional convention of 1849, at which delegates pressed the need to guard against corporations. They proposed prohibiting special corporate charters, establishing stockholder liability, and even prohibiting banks and paper money.[22] The Jacksonian presence continued to be felt in the legislatures of the 1850s. It was reflected in the battles over distribution of state lands. Even before formal government was set into place in California, Jacksonian ideals inspired customary mining laws—the rules early Californians developed to govern their "diggings."

Governing the Mine Fields

no formal law over minerals

The first miners to reach the goldfields did not find any formal law in place when they arrived. Most of the early mining was done on land that was located within the public domain. The federal government had not established any rules to regulate exploitation of the area's minerals other than following a long-held policy to reserve mineral-bearing lands from sale or homestead. Nor had any state or territorial government authority set up rules to determine who had the right to what claim, for how long, and under what conditions. It was left up to the miners themselves to preserve some modicum of order. In the eyes of some observers, the mining camps the newcomers organized came to represent the epitome of a free society.[23] On the surface, at least with respect to the distribution of property, this observation seemed to be true.

customary laws

The customary mining law that developed in these early times was based upon the simple principle of "discovery and appropriation." The result was a model of practicality and a tribute to pure individualism. The rule of discovery gave to all miners a property interest in whatever minerals they could find. At the same time, the rule of appropriation attempted to limit each miner's or group's claims to what they could take, doing so in two ways. First, claims could be no larger than one person could reasonably be able to work. Second, claims that remained unworked for a specified time were forfeited. In the early years of the gold rush each mining region developed its own version of the customary mining law. Although specifics differed from place to place, the mining regulations adopted for Jackass Gulch were typical. Section one of the regulations held that "each person can hold one claim by virtue of occupation but it must not exceed one hundred feet square." Section five read, "As soon as there is sufficiency of water for working a claim, five days absence from said claim, except in case of sickness, accident, or reasonable excuse shall forfeit the property."[24] Acting in relative isolation, the miners thus attempted to provide equal opportunity for every person to strike it rich. They also tried to prohibit absentee ownership and what the Jacksonians would have referred to as monopoly.

The method for establishing a mining claim was simple; it required only that the miner claiming the property mark an area, usually by driving stakes into the ground. Often the claimant would put up a sign such as one posted in Shasta County:

Notis: To all and everybody. This is my claim, fifty feet on the gulch, cordin' to Clear Creek District Law, backed up by shotgun amendments.

[signed] THOMAS HALL

For some historians, Thomas Hall's "Notis" symbolizes a quaint aspect of a spontaneous yet effective system of government developed in the mining districts. For others, it reflects the underlying violence by which property rights were enforced.[25]

Violence certainly was an aspect of life in the camps. Even in its absence, however, customary mining regulations were far from perfect. Codes usually were unclear and were inadequately followed, possibly because their details varied from one district to another. Furthermore, they were not enforced with regularity. Without formal government, criminal prosecutions and even property disputes were sometimes decided by a vote of the entire camp. Such proceedings carried an air of pure democracy, but they also had the flavor of vigilante-style justice with all its prejudice, fear, and hate.[26]

Despite their imperfections, there was apparently no desire to abandon the customary mining codes. The codes certainly satisfied the early miners. During the first few years of the gold rush most prospectors worked at what is called placer mining. This method involved the recovery of gold nuggets or flakes that had been freed when a vein of ore was exposed to the elements.[27] Usually these flakes and nuggets were found in riverbeds or streambeds or along the bank. Mining these claims was a simple process of separating the gold from silt and rock. Using pans or rockers, miners could work alone or in small groups. Because placer mining involved so little investment and so little cooperation, the miners' existence tended to be nomadic. When a claim played out, miners simply moved on. Few placer miners had any desire to own the land upon which their claim rested; ownership of the right to mine the minerals was the only property interest of importance to them.

Even so, as more miners arrived and as miners moved from place to place, there was a tendency to formalize customary codes. The first step involved miners organizing mining districts and promulgating uniform regulations for the diggings within the district. Changes in mining operations also increased the demand to formalize the rules. As surface gold became more scarce, miners had to dig more along river banks in order to recover ore. As a consequence they developed a new method, hydraulic mining, which used water pressure to blast away creek beds and cliffs. The resulting slush would be carried along a sluice to a rocker, where gold would be separated from the rock and gravel. Hydraulic mining involved more investment, more cooperation, and more potential for conflict among miners as well as the potential conflict between miners and downstream property owners.[28] Later in the decade, an even more involved and expensive mining process dominated the industry. Lode mining, or quartz mining as it was called in California, required miners to dig below bedrock in search of veins of gold. They dug tunnels, shored the walls of the mine, and hauled gold-bearing rock to the surface. Once on the surface the gold-bearing rock had to be smashed, using stamp mills, or ground, with a device called an arrastra. The quartz mining process usually involved a substantial investment and a significant number of workers; consequently, it increased the pressure for more formalized regulations. Quartz miners were among the first to attempt drawing up uniform rules for the industry and some of them favored giving miners a more substantial property interest in their claims.[29]

In 1851 Assemblyman Stephen Field successfully sponsored a bill in the state legislature that gave official recognition to customary mining codes. Although Field would later make political hay out of his "support for the mining population of the state," his legislation did nothing more than recognize a system of property distribution and dispute resolution that already existed. As part of Field's Civil Practice Act the customary codes would continue to govern decisions in actions involving mining claims, so long as the codes were not in conflict with the constitution and other laws of the state.[30] Customary mining codes thus became part of the state's formal law. Their underlying principle—discovery and appropriation—did not change. But mining codes were meant only to govern relations and disputes among miners prospecting on public land. The simple principles of the mining codes would not necessarily apply when miners found themselves in conflicts with landowners, creditors, or other elements of the society.

The rawness of the circumstances is what makes the development of California's customary mining law so interesting. Here was a group of people thrown into a legal vacuum, struggling to find the right balance between their desire for unrestricted opportunity and their need for an orderly society. The niceties of precedent and weight of superimposed legislation did not muddle the expression of their hopes and ideals. As the decade progressed, the evolution of customary mining law would be overshadowed by a battle over the control of the formal law of the state. Stephen Field would play a key role in determining the outcome.

Homesteads and Land Monopolies

Newcomers scrambling for land faced a legal situation quite different from that of the miners prospecting for gold. Rather than a legal vacuum, settlers found two systems of law, Mexican and American, that affected land ownership. As demonstrated by the squatter riots in Sacramento and throughout the state and by a later proliferation of lawsuits, the result was as often anarchy as it was order.

The confusion began with Article 8 of the Treaty of Guadalupe Hidalgo, in which the United States promised that "property of every kind now established [in the ceded territory], shall be inviolably respected." The original text of Article 10, taken along with a subsequent agreement, the Protocol of Querétaro, made the meaning of this language more clear. All grants of land made by the Mexican government were to be respected as valid to the same extent that they would have been valid if the territory had remained under Mexican rule.[31]

On the eve of U.S. assumption of control in 1846, virtually all private ownership of land in California took one of two forms. In some cities and towns property rights resulted from the Mexican policy of granting four square leagues (each league being about two and three-fifths miles) of land to every organized pueblo.[32] In all other areas, property ownership originated with the government's grant of a rural estate called a rancho. W. W. Robinson, who made a study of land in California, tells us that in 1846 there were more than 500 such ranchos in the state. Rancheros, he reported, owned much of the best land in the San Francisco Bay region and the entire coastal area south to San Diego. They also owned much of the central valley, which ran along the Sacramento River and its tributaries.[33] Although a few ranchos were as small as twenty acres, most were measured in the thousands of acres and some were gigantic. The rancho of Mission de San Fernando in Los Angeles County, for example, was 115,000 acres. And one man, Jose de la Guerra y Noriega, claimed four ranchos totaling almost 216,000 acres. Together, the ranchos accounted for between 13 and 14 million acres, or about 13 to 14 percent of the state.[34]

Of the ranchos existing in 1846 all but a few were of Mexican origin. The Spanish did grant a limited number of ranchos to private individuals as a way of rewarding veterans and colonizing California, but the practice increased substantially under Mexican rule. The purpose of colonization remained the same, however. Mexican laws expressly stated that ranchos would be granted for cultivation and inhabitation, and many of the rules governing property reflected that purpose. An 1824 law prohibited granting ranchos for land within ten leagues of the seacoast, limited the size of grants to a maximum of eleven square leagues, prohibited transfer to the church, and prohibited absentee ownership. A subsequent law passed in 1828 set up a procedure to be followed in order to perfect, or to complete, a grant. The prospective grantee was to file an application, which was to include a map of the proposed grant, with the governor of California. The governor would then seek final approval from the national authority or "Supreme Government," which was then to issue a document in the nature of a deed that the governor was required to keep on file. The 1828 law included two other rules of significance. One, which took some authority away from the governor, provided that land granted under this act was not to be held indefinitely without prior approval of the supreme government. The other, which held that grantees would forfeit the property if they failed to live on and cultivate the land, reinforced the Mexican government's aversion to absentee ownership.[35]

In theory, the impact of the Treaty of Guadalupe Hidalgo should have been very straightforward. Land granted to individuals under Mexican rule would remain in the possession of those individuals. All other land in the ceded territory would become part of the public domain, much of which would be available to settlers under American homestead and preemption laws. Early land disputes in California therefore had at their heart the matter of determining into which category a particular parcel fell. That task must seem simple enough to modern homeowners who tend to assume they have a clear chain of title for their piece of property. As in most legal disputes, however, nothing about the California land issue was either simple or clear.

A major source of confusion was that few of the Mexican grants complied 100 percent with the Mexican law. Some of the ranchos were located in prohibited areas. Some grantees failed to record their documents. Some failed to obtain approval from the supreme government. Still others failed to inhabit the land. In practice, however, the Mexican government was completely lax in enforcing these and other infractions of the formal rules governing land grants. That in turn raised the question of whether the Mexican government's actual practice or customs, rather than the letter of their law, should govern American determinations of the validity of claims.

The Mexican government's failure to enforce its laws strictly led to another related problem. Laxity of deed recording left people to rely on memory and oral testimony to prove the validity of purported claims. This practice, of course, left the door wide open for fraud. Mexican law required that a survey or plat, called a *diseño,* be filed along with the application for

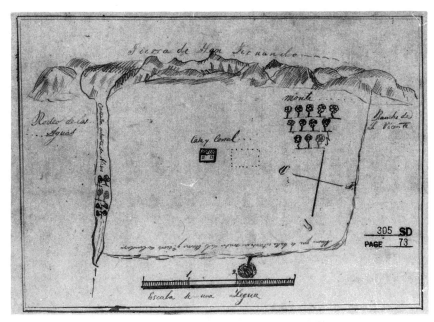

A *diseño* typical of those used to designate the boundaries of Mexican land grants in California. (Courtesy Bancroft Library)

a land grant. Although they were the only evidence of the boundaries of a particular claim, these *diseños* were incredibly crude sketches. They may have been useful to carve out a claim in an uninhabited frontier, but they were completely inadequate to the task of settling disputes as the territory became more heavily populated. Furthermore, possibly because some of the territory was unexplored at the time grants were made, Mexican governors occasionally awarded "floating grants," which gave the grantee an exclusive right to choose for his rancho an unspecified parcel from a much greater bloc of land.

The shift from Mexican to American rule presented an award-winning recipe for conflict. Land-seeking Americans who entered California in the 1840s and 1850s were inevitably going to settle on land they found uninhabited or thought was unclaimed. Some settlers were bound to build homes, cultivate, and make improvements on property that other people claimed by virtue of a paper title traced back to still untested Mexican grants. Given the uncertainty of most claims and the vagueness of their boundaries, many settlers may have been justified in thinking that the land upon which they settled was public domain and ripe for the claiming.

58 Justice Stephen Field

Others probably were shrewdly taking advantage of the confusion that a transfer of sovereignty left in its wake. One thing was certain, however: the confused conditions of land titles in California created a situation in which the U.S. government's delay in recognizing claims based upon Mexican grants was bound to create a legal imbroglio. Yet those same conditions made delay inevitable.

The clash between the Mexican policy of populating the region by granting large ranchos and the American policy of granting small homesteads certainly intensified the conflict over land in California. At the same time, however, the federal government's first response to the problem, the California Land Act of 1851, reflected a clash between two American traditions. One was the Anglo-American legal tradition with its deep respect for property rights. The other was an American frontier tradition of homestead—the idea that people had a fundamental right to claim public land, make the improvements, and eventually acquire a small farm at a modest price.[36]

This clash of traditions came out in the congressional debates over how the new law should place the burden of proving ownership. Thomas Hart Benton, a powerful Missouri senator, championed the grant holders' cause. Benton proposed a measure designed to ensure swift and easy confirmation of claims based on Mexican land grants by creating an office of Recorder of Land Titles. People who claimed rights under a Mexican grant would simply register their claims with the recorder. Registry would secure ownership of the property unless the U.S. attorney challenged the claim.[37] In essence, this proposal assumed the validity of every title except those in which there was clear evidence of fraud.

Benton had been a vocal supporter of land reform in his early career. Coining the phrase "the land belongs to the people," he helped make preemption a powerful political issue in 1829.[38] But the senator's personal interests apparently influenced his position regarding the California Land Act. Benton's two sons-in-law both claimed title to large land grants in California. One, William Carey Jones, was sent west by Pres. Zachary Taylor to study the condition of land titles. In contrast to an earlier report by Henry W. Halleck, which emphasized the weakness of many California land titles, Jones reported that most claims of Mexican land grants rested on valid ground. While conducting his research, however, Jones invested in several large ranchos. Benton's other son-in-law was John C. Frémont, the famous explorer, pioneer, and owner of the rich Mariposa grant. As one of California's first senators, Frémont joined Benton in the Congress in 1850, where he helped advance the cause of those claiming Mexican grants.[39]

Even though they were driven by self-interest, Benton's and Frémont's arguments had a general appeal. Benton advised the Senate that "there must be a hundred thousand people out there, for aught I know, who want the land of a few." Supporters of his approach warned that any delay in recognizing the claims of these grant holders would encourage squatters, deter investment, and retard the development of the state. Delay, they claimed, would result in the United States violating its obligations under the treaty with Mexico. It would put money in lawyers' pockets and result in confiscation of lands.[40]

Congress rejected Benton's proposal in favor of a plan introduced by California senator William Gwin. The version that eventually became the Land Act of 1851 instituted a much more deliberate and probing procedure for testing the validity of grant claims. The act created a Land Commission composed of three members appointed by the president.[41] Every person claiming land under a Mexican grant would be required to appear before the commission to prove his or her claim; if the commission approved the claim the grant holder would receive a patent from the U.S. government. This document, like a deed, served as evidence of ownership under U.S. law. If grant holders failed to present their claim within two years, or if the commission rejected the claim, the land in question would become part of the public domain. One aspect of the act that opponents found especially objectionable was that either the claimant or the government had a right to appeal the decision first to the U.S. district court and then to the Supreme Court. The appeal process, they complained, would cause even more delay and insecurity.

Contemporary historians joined Benton, Frémont, and their supporters in criticizing the act.[42] In part they played on sympathy for the destiny of the Californios—the people who had settled the land under Mexican rule. Benton told Congress that the law would threaten ranchos that could be traced back to grants from the king of Spain, illustrating the longevity of the grants by pointing out that they were made about the time Americans were fighting the Revolution.[43] His implication, that the 1851 act would take from Californians the land they had long held, has carried over to today. "In California thousands of gold-rush immigrants encroached on the California land grants and demanded that something be done to 'liberate' the land," writes one modern critic. The result, he says, was the Land Act of 1851.[44] There was a serious flaw in Benton's argument, however. Few of California's great ranchos were the product of long-held grants. Other than a handful of remnants from Spanish rule, the oldest grants came into existence between 1834 and 1842 as part of a drive to secularize property held by missions. Most of the grants were of even more recent origin. Of the 813 claims that eventually came before the Land Commission, historian Paul Gates counted 494 granted in the 1840s. One hundred fifty-five of these originated in 1845 and 1846, the last two years before American rule. In the last seven months of his service California governor Pío Pico approved fifty-six grants of one league or more, totaling 1,756,000 acres.[45]

This lament for the plight of old rancheros was not an essential element of the Benton forces' argument, but it did have some bearing on how the equities of the matter might be perceived. Even more fundamental to the grant holders' theory was their concern for property rights. Benton reminded Congress that "with the treaty of Guadalupe Hidalgo people changed their allegiance, but their rights of property remained undisturbed."[46] Josiah Royce, a contemporary historian, expanded on the theme by maintaining that the act encouraged squatter wars and disrespect for property. Sacramento squatters, he said, did not merely dispute John Sutter's title; they disputed all titles.[47]

In Benton's view, the delay built into the Land Act amounted to a slow, costly, and painful confiscation. To him the act assumed every title to property to be a fraud and required the grant holder to run the gauntlet formed by the Land Commission and two courts of appeal to prove otherwise. Frémont resorted to the dramatic to make the case for grant holders: "To what have we returned?" he asked. "I know of no time in which anything was done so cruel as a method of depriving people of their property."[48] But the link between Frémont's idealism and his personal economic interest became more evident than ever when he wrote to a friend that "as a landholder" he considered defeat of Gwin's bill "of vital importance to the security of our property."[49]

Although he stated it in the extreme, Benton captured the spirit of the act. The new law placed the burden of proof on people who claimed to hold Mexican grants, and its presumption favored placing as much land as possible in the public domain. That does not mean, however, that those individuals who supported the act were opposed to private property, a point Gwin made in debate. The people of California had no desire to violate the right of property guaranteed to any portion of the inhabitants of the state under the treaty with Mexico, he said. "All they desire is that some competent and impartial tribunal . . . will decide *what is private property,* and it will be respected."[50] Everybody, it seems, favored property. The real issue in this dispute was who would get which property.

Implicit in the grant holders' appeal was the notion that, once land had taken the form of private ownership, government did not have the authority to interfere with an individual's property rights. The California Land Act, they would argue, did just that. Even worse, it represented government redistribution of property. Stated in those terms alone, the grant holder's appeal surely would have appalled, or at least confused, anyone whose pulse still throbbed to the beat of Jacksonian ideals.

Many people of the Jacksonian mold, however, did not see the situation in quite the same light. On the contrary, they equated ranchos with monopoly and privilege. The treaty with Mexico protected land grants, they might agree, but the American government had a duty to protect the public domain. It should make absolutely certain that only legitimate land grants were recognized and thus should interpret strictly both the treaty and the Mexican law under which the grants were awarded. The existence of large ranchos ran contrary to a nineteenth-century reform movement that rested on the idea of the yeoman farmer. Henry George may have best captured the spirit of that movement with one simple statement: "While every man has a right to as much land as he can properly use, no man has a right to any more."[51]

The idea preceded Henry George, however. It was reflected in the development of federal policy regarding public lands. The government's earliest policy for disposing of federal land was to treat it as a revenue-making opportunity and to sell it at auction. Squatting on federal lands was thus illegal in the early years of the century, but it was not unusual. Pioneers tended to outpace the federal government, moving on to the land before officials could survey it. In 1815 Pres. James Madison proclaimed that people who had unlawfully settled on public land should be ejected by the army and prosecuted for trespass.[52]

Despite Madison's strong words the government tended to tolerate, rather than prosecute, squatting. There was a natural tendency to sympathize with the pioneers who opened western lands for settlement. Periodically, sympathy for squatters, who were in jeopardy of losing the land on which they had settled and the improvements they had made, forced Congress to pass preemption laws. The early preemption laws gave those particular squatters the option to purchase their improved property at a minimal price. In the 1820s land reformers pressured the government to make this periodic response into a general policy applying to all federal lands. They succeeded when President Jackson signed the Preemption Act of 1830. Still, the concept of preemption remained retrospective: it gave rights only to those people who had already settled on the land. It remained for the Preemption Act of 1841 to take the idea one step further. Completely reversing previous federal policy, the act called for the government to dispose of public land by offering small plots (typically 160 acres), at minimal prices, to actual settlers who would be willing to cultivate it.[53] Homestead law was the next logical step in the evolution of land reform. It proposed disposing of the public domain by giving free land to poor people. Once again the concept incorporated a limit on the size of the grant, usually 160 acres. The idea remained to provide land to actual settlers.

The term "actual settlers" indicated the change in emphasis that the land-reform movement proposed. Reformer George Washington Julian reminded Congress in 1851 that the new approach abandoned the idea of treating public domain as a source of revenue. At the same time, he said, "It abandons the policy of 'frittering it away' by grants to the States or to chartered companies for special and local objects; and it makes it free, in limited portions, to actual settlers, on condition of occupancy and improvement."[54]

Julian found justification for this policy in natural law. The friends of land reform did not intend to interfere with the laws of property or the vested rights of property owners, he maintained. Reformers did not advocate any "leveling" policy designed to strip the rich of their possessions by a sudden act of legislation. Their demand, Julian explained, was simply that "In laying the foundations of empire in the yet unpeopled regions of the great West, Congress shall give its sanction to the natural right of the landless citizen of the country to a home upon its soil."[55]

Julian also summoned the spirit of Andrew Jackson. Independent farmers, he quoted Jackson as saying, "are everywhere the basis of society, and true friends of liberty."[56] With this idealization of a country dominated by small farms owned by self-sufficient and independent individuals, Julian flaunted Jacksonian roots. So did the corollary theme that large blocs of land should not be controlled by single individuals. In this vein, California reformer Henry George warned his fellow westerners: "The danger that we have to fear is not overcrowding, but the monopolization of our lands— not that there will not be land enough to support all, but the land will be so high that a poor man cannot afford it."[57] Julian undoubtedly agreed. A speech later in his career reminded reformers that the role of government was to prevent monopoly and speculation in order to protect individuals' personal and property rights. Monopoly, he insisted, was the enemy of liberty.[58]

Free Labor and Free Land

At times George Julian sounded much like Old Hickory himself, but his speeches reflected another influence as well. In addition to Jacksonian Democracy, Julian also turned to the philosophy of free labor to support his proposals for homestead laws. His arguments deftly combined two aspects of free-labor theory. First, he maintained that a homestead law was an antislavery measure. Then he drew on another concern of free-labor ideology, the continued independence of the white working class.

Julian made the homestead movement into an antislavery measure by maintaining that slavery thrives only on large estates. "In a country cut up into small farms, occupied by as many independent proprietors who live by their own toil, [slavery] would be impossible," Julian argued; "there would be no room for it." The freedom to obtain public land, he continued, would weaken the slave power by lending the government's official sanction to "the natural right of man, *as man,* to a home upon the soil, and of course to the fruits of his own labor."[59] Julian was neither alone nor unique in this argument. In the 1850s the homestead issue increasingly became folded into the issue of the extension of slavery, abolitionists favoring homestead laws, slaveholders being opposed.[60] In 1847, wondering whether the new land acquired from Mexico would become the property of free workingmen of the North or be sequestered by slaveholders of the South, David Wilmot introduced into Congress a proposal to exclude slavery from the territories. The Wilmot Proviso failed, but it became a rallying cry for many antislavery Democrats, including Stephen Field's brother David Dudley Field.[61]

In one particular speech, Julian extolled the virtues of free labor by comparing Virginia to Ohio. Virginia was "dwindling and dying under the curse of slave labor," he observed, but Ohio was "teeming with abundance." The secret of Ohio's success, Julian reasoned, lay in the distribution of its property and its tradition of free labor. The state thrived because the owners of the soil were its cultivators. Liberty was preserved because their self-interest and the public good were linked. Most important, he argued that Ohio thrived because there labor was considered honorable and independent instead of being looked upon as degrading.[62]

Despite this passionate comparison of slave state to free state, abolitionism was not the subject of this particular speech. Julian was actually advocating homestead legislation. Even in Ohio, Julian warned, "the curse of land monopoly, or *white* slavery, is beginning to exhibit its bitter fruits, as it will everywhere if unchecked by wise legislation."[63] As he explained it, land monopoly first deprives the laboring population of their natural right to the soil and then prescribes the terms upon which it will give them food and shelter. Noting that the price of labor, as everything else, depends on supply and demand, he continued: "Land monopoly, by its unholy exactions, makes sure of a large supply, and then presents to the famishing laborer the alternatives of death by starvation, or life on such terms as its own *mercy* may dictate."[64] Julian's analysis may have been simplistic and his fuming extreme, but he was far from being the only reformer to liken the effect of land monopoly to slavery.

The goal of free labor was not limited to ending slavery in the South. Although slavery was the antithesis of free labor, the free-labor movement was even more concerned with the interests of America's white work force. It represented a long struggle for freedom from all sorts of controls that were available to employers, which early in the century had taken the form of legal control. Traditional Anglo-American law of master and servant treated wage laborers as free only in the sense that they had the right to sell their labor to another. Once they did, however, laborers were under the direct legal control of their employer, who could set the terms of their employment, prohibit them from leaving, and even administer corporal punishment. By mid-century many of these forms of legal compulsion had disappeared, but as proponents of free labor soon recognized, economic compulsion could just as effectively threaten the liberty of the working class.[65]

Faced with a kind of compulsion much more subtle than slavery, free-labor theory struggled with defining liberty. Reformers argued the benefits of free labor on economic development, social mobility, and political democracy. Like modern labor activists, they sought higher levels of compensation, better working conditions, job security, and control of the workplace.[66] Even though they had some difficulty in precisely defining free labor, there were definite common themes in the movement, one of the most common being the "dignity of labor." The object of free labor, reformers said, was "to make labor honorable."[67] Legal self-ownership and autonomy were minimal requirements for achieving this level of dignity.

The most extreme free-labor advocates believed honor could not be achieved by wage laborers at all because working for wages was itself an indignity. "Wage slavery," as they called it, was an affront to the traditional artisan ideal of economic and personal independence. For these people, wage labor could be justified only as a temporary condition. Even less intense advocates of free-labor ideology subscribed to this idea to some extent. To all of them free labor meant labor with economic choices and with the opportunity, or at least the hope, of quitting the wage-earning class.[68]

Opponents sometimes charged that homestead laws reflected the influence of socialism or "agrarianism." But the homestead movement rested upon a foundation that was quite different from that supporting either the utopian or Marxian forms of socialism.[69] Rather than planning for a new social order in the future, advocates of homestead legislation looked back to older times for their inspiration. Homesteaders did not want to change society; they wanted to preserve and expand democratic society and the liberty they believed they had already obtained. The danger they feared was also rooted in the past. In their view, land monopoly foreshadowed a return to a feudal society dominated by landed aristocracy. Such a society would reduce the options for the laboring class and would threaten the autonomy, control, and dignity that free labor required.

The homestead movement's reliance on the theories of Jacksonian Democracy and free labor made it clear that the ideas California settlers pressed in 1851 were part of a larger and longer lasting battle against monopoly and against privilege. By the time of the gold rush, homestead reformers had made substantial progress. The idea of preemption and homestead may not have captured public policy fully, but it certainly had been popularized. Furthermore, the government's generous distribution of land in Washington and Oregon reinforced the belief that land on the Pacific Slope would be available to settlers.[70] In that atmosphere, it is not surprising that people who came to California expecting to mine a claim or to make a homestead would find it difficult to believe that some 700 individuals might be permitted to monopolize 13 or 14 million of the state's choicest acres.[71]

Land Grants in the Courts

Because it placed the burden on grant holders to prove the validity of their claims, the California Land Act appeared to be a victory for settlers.[72] Built into the new law, however, was a directive that would dampen any benefits the settlers hoped to achieve. The act specified that certain criteria should guide the commission and the courts in deciding the validity of each claim. The Treaty of Guadalupe Hidalgo was obviously among these guidelines as were the decisions of the U.S. Supreme Court. In addition, however, the act specified that the "laws, usages, and customs of Mexico and American principles of equity should also guide the decisions."[73] Adding usages, customs, and equity into the decisionmaking formula was a fair and reasonable idea, but it gave a great deal of leeway to the Land Commission and the courts, leeway that quickly reduced the burden that grant holders faced.

The first major case under the new land act tested the validity of John C. Frémont's title to property known as Las Mariposas. Frémont, a famous explorer, a leader of the Bear Flag Revolt, and one of the more colorful personalities in the battles to wrest control of California from Mexico, would eventually become a U.S. senator and the first presidential candidate of the

Republican party. He purchased the rights to Las Mariposas on February 10, 1847, while the Treaty of Guadalupe Hidalgo was pending ratification. Legend has it that Frémont asked Thomas O. Larkin to serve as his agent for the purchase of a plot he had picked out in the hills of San Francisco. Larkin, however, decided to buy the plot for himself. He then used the $3,000 Frémont had entrusted to him to buy a rancho in a wild tract near the Sierra Nevada. Outraged at first, Frémont threatened to sue Larkin to recover his money. But his temper ebbed when he began to realize that the Mariposa tract could be one of the most valuable pieces of property in California.

The title that Frémont purchased was based on an 1844 grant from Gov. Manuel Micheltorena to Juan B. Alvarado. Alvarado received what became known as a "floating grant." This meant that the precise boundaries of the rancho were not designated in the grant itself. Rather, Alvarado received the exclusive right to lay out a rancho of ten square leagues (approximately 44,787 acres or 70 square miles) from within a larger specified area estimated to be as much as 900 square miles.[74] The enormous area from which he had to choose was bound by "a point within the [Sierra Nevada] Mountains and the Chanchilles, Merced, and San Joaquin Rivers." It had rich valleys and abundant water for farming and ranching. But the region's richest blessing, although neither Frémont nor Alvarado knew it at the time, was that it sat right on the edge of the mother lode.

Governor Micheltorena placed a number of explicit conditions on the grant. The first of these provided that Alvarado could not "sell, alienate, or mortgage the property." The second required that Alvarado build a house within a year and inhabit the property. Alvarado, in other words, did not own the property at all in the sense that most of us understand ownership; he controlled and possessed it so long as he lived on it and used it. According to the terms of the grant, however, he could not sell it. In addition, the grant required that Alvarado obtain from the local alcalde a patent that would mark the boundaries of his rancho. He then was required to survey it and to place proper landmarks on the property. Three years later, at the time of sale to Frémont, Alvarado had done absolutely nothing to satisfy the conditions of his grant. Furthermore, the grant failed to comply with general procedures that Mexican law required. No *diseño* of the grant had been filed, and the grant had not been approved by the supreme government.[75]

Frémont held the grant to Las Mariposas five more years before he had the opportunity, in January 1852, to present his claim to the Land Commission. During that period he did take some steps toward assuming ownership. In 1847 he hired an agent to inhabit and cultivate land within the area

of the grant, but Indians drove the agent out. In 1849 he commissioned
a survey. He also entered into an agreement with a company of Mexican
miners to share the profits of an expedition. Although Frémont expressed
his intention to make Las Mariposas his home, he actually spent little time
there during the period between his purchase and the Land Commission
hearings.[76]

All other arguments aside, it is fair to say that the letter of Mexican law
had not been followed with respect to this grant. The Land Commission,
however, tended to rely on custom and usage rather than on the letter of
the law. It ruled, for example, that approval of the departmental assembly
was not essential and that failure to inhabit the land was not crucial.[77] Using these guidelines, the Land Commission confirmed Frémont's claim. This
was only the first step of the legal proceedings, however. Representing the
government's interest in designating the land as public domain, U.S. Attorney General Caleb Cushing appealed the case to the U.S. district court in
San Francisco. There, Frémont received a different reception. District Judge
Ogden Hoffman, who heard the first cases under the land act, tended to require strict observance of Mexican law. In this case, focusing on Alvarado's
failure to inhabit the property, the judge ruled that the conditions of the
grant had not been satisfied.[78] Frémont's claim to Las Mariposas, he concluded, was not valid. The stage was now set for a test case in the U.S. Supreme Court.

It was Frémont who was to taste the final victory. In 1854 the Supreme
Court voted 6 to 2 that his claim to Las Mariposas was valid, with Chief
Justice Roger Taney writing the opinion for the majority. Taney was an old-
style Jacksonian who, in earlier cases testing claims in Louisiana and Florida, had required strict compliance with Spanish law.[79] In Frémont's case,
however, he displayed an uncharacteristic willingness to take notice of customs and usages, which he described as "the common or unwritten law of
every civilized country."[80] He distinguished the prior cases by noting that
grants in Louisiana and Florida took the form of concessions that only gave
the grantee permission to make a claim and then present it to the government. California grants, he said, differed in that they actually conveyed title.
In order for Alvarado's grant to be held invalid, he continued, the Court
would have to find that Alvarado had acted or failed to act in a matter that
forfeited his existing rights. Taney concluded that Alvarado's failure to inhabit the property did not forfeit his rights. In the first place, he said, the
public had no interest in having the rights forfeited. Second, Taney reasoned
that Alvarado had not been guilty of unreasonable delay since, during the
time of Mexican rule, the area was controlled by hostile Indians. Finally,

and not entirely accurately, Taney observed that there was no conflict with other individuals over ownership of the land but only conflict with the government.

Taney then dismissed two other objections to Alvarado's title. Governor Micheltorena's condition that Alvarado could not sell or alienate the property, Taney said, was invalid under Mexican statutory law. A provision of Mexican law that prohibited sale of land grants to foreigners was inapplicable because, at the time Alvarado conveyed the grant to Frémont, the territory was under control of American forces.

Justices John Catron and John Campbell disagreed. Catron disputed Taney's reasoning that this case was somehow different from those earlier claims in Louisiana and Florida. Colonization was the great object of the laws controlling all these grants, he said. American courts had long recognized that, if a Spanish grant contained the condition of habitation, the grant was void unless the condition was performed within the time prescribed. "To hold otherwise," Catron argued, "would be to subvert the manifest design of the colonization laws of Mexico, by reserving indefinitely, to single individuals, large bodies of uncultivated and unoccupied lands."[81] The "floating" nature of the Las Mariposas grant strengthened Catron's reasoning. The idea that the Mexican government designed to leave in force for an indefinite length of time such a large undefined concession "that might be surveyed at the election of the claimant at any time and at any place" was, he thought, "too extravagant to be seriously entertained."[82] With that, Catron struck at the heart of the matter. He might have agreed with Taney that the treaty with Mexico and the Land Act of 1851 allowed the Court to consider customs, usages, and equities. For Catron, however, the equities of the matter simply ran against Frémont's claim.

Catron realized that the *Frémont* case would have a disastrous impact on those people who had settled California territory under the assumption that it was public domain. California is filled with settlers who had been drawn to the West by the government's homestead policy, he argued. Settlers had expended much labor and money in the faith that a preemption right was safe title and that it protected their claim from floating Mexican concessions such as that made to Alvarado.[83] Justice Peter Daniel expressed the settlers' views even more candidly one year later, in another case. Daniel warned that the *Frémont* decision had the effect of "inciting and pampering a corrupt and grasping spirit of speculation and monopoly."[84] "Under the countenance of this Court," he observed, "*Principalities* are won by an *Affidavit,* and conferred upon the unscrupulous few, to the exclusion and detriment of the many, and by the sacrifice of the sovereign rights of the United States."[85]

Some scholars have argued that the *Frémont* case rewrote Mexican law and circumvented the purpose of the California Land Act of 1851. Others maintain that Taney's reliance on custom and usages demonstrated a deep respect for and understanding of Mexican law.[86] Whichever opinion might be correct, one result was certain. The decision reduced the potential burden on people claiming land under Mexican grants, thus making it easier for them to establish that their claims were valid. If settlers saw in the outcome of this case the image of a landed aristocracy laying claim to California, their fears were not assuaged when Frémont visited the White House and was handed the title to Las Mariposas by President Pierce himself.[87]

3

SHOWDOWN AT LAS MARIPOSAS

Important as the *Frémont* case was, it did not put an end to disputes over lands claimed under Mexican grants. It did not even settle all the disputes regarding Frémont's grant. The Court had ruled only that the land Frémont claimed did not belong to the public domain, thus resolving the dispute between Frémont and the U.S. government. But the Supreme Court's opinion did not have a direct effect on conflicts between Frémont (or other titleholders) and third parties. Grant holders continued to worry that their property was in jeopardy, and settlers still complained about floating grants, unfair surveys, and outright fraud.[1] Disputes over the ownership of property persistently made their way into the state and federal courts. And Stephen Field, who served as a judge in both forums, would have a major influence on the outcome of those disputes and on the way that land was distributed in California. His term on the state bench lasted from 1857 to 1863. The opinions he wrote during the first years as an appellate judge probably did not represent his fully matured views regarding the nature of liberty and the extent of government power, but his record in the California land cases may have sealed his reputation in his home state.

Run for the California Supreme Court

California settlers were sometimes hopeful but often suspicious of the legal system. Although settlers sometimes turned to the state court with a charge that a titleholder was claiming title under a fraudulent Mexican grant, many of the land cases in the state courts started as proceedings to eject settlers from their homestead claim. Ejectment was the process by which a person who held paper title to a piece of property could seek a court order forcing a person who was occupying the property but who had no right to be there to leave. The boundaries of Mexican grants were notoriously vague. In the years between Mexican rule and establishment of the Land Commission many homesteaders settled in areas that were later ruled to be part of a grant. Once the Land Commission recognized a grant, the prospect that settlers might be cast off their homestead became very real. "Who can lie down at night without fear lest morning may surprise him with some unheard of grant drifted over his property?" lamented one settler.[2] Some of these settlers thought they had been living on public land, or they may have gambled that the Land Commission would reject potential claims to the land. Whatever their justification, many refused to move even after another person's rights to the land under a Mexican grant had been verified. Some of the resulting disputes ended in violence. Others were handled informally, the settlers either buying or renting the property. Still, many of the conflicts between owners of verified claims and settlers wound up in the California courts as ejectment suits.

The California courts became involved in land disputes in other ways as well. In 1856, for example, the California legislature passed an "occupancy law." Under this statute, once a jury had settled on the value of improvements settlers had made to the land, the owner of a verified grant had the option of either selling to the settler at fair value less the value of improvements or of paying the settler the value of improvements minus rent and damages. The occupancy law satisfied one of the settlers' major grievances. It did not give them the land on which they had made a home, but at least it required that the owners compensate them for improvements they had made. Settlers barely got a taste of their legislative victory, however, before the courts snatched it away. Early in 1857 the California Supreme Court ruled that the new occupancy law was invalid.[3] One miner's reaction was typical: "To tell a man to go to the law is a mockery. Law is *intended* to do justice between man and man, to protect the weak against the strong, the poor man from the oppression of the rich: it never contemplates the measurement of purses—yet such is its working."[4] Settlers and miners quickly found out that success in the legislature was not enough. Californians elected their judges by popular vote, and settlers and miners realized that in order to fully protect their interests, they would need to be certain that the state's courts were composed of judges who shared their sentiments.

It was in this atmosphere that Stephen Field decided to run for justice of the California Supreme Court. The road to his eventual election began as a small part of one of the epic battles in the state's political history—the struggle between David Broderick and William Gwin for control of the Democratic party. In 1857 Broderick had still not satisfied his prediction of becoming a U.S. senator. In those days, senators were still selected by state legislatures rather than by popular vote. Broderick had managed to block Gwin's reelection in 1855 when the legislature, ending in stalemate, failed to make a choice. The success of the Know-Nothing party in 1856 forced him and Gwin to cooperate in blocking selection of a senator that year as well. The legislature that convened in January 1857 would therefore choose two senators. One was to fill the four years remaining of the seat that had become available in 1855; the other was for a full term. Broderick's forces in the 1857 legislature were strong. Sensing a possibility of controlling both seats, he arranged for the full-term seat to be voted upon first. On the first ballot Broderick defeated the incumbent, John B. Weller, by a vote of 42 to 34. He had finally reached the office to which he had aspired when he left for California.[5]

More political intrigue was in the making for selecting the senator for the short term. Broderick, not fully satisfied with his own election, now resolved to crush Gwin or at least to break the Chivalry wing's monopoly on federal patronage. Shortly after deciding on Broderick, the legislature nominated six men for the short term: William Gwin, Milton S. Latham, Joseph W. McCorkle, B. F. Washington, A. P. Crittenden, and Stephen J. Field. The real battle, however, would be between the two leading candidates, Gwin and Latham. Crittenden dropped out after the first ballot; Washington soon followed. James O'Meara, a contemporary political observer, noted in hindsight that Field had no visible chance of being elected senator but participated in the race to pave the way for his nomination to the California Supreme Court, "a position more congenial to his nature and training and much coveted by him."[6] To this end, O'Meara reported, Field's support was at the disposition of Broderick, who, in return, promised Field the supreme court nomination at the Democratic convention, which would be held the following summer.[7] Field later disputed this account. Recalling the friendship Broderick extended to him during the legislative session of 1851, Field claimed that he stood by Broderick out of a sense of loyalty and often at a great inconvenience.[8] In any case, Field never garnered more than seven votes, but those votes might have been crucial. He and McCorkle, another Broderick supporter, stayed in the race while Broderick parlayed with the front-runners.

Broderick planned to trade his support to any other candidate who would sign a written agreement giving Broderick full control of federal patronage. With other candidates in the running, neither Latham nor Gwin could round up the votes needed for election. This gave Broderick the leverage he needed. He first approached Latham with the proposal that he sign off on patronage in exchange for the needed votes. When Latham refused, Broderick turned to Gwin, who agreed to relinquish his share of control over patronage. On cue, Field and McCorkle threw most of their votes to Gwin, who won election on the fourteenth vote.[9]

Some people believed that Broderick later paid Field back by arranging that the Democratic party nominate him for the supreme court. According to Field, however, the friendship between the two men was broken soon after Broderick was elected to the Senate. Field recalled that Broderick subsequently "announced his opposition to my nomination [to the court]."[10] Regardless of whether Broderick was behind him or against him, Field's nomination as the Democratic candidate for supreme court certainly was not fully ensured. On the opening day of the Democratic convention the *Alta California* reported that the most vigorous fight would be for judge of the supreme court. Field and his two opponents, Judge Peter Burnett and John H. McCune, were reported to be "working like beavers for proxies." Field prevailed when, on July 14, 1857, the convention nominated him by a fairly close vote as the party's candidate for the state supreme court.[11]

In the wake of the Democratic convention it was soon apparent that Stephen Field was not a favorite of miners and settlers. At the same time the Democrats were meeting, a group of settlers and miners attempted to organize their own political party. Organizers of the new group complained of floating grants and the government's generosity toward individuals claiming land under immense foreign grants. They called for compensation for settlers displaced by land grants and for laws framed to favor the actual possessor of land. They maintained that, with respect to Mexican land grants, mineral rights did not convey with the title to the surface. Perhaps most significantly, they expressed the belief that "of all the departments of government, the Supreme Bench is by far of the highest consequence to us." "What good is it to pass legislation," they asked, "if the judiciary is disposed to annul all enactments for the benefit and protection of the Settler and possessor of the sod?"[12]

The potential defection of the settlers and miners at the general election worried some Democrats. Field, many admitted, was "a man whose interests were known to be opposed to those of the settlers." Some observers worried that his presence on the ticket would mean defeat for the party in the fall.[13] The Settlers' Convention did nominate a slate of candidates for the general election, but it was composed mostly of men who had already been nominated by the Republicans. Still the Settlers' party ticket had the effect of putting a group of miners and settlers to work against the Democratic party in general and against Field in particular. "The settlers are holding meetings in various portions of the State and endorsing [Republican candidate] Judge Bennett," reported the *Sacramento Bee*. "Hence the friends of Field, the greatest lawyer in the state should bestir themselves actively from this time forth. A special effort will be made to defeat him."[14]

Less than a month before the general election, however, the *Sacramento Union* predicted that Field's opponent Nathaniel Burnett did not "stand a ghost of a chance." The Settlers' party might draw off some support from the Democratic candidates, it reasoned, but the remaining settler vote along with the Broderick Democrats would make up the majority. The *Union* won bragging rights as the better political prognosticator when the general election held on September 2, 1857, turned into a Democratic landslide. The voters of California elected the entire Democratic ticket, including Field, who would later be able to boast that he had received more votes than both of his opponents together.[15]

Field's six-year term was scheduled to begin on January 1, 1858. When Chief Justice Hugh C. Murray died in September, however, the governor appointed Field to fill the vacancy on the court. He took his seat on the California Supreme Court on October 13, 1857.

Judge Field

Fellow supreme court judge Joseph Baldwin recollected that, when he and Field joined the bench, the California Supreme Court was challenged with molding a system of law from what was little better than chaos. No general or common source of jurisprudence was established, Baldwin recalled. Mexican traditions mixed with conflicting precedents from Great Britain and the eastern states. Worse still, the court was an elected body operating in a highly charged atmosphere that accompanied the formation of the new state. The terms of the three-member court were staggered, and a constant turnover resulted in a lack of consistency in its opinions. In Baldwin's view, Stephen Field, more than any other man, gave "tone, consistency, and system to our judicature, and laid broad and deep the foundation of our civil and criminal law."[16]

Field's impact on the court was not immediate. He joined a body made up of Peter H. Burnett and David Terry, a man who would turn out to be his lifelong nemesis. For a little more than a year, the two men teamed up in opposition to Field, whose name appeared on only a few cases of minor importance. On October 2, 1858, when Joseph Baldwin replaced Burnett, the court's course began to change. Field still authored only a few opinions in 1859, but it became common to see his name attached to opinions as a concurring vote. By the end of the year it was clear that he and Baldwin would control the direction of the California Supreme Court for some time to come.[17]

Baldwin was correct in his assessment of Field's impact. He and Field, later joined by W. W. Cope, undoubtedly did give consistency to California jurisprudence. They also brought an unprecedented degree of harmony to the court. Historian Charles McCurdy admiringly suggests that they accomplished this by striking "a balance between the competing interests and ideological commitments of California's early Anglo American occupants."[18] Strike a balance they surely did; but California's settlers and miners may have had reason to suspect that their interests did not weigh heavily on Field and Baldwin's scale. Many critics would complain that, rather than interpreting the law, Field settled cases by imposing his own will. Instead of following precedent, they argued, Field based decisions on his own personal philosophy or sentiments.

Many of the cases the California Supreme Court decided during Field's six-year term were plain vanilla in that they simply applied a rule for settling disputes. In these, Field's record of providing consistency is irreproachable. But such cases did not say much about how Field would weigh competing interests. They had little publicity, and they carried no grand ideological implications. Even the usually volatile land and mining cases often were simply personal disputes that required an arbitrator and needed a set of rules to allow society to function in an orderly fashion. Few cases were so glaring as to pit monopolist land speculators against simple homesteaders; more often the cases were of settler against settler or miner against miner.[19] Cases involving city lots often pitted one generation of speculator against the next.[20] Still others were disputes between competing claims based on Mexican land grants. In *Waterman v. Smith,* for example, two people claimed the same property on the basis of floating grants that overlapped. One had received a U.S. patent and thus had in hand a survey of the exact boundaries of his claim. The other's patent application was pending. Field ruled that the one who had received the government survey prevailed, even if the land he claimed encompassed land that the other occupied.[21] "First in time first in right" was the general rule Field used to settle this dispute, and he consistently applied it in later cases as well. Later he explained that in conflicts among miners and among settlers he relied upon the presumption that ownership vested in the first person to have appropriated the property. He warned, however, that this presumption would not be applicable against a person who held superior title.[22]

Title based upon a land grant was, if proven to be valid, superior title in

Field's eyes. The reason was quite logical. A settler's or miner's claim rested on the idea that each had a right to appropriate public land. In a sense, the U.S. government was giving them the property. Land that had already been granted to an individual during Mexican rule, however, did not belong to the United States and it was thus not the government's to give away.

The general precedent for determining what land legitimately belonged to individuals and what land belonged to the government grew from the Land Act of 1851 and the *Frémont* case. When Field was elected to the state bench, however, there remained a need to fill in the details of this general rule. Much of that filling in was done in the state courts, where grant holders would seek a court order to eject squatters from their land. Settlers who faced ejection used resourceful and imaginative legal arguments in their defense. In cases where a U.S. patent had been granted to the landowner, some settlers continued to challenge the patent itself. These settlers claimed either that the grant was a result of fraud or that the grant holder had violated a legal technicality. Field consistently ruled that a patent was conclusive evidence of the validity of the grant. An ejectment proceeding, he reasoned, was not the place for such a challenge; it was too late. The person claiming fraud should have done so directly at the time of the hearing on the original claim.[23]

Another approach settlers took to protect their interests was to pressure the legislature to set limits on the time that holders of a patent could enforce their claims. An 1856 statute labeled "An Act for the Protection of Actual Settlers and to Quiet Land Titles" required that any suit for ejectment be commenced within two years from the date of the patent. But the California Supreme Court overruled the act in 1861. Reasoning that the new statute of limitations was aimed only at land claimed under a Mexican grant, it ruled that the provisions were a violation of the Treaty of Guadalupe Hidalgo and thus unconstitutional.[24] One year later another ejectment suit tested another time limit. This time the settler claimed rightful ownership of the property under the provisions of the state's general adverse possession law. Under this statute a holder of paper title who had not been in physical possession of the property for five years was barred from bringing suit to remove a person in possession. Because this law applied to all titleholders, whether or not they held on the basis of a Mexican grant, Field ruled that the limitation was valid. There was no victory for the settler in this particular case, however, for Field also ruled that the time period began to run not from the date the patent was issued but only after all of the hearings relating to the patent had concluded. Using Field's clock, the time had not been exhausted in this case.[25]

In these cases and many others, Field made a reasonable choice among possible outcomes. His presumptions may have favored grant holders in many instances, but there was a consistency, rationality, and predictability to his reasoning. Field's record in these cases demonstrated that he had a keen appreciation for law as order. Other cases, however, demonstrated that he also understood law as power.

Hints of this awareness began to show up very quickly in his term. In *Ferris v. Coover*, one of the many cases involving John Sutter's grant in the Sacramento area, Field ruled that the oral testimony of Sutter and his surveyor could be admitted to explain the grant's boundaries.[26] Settlers feared such loose application of the California Land Act; oral testimony, they thought, left the door wide open for fraud. Yet there was another aspect of Field's opinion that should have concerned them just as much. The defendants in this case argued that the boundaries defined by Sutter's survey contained slightly more area than the eleven leagues he had been granted. They claimed, in other words, that there was a surplus. Since Sutter had failed to set aside his land accurately from the public domain, they reasoned that the property they had claimed was part of the surplus rather than part of the Sutter grant. Field did not agree. The government alone could determine and set aside the surplus, he said, and until it took action, the right of the grantee remained good to the possession of the entire tract.[27]

In this case that seemed a reasonable rule. The dispute in *Ferris v. Coover* involved a fixed area. The measurement by which it was defined under Mexican law—eleven leagues, or *sitos de ganada mayor*—was a large unit. It was meant to measure raw and empty land, not town lots, and therefore was not necessarily intended to be precise. Complaints that the Mexican government had too liberally and lavishly granted property might be justified, Field reasoned. "But the United States have bound themselves by a treaty to acknowledge and protect all bona fide titles granted by the previous government; and this court [has] no discretion to enlarge or curtail such grants, . . . by stringent technical rules of construction, to which they were not originally subjected."[28]

The rule that a grantee had the right to an entire tract, including surplus, until the government had acted was not as passive as Field made it appear. Under the letter of Mexican law, a grantee did not receive full rights to the property until it had been segregated from the public domain. In the conditions of Mexican California, the rule was not strictly applied.[29] But it is clear that the design of this Mexican colonization law was to avoid reserving indefinitely to single individuals the rights to vaguely identified property. Although Field emphasized that he was talking about grants for a specific tract of land, the *Ferris v. Coover* ruling had serious implications for people who had settled within or near floating grants such as Las Mariposas. It took only a slight expansion of Field's logic to conclude that a grantee would have the rights to an entire floating tract until a patent was issued and a survey completed. This idea was at the heart of the continuing conflict surrounding John C. Frémont's claim to the rancho Las Mariposas.

The presence of gold only magnified the conflict. Frémont himself claimed one of the early strikes, a quartz mine he called Mariposas. In 1850 he leased his claim to the Mariposa Mining Company, which was controlled by the politically connected San Francisco banking house, Palmer, Cook, and Company. About the same time a prospector named John R. Johnson discovered and claimed a better part of the mother lode. Within the year, Johnson joined with John L. Moffit and others to form the Merced Mining Company, which set out to exploit "the great Johnson vein" with operations at the Mt. Ophir, Josephine, and Pine Tree mines. Frémont and the Merced Mining Company thus became the two major players in the drama that unfolded in the Mariposa region, but countless other prospectors "combing the hills with pick, shovel, and magnifying glasses discovered hundreds of veins."[30]

The potential wealth of the region was staggering. The gold was there, but mining the quartz veins was a tedious process. It required not only digging the gold-bearing quartz from the earth but also moving it to a mill where the quartz was smashed and the gold extracted. The expense of timber, machinery, labor, and supplies made this a costly undertaking, especially for large operations expecting to turn profits huge enough to satisfy anxious stockholders. Inexperience in mining the area, inadequate machinery, and inept management cost the major companies dearly. At its Mt. Ophir works, Merced had spent $130,700.07 and produced only $5,214.00 in gold.[31] In 1852 both the Mariposa Mining Company and the Merced Mining Company shut down their operations and turned to foreign investors to revitalize their claims. Merced leased its interest to Nouveau Monde Gold Mining Company, which was headed by Emperor Napoleon and backed by British and French capital. Frémont's agents formed at least seventeen joint stock companies that sold shares primarily to British investors. By 1855 these companies had also failed.

During this time no one knew for certain if the U.S. government would validate Frémont's claim to Las Mariposas. Although some people complained that investment in the region was frozen pending the outcome, the consequent uncertainty did not slow down either prospecting or investment, partly because Frémont's land grant, as originally surveyed, did not cover most of the rich mining region.[32] After Frémont filed his claim in 1852, the Land Commission ordered that a survey of the claim be made according to Frémont's wishes and his 1849 *diseño*. Following the commission's order, surveyor Allexey W. Von Schmidt drew a panhandle-shaped map of Las Mariposas. Half of the land was a six-by-five-mile rectangle that included the town of Mariposas and adjacent mineral lands. The other half of the rancho ran in a long narrow line encompassing farming and grazing lands for thirty miles down the watershed of the Mariposa River. For the most part it appeared that conflict over mining operations had been avoided since the survey did not extend north into the central region of the mother lode. Most claims in the region, it seemed, would continue to be recognized on the basis of traditional mining law—discovery and appropriation. By the time the U.S. Supreme Court finally validated Frémont's claim to Las Mariposas in 1854, Merced Mining Company had resumed control of its operations and was having better success. Smaller companies and individuals also operated profitably in the region.

Astonishingly, as part of its ruling in *Frémont v. United States,* the Supreme Court ordered that a new survey be taken.[33] This directive created an incredible opportunity, which Frémont eventually turned to his advantage. Following the Supreme Court's directive, the U.S. district court appointed former Texas ranger John C. "Jack" Hays to make the new survey. In order to make the rancho more compact, Hays proposed cutting off the long extension down the Mariposa River but retaining the six-by-five-mile rectangle as Von Schmidt had laid it out. Hays then asked Frémont's manager, J. E. Clayton, for suggestions about where the remainder of the grant should be located. The resulting Hays survey in 1855 created an estate that was very different from the rancho laid out in the Von Schmidt survey of 1852. It certainly was a much more compact area, but the new survey also shifted onto Frémont's estate most of the valuable mineral lands in the region, including Merced Mining Company's Mt. Ophir, Josephine, and Pine Tree mines.[34]

Miners and settlers in the area had been preparing for the worst. In July 1855 they formed a committee "to defend our rights against the pretended claim of John C. Frémont." In 1852 they had sworn that "having derived our title from old Uncle Sam and being in actual possession . . . we will not yield possession until compelled to do so by the highest legal tribunal of the country." Now that tribunal had spoken. But the general public of Mariposa still considered the final location of Frémont's claim to be "an outrageous bare-faced piece of downright stealing" and "one of the most magnificent swindles ever yet perpetrated upon the people of this state."

Whatever the legalities, they believed that the courts had no authority to place the Frémont grant upon the mineral lands of the Sierra Nevada.[35]

The next year, 1856, the new Republican party chose John C. Frémont as its candidate for president of the United States. Preoccupied with politics, Frémont did not take any steps to secure possession of the property that was now Las Mariposas or to evict the miners and settlers living and working on that land. Invisibility did nothing for Frémont's popularity in the region, however. In Mariposa County Frémont made a pathetic showing of 165 votes to the Democratic candidate Buchanan's 1,254.[36]

F tries to eject miners + they won't claim he doesn't own gold lmins

Biddle Boggs

Although Frémont's claim to the land in the mining region appeared to be beyond dispute, there was still hope for the miners. Most people believed that mineral rights did not belong to the land owner. That was the rule under Mexican law, at least, and it would be a major issue in the final battle over Las Mariposas. "You say that the highest Judicial tribunals have confirmed his grant," J. Boling wrote to the *Alta*. "This I do not deny, but I do deny that these high tribunals of Justice have decided or confirmed the *minerals* (the great bone of contention) in that grant of land is to belong to Frémont; and until they do so, I for one will use all my energy and resources to prevent him from wrenching, by force or otherwise, the hard earned labor of those men who have in good faith acquired their possessions."[37]

The fireworks began in January 1857 when Frémont's agent, J. E. Clayton, published a demand that Merced Mining Company turn over possession of their Mt. Ophir works, including all the machinery, buildings, and outhouses, and leave the premises. The Merced Mining Company quickly won an injunction in the state court that prevented Clayton from enforcing his demand and to keep the Frémont interests from working the Merced claims. Frémont appealed to the California Supreme Court. In a decision upholding the injunction, Justice Peter Hart Burnett emphasized the urgency of Merced's plea. The only value of a gold-mining claim, he reasoned, consists of the mineral; allowing it to be taken away would destroy the very substance of the estate.[38] The first minor legal skirmish was thus a victory for Merced. More important, however, miners saw that they could depend on justices Burnett and Terry. Field was not yet on the court. Burnett's opinion relied on legal theories that most miners favored and thereby provided a signal of the court's leanings. The most important of these theories came from the California case *Hicks v. Bell,* which held that minerals on public land belong to the state. Neither the state nor the federal government had expressly granted miners a right of property in their claims, the court had admitted, but by allowing miners to take gold from the public domain both governments had implied that miners had some kind of right.[39]

Even after the injunction, Frémont continued his efforts to drive Merced off the land he claimed. In April 1857 he leased Mt. Ophir to a man named Biddle Boggs, who then filed suit to eject Merced from the property. John R. Howard, the son of Frémont's business associate, described Boggs as "the most 'Dickensy' character I ever knew." He was a jack-of-all-trades on the Frémont estate, "tireless on foot or horseback, lazy as to all regular employment, shrewd of judgment, deliberate in speech, with a perfectly delightful conceit in his own wisdom and importance."[40] And, it was unlikely he could afford the array of legal talent that gathered in the Mariposa Courthouse to represent his interests. Among the eight attorneys representing Boggs and Frémont were Joseph Baldwin and William T. Wallace, both of whom were soon to become justices of the California Supreme Court, and former California Supreme Court justice Solomon Heydenfeldt. Merced's attorneys included the powerhouse San Francisco firm Halleck, Peachy and Billings.[41]

Although sympathizers for both sides packed the courtroom, most independent miners hitched their future to Merced's. Whether large operations or lonely prospectors, they were, in one sense, kindred souls. Merced's claim, after all, hinged on theories that supported a public right to mine for the minerals in California. The same general ideas formed the basis for most of the prospecting claims in the state. Most of the miners in the audience must have been disappointed, therefore, when this second preliminary skirmish resulted in victory for Frémont. On July 2, 1857, District Judge Edward Burke ruled that Merced had no equitable rights to the minerals at the Mt. Ophir works. Consequently, he concluded, Frémont was entitled to possession of the disputed property plus damages for loss of revenue.[42]

Frémont's claim to the minerals beneath Las Mariposas was still not completely secure, however. Less than a month later Merced Mining Company filed an appeal to the California Supreme Court. Merced maintained that under Mexican law, the law upon which Frémont's claim was based, ownership of minerals did not pass to a grantee along with the surface rights. Frémont's attorneys argued that it did not matter whether title to minerals passed to grant holders under Mexican law. Under U.S. law ownership included both the land and the minerals under the surface. Once the United States had issued a patent, they reasoned, its law should govern. Besides, they said, to hold that one man had the right to bring a troop of men to dig up another's farm in order to hunt for gold or silver would be "an odious doctrine." It would amount to taking private property and appropriating it to the private uses of another.[43]

In March 1858 the California Supreme Court delivered an opinion in *Biddle Boggs v. Merced Mining Company*. Judge Peter Hart Burnett's opinion for the court was, once again, all that Merced and independent miners could have hoped for. First, Burnett addressed the issue of who owned the mineral rights. When it passed the California Land Act of 1851 Congress did not grant any *new* rights, Burnett observed; the purpose of the act was to confirm *old* titles. Hence the U.S. patent that recognized Frémont's claim to Las Mariposas could not vest in him any title that was not already included in the original grant. Since the laws of Mexico reserved all mineral rights to the state, title to the minerals beneath Las Mariposas did not pass to Juan Alvarado when he received the original grant. By drawing the chain of title in this manner, Burnett reached the logical conclusion that Alvarado had no mineral rights to give when he sold his property to Frémont. The state still owned the minerals, and when Mexico signed the Treaty of Guadalupe Hidalgo, its rights passed to the U.S. government.[44]

But what was the United States to do, and what had it done, with those minerals? The answer to this question, Burnett implied, would determine whether prospectors had a right to mine for government-owned gold on privately owned land. Burnett began with a practical observation. The government's right to the gold, he said, necessarily carries with it the right to enter private property and search for and dig that gold. The ownership would be worthless without the power to take possession of the minerals. Burnett then noted that the government had not done the work of mining itself; rather, it had adopted a policy of allowing private individuals to mine the gold. Thus, the federal government had implicitly transferred its right to dig for those minerals to miners, he reasoned. The government had, in other words, given them what amounted to a general license. It followed, according to Burnett, that government policy, combined with traditional mining law, had the practical effect of giving the owners of mining claims a good vested title to the property of their claim, even if that claim lay within the boundaries of a confirmed Mexican land grant.[45]

Justice David Terry agreed with the outcome of *Biddle Boggs* but wrote a separate opinion saying that it was sufficient to rule that Frémont did not own the rights to the minerals under his land. Stephen Field, who had just recently been elected, dissented without comment.[46] Merced Mining Company and the independent miners of Mariposa County apparently had secured a final victory. For them the decision meant that Frémont had only the same claim to minerals on Las Mariposas as did other miners—"He could not claim the fruits of labor of others nor prevent their operations."[47] The result of *Biddle Boggs* was not as certain as it appeared, however. Frémont's forces quickly filed for a rehearing in the California Supreme Court. This type of motion is usually a technicality, and rehearing is seldom granted. Frémont's legal maneuver therefore would not have been particularly threatening to miners had it not been for intervening factors.

While the legal battles were proceeding, both Frémont and Merced continued mining operations. Frémont's men began to work a tunnel called Black Drift, which ran right next to Merced's Pine Tree and Josephine operations. Bad feelings and close proximity created a powder keg. As late as September 1857, the *Alta California* was able to report that no violence had occurred despite the unsettled affairs in Mariposa.[48] That changed on July 9, 1858, when an armed group, estimated at 75 to 120 armed men, tried to jump Frémont's Black Drift tunnel. The group called themselves the Miners and Settlers or the Hornitos League—Hornitos being the name of a nearby town with a reputation for lawlessness. Whether the men were employees of Merced, lawless thugs, or aggrieved miners is impossible to say. John Frémont's wife, for one, thought they were a mixture. In any case, when the Hornitos League party made their way into the entrance of Black Drift they found, to their surprise, that the tunnel was occupied by a small group of Frémont's men. The former decided to lay siege to the entrance and starve out the miners inside.[49]

When he learned of the situation, Colonel Frémont set out for the mine with another small group of his men. The siege then settled into a tense stalemate, with Frémont's men in the mine, the Hornitos men at the entrance, more Frémont men surrounding them, and even more Hornitos sympathizers blocking the roads out of the county. Tension increased when the wife of one of Frémont's miners boldly forced her way into the tunnel with food and ammunition. It rose again when rumors spread that the Hornitos men had found a back way into the tunnel. John Raymond Howard remembered that one of the Frémont men, "a tall, broad-shouldered giant, clad in brown velvet, with belt and shiny appurtenances, a wide sombrero shading his blond curling hair and tawny mustache," stood up and shouted a warning. "Click-click-click went the cocking of firearms on all sides," he remembers; "everyone seemed to be waiting for someone else to begin the fray."[50] But no one did, and the stalemate continued for several more days. "Frémont's men are well fortified in their tunnels," reported the *San Fran-*

cisco Evening Bulletin, "and if attacked by the party which has surrounded them, there will be a terrible slaughter."[51]

On July 12 a group calling themselves a committee on behalf of the citizens of Mariposa County sent written terms to Frémont. If Frémont would withdraw his forces and quit mining the shaft, they proposed, they would also withdraw, placing the mine in the hands of two neutral individuals until the supreme court finally decided the motion for rehearing in *Biddle Boggs*. Frémont, calling the demands a flagrant violation of common right, would hear nothing of it. "I hold this property by law, by occupation, and even by mining regulations," he replied. "This demand you make upon me is contrary to all my sense of justice, and what is due to my own honor."[52]

Although the roads were blocked, a young Englishman staying with the Frémonts managed to slip through the back country with a message to the governor. Time, along with rumors that the state militia was moving in the direction of Mariposa, weakened the Hornitos men's resolve. The siege quietly dissipated, leaving Frémont in control of the mine.

The drama that the siege at Pine Tree mine produced in the summer of 1858 was matched only by the political intrigue surrounding the supreme court. Judge Peter Hart Burnett, author of the *Biddle Boggs* decision, was nearing the end of his term. At the same time, the slavery issue began to influence party politics in the state. The Democratic party actually split in two, with the Lecompton (proslavery) and Anti-Lecompton (free-states) groups holding separate conventions on the same days. With state elections coming up, the Lecompton group chose Joseph Baldwin over incumbent Burnett as candidate for supreme court. The Anti-Lecompton convention chose John Curry, who was also the Republican nominee.[53] Although the slavery debate began to cloud local issues more than it had earlier in the decade, local issues remained in the forefront in this contest for the supreme court. The choice was clear to California's miners and settlers: they knew they could depend on Burnett, and they knew just as well that Baldwin's leanings would be toward Frémont.

"The Lecompton–Anti-Lecompton debate should be of no concern in election of Supreme Judge," the *Alta* advised. Both sides agreed. Nothing was so important to the people as election of a proper person to fill the seat on the supreme court, said Baldwin supporters. They called for consistency, honesty, and intellect on the bench. Under past courts, they argued, "titles to property have been unsettled, well settled principles of law have been overturned, the rulings of the court have been variable, fluctuating, and often contradictory; and as a necessary result, we have been floating on a sea of uncertainty and doubt, in respect to our most sacred rights of person and property." The public, they concluded, should no longer submit to the rule of men who color their decisions in accordance with what they believe to be the temporary public sentiment.[54]

The miners' and settlers' attack on Baldwin was fierce. They questioned his honesty, his integrity, and his intelligence. They painted him as the candidate of politicians and demagogues. "We have seen him arm in arm with pot-house politicians, with legislative brokers, treasury thieves and public gamblers," reported the *Bulletin*. Worse yet, opponents claimed, Baldwin was the candidate of "that objectionable class . . . the tricky and scheming lawyers."[55]

If this were not enough, settlers and miners needed only to recall that a few months earlier Baldwin had argued the *Biddle Boggs* case on rehearing—as one of the attorneys for Frémont.[56] Settlers and miners considered the *Biddle Boggs* decision to be a vindication of their position on the land issues. Now their greatest concern was that the court would grant a rehearing and change its opinion. Naturally settlers and miners condemned Baldwin for his role. One reported that "we regard the doctrines of Mr. Baldwin, as expressed in his brief, as subversive of and fatal to the holding and enjoyment of property in the mineral districts in this state."[57] If politicians are successful in electing Baldwin to the bench, warned another, "[a man's] very homestead, bought and paid for, under a solemn decision of the Supreme tribunal made last year, might be wrested from him by an adverse decision of the same tribunal made to-marrow."[58]

Despite heavy opposition from the miners and settlers, Joseph Baldwin was elected to the supreme court on September 1, 1858, and took his seat on October 2. With Burnett gone, David Terry and Stephen Field canceled each other on issues relating to land policy. Terry, who had proven to be a staunch and outspoken supporter of the settlers and miners, was unlikely to compromise. He and Field both possessed the same unbending will, and they seemed to clash on virtually every kind of issue. Baldwin's presence may actually have presented a quandary. Under normal conditions, he would be the deciding vote, and there was no question that he would side with Field. The two, who saw eye to eye on every issue, soon became the best of friends. Baldwin even named his son, Sidney Field Baldwin, in Field's honor.[59] But Baldwin's recent status as Frémont's attorney made it difficult for him to participate in the *Biddle Boggs* case. Although the standards of judicial ethics were different in those days, such a close connection would have been difficult to justify and possibly would have weakened the value of any decision the court made.[60] Apparently in deadlock, *Biddle Boggs* sat on the court's docket for almost an entire year. It remained dormant until David Terry's actions off the bench ended the stalemate.

Terry's term on the supreme court was due to end in January 1860. In the Fall of 1859 he sought the nomination of the Lecompton Democrats. Always a vocal and loyal southerner, Terry spoke passionately to the convention about the right to own slaves and the doctrine of states' rights. He also had harsh words for Anti-Lecompton forces whom he referred to as "personal chattels of a single individual, whom they are ashamed of."[61] Anti-Lecomptonites, he said, belonged "heart and soul, body and breeches" to Sen. David Broderick. Somewhat surprisingly the Lecompton Convention chose W. W. Cope over Terry as its candidate for the supreme court. But the event ultimately had a more important impact on California political history. Broderick, apparently insulted by Terry's comments, struck back. In earshot of one of Terry's friends, he said, "I have hitherto spoken of [Terry] as an honest man—as the only honest man on the bench of a miserable, corrupt Supreme Court—but now I find I was mistaken. I take it all back. He is just as bad as the others."[62]

Although dueling was outlawed in California, David Terry was one of those individuals who clung to its outmoded code of honor. When he learned of the insult, he resolved to "receive satisfaction" from Broderick. Terry waited until the general elections were over. Then he sent his challenge. Broderick accepted, and the date was set for Monday, September 12, 1859, at 5:30 A.M. The duel was delayed when the San Francisco chief of police arrested the would-be duelists for disturbing the peace. They were quickly released, and on the morning of the next day, the two men faced off. In a matter of minutes, Broderick lay mortally wounded; three days later he died.

Rumor spread that the duel was rigged and that the entire event was a conspiracy perpetrated by southerners. Broderick, never before so popular and admired, became a martyr for the northern cause. The duel had a significant effect on the supreme court as well. Terry, now a political pariah, resigned before the end of his term, which allowed the governor to appoint W. W. Cope in his place. Cope then won the general election in November, and the path was paved for a final decision in *Biddle Boggs*. Cope's appointment changed the balance on the court so that it was no longer necessary for Baldwin to participate. Field, who had become chief justice when Terry resigned, wrote the opinion in the second *Biddle Boggs* case.[63] It proved to be exactly what the miners had feared.

The second *Biddle Boggs* case addressed an issue that had not been part of the earlier decision. The Merced interests added to their legal argument a new element founded upon theories of fraud and equitable estoppel. Frémont, they reasoned, had never before claimed the mineral-rich lands in question. Acting on the basis of Frémont's earlier survey and his actions, other people had staked claims in these areas, expending hundreds of thousands of dollars and their own labor to develop these claims. It would be unfair, the argument ran, to now take this property from them.

The charges of equitable estoppel and fraud had more emotional appeal than legal merit. Equitable claims such as these faced technical legal hurdles. To win under a theory of fraud, Merced would have to prove Frémont had intended to deceive them or that Frémont had misrepresented his claim. Merced would also be required to prove that Frémont intended for Merced to rely on that misrepresentation. Either argument would be a difficult task since technically the U.S. Supreme Court, not Frémont, had ordered that a new survey be taken. Also, even though Frémont had agreed to the result, the federal government had commissioned the new survey that encompassed the mineral lands. Field had no difficulty disposing of the fraud claim; it had no basis, he ruled. Besides, Field reasoned, Biddle Boggs and Merced were the parties to this suit. Frémont's rights could not be impaired in a suit between third parties.[64]

Equitable estoppel required the same kind of proof. Even if Frémont had made misrepresentations about the location of his claim, Merced would have to prove that he willfully made them and that he intended to deceive Merced and other miners. Once again, Field had no problem disposing of the claim. Merced knew the grant was a floating one, he pointed out. To transfer Frémont's rights to them now would result in the highest degree of inequity.[65]

Technical rules of law did not convince miners and settlers. With just a bit of sarcasm, Horace P. Russ of the Quartz Miners' Association reported what the court had said to Frémont regarding the mineral lands.

Yes, take them; they are yours. You did not claim the land when these people were building the works, in fact you disclaimed it, but that was a mistake for which you must not be prejudiced; you did not find the vein or make the tunnel, or build the mills, or level the roads; you have done nothing except manage a survey skillfully; but take the property, the law gives it to you.[66]

With the equity claims out of the way, Field turned to the issue that had dominated the first *Biddle Boggs* decision. Directly reversing the earlier case, he ruled that Judge Burnett's theory that the government had given miners an implied license to take the minerals had no merit. There could be no license in the legal meaning of that term, he reasoned, because such a license could be created only by an act of Congress, and Congress had adopted no specific legislation on the subject. Field had always maintained that requiring strict construction of Mexican laws would be an injustice to grant holders. Now he was requiring strict construction of American law — regardless of any injustice it might bring to miners and settlers.

The doctrine of unlimited general license to take minerals from private lands was, Field said, "pregnant with the most pernicious consequences." What value would there be to a title for one man, with a right of invasion for the whole world, he asked?

There is something shocking to all our ideas of the rights of property in the proposition that one man may invade the possessions of another, dig up his fields and gardens, cut down his timber and occupy his land, under the pretense that he has reason to believe there is gold under the surface, or if existing, that he wishes to extract and remove it.[67]

The second *Biddle Boggs* opinion did not determine who owned the minerals under private land. Field had assumed, for purposes of the case, that they belonged to the United States. Neither did the opinion completely reject the notion of implied license. It simply held that any presumption of an implied license did not take precedence over the rights of private landowners. Miners thus did not have a right to enter private land. But the effect of the opinion, as a practical matter, was to shift the implied license to extract materials from miners to landowners. In a way, it gave Frémont a monopoly of access to the public resource within the area he claimed.

Devastating as this decision might have been to miners and settlers, the court had not gone so far as to rule that mineral rights belonged to the landholder. Perhaps the *Biddle Boggs* decision was only a stopgap measure made necessary because of Baldwin's earlier participation in the case as Frémont's attorney.[68] One year later, in combined cases of *Moore v. Smaw and Frémont v. Flower,* Field did rule that the right to minerals passed to the landholder who had received a U.S. patent.[69] Field professed to believe that "the court could not, without doing injustice to individuals, give to the Mexican laws a more narrow and strict construction than they received from the Mexican authorities who were entrusted with their execution."[70] In *Moore v. Smaw and Frémont v. Flower,* however, he was willing to give to the grant holder an interest that Mexican law definitely did not give — mineral rights. The Mexican law, under which ownership of the minerals would remain with the state, was based upon an archaic theory of *jura regalia* under which mines of value were held for the crown, Field reasoned.

In America the government does not own property by right of sovereignty but by right of ownership, like everyone else. Unless it had expressly reserved mineral rights, when the government gave a patent to landowners, it transferred everything. Field's opinion was a masterpiece of legal reasoning.[71] But it required a leap of legal logic that nonlawyers were unlikely to appreciate.

The beauty of Field's opinion was that it put miners in the awkward position of having based their claim on a particularly odious form of sovereignty (*jura regalia*). The opinion placed landowners on the philosophical high ground, claiming that their rights represented freedom from government interference. In this respect it was a good Jacksonian argument. When applied to protect small property holders, as it later was in *Dubenspeck v. Grear,* this appeal to the sanctity of private property had an attractiveness for everyone raised in that tradition. Even the pro-settler and pro-miner *Sacramento Union* admitted the "luminous and voluminous" opinion reflected some credit upon the ability of its author.[72]

However much some intellectuals among the miners might admire the opinion, most miners were more aware of the practical effect the opinion would have on their way of life when it applied to Frémont's vast claim. Mining rights must be free to all so that the poor might have the same opportunity as the rich, cried one letter writer to the *Union.* Predicting the worst, the author warned that to allow the mining districts to be monopolized by a few landholders would result in their having the white laboring population as much under their control as a southern planter had his black slaves.[73] Although exaggerated and racist, the letter accurately reflected miners' fears that the court's policy would reduce them to wage earners or peasants. Their fears were not totally unfounded. By the 1860s it was becoming obvious that the California dream of an egalitarian paradise would never materialize.[74]

The second *Biddle Boggs* opinion did not bode well for settlers, either. It reflected a long-cherished prejudice against squatters and squatters' rights, said the *Union,* and a belief that "no amount of evidence could shake the opinion of the Court in the infallibility of land patents—no matter how acquired."[75] Field made no secret of his insistence on the infallibility of land patents or of his belief that the government should make every effort to protect rights based on Mexican land grants. He was proud of his stance, and in the many land cases he faced in his judicial career, he seldom deviated.[76] Admirers maintained that Field's record reflected his superior intellect, devotion to principle, creative power, and courage. They were certain that the path he chose to follow would protect property rights and enhance the economic development of the state. He had neither courted personal popularity nor shrunk from unpopularity through his decisions, wrote John Norton Pomeroy.[77]

It was not only the policy outcome of the *Biddle Boggs* decision and *Moore v. Smaw and Frémont v. Flower* that frustrated miners and settlers but also the fact that the court had seized the power to determine that policy. Field's opinion amounted to legislation and was undemocratic, complained a letter writer to the *Alta*. Public use, custom, and opinion had not done away with the Mexican mining laws, the writer argued. America's written law had not repealed them. The people had adopted them, and equity protected all rights secured by them.[78] Yet Judge Field had ignored them. It was not the last time Field would be charged with legislating from the bench.

To many miners and settlers Las Mariposas now seemed like a small principality. The result of Field's opinions, wrote the *Sacramento Union*, was that every species of property included within the metes and bounds of the "notoriously fraudulent survey" belonged to Frémont: "The Court House, even, is at the mercy of the Colonel, and its occupants are liable to vacate the building at his bidding."[79] Although clearly exaggerating, the *Union* was not far off the mark. In the town of Mariposa and other settlements, people were forced to pay Frémont for the land upon which they had settled and believed they already owned. Merced Mining Company lost everything it had developed; its claims, its equipment, and its investment went to Frémont. With Frémont controlling both the land and the minerals, independent mining companies could work only under leases from him. Placer miners were affected as well when Frémont instituted a "tax" for the privilege of working the region.[80]

Although Frémont emerged as the winner of this long legal battle, he was not destined to keep Las Mariposas for long. In 1863, desperately in debt, he turned to New York financiers Morris Ketchum, James Hoy, and George Updike to bail out his mining operations. The group formed a company that bought Frémont out, leaving him little interest in Las Mariposas and no control. The miners and settlers of Mariposa County must have had mixed feelings about Frémont's destiny. The vengeful among them surely found some satisfaction in his downfall. But the Jacksonian streak in them was just as surely amazed and depressed that the great wealth of the Sierra Nevada had simply dissipated and ended up in the pockets of bankers and financiers.

Justice Field's brother, David Dudley Field, represented Frémont in the transaction with Ketchum, Hoy, and Updike. His fee was 2,000 shares of Mariposas stock (worth $200,000 at par value). Many people thought Frémont had been cheated and that David Dudley Field had been part of the conspiracy.[81] Frémont, however, apparently held no animosity toward the judge or his brother. He later employed David Dudley Field's services again in his final financial disaster, the bankruptcy of the Memphis and El Paso Railroad.[82]

The business relationship between Frémont and David Dudley Field must have added fuel to charges that Justice Field had a financial interest in the outcome of *Biddle Boggs*. Complaints of this sort were not uncommon during the 1850s. Charges of corruption seemed to accompany every significant case before the supreme court and every election of supreme court justices. With respect to *Biddle Boggs,* a pamphlet, "The Gold Key Court or the Corruptions of a Majority of It," claimed that both Baldwin and Field had profited. Field, it said, had received $50,000 in Frémont bonds for his services in reversing the former judgment of the court.[83] As might be expected, there is no hard evidence that Field was involved in any bribery scheme. The only certainty is that he was of like mind with those individuals who had an interest in Frémont's success. He admired men like Frémont and John Sutter, respected Frémont's attorney, Heydenfeldt, and became great friends with Baldwin. These men shared a belief that the fate of the nation depended on the sanctity of private property. Their faith may have appeared convenient in the way it was applied to the California land cases, but in the absence of any other evidence, one can only assume it was genuine.[84]

It is difficult to determine how much political fallout the Frémont land cases produced. Within four years of *Biddle Boggs* Field and Baldwin were no longer on the court. Although the court did not always rule in favor of large landholders, the two men certainly had not made many friends among the miner and settler elements in the state.[85] If aroused, this group of voters might have had enough of a following to influence the outcome of an election. But the miners and settlers would never have the chance to vent their hostility at the polls. The nation was moving toward civil war, and after Abraham Lincoln's election in 1860, the local issues of landownership and mining rights were quickly swallowed up by the nation's crisis.

When news of Fort Sumter reached California in April 1861, the California Democratic party divided on the question of loyalty to the Union. Loyalists, often referred to as Union Democrats, designated themselves the Douglas Committee. Democrats who sympathized with the South or whose support for the Union was conditional became known as the Brackinridge Committee. Joseph Baldwin's term on the supreme court was ending that same year. Most indicators placed Baldwin as an advocate of states' rights. He had, after all, received his first nomination for the supreme court post in 1858 from the Lecompton wing of the Democratic party. When the Brackinridge Committee nominated him to run for reelection to his seat, however, Baldwin declined. It did not make much difference. If he had run on the Brackinridge ticket, Baldwin would not have had a chance. There was some talk of secession in California and some talk of establishing a Pacific republic, but a large majority of Californians favored loyalty to the Union. Given the mood of the state, and with the Democratic party hopelessly divided, Republicans won a landslide victory in the November election. On January 1, 1862, Republican Edward Norton took a seat on the California Supreme Court. Joseph Baldwin returned to the private sector.[86]

Republican president Abraham Lincoln saved Stephen Field from the same fate. Field's term would expire in 1863. Although he did not publicly align himself with either wing of the Democratic party, Field always remained loyal to the Union. Nevertheless, as a Democrat, his prospects for reelection did not look very good. All signs pointed to the end of Field's career as a judge. But Lincoln was looking for a westerner to fill a new seat on the U.S. Supreme Court. As chief justice of the California Supreme Court, Stephen Field had the qualifications to be a reasonable candidate for the post. Although it probably did not help that he was a Democrat, Field had influential friends in California and in Washington, D.C. Early in 1863, Lincoln made his decision. In March he nominated Stephen Field as associate justice of the Supreme Court of the United States.

4

THE TENTH JUSTICE

Stephen Field would sit on the U.S. Supreme Court from 1863 to the end of the century. His seat on the high court made him one of the most important figures in state and national politics. From that vantage, he influenced the direction of American constitutionalism in the wake of the Civil War and stood at the center of a struggle to define the nature of liberty in a nation that was speeding toward modernization. Yet as with many such occurrences, Stephen Field's appointment to the Supreme Court depended upon a fortuitous alignment of circumstances and influence.

The Civil War created the circumstances. Although a Confederate retreat at the Battle of Antietam gave President Lincoln the opportunity to announce the Emancipation Proclamation in September 1862, the war was not going well for the Union late that year or early in 1863. The Union victory at Gettysburg was still more than six months away when Lincoln considered Field's appointment to the Court. In the emergency, neither the president nor the Radical Republicans who controlled Congress were confident that the Supreme Court could be counted on to support their policies. With five members who had supported the proslavery position in the *Dred Scott* case, the Court was "a long way from being made safe for Republicanism."[1]

Many northerners and abolitionists pointed to organization of the federal courts and traditions regarding Supreme Court appointments as the cause for what they believed was an overrepresentation of southern interests. The lower federal courts were organized into nine circuits, with each Supreme Court justice assigned to supervise one particular circuit. Supervision included "riding circuit," a duty that required the justices to travel outside of Washington, D.C., to hear cases along with the lower federal judges in their circuit. By tradition, geography became a major factor in the decision of who would be appointed to the Supreme Court. Presidents tended to choose people from within the circuit to which they would be assigned. Opponents of slavery complained that this system resulted in a disproportionate number of southern men sitting on the bench. And their complaints appeared to be justified. Five of the circuits, containing about 11 million people, were made up exclusively from slave states. The remaining four

Justice Stephen Field, taken about the time of his appointment to the United States Supreme Court. (Oregon Historical Society, Negative No. ORHI 77527)

circuits, which covered northern states, contained more than 16 million people.[2] Thus the court's makeup was a prime example of what abolitionists called "the slave power." They argued that the South was overrepresented in all branches of the federal government and that a small group of slave-holders had a vise grip on national policy.[3]

Republicans, who wanted to pack the Court with judges who would "help keep the power of the Court right," responded with a plan to reorganize the federal judiciary.[4] One aspect of their plan would change the boundaries of the existing circuits, with the result of shifting two circuits to the more populated North. The second element would create a tenth seat on the bench for a justice who would have responsibility for the Pacific Coast.[5]

Congress had already created an independent judicial circuit for California and the Pacific Coast in 1855. Since no Supreme Court justice was charged with responsibility for the circuit, circuit court judge Matthew Hall McAllister served as the highest federal judicial officer. By most accounts he served the region ably. In 1863, however, McAllister was nearing the end of his career, and there was some question about his ability to continue in the job. He resigned in January 1863, less than two months before Congress passed the legislation creating the tenth seat on the Supreme Court. The seat was now wide open, and Stephen Field was reasonably well positioned to be considered for the appointment.[6]

There was no requirement that a westerner be appointed as justice for the new circuit. But California was relatively isolated, and although it appeared staunchly loyal in the 1860 elections, there remained a strong southern element. The president thus believed it was important to the Union cause to appoint a Californian to the new seat. Death and resignations among the members of the Supreme Court made Lincoln's decision to appoint a Californian even easier. When Justice Peter Daniel of Virginia died in 1860, Republicans blocked Pres. James Buchanan's nominee, leaving the choice for the incoming president. John McLean of Ohio died in April 1861 and John Campbell resigned when his home state, Alabama, seceded from the Union. McLean's seat immediately went to Noah H. Swayne, another Ohioan. To ensure that the two seats vacated by southern judges would go to loyal Republicans, Lincoln waited until Congress had redrawn the circuits. Then he appointed David Davis, a friend from Illinois, for one redrawn circuit and Samuel Miller of Iowa for the other.

Having satisfied other pressures of geography, politics, and friendship, Lincoln was free to look to the West for his fourth appointment.[7] Stephen Field was one logical choice. Field was the highest judicial officer in the

State. He was a Democrat, but at least in one public speech, he had declared himself to be a loyalist. With the nation at war, the completion of a
transcontinental telegraph in October 1861 became an important symbol of
linking the West to the North. One of a series of "first messages" over that
line was sent from Stephen Field, chief justice of the California Supreme
Court, to Pres. Abraham Lincoln. Declaring that Californians wanted their
first message across the continent to express their loyalty to the Union, Field
predicted that the telegraph "will be the means of strengthening the attachment which bind both East and West to the Union."[8]

Circumstances were thus ripe for Field's nomination. The political influence that made it happen probably came from his older brother David
Dudley. Family lore has it that, in a personal interview with the president,
a prominent New Yorker named John Gray recommended Field's appointment. "Does David want his brother to have it?" Lincoln was said to have
asked. "Yes," said Mr. Gray. "Then he shall have it," replied the president,
and the nomination was sent to the Senate that afternoon.[9] It is impossible
to know just how much influence David Dudley Field may actually have
had. But there is no question that his links to the antislavery movement were
old and deep. David Dudley, a New York lawyer, got his start in politics in
the 1840s as a Barnburner Democrat. These followers of Martin Van Buren
fought with the main faction of the party partly over patronage and partly
over expansion of slavery. David Dudley's antislavery feelings were made
clear however, at the New York State Democratic Convention of 1847,
where he attempted to place the Wilmot Proviso (to restrict the expansion
of slavery) on the party's platform. He was among the disillusioned Democrats who aligned with conscience Whigs and abolitionists to form the Free-
Soil party in 1848. By 1856 he had given up on the Democratic party altogether—calling it the "tool of a slave holding oligarchy." That same year he
joined the Republicans.[10]

Secretary of the Treasury Salmon P. Chase was undoubtedly David
Dudley's closest ally in the Lincoln administration. The two corresponded
regularly, with Field advising the secretary on everything from the conduct
of the war to contracts for war supplies. When the Legal Tender Act of 1862
was challenged in New York's courts, the Treasury chief assigned David
Dudley the important task of defending it. David Dudley had other friends
who may have had Lincoln's ear from time to time. He worked on lawsuits
with Union Democrat Reverdy Johnson, corresponded with Lyman Trumbull, and he may have had access to the president himself. He was an early
supporter of Lincoln, and in 1860, when Lincoln spoke at Cooper Institute

in New York, David Dudley Field was among the group that joined him on the platform.[11]

Stephen Field had plenty of supporters in addition to his brother. The entire California congressional delegation united to work for his appointment. Senator Milton Latham, who had been a fellow Broderick crony in the Senate contest of 1856, vigorously supported Field. So did the budding railroad magnate Leland Stanford, who was then governor of the state. In January 1863 friends asked Field if he would agree to replace McAllister as the circuit judge for California. Field rejected the offer, replying that he could not accept the position because he preferred to remain chief judge of the supreme court of the state rather than be a judge of an inferior federal court. "But if a new justice were added to the Supreme Court of the United States," he continued, "I would accept the office if tendered to me."[12] The California delegation apparently thought Lincoln intended to use the circuit judge appointment as a stepping stone to the Supreme Court. Ignoring Field's rejection of their advances, they continued to press for him. On February 23, 1863, Lincoln appointed Stephen Field to the circuit judgeship. Less than two weeks later, on March 6, 1863, when Congress enlarged the Supreme Court, the president appointed Field to fill the tenth seat. The Senate confirmed his appointment on March 10, and he was sworn in on May 20, 1863—his father's birthday.[13] The Court would have ten justices for only a few years; in 1869 Congress returned to a nine-member court. Field's circuit, covering California and the West Coast, then became the Ninth Circuit.

California Justice

Perhaps Field's comment that he would prefer to be the chief judge of the California court than an inferior federal judge says more about his attitude and character than anything else. He appeared to be a man who liked to be in charge. Although Field would spend a greater part of each year in Washington, D.C., his appointment to the Supreme Court did not sever his ties to California. Indeed, his influence within the state increased. His importance in the state grew in part from his duty of riding circuit. Each summer for most of his thirty-four years on the Court, Field traveled back to the Pacific Coast. In his early years on the Court, he made his way back and forth over roughly the same route he had taken as a forty-niner. During the 1860s the Panama route was a little more comfortable because he crossed the isthmus by train. Later, with the completion of the transcontinental railroad, he was able to travel across the continent by rail, but the trip was still arduous. And when he arrived, there was more travel. His circuit ran the entire length of the Pacific Rim, from Los Angeles to Portland.

Difficult as the duty of riding circuit was, Field must have found some satisfaction in it. When acting as circuit judge, he was the highest judicial authority in the West. Besides, the regular trips allowed him to touch base with home and to stay closely attuned to the California political scene. In the 1860s many of the political battles continued to revolve around distribution of land in the state. Field influenced the outcome of these battles in two ways. First, he used his position as a Supreme Court justice to extend the rule of law he had developed as a member of the California court.[14] There was nothing unexpected or unconventional about that. But Field was also willing to use his judicial status to influence the political process. When conflicts erupted over ownership of valuable lots in San Francisco, for example, Field seized the issue and used every means at his disposal to direct the outcome. Thus he influenced the land disputes in a second way that went far beyond the normal role of a judge.

In his first decade on the Supreme Court, Field had numerous opportunities to reinforce the land-dispute rulings from his days on the California court. People who hoped to validate their claims to land grants continued to find comfort in his liberal interpretation of Mexican law. In his first year on the Supreme Court, Field followed his own California precedent in holding that strict compliance with the formalities of Mexican law was not required.[15] He went beyond reiterating existing rules, however. Giving claimants every benefit of the doubt, he ruled that the words "five leagues more or less" in a grant supported a grantee's claim to eleven leagues. The phrase was not a limitation on the quantity of land granted, he reasoned, but a conjectural estimate of the amount of property described.[16] Where fraud was clear, Field did not hesitate to rule against the claimant.[17] But in his opinions, the benefit of the doubt usually seemed to go to the claimant. In *Malarin v. United States* he validated a grant of two leagues even though the original document had been altered, changing it from one league to two.[18] In another decision the same year, he validated a grant even though it was dated after the time Mexican authorities said they had quit issuing grants.[19] In still another he held that the decree of the Board of Land Commissioners was valid even if it granted different land to an individual from that which was described in the original grant.[20] Field also strove to smooth the procedure affecting suits over land titles, making it as favorable as possible to the claimants.[21] He undoubtedly believed that the United States had a duty to protect even the imperfect and equitable titles of Mexican grantees.[22]

Where settlers were involved, however, Field's generosity abated. The most revealing cases involved the issue of whether homesteaders had an equitable interest in property they had settled upon, even though they had not yet fulfilled all the requirements of federal preemption law. Roughly speaking, the law required that a homesteader occupy the land, cultivate it, and pay a small fee. In *Frisbie v. Whitney* Field joined a majority of the Supreme Court in ruling that the act of occupying land and cultivating it did not give homesteaders a vested interest in their claims. Until they paid the fee, the government technically still owned the land.[23]

Although Justice Miller wrote the *Frisbie* opinion, some California homesteaders insisted on attributing the outcome to Field. Shortly after the decision, W. Hastings, a lawyer, petitioned the U.S. House of Representatives to impeach Field and California federal district judge Ogden Hoffman. According to Field, Hastings was a man carrying a grudge. Less than a year earlier in an unrelated incident, Hoffman had disbarred Hastings from practicing law in California federal courts.

Hastings could have been a crackpot, but he found United States congressman George W. Julian willing to sponsor a petition for the impeachment of Field and Hoffman. The charges that Julian leveled against the two judges were extremely general. The petition for impeachment claimed that they had disregarded the law of evidence, appointed dishonest clerks, and misdirected juries. But Julian had a reputation as the champion of homesteaders. His willingness to sponsor the impeachment proceedings and the timing of the episode—shortly after the *Frisbie* case—provides a strong indication that the impeachment effort was really instigated because of the judges' record on land issues. Julian tried twice to have the impeachment proceedings adopted. Both times he failed. Finally, the House Judiciary Committee reported it to the floor of the House with a recommendation that would kill it, and there the matter ended.[24]

A few years later Field had an opportunity to expand the *Frisbie* opinion when Congress gave the Yosemite Valley to the state of California. J. M. Hutchings claimed 160 acres of land within the area that was to become the park. Shortly before the federal government had transferred ownership to the state, Hutchings had bought the land from a man who thought he had a right to it under federal preemption law. Hutchings also paid the former owner of the land for buildings and improvements. Neither Hutchings nor the former owner had paid the required fee to the federal government, but

Yosemite Valley Case

they had satisfied all the other requirements necessary to claim a homestead. Thus Hutchings believed he had an equitable right to the property.

The Yosemite Valley Case drew former congressman and homestead activist George Julian to Hutchings's defense. Julian, who had also helped prepare the brief in *Frisbie,* reminded the Court that preemption involved several requirements. Payment of the fee to the government was no more vital or sacred than any other, he maintained. Besides, the government had never surveyed the land that Hutchings claimed or imposed a charge. Julian reasoned that the government's failure to officially delineate boundaries and charge the fee made it impossible for homesteaders to fulfill all the technical requirements of the homestead law. Once the land was occupied and cultivated, he continued, the settler had a vested interest in it. The government was bound by its good faith to protect the settler at this stage of his claim. It could not simply divest the homesteader and give the land to another.[25] Julian tried valiantly to distinguish *The Yosemite Valley Case* from *Frisbie,* but the legal ground upon which he based his argument was weak.

Writing for the Court, Field ruled that Hutchings had no right to the land until he had paid the purchase fee. In contrast to his treatment of grant holders, Field was willing to hold settlers to the technical requirements of the law. The homestead acts gave settlers no equitable rights, he reasoned: "The acts of Congress give to the settler only a privilege of preemption *in case the lands are offered for sale* in the usual manner."[26] In this case Hutchings had no rights because the federal government had never offered the land for sale. But Field's language had even larger implications for the underlying theory of homestead laws. Julian and other advocates thought of homestead as a right. Like the preemption statutes of the 1820s, Field's opinion treated it more like a privilege that Congress could grant or deny at its discretion. To Julian, this view must have looked like a major step backward for the homestead movement, a step that returned it to the principles predating the Preemption Act of 1841.[27]

The Yosemite Valley Case pitted George Julian against Stephen Field in a battle over ideology, but in some other land disputes the ideological aspects were not so pronounced. The most notorious of these involved title to town lots in San Francisco. It was in these disputes that Stephen Field graphically displayed his willingness to take control of an issue and see it through to a final outcome—even if it meant going beyond a judge's usual role of interpreting the law.

Although the San Francisco land cases raised questions about the validity of Mexican grants and preemption, there was more avarice than ideology in the mix that made up this dispute. Chain of title to land in the city was a complete mess. "I have known as many as six claimants for one lot," reported one early resident.[28] There were all kinds of claimants, ranging from the simple squatter who occupied one lot to bold schemers who claimed to possess Mexican land grants giving them title to virtually the whole city. Many were speculators who traced their title to a variety of sources, virtually all of which were of dubious validity.[29]

Many of the people who claimed lots near the waterfront based their claims on what was known as alcalde grants. Under Mexican law, each town or "pueblo" was allowed four square leagues of land. The law's intention was for the alcalde of the pueblo to encourage settlement by giving away part of this land in small lots to individual settlers. Some town lots in San Francisco could be traced to the time of Mexican rule. But American alcaldes, governing during the transition period, had made most of the grants. Although the validity of many of these later grants was questionable, the main issue that arose when the dispute over San Francisco titles came to a head was whether San Francisco had ever been a pueblo. If not, none of the alcalde grants would be valid.

A second group of speculators and investors claimed large parcels of land on the fringes of the city, tracing their title to the right of preemption. Few of them, however, were actual homesteaders. They tended to be individuals or investment companies who purchased large blocs of land for investment purposes. In most instances, even the original settler may have claimed the land only for the purpose of selling it for a profit. Whatever the case, their title depended on the land being declared part of the public domain.

Another complication was created when the city attempted to pay its creditors by allowing supposed city property to be sold off at execution sales. It began in 1852 when a group of creditors won judgments against the city for failure to pay its bills. In order to satisfy the judgments, the cash-poor city auctioned off large blocs of valuable property at amazingly low prices. The transactions, popularly named the Peter Smith Sales after the city's most prominent creditor, posed a serious threat to many older investors. The Peter Smith deeds could be valid only if the city, as heir to a Mexican pueblo, actually owned the property it had conveyed. But if the city was a pueblo, investors holding land in the outlying areas and tracing their title to preemption rights stood to lose countless millions of dollars worth of valuable real estate. To further complicate matters, if it were determined that the city had never been a pueblo, owners of property in the central business district who traced their ownership to alcalde grants stood to lose even more.

The struggle for ownership of San Francisco lots began while Stephen Field was still sitting on the California court. Established investors prevailed upon the city government to pass legislation in 1855 that would clear their title. Known as the Van Ness Ordinance, it relinquished the city's claim to property in the urban area and recognized the title of people who had been "in actual possession" of the property on or before January 1, 1855. The practical effect of the Van Ness Ordinance was to recognize the title of the older investors and to freeze the Peter Smith interests out. Almost simultaneously, however, holders of Peter Smith deeds began to file suits in the state trial courts to eject anyone who was then in possession of the land they claimed. When these cases were appealed, Field and the California Supreme Court were called on to decide whether a pueblo had ever existed on the site of San Francisco.

California's state judges faced the same dilemma that had perplexed the city council. If it ruled that there had been a pueblo on the site of San Francisco, older investors in the central business district would be secure in their title but older investors in the outlying area would lose their land to the holders of Peter Smith deeds. If it ruled that no pueblo had existed, the Peter Smith deeds would be invalid, but ownership in the central district would be in jeopardy because it was traced to alcalde grants. The court responded in 1860 with *Hart v. Burnett.* To the amazement of almost everyone, Judge Joseph Baldwin provided a solution that protected the interests of all classes of older investors. Field heartily concurred with his friend and undoubtedly played a hand in developing the theory of the case.

It was an enviable display of nimble legal reasoning. The court first ruled that some form of pueblo had indeed existed on the site since 1834. The city was thus entitled to four square leagues. Nevertheless, Baldwin reasoned, the property was not granted to the city as absolute property with an unlimited right to dispose of it. Rather, the city held the property as a "public trust" for the benefit of the entire community. This interpretation did not mean that it could not sell property at all. Sale of public property to promote the growth of the city and the comfort and convenience of its inhabitants was consistent with the public trust. If Baldwin had stopped there, Peter Smith purchasers might have joined holders of central-district lots in breathing a sigh of relief. But he was not finished. One matter that was inconsistent with the public trust, he said, was for the city to subject the trust property to forced sale in order to satisfy debts. Under this public trust doctrine, the Peter Smith deeds were therefore invalid. Older title to both the alcalde grants in the central city and the preemption lands in the outlying areas were, for the moment, secure.[30]

"Property to the value of many millions was thereby rescued from the spoiler and speculator and peace was given to a thousand homes," Field later recalled. But not everyone was happy with the outcome of *Hart v. Burnett*. Field rather dramatically described the public's reaction to the decision:

Yet from this just and most beneficent judgment there went up from a multitude, who had become interested in the sales, a fierce howl of rage and hate. Attacks full of venom were made upon Judge Baldwin and myself, who had agreed to the decision. No epithets were too vile to be applied to us; no imputations were too gross to be cast at us. The Press poured out curses upon our heads. Anonymous circulars filled with falsehoods, which malignity alone could invent, were broadcast throughout the city, and letters threatening assassination in the streets or by-ways were sent to us through the mail.[31]

Field believed, however, that the public eventually saw the wisdom of his thinking. Within a year, he boasted, the people appreciated the great good the decision had conferred upon the city. Field's observations notwithstanding, bad feelings continued.

The outcome of *Hart v. Burnett* is considered a landmark in public trust doctrine. An even more interesting aspect of the case is how Stephen Field, having helped formulate a solution to the problem of San Francisco land titles, worked to ensure that his solution would prevail. Early in 1862, while Field was still chief justice of the California Supreme Court, Hart (the loser in the case) filed a motion for writ of error, which would start an appeal to the U.S. Supreme Court. The U.S. Court granted the motion and ordered the state court to send its files up for review. When presented with the writ of error, however, Field refused to recognize the federal court's order. The supreme court of this state, he wrote, does not recognize an unlimited right of appeal to the Supreme Court of the United States. He agreed that, in certain circumstances, the federal Judiciary Act of 1789 provided for appeal to the United States Court from "a *final judgment* or decree in any suit, in the highest court of law or equity of a State in which a decision in the suit could be had." But in this case, he said, his court had remanded the case to the lower state court for a new trial. Field reasoned that there had been no final judgment in the case. The writ of error, he concluded, was therefore invalid.[32]

Although Field avoided sending the case to the U.S. Supreme Court, the California court would still not have the last word on the subject. At the same time that disputes were being fought in the state courts, the federal

Board of Land Commissioners ruled that the city was a pueblo but validated only three rather than four square leagues. Under the Land Act of 1851 the commission's decision was then appealed to the federal district court, which raised anew the question of whether the city was a pueblo. And as the new case unfolded in the federal venue, it created a series of events that were astounding for the usually staid world of legal process.[33]

The city prepared an appeal to Judge Ogden Hoffman's federal district court, but the case languished until after Field's appointment to the federal bench in 1863. Then Field moved quickly to gain control over the case. He had an ally in Sen. John Conness, who, on January 12, 1864, introduced a bill in the U.S. Congress that would have transferred from Hoffman's district court to Field's circuit court all cases concerning claims to land situated wholly or in part within the city or county of San Francisco.[34] When Conness's bill failed to pass, the two men took a less direct approach. In February Conness introduced another bill that would permit district court judges to transfer land cases to the circuit court and that required transfer of cases in which the district judge had an interest in the land. Field was finally successful. Hoffman denied having a financial interest in San Francisco land; nevertheless, he transferred the San Francisco pueblo cases to the circuit court.[35] Then, in *San Francisco v. United States,* Field again ruled that a pueblo had existed on the site of San Francisco. Regarding the extent of the land, he overruled the Board of Land Commissioners and ruled that the city was entitled to four square leagues. Regarding the authority of the city to dispose of the land, he simply referred the reader to the opinion in *Hart v. Burnett.*[36]

The dispute still was not quite over. Two attorneys ostensibly represented the interests of the United States in the case. Delos Lake was the U.S. attorney in charge of the case. In theory, his duty was to protect the public domain by making sure that any claims to Mexican land grants were valid. In addition, the federal government hired John B. Williams as special counsel for the United States; his duty was to represent settlers' interests. His interest, therefore, was to narrowly construe Mexican grants in order to keep land in the public domain and available for settlers. This was not an unusual arrangement at the time. Williams had often participated in this capacity in land cases before Judge Hoffman's court.[37]

Although his duty to represent the federal government's interest implied that Lake would also want to construe Mexican grants narrowly in order to keep land in the public domain, he was in general agreement with Field about the outcome of the case. After several informal ex parte meetings with Justice Field—that is, meetings in which no other parties were present—Lake officially conceded to the existence of a pueblo on the site. Williams was thus the only attorney dissatisfied with Field's opinion. When Field handed down the opinion, Williams filed a motion in Field's court for rehearing. In the affidavit accompanying his motion, Williams claimed that the clerk of the court had suppressed his brief, that Field had never considered it, and that Field had excluded him from ex parte discussions that resulted in Lake's concession. Williams, whom Field thought of as nothing more than a self-styled "special counsel to the United States," may have had good cause to suspect that he had been mistreated. Nevertheless, as anyone might have guessed, Field denied the motion for rehearing.[38]

Williams then filed another motion in the circuit court, a motion for appeal to the Supreme Court of the United States. When Field denied it, Williams realized he would get nowhere in Field's court. He then petitioned directly to the Supreme Court for a writ of mandamus, a document that would order Field, wearing the hat of circuit judge, to send the case to the Supreme Court. In a response that could only be interpreted as a rebuke to their fellow justice, Field's colleagues on the high bench voted 5 to 4 to grant the mandamus and order the case to be sent up on appeal.[39]

Officially, Field could do nothing more than dissent from the majority opinion. But he was not through. Once again acting with Senator Conness, he turned to legislation to accomplish his purpose. On March 8, 1866, Congress passed legislation entitled "An Act to Quiet Title to Certain Lands Within the Corporate Limits of the City of San Francisco." This statute, by which the United States would concede title to most of the land within the city, expressly confirmed Field's ruling in the circuit court. The appeal before the Supreme Court was thus moot. In its next term, the Court dismissed the case.[40] Field had tenaciously used every means, even those not conventionally at his disposal, to reach the outcome he preferred.

That year, Field received a package bomb in the mail. Pure luck kept the judge from setting it off. When the package was opened, it was found to have a clipping from a San Francisco newspaper dated October 31, 1864, reporting Field's decision in a stage of the San Francisco pueblo case.[41]

Liberty and Loyalty

California land cases were not, of course, the only subject to occupy Field's time in his new post. As important as that subject was in California, the nation as a whole had other problems to worry about. The battle of Gettysburg was still more than a month off when Field was sworn in. Obviously, people were more concerned about the progress of the war and preservation of the Union than about the new judge. In California, however, the two issues combined in Field's first reported case as a federal judge. It involved an incident that was sometimes as comical as it was daring. Asbury Harpending, a Kentuckian who had made a fortune in the goldfields, believed that Confederate sympathizers in California could outfit a ship of war and then sail the Pacific, preying on the Union navy and the merchant trade between California and the East. Traveling to Richmond, he received letters of marque from Jefferson Davis, documents that essentially gave him permission to make war on Union ships as a privateer for the Confederacy.

Armed only with his letters of marque, Harpending returned to California to gather money and supporters. He found the pickings slim. Only Ridgley Greathouse, another Kentuckian who had also made a fortune in the state, was willing to contribute to the cause. Together they had enough money to buy a ship and pay for the crew and munitions necessary to carry out the plot. Joined by a young Englishman, Alfred Rubery, they set the plan in motion. It seemed fairly well thought out. The group bought a small, fast schooner, the *J. M. Chapman,* docked at the Jackson Street wharf. Through a Mexican friend they bought cannon powder and other weapons and ammunition, then loaded it on board in crates labeled machinery. They also hired a captain, William C. Law, a seafaring man with three fingers missing from one hand, a sinister, villainous face, and a shady past.

The major weakness in this covert plan was that most of San Francisco seemed to know about it. The group came and went as if the *J. M. Chapman* was docked in the heart of the Confederacy, making only feeble attempts to cover up their activity. They discussed the plan in public taverns. Harpending boasted about his commission in the Confederate navy as he continued to solicit supporters. And they hired a captain who turned out to be either a traitor or a drunk. Federal authorities closely watched the group as the plan played out. When the night to sail came, Union forces were ready. The sloop-of-war *Cyane* and a steamer tug filled with police and marines lay in waiting. On March 14, 1863, overhearing that federal authorities planned to seize their ship, the aspiring privateers gathered their crew and made preparations to sail; by morning they were on board, except for Captain Law. Harpending grew nervous, suspecting treachery. As soon as the tide was favorable, he set sail without the captain. When the *J. M. Chapman* moved, the *Cyane* immediately launched boatloads of marines to intercept. Hoisting sail, Harpending tried to get under way, but there was no wind and the conspirators were quickly overtaken. Federal troops poured on board.

Below decks they found a magazine filled with ammunitions and the crew trying to burn or even eat incriminating papers. Captain Law came on board sometime later and was arrested with the others.[42]

The first indictments in the case charged the conspirators and about sixteen other San Franciscans with treason under an 1862 federal statute. Interestingly, one of them was Joseph Baldwin, Jr., the son of Field's friend and fellow judge on the California Supreme Court. Charges against the sixteen were dropped, however. When Law turned state's evidence, only Greathouse, Harpending, and Rubery were left to stand trial.[43]

United States v. Greathouse was tried before a jury in the federal district court. Field, who was riding circuit, presided over the case along with District Judge Ogden Hoffman. The trial dominated San Francisco news for weeks in fall 1863. Lawyers for the group argued that the defendants were not treasonous conspirators but soldiers of the Confederacy acting under the rules of war. In his charge to the jury, however, Field responded that, even if this were so, it would not apply to plotters who were operating in a state that had not seceded. The federal courthouse was packed when the jury read its verdict. Greathouse, Harpending, and Rubery were found guilty as charged. Prior to the Civil War, the only applicable federal statute made treason punishable by death. The 1862 statute implemented an administration decision to display leniency and still treat Confederate sympathizers as traitors.[44] The statute carried a maximum penalty of ten years in prison, a $10,000 fine, and forfeiture of slaves, and Field imposed the maximum penalty allowed. To his dismay, however, Judge Hoffman released the prisoners after President Lincoln issued a general amnesty proclamation on December 8, 1863.[45]

Unlike Greathouse and his co-conspirators, many people who were accused of seditious activity or disloyalty during the Civil War did not have their guilt or innocence determined in the civilian courts. Declaring martial law in September 1862, Lincoln ordered that any person "guilty of any disloyal practice affording aid and comfort to the rebels against the authority of the United States, shall be subject to martial law, and liable to trial and punishment by courts-martial or military commission."[46] That order gave the military jurisdiction over such cases. At the same time, the president effectively removed the courts from the process by suspending the writ of habeas corpus. In *Greathouse* Field had demonstrated an intolerance for disloyalty. When questions about military jurisdiction and suspension of the writ of habeas corpus reached the Court, however, he would show a fervent commitment to liberty.

The writ of habeas corpus, an order that a prisoner be brought before a

Suspension
of
habeas
corpus
+
mil
trivinals

court, is intended to protect individuals from being held in custody without being charged for a crime and tried. Although it is today overshadowed by other guarantees of liberty, the authors of the Constitution thought of the writ of habeas corpus as a major barrier against despotism. So important was it to them that it is one of the few direct guarantees of liberty written into the original body of the Constitution. Article 1, section 9 declares, "The Privilege of the Writ of Habeas Corpus shall not be suspended, unless when in Cases of Rebellion or Invasion the public safety may require it." Because Article 1 is the part of the Constitution that sets out the powers of Congress, there is a question of whether President Lincoln had authority to suspend the writ. In early 1863, however, Congress backed the president's action when it also ordered the writ suspended.[47]

There certainly was cause for suspension. The country was in a state of armed insurrection. Rebel sympathizers were not confined to the South; they also inhabited the key border states and even the North. It could not have been easy to distinguish friend from foe. And it must have been a relatively simple matter to cross battle lines, to carry messages or supplies, or to organize clandestine operations like the one that Ridgley Greathouse attempted. The danger was very real and, in the theater of war, military commanders had neither time nor patience for the niceties of legal process.

Yet just as the danger of war was real, so was the threat that trial by military commission posed to civil liberty. The justification for military commissions might be evident in time of war, near the battle lines, and in states where the rebellion was occurring. But could the commissions be justified in places away from battlegrounds or in states that had never seceded? What about after the war had ended? Certainly there was still some danger in these latter circumstances, but the farther one moved from the battle, the less the suspension of civil liberties could be excused. Even under the most justifiable of circumstances there would be abuses of the military process. David Dudley Field had a legitimate point when he argued that military commissions were organized to convict.[48] The mere accusation of disloyalty could lead to a person's being imprisoned.[49]

The case of Lambdin Milligan did not involve such an overt abuse of military power. Milligan was a leader of a clandestine group of Confederate sympathizers, the Sons of Liberty. Toward the end of the war, the group developed a detailed strategy to save the Confederacy by encouraging insurrection in midwestern states. Besides calling their followers to arms, the Sons of Liberty also planned to release southern prisoners held near Chicago and then fight their way south. They hoped their actions in the Midwest would create such havoc that Sherman would turn from his march to the sea. When the plan fizzled, Milligan was among the leaders of the group who were arrested and tried for treason before a military commission. Early in 1865, the military commission found the prisoners guilty and sentenced them to death. Attorneys immediately filed for a writ of habeas corpus in the federal circuit court asking that the prisoners be turned over to civil authorities. The Civil War ended in April 1865, and friends of the prisoners pleaded with the president for leniency. On the eve of the scheduled execution Milligan and his friends were still hoping that the court would issue the writ of habeas corpus, but it was not forthcoming. Only Pres. Andrew Johnson's last-minute commutation of the death sentences gave the circuit court time to react. The two judges who sat on the case split on whether to issue the writ of habeas corpus, a result that caused the case to be sent to the Supreme Court.[50]

Among the prominent group of attorneys pleading Milligan's case before the Supreme Court was David Dudley Field. The justice's brother argued that trial of civilians by military tribunals, whether in war or in peace, was a notion inconsistent with liberty.[51] A unanimous Court, which included Stephen Field, agreed, ruling that military trials of civilians were illegal wherever civil courts were functioning, as they were in Indiana when Milligan was convicted. Justice David Davis wrote the Court's opinion. The Constitution provides that the writ of habeas corpus may be suspended in certain grave circumstances, he admitted, but not for the mere convenience of the administration. Suspension of the writ is proper only in times of immediate peril, when the threat to government is actual and real and invasion or rebellion has effectually closed the courts and deposed civil government. Imposition of martial law on any other basis, he reasoned, destroys every guarantee of the Constitution and effectually renders the military independent of and superior to the civil power. Civil liberty and this kind of martial law cannot endure together, he continued; the antagonism is irreconcilable, and, in conflict, one or the other must perish.[52]

Although *Ex parte Milligan* is remembered as a victory for civil liberties, the case was not popular in all quarters by any means. Radical Republicans in particular viewed the decision as a threat to the congressional plan for Reconstruction. The case itself may have had little practical impact. Military tribunals continued to operate from the date of the decision in 1866 at least until 1870.[53] But the implication of this case—that the Court could overrule legislative strategy for dealing with the former Confederate states—inflamed an ongoing debate about the reaches of judicial power.[54] This aspect became even more evident later in another test of the jurisdiction of military commissions, *Ex parte McCardle*.

McCardle

Under the Reconstruction Acts of 1867 most of the former Confederate states remained under military control until they adopted new constitutions and were readmitted to the Union. In one of those states, Mississippi, newspaper editor William McCardle was arrested for publishing articles critical of the government's policy and held for trial before a military commission. McCardle petitioned the U.S. circuit court for a writ of habeas corpus. The court first granted the writ, then later remanded McCardle back to military custody. He then petitioned for appeal to the Supreme Court.

A recently enacted statute, the Habeas Corpus Act of 1867, expressly provided that the final decision of a U.S. district court on a motion for habeas corpus could be appealed to the circuit court and then to the Supreme Court. Given its statutory jurisdiction over the matter, the Supreme Court accepted McCardle's appeal.[55] Soon after oral arguments were presented, however, Congress revoked the Court's jurisdiction to take appeals in habeas corpus cases that had originated in the federal courts. "I have lost confidence in the majority of the Supreme Court," Congressman James F. Wilson told the House; "I believe they usurp power whenever they dare to undertake to settle questions purely political, in regard to the status of the States, and the manner in which those States are to be held subject to the law-making power."[56] Within the month, Congress passed a bill repealing the jurisdiction it had given the Supreme Court in the Habeas Corpus Act of 1867. When the president vetoed the bill, Congress mustered the two-thirds vote to override.

The Court never reached the merits in the *McCardle* case. It purposefully delayed announcing a decision until Congress had revoked its jurisdiction and then dismissed the case for want of jurisdiction.[57] Stephen Field joined in protest with fellow Democrat Justice Robert C. Grier, who let his feelings about the turn of events be known. Grier emphasized that the case involved the liberty and rights not only of the appellant but of millions of citizens. Then he admonished his colleagues on the bench: "By the postponement of the case we shall subject ourselves, whether justly or unjustly, to the imputation that we have evaded the performance of a duty imposed on us by the Constitution, and waited for legislation to interpose to supersede our action and relieve us from our responsibility. I am not willing to partake of the eulogy or opprobrium that may follow." Field curtly added, "I am of the same opinion with my brother Grier, and unite in his protest."[58]

In *McCardle,* Field and Grier were united in a desire to protect both individual liberty and judicial authority. A later habeas corpus case put a different twist on Field's attitude, however. *Tarble's Case* involved an underage army recruit who was being held for trial before a military commission on charges of desertion. It differed procedurally from *McCardle* in that a Wisconsin court, rather than a federal court, issued a writ of habeas corpus, which allowed the Supreme Court to accept an appeal. Field wrote the Court's opinion. Overruling the Wisconsin court's writ, Field declared that state judges could not issue habeas corpus for return of a prisoner held in federal custody. His reasoning was based upon federalism. The state and federal government was each sovereign within its own sphere, he said; the state could not interfere with enforcement of federal laws.

Logical as it may be from the standpoint of federalism, Field's reasoning arguably denied a large class of citizens protection against arbitrary imprisonment.[59] In this case Field thus seemed to abandon some of his earlier passion for liberty. Field did not, however, abandon the other aspect of Grier's dissent in *McCardle*. He remained protective of the power of federal courts. "If the power asserted by the State court existed," he argued, "no offense against the laws of the United States could be punished in their own tribunals, without permission . . . of the courts of the State in which the parties happened to be imprisoned."[60] The major factor underlying Field's opinion, it seems, was a concern for the supremacy of federal courts.

Patterns were beginning to emerge in Stephen Field's jurisprudence. On the California Supreme Court he had defended the independence of state courts. Now a justice of the Supreme Court of the United States, Field jealously guarded the power of his new forum. In California land cases, his opinions tended to favor large and powerful owners. His postwar opinions on the federal bench tended to trace the politics of the Democratic party. To settlers and miners of California and later to Republicans it may have seemed that power and politics, rather than principle and precedent, drove much of Field's decisionmaking. Yet it would be a mistake to assume that he was not also guided by a sincere desire to preserve individual liberty. That element of Field's thinking was evident in two cases that were decided in the same year as *Ex parte Milligan*. The cases, *Cummings v. Missouri* and *Ex parte Garland*, are popularly known as the *Test Oath Cases*.

At the end of the war the federal government and many states passed laws that required people to swear an oath of loyalty before they could assume a position of authority in the government or even in the private sector. The ostensible reason for loyalty oaths, or "test oaths," was the same as the reason for military rule and suspension of the writ of habeas corpus: in this *civil* war, it had often been difficult to identify one's adversary. Indeed, at the beginning of the war, southern sympathizers held many high places in the federal government. Some resigned, some remained loyal to the Union.

But any disloyalty that might come from that quarter could pose a serious threat to the Union even after battlefield victory.[61] With the battles ended proponents of the loyalty oath feared that former southern sympathizers would return to positions of authority in government and society and thus threaten the fruits of the Union victory. Loyalty oaths, they argued, would help ensure this possibility did not happen.

The raw politics of test oaths were quite obvious. Republicans were a new party composed of factions ranging from radical to conservative and including disaffected former Democrats such as David Dudley Field. Although they dominated national politics at the end of the war, the factions were becoming more contentious. If the party was to stay in power, some Republicans thought, it would be necessary to keep the Democrats hobbled. The South had always been a strength of the Democratic party. What better way to reduce that strength than to withhold from former rebels the right to vote and hold office?

Staunch opponents of slavery subscribed to a more public-spirited rationale for loyalty oaths as well. Many people believed it would be absurd to allow former leaders of the rebel government to regain power as state and national officials. To do so, they feared, would reestablish the control of the planter class—the slave power—and return the country to the same stalemate that had led to the war. The theory of the slave power held that, prior to the war, the planter class in the South was easily able to dominate local politics. Because southern representation in the national government was disproportionately large, followers of this theory thought that this relatively small group of slaveholders was able to control national policy. In the minds of slavery's opponents, the slave power, thus empowered, had conspired to subvert the true purpose of the Constitution by installing slavery as a national rather than as a local institution.

Before the war, the slave power had been the perfect ideological villain to draw various factions of antislavery advocates together; after the war, for some, it justified oaths of loyalty. The theory was meant to appeal to white self-interest as much as to any particular concern for black slaves. It presented the slave power as a conspiracy that threatened liberty, democracy, and free labor. As Salmon P. Chase explained, antislavery, as opposed to abolitionism, meant "a hostility to slavery as a power antagonistic to free labor, as an influence perverting the government from its true end and scope."[62]

Whether requiring an oath of loyalty could effectively accomplish any of the purposes for which it was intended is subject to question, but some people believed it could. Furthermore, the oaths must have appealed to some people's desire for vengeance, which partially explains why legislators enacted oaths in an unusually stringent form. These "ironclad oaths," as they were called, required not only that individuals promise to be loyal to the Union and the Constitution but also to swear that they had never been disloyal. The oath federal officers were required to take under the act of July 1862 was typical:

I, A. B., do solemnly swear (or affirm) that I have never voluntarily borne arms against the United States since I have been a citizen thereof; that I have voluntarily given no aid, countenance, counsel or encouragement to persons engaged in armed hostilities thereto; that I have neither sought nor accepted nor attempted to exercise the functions of any office whatever, under any authority or pretended authority in hostility to the United States; that I have not yielded a voluntary support to any pretended government, authority, power or constitution within the United States, hostile or inimical thereto.[63]

The politics and dangers of the test oaths were particularly obvious in Missouri. In no other place did the Radical Republicans' control depend more on their ability to keep Democrats from the polls and out of powerful positions. And in no other place did vengeance provide a more obvious motivation for loyalty tests. In addition to restricting the activities of people who had actually participated in the Confederate cause, amendments to the state constitution in 1865 placed severe restrictions on anyone who had even sympathized with people who had so participated. Anyone who had ever "by act or word, manifested his adherence to the cause of such enemies, or his desire for their triumph over the arms of the United States; or his sympathy with those engaged in exciting or carrying on a rebellion" was denied, among other privileges, the right to vote. Such people were also disqualified from holding public office or "any office of honor, trust, or profit." They could not be corporate officers, teachers, lawyers, or members of the clergy without first taking an oath that they had never participated in the rebellion or expressed or felt sympathy with people who had.[64]

John A. Cummings, a Catholic priest in Missouri, refused to take the oath. When he continued to minister his faith, Father Cummings was fined $500. He appealed his conviction to the Missouri Supreme Court, where he was unsuccessful. Then he took his case to the U.S. Supreme Court. Cummings was lucky to have powerful political forces lined up behind his quest for justice. Francis P. Blair, a loyal but conservative Missouri politician, opposed the loyalty oath. After a chance meeting with Father Cummings, he proposed using the priest's plight as a test case. Blair enlisted the legal services of his brother Montgomery Blair, constitutional lawyer Reverdy Johnson, and Judge Field's brother David Dudley.[65]

To the modern eye, their task must appear to have been relatively easy. The Missouri loyalty test trampled over rights that we think of as given: most graphically the First Amendment guarantee of freedom of religion. Free speech, the guarantee of due process, and the right against self-incrimination also come to mind. Cummings's attorneys made these points, but they had a major problem. These guarantees were found in the Bill of Rights, which, under standard constitutional doctrine in 1867, protected individuals against the federal government only, not against the states. The original Constitution, aimed primarily at defining the powers of the federal government, places few restrictions on the ability of a state to interfere with a person's liberty. One of these restrictions is the provision of Article 1, Section 10, that no state shall pass ex post facto laws or bills of attainder. These were the guarantees of the Constitution to which the Cummings defense team hitched its argument.

Ex post facto laws make an activity punishable as a crime in instances when that activity was not criminal when committed. A bill of attainder is a legislative act that inflicts punishment on a person or group without a trial. In a sense, the ironclad oath would seem to fit under these definitions. It involved repercussions for past activities, and it could adversely affect one's life without a trial. But the prohibition against ex post facto laws and bills of attainder apply only to laws of a criminal character—laws that inflict a punishment. A threshold question before the Court, then, was whether the effect of failing to swear to a loyalty oath constituted a punishment.

"What is a punishment?" asked David Dudley Field in his argument to the Court. Answering his own question, he defined punishment as the infliction of pain or privation:

To inflict the penalty of death is to inflict pain and deprive life. To inflict the penalty of imprisonment is to deprive of liberty. To impose a fine is to deprive of property. To deprive of any natural right is also to punish. And so it is punishment to deprive of a privilege.[66]

Applying this abstract definition to Cummings's case, David Dudley Field maintained that depriving a Christian minister of the right to preach was a punishment not only because it deprived him of an abstract natural right but also because it deprived him of his property. Preaching was Father Cummings's means of making a living, he argued; it was his profession: "Is not his interest in his profession property?"[67]

Arguing the case for the state of Missouri, George P. Strong implicitly admitted that preachers might have something on the order of a property interest in their profession—but not an inalienable property right. Every private calling is subject to such regulations as the state may impose, he reminded the Court.[68] To the extent that a loyalty test might affect a person's ability to engage in a profession, it did nothing more than regulate. The Missouri loyalty test was not an ex post facto law or a bill of attainder because Father Cummings had not been subject to criminal action, Strong maintained. He had not suffered a punishment. "He is surely not deprived of life or liberty, and the right to pursue his profession is not such an absolute right of property as to be above the control and regulation of State law."[69]

Given its extreme nature, the question of whether Missouri's loyalty test could amount to a punishment was not an easy one. Reverdy Johnson summed up the problem. It is said that what Missouri has done is merely to exercise her sovereign power to regulate the qualifications of those who are to hold office and pursue certain professions, Johnson said. "In one sense this is so; but is it the sense in which the [loyalty test] provision has been incorporated in the [Missouri] constitution? To prescribe age, property qualifications, or any other qualification that anybody has an equal opportunity of acquiring, is one thing; to disqualify because of imputed crimes, is quite another thing."[70] In a close decision, the Court held the Missouri test oath provision unconstitutional. Justice Field, writing for the majority, agreed with his brother.

The disabilities created by the Missouri constitution must be regarded as penalties, Field wrote. Saying that he disagreed with the state's argument that to punish means to "deprive [one] of life, liberty, or property, and that to take from him anything less than these is no punishment at all," Field made a rather vague stab at defining both punishment and rights.

The learned counsel does not use these terms—life, liberty, and property— as comprehending every right known to the law. He does not include under liberty freedom from outrage on the feelings as well as restraints on the person. He does not include under property those estates which one may acquire in professions, though they are often the source of the highest emoluments and honors.[71]

Under appropriate circumstances, Field continued, the deprivation of any previously enjoyed rights, civil or political, might be considered a punishment.

Field did not limit himself to those rights found in the Constitution. He also turned to the Declaration of Independence. Its guarantee of the pursuit of happiness, he said, includes a right that all avocations, all honors, all positions, are alike open to everyone and that in the protection of those rights all are equal before the law.

Field described the nature of this right even more forcefully in the other test oath case decided on the same day. *Ex parte Garland* involved an iron-clad oath that Congress required of attorneys who practiced before federal courts. Overruling the federal test oath, Field wrote: "The attorney and counselor being, by the solemn judicial act of the court, clothed with his office, does not hold it as a matter of grace and favor. It is a right of which he can only be deprived by the judgment of the court, for moral or professional delinquency."[72]

Once the Court had determined that the disabilities imposed by the loyalty tests constituted a punishment it was an easier step to find that they were ex post facto laws and bills of attainder. The ironclad loyalty test was unquestionably directed at past acts. What is more, it subverted the presumption of innocence. That the statutes creating such oaths were not written as criminal laws and that one could avoid the penalty by taking the oath was of no consequence to Field. The Constitution, he said, "deals with substance, not shadows."[73]

The dissenters in *Cummings* and *Garland* thought Field was making shadow figures of his own. For them, the loyalty test was nothing more than a qualification and a reasonable one at that. Writing for the group, Justice Samuel Miller pointed out that the loyalty oath merely required applicants to swear that they have not been guilty of treason to the government in the past and that they will bear faithful allegiance to it in the future. What better reason could there be for disqualifying a person from high positions in a time when the nation had just gone through a civil war? Miller emphasized his point with a direct reference to *Garland:* "That fidelity to the government under which he lives, a true and loyal attachment to it, and a sincere desire for its preservation, are among the most essential qualifications which should be required in a lawyer, seems to me to be too clear for argument."[74]

The loyalty oath imposes no criminal offense, Miller argued. It does not pronounce any sentence or inflict any punishment. It applies equally to all persons pursuing a trade, not to any particular person or class. "Where is this ex post facto law which tries and punishes a man for a crime committed before it was passed?" Miller asked with just a touch of sarcasm. He could find it only in the majority's "elastic rules of construction."[75]

Even people who agreed with the outcome of the *Test Oath Cases* would have difficulty denying that Field stretched the Constitution to get there. He applied an expansive view of judicial power to overrule both an act of Congress and a state law. He employed considerable imagination in defining ex post facto, bill of attainder, and punishment. More significantly, he invented a new right. Nowhere does the Constitution expressly guarantee a right to engage in a trade or profession.

Field's idea of a right to engage in a trade or profession also had the potential of imposing an unheard-of limitation on the power of government. Would all regulations subsequently be subject to challenges that they were ex post facto laws and bills of attainder? That seemed unlikely. Field's expansive use of these provisions of the Constitution worked in the *Test Oath Cases* only because the effect that loyalty tests had on the people who refused to take the oath looked like criminal punishment. Ordinary regulations of trades and professions were unlikely to have the same appearance. At virtually the same moment, however, Congress' Joint Committee on Reconstruction was working out the details of the Fourteenth Amendment. Its provisions would ultimately give Field's new right a broader impact.

Liberty and the Right to Pursue a Calling

The Fourteenth Amendment was one of three "Reconstruction amendments" ratified after the Civil War. The Thirteenth Amendment abolished slavery; the Fifteenth, ratified in 1870, provides that the right to vote shall not be denied on account of race, color, or previous condition of servitude. The purpose of the Fourteenth Amendment was more ambiguous. Soon after the Thirteenth Amendment was ratified in 1865 it became apparent that abolition alone did not adequately secure the liberty of former slaves. Southern states reacted with statutes known as "black codes" that used vagrancy laws and other misdemeanors to return the former slaves to what amounted to an indentured status. Section one of the Fourteenth Amendment was aimed at eliminating such practices and guaranteeing the fruits of liberty to the freedmen. That undoubtedly was its most direct and obvious purpose, but the amendment's framers chose to write the key provisions in broad, sweeping, and vague language:

All persons born or naturalized in the United States and subject to the jurisdiction thereof, are citizens of the United States and of the State wherein they reside. No State shall make or enforce any law which shall abridge the privileges or immunities of citizens of the United States; nor shall any

State deprive any person of life, liberty, or property, without due process of law; nor deny to any person within its jurisdiction the equal protection of the laws.

These phrases, "privileges and immunities of citizens of the United States," "due process of law," and "equal protection of the laws," convey a commitment to the principles of liberty and equality. They also implied that Congress intended to make some change regarding the power of state governments to restrict private liberty. But they are as vague and flexible as they are sweeping. Perhaps for that reason, the Fourteenth Amendment, ratified in 1868, quickly became both one of the most important and one of the most confusing and controversial provisions of the Constitution. Its meaning continues to be hotly debated more than 130 years later.[76]

The first major case to interpret the Reconstruction amendments involved a Louisiana law designed to "promote the health of the City of New Orleans" by centralizing and regulating the slaughtering industry.[77] There was no question of the need to control butchering in the city. Circumstances following the Civil War caused New Orleans to become a hub in production of meat products for the nation. The butchering industry was thus crucial to the city's economic recovery. That very same growth, however, escalated an already existing health hazard. Butchers regularly dumped offal (which William J. Novak aptly calls "the hazardous waste of the nineteenth century") into the Mississippi River. Because most slaughterhouses were located upstream, their dumping practices regularly contaminated the city's water supply. A New Orleans health official graphically described the problem: "Barrels filled with entrails, liver, blood, urine, dung, and other refuse, portions in an advanced stage of decomposition, are constantly being thrown into the river but a short distance from the banks, poisoning the air with offensive smells and necessarily contaminating the water near the bank for miles."[78] New Orleans, not surprisingly, had the reputation as one of the most unhealthy cities in the United States. Repeated cholera epidemics provided ample motivation for reform.[79]

Attempts to regulate the butchering business reached the legislature almost as soon as the state returned to civilian rule following the Civil War. Ultimately, the state settled on a centralized slaughterhouse located south of the city as the means of controlling the problem. In 1869 the Louisiana legislature gave Crescent City Live-Stock Landing and Slaughter-House Company an exclusive twenty-five-year franchise to build and operate the central slaughterhouse and stockyards for the city of New Orleans and for Orleans, Jefferson, and St. Bernard parishes. The statute prohibited slaughtering for profit in any other location. It also regulated the fees that the company was to receive when individual butchers landed animals or slaughtered animals at the site. Yet the statute technically did not create a monopoly. On the contrary, it required that the company build "a grand slaughter-house" of sufficient capacity to accommodate all butchers, and it prohibited the company from refusing to allow any butcher to slaughter animals in its facilities.[80]

Building a centralized facility in a safe location was not a unique approach to solving the health problems associated with butchering. The French and English had long since introduced a system of centralized public abattoirs, as the slaughterhouses were called. By 1869, New York, San Francisco, Boston, Milwaukee, and Philadelphia had followed suit.[81] Nor was this idea of regulating a trade by providing a centralized facility in which to carry it out unique to slaughtering. The centralized public market, a longstanding tradition, was still a part of the American economic scene into the 1870s. Furthermore, standard legal precedent of the time supported a municipality's power to build and regulate public markets and to restrict the sales of goods in other places.[82] Nor was Louisiana's decision to accomplish its goal by giving an exclusive franchise to a private company unusual. This method was fully supported by common law and recognized in constitutional law. The New Orleans central slaughterhouse fit neatly into the mid-nineteenth-century idea of a well-ordered market and was supported by recent trends for regulating businesses that tended to be hazardous to the public health.[83]

What actually galled the citizens of New Orleans was the means that their legislature chose to carry out the plan. States regularly allowed private corporations to build quasi-public facilities such as bridges, toll roads, and ferries and to grant them an exclusive franchise to carry on a public function. That was a common practice in the nineteenth century, and is still seen today. But the New Orleans slaughterhouse law had an odor of the kind of exclusive privilege that would have raised the hair on the back of an old Jacksonian's neck.[84] Proponents maintained that the slaughterhouse law was intended to protect the public health and, therefore, it was carrying out a public function. Opponents disagreed. This was not a health measure, New Orleans newspapers charged; it was a monopoly pure and simple. Opponents portrayed the central slaughterhouse as a monopoly granted to outsiders who had no experience in the slaughtering industry. The price of meat would rise, they claimed, while those speculators grew rich.[85]

The most forceful resistance to Louisiana's new slaughterhouse law came from established New Orleans butchers, who naturally did not want to move their businesses to a new location. A group of butchers even tried unsuccessfully to circumvent the law by planning a central slaughtering facility of their own.[86] Legal fireworks began when, in May 1869, an organization representing the butchers sought an injunction in the state courts to prevent the company from implementing the terms of the slaughterhouse statute. This action set off a messy flurry of suits and countersuits in the state trial courts—more than 200 cases resulted. Early in 1870 the cases were combined and brought before the Louisiana Supreme Court. On April 11 the state court announced its decision upholding the statute and thus giving victory to the company.[87]

This decision normally would have been the end of the matter. At the time, these types of regulations were generally thought to be within a vast sphere of activities referred to as the state police power. Police power was a term picked up from several opinions written by Chief Justice John Marshall.[88] Marshall used it simply to distinguish the functions of the state governments from the functions of the federal government. The concept of police power admitted that the federal government was supreme in its sphere of activity, but that sphere included only powers that were enumerated in or implied by the Constitution. All other functions of government were left to the states. Under what was then the conventional view of federalism, it thus would have been up to the state legislature to determine the preferred method of regulating slaughterhouses. Appeal, if warranted, would be to the state courts to determine if the legislature had exceeded its authority or failed to conform to proper procedure. The pattern of a similar case from Illinois was typical. There, the state court ruled that Chicago had exceeded its municipal authority when it set up a centralized slaughterhouse.[89] The New Orleans butchers tried that approach and lost. Thus they hoped to find a theory that would send their case to the federal courts.

Former U.S. Supreme Court justice John Campbell, who represented the butchers, needed all the ingenuity he could muster to develop that theory. Demonstrating great foresight, he began laying the theoretical foundation for an appeal to the federal bench while he was arguing his case in the state court. All courts of the country had a duty to protect fundamental rights against unreasonable legislative intrusion, he told the Louisiana judges.[90] In his argument to the U.S. Supreme Court, Campbell took this vague notion of rights and honed in on the new amendments to the Constitution. First, he reasoned that the slaughterhouse law violated the Thirteenth Amendment prohibition against slavery by reducing butchers to a state of indentured servitude. More important, he argued that the Fourteenth Amendment had completely altered the powers of state governments. Campbell's position was that the amendment, taken as a whole, gave the federal courts the authority to secure individual liberty, individual property, and individual security and honor from arbitrary, partial, proscriptive, and unjust legislation of state governments.[91]

John Campbell's legendary legal skill was not enough to convince the Supreme Court that the Fourteenth Amendment went that far. Writing for a 5-to-4 majority Justice Samuel Miller reasoned that under the American system of government, the states have the power to regulate businesses such as the slaughtering industry. This authority—called the police power—was based not only upon the principle that every person ought to use his property so as not to injure his neighbors, Miller said, but also upon the principle "that private interests must be made subservient to the general interests of the community."[92]

Under standard legal doctrine of the time, the constitutional limitations on the police power of the states were very few. Federal courts did overrule acts of state legislatures, but the scope of their authority to do so was quite narrow. State laws that interfered with Congress' power to regulate interstate commerce were subject to the scrutiny of the federal courts. Article 1, section 10 of the Constitution contained a few specific limitations on state power. In addition to that article's prohibition of ex post facto laws and bills of attainder was the provision that "no state shall pass any law impairing the obligation of contracts." Beyond that the Constitution left the states to function for themselves. Not even the federal Bill of Rights applied to their activities.[93]

The essence of Campbell's argument was that the new amendments to the Constitution changed both the nature of the police power and the character of American federalism. The amendments, he argued, placed a previously unknown limit on the states by allowing the federal government great latitude in enforcing individual rights against state legislation. Justice Miller was willing to recognize the obvious. The Reconstruction amendments did change the relative powers of the national and state governments in some way. But Miller was unwilling to admit that they were intended to "reshape American federalism." Instead, he said, the amendments had a much more limited purpose.

Miller was not explicit about what that purpose might be, but he did give some indication of its nature. "No one can fail to be impressed with the one pervading purpose found in [the Reconstruction amendments], lying at the foundation of each, and without which none of them would have been even suggested; we mean the freedom of the slave race, the security and firm establishment of that freedom, and the protection of the newly-made

freeman and citizen from the oppressions of those who had formerly exercised unlimited dominion over him."[94] This was not to say that only the
Negro could share in this protection, Miller continued; rather, it was a
guideline founded on the idea that in construing the amendments the Court
should look to their pervading spirit and the evil that they were designed to
remedy.[95]

As well as addressing the power of the states, the *Slaughter-House Cases*
spoke to the nature of rights. Although Campbell sought protection for the
butchers under all of the provisions of the Thirteenth and Fourteenth
Amendments, Miller's opinion centered on the Fourteenth Amendment's
guarantee: "No State shall make or enforce any law which shall abridge the
privileges or immunities of citizens of the United States." Justice Miller gave
the language a much narrower interpretation than Campbell would have
liked. Certain rights are derived from being a citizen of the United States,
Miller reasoned, and other rights are derived from being a citizen of a state.
The privileges and immunities clause, he ruled, protects only the former.

Miller gave some examples of what he considered to be rights of citizens
of the United States. He mentioned the right of peaceable assembly, the
privilege of habeas corpus, and some others, but he did not intend to pronounce an exhaustive list. And because Miller was not explicit about what
rights belonged in which category, his comment remains the subject of controversy today.[96] Most important, however, Miller saw the privileges and
immunities clause as protecting some finite set of rights that were based
directly on the language of the Constitution. It was unnecessary to go any
further in describing these rights, he said, because the rights the butchers
claimed, if they existed at all, certainly did not fall into the category of
privileges and immunities of citizens of the United States.[97]

Stephen Field's disagreement with the majority was as complete as could
be imagined. Over time, Field showed great concern for federalism and
states' rights, but his dissent demonstrated his belief that the Reconstruction amendments had changed the powers of the national and state governments in some important ways. If Miller's narrow reading was correct, he
warned, the amendments were "vain and idle enactment[s] which accomplished nothing."[98] Using fine Jacksonian language, Field railed against
what he thought of as the slaughterhouse monopoly:

The Act of Louisiana presents the naked case, unaccompanied by any public
considerations, where a right to pursue a lawful and necessary calling, previously enjoyed by every citizen, and in connection with which a thousand
persons were daily employed, is taken away and vested exclusively for
twenty-five years . . . in a single corporation.[99]

He was, of course, not entirely accurate. Butchers were not prohibited from pursuing their calling. The law required only that they pursue it in a particular location and pay a fee to the company that ran the operation.

Disregarding this detail, Field presumed that "abstract justice" supported the butcher's appeal.[100] There was no direct constitutional provision against a monopoly, Field admitted, "yet the whole theory of a free government is opposed to such grants."[101] Besides, he continued, the monopoly violated New Orleans butchers' right to pursue an ordinary trade. Field's attachment to this right to pursue an ordinary trade was longstanding. It had been a personal crusade in the justice's early career, when Judge Turner had attempted to disbar Field, then a young California lawyer, and it was a significant element of *Ex parte Garland* — perhaps it is not coincidental that *Garland* also involved an attorney's right to practice law.

Abstract justice is one thing, constitutional guarantees are another. Yet Field had no difficulty finding that the Fourteenth Amendment restricted a state's ability to interfere with the right to pursue a trade. His emphasis, like Miller's, was on the privileges and immunities clause. Field defined privileges and immunities quite differently, however. "The privileges and immunities designated are those *which of [natural and inalienable] right belong to the citizens of all free governments,*" he said. "Clearly among these must be placed the right to pursue lawful employment in a lawful manner, without other restraint than such as equally affects all persons."[102]

Natural rights, then, not the language of the Constitution itself provided the means by which Field would transform abstract justice into a tangible constitutional guarantee. Although Field did support his opinion with references to the legal doctrine of the day, he was most convincing when he entered the realm of political, economic, and even religious philosophy.[103] The right to pursue a trade or calling was an ideal reflected in the desire of the Declaration of Independence to guarantee the pursuit of happiness, Field argued. It was implemented in France and was recognized as a natural right of Englishmen. It lay at the heart of Adam Smith's economic theories. And it was the gift of the Creator.[104]

It is doubtful that the authors of the Fourteenth Amendment had all these concepts in mind when they sat down to write the privileges and immunities clause. Some of today's historians argue that Field's opinion was, nonetheless, the end product of American traditions that predated the Civil War — specifically the traditions of Jacksonian Democracy and free labor. Field certainly employed the rhetoric of those traditions. Summing up his interpretation of the law, Field said, "There is a recognition of the *equality of rights* among citizens in the *pursuit of the ordinary avocations of life,* and a declaration that all *grants of exclusive privileges,* in contravention of this

free labor

equality, are against common right, and void."[105] How much more Jack-sonian could one sentence be? How much more could it express the idea of free labor?

But inspired rhetoric is more appropriate to political debate than to judicial opinion.[106] Law values consistency, precision, and direction. With these values in mind, it would be reasonable to ask where was Field's com-mitment to the right to pursue a trade or calling in the California land cases. Field may have seen *Biddle Boggs* as a case involving John Frémont's prop-erty rights rather than as one involving a grant of exclusive privilege. If pressed, he might say that, unlike the *Slaughter-House Cases,* the interfer-ence with the miners' right to pursue their trade came from a private source rather than from government. These distinctions may impress a lawyer or philosopher, but they would have mattered little to California miners and settlers, to whom Field's opposition to exclusive privilege in Louisiana surely would have seemed ironic.

Nor would old Jacksonians, who opposed centralization of government, been too happy with the extent to which Field's ideas would give federal courts oversight of state legislation. Justice Miller picked up on this theme. He worried that the broad interpretation Field endorsed would make the Court a "perpetual censor upon all legislation of the states."[107] Time would prove Miller's worry prophetic. Field's right to choose a profession or trade eventually evolved into an even more sweeping theory called liberty of con-tract. Although this theory would not be fully developed until shortly be-fore Field's death, from the last part of the nineteenth century to the 1930s it would give the Court a virtual veto over a wide range of state economic legislation.

Stephen Field was not the only dissenter in the *Slaughter-House Cases.* Joseph Bradley wrote a separate dissent, and his analysis of the case involved two steps. First, he asked whether it is one of the rights and privileges of citizens of the United States to pursue a lawful calling, *subject to reasonable regulations as may be prescribed by law.* Concluding that it was, Bradley shared many of the ideas Field expressed. He added emphasis to one point, however, that was barely mentioned in the other opinions. Bradley reasoned that by its very nature the slaughterhouse law deprived butchers of their life, liberty, or property without due process of law. Eventually, the due process clause, rather than the privileges and immunities clause, became the vehicle for applying liberty of contract to the rights the Court would guarantee. Nevertheless, the effect would be the same; the Court would assume the authority to oversee all sorts of state economic regulation.[108]

A second part of Bradley's dissent asked whether a monopoly, or an exclusive right given to one person at the expense of all others, was a reasonable regulation that the legislature had a right to impose. His conclusion that a monopoly was not reasonable regulation should come as no surprise. Even more interesting, his reasoning emphasized the danger of monopoly as much as limits on the power of government. Granting monopolies is bad, he said, because they constitute "an invasion of the rights of others to choose a lawful calling, and an infringement of personal liberty."[109] In their 1873 *Slaughter-House* dissents the difference between Field and Bradley seemed merely one of emphasis. A few years later, however, the two would split in *Munn v. Illinois,* another case involving charges of monopoly. Then their opinions would reflect more substantial differences in their attitudes about the powers of government and about monopoly as the source of privilege and a threat to liberty.

Inherent in Field's natural law approach to interpreting the Fourteenth Amendment was the danger that it was as vague as the language of the amendment itself. It gave the Court open-ended and arbitrary power, which became obvious almost as soon as the Court delivered the *Slaughter-House Cases* opinion. On that same day the Court was to decide whether Illinois had properly refused to admit Myra Bradwell to the bar. When Bradwell claimed that she had the same constitutionally protected right to choose a profession as did the New Orleans butchers, Field and Bradley were not impressed.

Bradwell was a remarkable woman who later founded the *Chicago Legal News* and turned it into one of the most important legal publications in the nation. In 1869, after having studied law in her husband's office, she passed the Illinois bar exam with high honors. Bradwell then petitioned the Illinois Supreme Court for a license to practice law. The court rejected her application, reasoning that as a married woman she was legally incompetent to enter into the kinds of contracts necessary in the profession. On rehearing, the state court simply ruled that Bradwell was not of the class of persons that the legislature had intended to be admitted to the practice of law.[110]

Renowned constitutional lawyer Matthew Hale Carpenter took Bradwell's case to the U.S. Supreme Court. Carpenter cited Field's opinion in *Cummings v. Missouri* for the proposition that every person has a right to choose a profession or trade and Field's opinion in *Ex parte Garland* for the proposition that this rule applied to the practice of law. He continued in a vein that should have been familiar to Field. If the right to pursue a profession was recognized as a privilege and immunity of every white citizen, he reasoned, "the Fourteenth Amendment clearly made it a privilege and im-

Bradwell
(Woman wants
to be admit to
bar)

munity of every Black citizen and, by implication, a privilege and immunity of every female citizen as well." Although the legislature may prescribe qualifications for entering this pursuit, he argued, they cannot, under the guise of fixing qualifications, exclude a class of citizens from admission to the bar.[111]

Having just rejected a similar argument in the *Slaughter-House Cases,* Justice Miller and the majority had no difficulty rejecting Bradwell's plea as well. "We agree with [Mr. Carpenter] that there are privileges and immunities belonging to citizens of the United States," Miller wrote, "but the right to admission to practice in the courts of a State is not one of them."[112] Myra Bradwell, they concluded, was not entitled to be admitted to the Illinois bar.

Justices Bradley and Field, who agreed that Myra Bradwell did not have a constitutionally guaranteed right to practice law, did not have the luxury of being so consistent. In stark contrast to their *Slaughter-House* dissents, Bradley wrote that the privileges and immunities of *women as citizens* do not guarantee a right to engage in any and every profession, occupation, or employment. "The natural and proper timidity and delicacy which belongs to the female sex evidently unfits it for many of the occupations of civil life," he observed. " The paramount destiny and mission of a woman are to fulfill the noble and benign offices of wife and mother. *This is the law of the Creator.*"[113]

In still another case argued at the same time as the *Slaughter-House Cases,* F. Bartemeyer claimed that the right to sell intoxicating liquors was one of the privileges and immunities guaranteed by the Fourteenth Amendment. Iowa's prohibition law, Bartemeyer claimed, deprived him of his right to choose a trade or calling, and it deprived him of his property without due process of law. Once again, Miller and the majority had no trouble ruling that the law did not deprive Bartemeyer of his rights. And, once again, Field and Bradley were put in the position of agreeing with the outcome while defending their *Slaughter-House* dissents.[114]

Field argued that the "oppressive and odious monopoly" distinguished Louisiana's slaughterhouse law from Iowa's prohibition statute. His emphasis on this distinction was both accurate and misleading. Certainly Field's *Slaughter-House* dissent targeted the "monopoly." But what if the state had outlawed all slaughtering in Orleans, Jefferson, and St. Bernard parishes? In that hypothetical, the element of special privilege would be lost, but the fundamental right to choose a profession would be the same. It is impossible to tell whether Field would have viewed such a sweeping prohibition of a common calling to be a reasonable exercise of the police power.[115]

The hypothetical does, however, illustrate that a tangible difference between the two cases was the nature of the trade or calling that the state proposed to regulate. "No one has ever pretended . . . that the Fourteenth Amendment interferes in any respect with the police powers of the State," Field wrote in *Bartemeyer.* "That power embrace[s] all regulations affecting the health, good order, morals, peace, and safety of society."[116] In Field's and Bradley's opinions the plan Louisiana chose to save downstream citizens from the ravages of disease was not such a regulation affecting public health or safety. Iowa's plan for saving depraved citizens from the ravages of drink was. Throughout his career, Field supported state legislation designed to promote Victorian morality. For him, prohibition laws always fell within the police power of the state.[117]

In his first decade as a member of the Supreme Court, Stephen Field played an important part in the nation's effort to define again the fundamental principles upon which the American system of government was established. With his opinions in the habeas corpus cases, the *Test Oath Cases* and the *Slaughter-House Cases,* he assumed the posture of a great defender of liberty. His staunch insistence that the right to choose a trade or calling was a fundamental guarantee of the Constitution reflected free-labor theory. And, at least, the language of his *Slaughter-House* dissent seemed to reflect the venerable Jacksonian opposition to special privilege.

Yet as the Civil War raged, and later when Congress, the president, and the Court worried about how to reconstruct the Union and struggled over what liberty meant to the recently freed slaves, another major change was taking place in American society. The country was moving fast toward a new economic structure. It was an economic structure characterized in part by technological revolution, advances in transportation, and concentrated corporate wealth. Like the Civil War, the changes occurring in the economy shook the traditional ideas about the meaning of liberty. In contrast to abolitionism, however, this development focused more directly on the question of what liberty meant for the people who supposedly had it. It produced new ideas about the source of threats to individual liberty and about the role government should play in preserving liberty.

Field would continue to defend liberty and to attack economic privilege—as he understood them. As the impact of changes in the economy began to be felt, however, Field's understanding of liberty and privilege assumed a form quite different from the understanding of other people who were steeped in the Jacksonian and free-labor traditions. Field's concern about "special privilege" would evolve into a concern about "class legislation" and, in the process, lose its Jacksonian aura. The "right to choose a profession or trade" would develop into "liberty of contract"—a constitutional doctrine that abandoned many of the ideals of free labor. These developments help explain how at the same time that friends admired Justice Field as a defender of liberty and an opponent of privilege, his critics saw him as a threat to liberty and a defender of privilege.

Completion of the transcontinental railroad and the transportation revolution provide a convenient symbol for explaining the country's economic transformation. Therefore, the next chapter will begin with the transcontinental railroad. That grand project was only part of a larger change that affected all parts of the country and all sectors of society. But the story of building and financing the transcontinental railroad—and the subsequent growth of railroad power and popular resistance to it—provides a vivid portrait of a growing rift among the people who had subscribed to the Jacksonian and free-labor ideals of antebellum America.

5

VISE GRIP ON THE FLOW OF COMMERCE

There is a frequently told story about Central Pacific Railroad president Leland Stanford driving the "golden spike." This final act in May of 1869 would link his railroad with the Union Pacific to form the first transcontinental railway. J. D. B. Stillman, a witness to the event, told the story with the theatrical flare that only a nineteenth-century journalist could conjure:

Stanford stood with silver sledge gleaming in the air, whose blow was to be heard farther, without metaphor, than any blow struck by mortal man; the realization of the ancient myth of Jupiter with the thunderbolt in his hand. The blow fell, and simultaneously the roar of cannon on both shores of the continent announced the tiding: It is done!

Stillman, who had traveled to the ceremony as a guest of the railroad, politely ignored the fact that Stanford missed! The specially made silver sledgehammer hit iron rail rather than golden spike, but it still made the electrical contact needed to trigger a prearranged telegraph signal along the route to both coasts. And, if Stillman is to be believed, jubilation broke out across the nation.[1]

No undertaking captured the imagination of nineteenth-century America more than the transcontinental railroad. The project represented the best of American ingenuity, a sheer force of will that symbolized the nation's ability to tame its own geography. The prospect of linking the East Coast to the West by rail had all the promise of today's computer revolution. It would create a highway of commerce that would dramatically affect the lives of nineteenth-century Americans. Even before California became a U.S. territory, visionaries—crackpots to some—had begun to press for government support of the project. A transcontinental link, they maintained, would encourage settlement of the plains. It would draw together the East and the West, making America truly one nation. Some even dreamed that it would prove to be a trade route from Asia, across America, to Europe.

There was nothing especially innovative about the transcontinental railway. The technology had been developed and thousands of miles of track had been laid in the East before the Civil War. Railroads were already in use. The scale of the project is what set it apart. Consequently, it serves as a convenient symbol of its era. All the promises that the transportation revolution offered to society were magnified when applied to the transcontinental line; all the problems it created were intensified. Americans, many of whom had long been wary of special privilege, saw in the transportation revolution generally and the transcontinental railway in particular an increase of corporate power to an astounding new level. At every stage— building, financing, and operating—the project caused some people to reassess their ideas about government authority and the nature of liberty.

Building the Transcontinental Railway

The national unity that the transcontinental railway promised also delayed the dream. Before the Civil War, jealousies over various proposals for either southern or northern routes caused the support for the project to stall in the quagmire of sectional politics. The outbreak of war gave it the push it needed, for Lincoln believed that the transcontinental line would go far in tying the western states to the northeast, thus assuring their loyalty.[2] Congress responded in 1862 with the Pacific Railroad bill. Amended in 1864, this legislation instituted a plan by which the national government would subsidize building a railroad from the Missouri River to the Pacific Ocean. The new law created the Union Pacific Railroad Corporation, which would be responsible for building the line westward. Eventually it would run from Omaha, through what is now Nebraska, and Wyoming to Promontory, Utah. At the same time the Central Pacific, an existing California corporation, was given the right to build eastward from San Francisco. That line would eventually go through California and Nevada to western Utah, where it would join the Union Pacific.[3]

Most Americans of the time were in awe of the Union Pacific's plan to build a railroad across a region of the country that they called "the great American desert." In the words of Poor's *Manual of Railroads* the transcontinental route would pass over a 2,000-mile void, uninhabited and uninhabitable and nearly destitute of wood and water.[4] This description was an exaggeration, to be sure. Although stretches of the route passed through large alkali desert, it also crossed fertile plains and mountain ranges. Most of the land in the eastern part was neither uninhabitable nor uninhabited. Plains Indians had supported themselves there and European settlers of Nebraska and Wyoming would soon convert much of it into productive farmland and ranchland. The land became less hospitable as the route moved westward to Utah, but even there, it was occupied by Native Americans and Mormon settlements.

Nevertheless, Poor's description gave an accurate sense of the challenge facing the Union Pacific. Crossing the Great Plains, the geographical barrier in the eastern part of the transcontinental route was horizontal rather than vertical. Even when the company's surveyors and engineers reached the Rocky Mountains, they were able to find what they called "an easy line." Work crews could lay four or more miles of track a day—when they had supplies. But the Union Pacific's relatively easy line crossed over a vast expanse of land that often failed to yield the wood needed for ties and fuel and that sometimes lacked the water and supplies needed to keep crews working. It was the same land that had taken the forty-niners months to cross and that cost many travelers their lives. And it was land that western civilization had only grazed.

In a sense the Union Pacific's accomplishment was an exercise of perseverance. The Central Pacific's, in contrast, was an exercise of muscle and a far more dramatic feat of civil engineering. The Central Pacific route from the West immediately ran into the rugged Sierra Nevada Mountains. Beginning at sea level, its line of construction soared. In just 105 miles it reached its highest point, a place called Summit, which rested at an altitude of 7,012 feet. Blasting through solid granite, the railroad workers inched along through fifteen tunnels, the longest being the 1,659-foot tunnel at Summit.[5] Harsh winters also slowed the Central Pacific's progress. The winter of 1866–1867 dumped forty feet of snow on the mountains; temperatures dropped to twenty degrees below zero.[6] The threat of avalanche required the company to protect its tracks by building massive snowsheds along the mountainside. Even where tunnel and snowsheds were unnecessary, the process of grading a level roadbed over hard rock, through redwood forest, or along sheer cliff was excruciating.

Progress through the mountains was agonizingly slow. On days when the Union Pacific might measure its progress in miles, the Central Pacific measured it in inches. By January 1, 1867, the Central Pacific had laid only 94 miles of track while the Union Pacific, working on level ground, had laid 305 miles; and the Central Pacific had begun work almost a year earlier than its rival. It took the Central Pacific more than a year to progress another 46 miles. Construction continued at this snail's pace until workers broke out of the mountains; then they raced across Nevada and into Utah, covering 363 miles in less than a year.[7] Central Pacific officers were understandably proud of their accomplishment. For many years after the road was completed, trains took a scheduled stop at a vantage point called Cape Horn to allow passengers to take in the splendid view from the mountainside and let them admire the Central Pacific's achievement.[8]

The Central Pacific's strategy for taming the Sierra Nevada did not depend upon advanced technology. Generally, it pushed forward with blasting powder and human muscle, and most of that muscle was supplied by Chinese laborers. It is estimated that the company employed between 8,000 and 14,000 Chinese workers to build the railroad.

The Central Pacific initially turned to Chinese labor because willing white workers were unavailable. Although most of the placer mining had been played out by the time construction work began on the railroad, white workers were still more interested in mining. The discovery of silver drew many potential workers to mines in Nevada. The work was better there, the pay was better, and there was always the dream of setting out on one's own. Most of the 2,000 white workers Charles Crocker hired in summer 1864 simply used their trip to the company's work camps at the end of the line as a point of departure for the mines.[9] Like their white counterparts, many Chinese gold miners also found themselves unemployed in the early 1860s. Given fewer opportunities, however, they were more willing to take work on the railroad.[10]

Company leaders quickly recognized the benefits of using Chinese labor. White workers sometimes abandoned the railroad at the hint of a better opportunity, but the Chinese usually stayed on.[11] They tended to be more dependable on the job as well, and absenteeism was a minor problem. They did not drink alcohol, and their habit of drinking tea may have protected them from tainted water.[12] Railroad supervisors also believed that Chinese workers were less likely to strike and more likely to do the work asked of them.[13]

Perhaps even more important to the railroad, Chinese labor was cheap. Chinese workers received the same thirty dollars a month as whites, but unlike the white workers, the Chinese did not receive board in addition to their wages. As a result the actual cost to the railroad was about two-thirds less than the cost for hiring whites. According to one estimate the railroad thus saved about $5.5 million over three years by hiring Chinese labor.[14]

Charles Crocker, the Central Pacific's construction chief, at first had misgivings about using Chinese labor, but they turned out to be courageous and tenacious workers. Laboring in gangs of thirty and working twelve hours a day, they picked their way through the mountains at an average of less than a foot a day. They worked underground in close quarters with hundreds of men picking and digging in the space of a small tunnel.[15] They worked above ground at dizzying heights. Disregarding danger, Chinese crews devised a method for carving the roadbed into the side of a mountain. They would ease one man over the edge of a sheer granite cliff. Sitting 2,000 feet over the American River in a woven basket tied to a cable, the volunteer would set a charge of blasting powder. Then he lit the fuse and hoped that his companions could pull him to safety before flying rock sent him to his death.[16] They also worked through bitter winters. In winter 1866–1867, Chinese working at the summit tunnel lived the life of a mole. After snow covered their camps, they tunneled through it to the bowels of the mountain, where they worked twelve-hour shifts. For months some workers never saw the light of day. Those who worked on the outside had to clear as much as fifteen feet of snow just to reach their work on the roadbed. Avalanches and snowslides carried men, even entire camps, down the mountainside; usually their bodies were not found until the spring thaw.[17]

Although most Californians supported the railroad during the construction phase, the one thing that did instill opposition to the Central Pacific from the beginning of the project was the company's policy of hiring Chinese labor. Chinese immigrants were the object of hatred and a target of harassment and discrimination almost from the time they began to arrive in California. This anti-Chinese sentiment was a product of racism and prejudice, melded with a fear that Chinese immigrants posed a fundamental threat to white workers. Whether Chinese labor actually threatened white workers' prospects for employment is subject to debate; some white workers thought it did. But more important, they thought that Chinese labor threatened the fundamental advances that had been made in the conditions under which they were employed. In this respect, the company's policy of hiring Chinese workers came into conflict with the ideals of the nineteenth-century free-labor movement. At least some white workers and proponents of free labor thought it did. Thus, although the ideals of free labor provide no excuse for racism and prejudice, understanding this aspect of the anti-Chinese movement is important for understanding nineteenth-century America's struggle to define liberty.

The ultimate goal for the people who opposed the Chinese was to restrict immigration or to exclude Chinese from the state altogether. This was, of course, beyond the state's power. Treaties with foreign nations and regulation of commerce fell within the federal government's authority, and the 1868 Burlingame Treaty with China followed a national policy of free immigration. It also added protections for Chinese residents in the United States by providing that "Chinese subjects visiting or residing in the United States, shall enjoy the same privileges, immunities, and exemptions in respect to travel or residence, as may there be enjoyed by the citizens or subjects of the most favored nation."[18]

Anti-Chinese antagonists persisted, nevertheless. From as early as 1852, Chinese individuals and the Chinese community were the victims of prejudice-induced murder, arson, assault, robbery, and burglary.[19] Antagonists also used the power of state law to harass Chinese immigrants. California imposed special taxes on Chinese. It barred them from some forms of employment or required them to have special licenses. It subjected businesses to which Chinese gravitated, such as laundry and cigarmaking, to special rules. It denied them the right to sit on juries and to testify in courts. Other laws were designed to make it difficult for Chinese immigrants to conform to their habits, customs, and traditions.

Anti-Chinese sentiment was strong enough in California to affect anyone involved in politics and law, Stephen Field included. Two opinions Field wrote while on the California Supreme Court were of particular interest to opponents of the Chinese. In one dissenting opinion Field voted to allow a "police tax" on all Chinese living within the state. The majority of the court overruled the tax on the theory that it interfered with the federal government's authority to regulate commerce. Field disagreed. The tax, he reasoned, was simply a tax on a class of persons already residing in the state. Since it was not imposed as a condition of landing on the shores of this country, it did not interfere with commerce.[20]

A more interesting case, and one that may have been a better indicator of Field's inclinations in the matter, involved a tax the state imposed on foreign miners. *Ah Hee v. Crippen* began when Mariposa County sheriff Crippen seized Ah Hee's horse after the Chinese immigrant failed or refused to pay the tax.[21] Ah Hee then sued for return of the horse, claiming that the tax, which was levied only on Chinese, violated a provision of the California constitution that secured to foreigners "the same rights, in respect to the possession, enjoyment, and inheritance of property, as to a native born citizen." Ah Hee also argued that the tax violated his right to be secure in his property. Field simply ignored the arguments that this tax violated Ah Hee's rights. The judge's silence on the matter could have been taken to imply that the Chinese had no rights. Read only that far, Field's decision could have placated anti-Chinese agitators.

Ah Hee had a fall-back position, however. The statute imposed a tax on all foreigners who took gold from "the mines of this state." Ah Hee's attorney maintained that, in choosing this phrase, the legislature did not mean to impose the tax on Chinese working in "all of the mines within the state" but only on those Chinese working in "mines belonging to the state." Field agreed, and concluded that Chinese miners who worked on private property were not subject to the tax.

Inquiring minds already knew that *Ah Hee v. Crippen* involved a Chinese miner working on John Frémont's Mariposa estate. The case came to the California Supreme Court just two years after Frémont won mineral rights in the bitter legal battle of *Biddle Boggs*. In the eyes of cynical Californians this case must have appeared to turn on a contrived technicality, one invented to protect Frémont's interests.

In Field's opinion, however, there were grand implications to the question put before the court. For the present he was willing to remain silent on whether Chinese had the same rights to property and to the fruits of their labor as those guaranteed to whites. More important to Field was that the state law, if interpreted as a tax on miners working on private land, would have interfered with Frémont's right to do what he pleased with his property. Frémont's patent from the U.S. government invested him with ownership of the precious metals on his estate, Field reasoned. He could extract the gold himself or arrange for others to do it; the state had no right to interfere.[22] Field's opinion in *Ah Hee v. Crippen* thus revealed the broader forces at play on the question of Chinese immigration. It graphically showed that anti-Chinese legislation raised questions about liberty that affected whites as well as Chinese.

Field's legal reasoning masked the intensity surrounding the issue. The countless anti-Chinese diatribes published during the era did not. One startling yet typical list of charges, for example, proclaimed that all Chinese were heathens. A Chinese woman is a prostitute from instinct, it said, and degrading to all around her. A Chinese man has none of the wants of a civilized man. He herds, in scores, in small dens and is a slave reduced to the lowest terms of beggarly economy. The Chinese laborer is no fit competitor for an American freeman, it continued, "American men, women and children cannot be what free people should be if they must compete with such degraded creatures in the labor market."[23] Hatred and prejudice were obviously part of the anti-Chinese equation. But the last of these complaints revealed that fear and a deep-seated, though misguided, sense of self-interest motivated many of the white workers who turned against the Central Pacific when it began to employ Chinese.

Many Californians believed that the Central Pacific was importing Chinese labor and increasing the Chinese labor force in the state as an alternative to hiring whites, a supposition that was only partially accurate. Although the company undoubtedly hired laborers directly from China, the Chinese population in California remained fairly stable during the years that the transcontinental railroad was being built. As some Chinese immigrants entered the country, others returned to their homeland. In 1867, for example, 200 more Chinese left California than entered.[24] Even the assumption that Chinese labor directly displaced white labor on the railroad was only partially accurate. White workers may have wanted to work but not necessarily in the same jobs or under the same terms and conditions as the Chinese. Nevertheless, many white laborers believed they were being deprived of the opportunity to benefit from the great enterprise that was taking place in the Sierra Nevada.

It may have been inconsistent for white laborers to want work but not to want the work that was being offered. Yet their position was consistent with the long-term development of the free-labor movement. For many, free labor was defined as an evolution away from conditions under which legal compulsions made wage labor only slightly different from indentured servitude. Thus one factor in defining the success of free labor was labor's "ability to resist infiltration and debasement from various forms of unfree labor."[25] The specters of black bondsmen, industrial "wage slaves," and subsistence "pauper-laborers" of the Old World represented the kind of debasement the movement most feared; so did the Chinese coolies.

Although Californians tended to apply the term coolie to any Chinese worker, the word actually had a more precise meaning. It referred to a form of indentured servitude that had begun in the 1840s. Much of this coolie trade sent Chinese contract laborers to South America and Cuba to work in sugar plantations and guano pits. Some of these coolies signed contracts, some were taken into service against their will. Regardless of whether they entered into agreements of their own free will, however, they were treated in many ways as indentured servants. They were bound to employers by contract, they were sometimes sold on the open market, and they were subjected to inhumane working and living conditions.[26]

An 1862 law prohibited American shippers from engaging in any form of coolie trade, but Californians were convinced that the coolie traffic continued.[27] Most Chinese arranged passage to the United States through a process that came to be called the credit ticket system. Under these agreements someone else, often a broker, paid the immigrant's passage; upon arriving in America, the immigrant was bound to seek work and pay a portion of his wages to the broker until the debt was paid off. The broker essentially had a lien on the laborer's wages, a lien that was sometimes sold to the employer. The credit ticket system differed from coolie labor in that most workers were free to leave one particular job for another. Some historians have concluded that the Chinese who came to California under this system were "mostly poor and uneducated, but they were responsible free men." Others think that the credit ticket system and coolie labor amounted to the same thing; the difference, they say, was largely one of degree.[28] Whichever is the case, the circumstances by which Chinese immigrants came to California did not help to dispel many Californians' belief that the coolie trade remained.

The conditions under which many Chinese worked and lived also added to that belief. Chinese workers came to America as laborers, hoping to make some money and return home. They came without wives and family and tended to live in close quarters, dormitory style. They worked longer hours than many whites, at jobs that most whites disdained. The railroad usually hired whites for skilled work and as foremen. The work reserved for the Chinese tended to be the most dangerous and backbreaking. They worked in gangs and sometimes even suffered under Charles Crocker's whip.[29]

Not everyone agreed that the condition of the Chinese worker in California amounted to indentured servitude. To charges that Chinese workers were coolie labor, Leland Stanford simply replied, "Their wages were always paid."[30] Stanford's point is well taken, but his response was surely not enough to convince most white workers that the conditions under which the Chinese worked represented the kind of free labor they had in mind.

It is ironic that some of the same kind of free-labor ideas that attracted many white workers to the cause of freeing slaves in the South moved others to try to drive Chinese immigrants out of California. Yet most historians have recognized that there was also a racist tinge to the antislavery movement. It was common for Republicans in the 1850s to couch their arguments for abolition in terms of benefits for the white laboring class rather than in terms of any concern for the circumstances of slaves.[31] Racial prejudice stood side by side with abolitionism. Even the desire to keep slavery out of the West was sometimes defended in terms of keeping the African race out and of preserving the new territories for free white labor.[32] The people who opposed the presence of Chinese in California were apparently not particularly unusual in failing to see an inconsistency in favoring free labor but believing that it could be appreciated only by whites.[33]

White workers exhibited this desire to drive out the presence of "unfree labor" in their reaction to another anti-Chinese proposal. In 1852, the same year that the California legislature imposed a tax on Chinese miners, that body rejected another measure called the Tingley Coolie bill. If passed, this legislation would have declared that all contracts made in China were enforceable in California. Workers who believed that coolie trade was still flourishing argued that this proposal would have the practical effect of validating contracts for indentured servitude. They opposed the bill, not because of concern for the welfare of Chinese workers or out of a concern that these labor contracts might be the product of fraud or coercion, but because they were not willing to give unfree labor the authority of law.

California's white workers may have seen the specter of southern slavery in the Tingley Coolie bill. They also may have seen something of their own past. In the not very distant past the theory of employer-employee relations was that of master and servant. Even those workers who had voluntarily undertaken their employment were subject to legal rules that kept them on the job and under the control of their employer. The law presumed that a worker's labor belonged to the employer and gave employers the right to control a laborer's person. Workers who attempted to leave their employment before the contract term had ended might be subject to criminal punishment or they might forfeit wages. Employers also had a right to sue anyone who enticed their employees to leave the job. Robert J. Steinfeld's enlightening study of the origins of free labor points out that the success of the movement, its very definition, rested on removing these legal compulsions from the workplace. The Tingley Coolie bill would, in this sense, have been a decided step backward.[34]

Steinfeld also recognizes that the success of the free-labor movement in removing these legal compulsions did not necessarily result in free choice for workers. "As the nineteenth century wore on, wage workers complained more and more bitterly that the power of property was making them slaves to their employers," he observes. Having won the right to own and dispose of their own labor, it was now more difficult and contradictory for workers to argue that they were still not free. Nevertheless, white workers were quickly beginning to understand that, in the rapidly developing nineteenth-century social and economic order, the major threat to freedom and dignity of labor would not come from governmental authority or the force of law. The more serious threat was from private economic power. Workers who benefited from the success of the free-labor movement now faced concentrated corporate wealth that produced employers who seemed too powerful to combat.[35]

Whatever may have been its underlying causes, the California anti-Chinese movement demonstrated that free-labor concerns did not end with the emancipation of southern slaves. The struggle for free labor, affected by new economic and social conditions, was merely transformed. Economic and social development had a similar impact on the ideals of Jacksonian Democracy. Americans did not abandon its language: the *Slaughter-House Cases* demonstrated that the ideals and villains of that era—liberty, democracy, privilege, and power—continued to dominate popular thought. Of all the disputes of the 1870s, those surrounding the financing of the transcontinental railroad would have been most familiar to old Jacksonians. As the decade progressed, however, the operation of the railroads and frustrations with corporate power ignited a wave of antirailroad feelings. Jacksonian and free-labor themes would begin to play out in a different manner from the way they had in the past.

Government Loans and Public Land

Financing the transcontinental railroad proved to be as massive an undertaking as was building it. The Pacific Railroad bill, as amended in 1864, provided two major types of government aid. One form of subsidy was government bonds. Under this plan, the government would give the railroad bonds at a rate of between $16,000 and $48,000 per mile of track laid. The bond would be issued only after the companies completed twenty continuous miles of road. Any holder of the bonds would be able to redeem them for their face value after the maturity date. In order to raise the ready cash they needed, the railroads would sell the government bonds on the open market for less than face value. At maturity, the railroads would be responsible for paying back to the government the face value of the bonds plus interest. In essence, then, these bonds constituted a loan to the railroad bearing 6 percent interest and payable when they matured thirty years after the railroad was completed. The companies also had the right to raise money by issuing their own private bonds and selling stock. In addition, the Central Pacific received substantial aid from state and local governments.

The other form of government subsidy to the railroads was land grants. The companies were to receive a right-of-way 100 feet on either side of the track they laid. They also were to receive a grant consisting of twenty sections (12,800 acres) of adjacent land for every mile of track they laid.[36] The idea of subsidizing the railroads with land grants seemed appropriate for the time. Although the Civil War was draining the federal government's cash supply, there was plenty of public land in the West to give away.[37] In theory, the railroads would be able to defer construction costs by selling the land as construction progressed. Like the bonds, land would be released only after a company had completed twenty miles of track. The companies were not given mineral rights, but they did receive the rights to timber and coal.[38]

The actual value of the financial aid that the government provided is somewhat elusive. Some members of Congress later complained of its excess. The federal government, they charged, was subsidizing the railroads with more than $100 million dollars. One historian calculated that the amount actually realized by the Central Pacific alone was more than $30 million.[39] Other scholars have argued that the government subsidy was not enough to build the railroad. Whatever the actual figure may have been, there is no question that it represented a large sum of money, especially by nineteenth-century standards.

Still, the government subsidy was only enough to prime the pump. As generous as the aid may have been, the government did not provide the railroads with any cash at all. It was incumbent upon the company leaders, therefore, to raise enough financing in either cash or private credit to get construction under way. Once construction began, the leaders had to continue to supply enough money to keep the project moving. The conditions of the subsidy complicated their problem since Congress did not give the promised bonds and land to the companies all at once. The conditions of the market also complicated the company leaders' task. The government bonds usually sold well below face value on the open market. The actual cash realized from their sale was considerably less than it may have appeared.

Despite the apparent difficulty in raising funds for the project, building the transcontinental railroad produced great wealth for many of the men connected with it. One only has to look at the names of towns and universities, especially in the West, to be reminded of that. It is easy to forget, however, that the transcontinental railroad was also a speculative venture. Its success depended upon savvy, persistence, energy, and the skullduggery of leaders who were willing to take a risk.

Collis P. Huntington, Leland Stanford, Charles Crocker, and Mark Hopkins gave the Central Pacific just that type of leadership. Collectively known as the Big Four, this group of successful Sacramento shopowners bought into engineer Theodore Judah's dream to build a railroad through the Sierra Nevada. They formed the company in 1861, one year before Congress passed the Pacific Railroad Act. Much of their first year in business was spent convincing Congress that the Central Pacific should be the company chosen to build the transcontinental railroad from the West. By most reports, Judah's influence and judicious distribution of company stock helped seal their success.[40]

Although Central Pacific stock was offered to the public, few outside investors were interested. For the most part, Huntington, Hopkins, Stanford, and Crocker started with their own money; and from 1861 until the road was completed in 1869 the company seemed chronically short of cash.

Collis P. Huntington represented the company's interests in the financial centers in the East. From his office in New York he worked something of a financial miracle. Using the personal credit of his partners, he was able to buy untold millions of dollars in raw materials, supplies, and machinery. The endless stream of rails, ties, locomotives, cars, and blasting powder moving into the port of San Francisco was a tribute to his perseverance and ability. It also showed that America's industrialists, merchants, and financiers who were willing to risk investing in his company smelled money in the great project.

The Union Pacific did not have much more luck attracting capital in the initial stages of the project. But one director, George Francis Train, did come up with a way of ensuring that the few individuals who controlled the company made a profit. In 1867 he established Crédit Mobilier of America. Train described his creation as the first "trust company" in the country.[41] Copied from a French prototype, Crédit Mobilier was completely owned by a group of directors of the Union Pacific. Its primary function was to shift money—money that came from the U.S. Treasury and the pockets of the Union Pacific's minor shareholders.

Because they controlled the board of directors of the Union Pacific, this select group was able to give contracts to their own company—Crédit Mobilier. The purpose of the contract was legitimate enough. Crédit Mobilier was supposed to build portions of the road and provide other services. But by giving wildly favorable terms and paying exorbitant prices, the controlling group was able to siphon money out of the Union Pacific and into the coffers of Crédit Mobilier. As contemporary critic Charles Francis Adams, Jr., put it, "They receive money into one hand as a corporation, and pay it out into the other as a contractor."[42] The profit they kept for themselves.

Adams admitted that much of what was known about Crédit Mobilier was the result of hearsay and street rumor. Nevertheless, by most accounts the profits were enormous. One congressional investigation reported that $23 million went into the pockets of Crédit Mobilier's owners.[43] Adams estimated that they received dividends exceeding 100 percent per annum on their original investment.[44] Regardless of the amount, undoubtedly American taxpayers and unsuspecting Union Pacific minority investors paid dearly.

In the West, the Big Four borrowed the technique. At first the Central Pacific contracted with independent construction companies to build the railroad. In 1864 Charles Crocker created a separate company to undertake construction, which carried out the Central Pacific's construction work until 1867. Then he and his three associates organized a separate company modeled on Crédit Mobilier. From that point on, all of the Central Pacific's construction work was done by a corporation innocuously named the Contract and Finance Company.[45]

Crédit Mobilier was elevated from an obscure scheme to a glaring scandal when in 1871 it became known that the company had distributed shares of its stock to influential government officials. Congressmen John B. Alley and Oaks Ames were implicated in having developed the scheme. Later, other political figures were implicated when they received gifts or cheap offers to buy the stock. Speaker of the House Schuyler Colfax (who was Grant's first vice-president), Sen. Henry Wilson (Grant's second vice-president), and future president James Garfield were among the most prominent. It proved difficult for a congressional investigation to determine whether they had acquired the stock through a simple purchase, as a result of insider trading, or as bribes. Consequently, they were exonerated, except for Alley and Ames, who received official censure.[46]

Although Congress hesitated to punish its own, it did pass a law designed to punish Crédit Mobilier and to cut losses to the government. The Crédit Mobilier Act of 1873 directed the secretary of the treasury to withhold all payments that the government owed to the railroad for delivery of the mail, troop transportation, and other services. It further ordered the secretary to apply that money to current interest that the railroad owed on the government bonds. Another section of the act directed the attorney general to bring suit against the owners of Crédit Mobilier, "to recover what was due either to the Union Pacific Company or to the United States."[47] Ultimately neither approach proved successful. Two years after Congress enacted the legislation the Supreme Court rendered the first provision invalid by ruling that the law establishing the transcontinental railway gave the government no right to withhold payments for current interest.[48] Then in 1879 the Court ruled that, although the Crédit Mobilier scheme constituted fraud, the fraud was against innocent minor stockholders of the Union Pacific. Ignoring the taxpayers who would eventually pay for the overcharges, Justice Miller's majority opinion reasoned that because the U.S. government had no direct interest in the contracts between the Union Pacific and Crédit Mobilier, it had no right to intervene.[49]

Not only did Stephen Field vote with the majority in both cases, but he desperately wanted to write the opinion in the first case. Chief Justice Waite, who wanted to be careful to assign the opinion "to someone who would not be known as the personal friend of the parties representing the railroad interest," gave it to Davis instead. "There was no doubt of your intimate personal relations with the managers of the Central Pacific," he consoled Field, "and naturally you, more than anyone else in the court, realize the vast importance of the great work that has been done."[50]

The Crédit Mobilier scandal involved concerns about corruption as well as concerns about privilege and liberty that had been familiar themes in Jacksonian America. Government dispensed privilege. Privilege created power. Power gave the privileged undue influence over government and thereby threatened individual liberty. The solution for old Jacksonian reformers had been less government. That approach carried over to some reformers of the post–Civil War era as well. E. L. Godkin, for example, offered a solution for corruption: "Get the government out of the protective business, the subsidy business, the improvement business and the development business."[51]

At the same time that the Crédit Mobilier scandal broke, however, other reformers were beginning to see the problem of preserving liberty in a new light. The difference was subtle but revolutionary. This change did not grow from a particular organized philosophical movement. Rather, reformers demonstrated by their actions that they were coming to see government not as a threat to their liberty but as an ally in the struggle to preserve their liberty. For them government was no longer just a source of privilege but also an authority that could be used to control the excesses and the power that privilege brought. Although railroads were not by any stretch of imagination the only possessors of great economic power, they served as a symbol. And nationwide, there was a strong desire to control the railroads. That desire motivated the antimonopoly movement in California and it motivated the Granger movement in the Midwest. Both of these movements exemplified the evolution that had taken place in reformers' thinking.

"Businesses Affected with Public Interest"

"You can get any man to be unfriendly with a railroad after it is built." With this one sarcastic, yet poignant, comment Charles Crocker captured the essence of relations between California and the railroad.[52] Most Californians wanted the railroad to come to their state. Then they wanted the railroad to come to their town. Once they had it, however, it seemed that most people were unhappy with it. Although Crocker may have been justified in thinking that the peoples' behavior was unappreciative, at least it was explainable. For many Californians the arrival of the railroad turned out to be disappointing, disruptive, and threatening. Yet it was also necessary if they were to survive in the new world that the technological and transportation revolution was creating.

Californians had great hopes for the transcontinental railroad. Admirers predicted that this new artery to the east would provide an outlet for California commerce, bring new immigration, and solve some of the state's post–gold-rush economic malaise. Historians who defend the railroad's record make the point that over the long term railroads made eastern goods cheaper in the West, gave farmers and merchants new markets, and created a host of new towns and urban centers.[53] But the railroad was disappointing in part because it did not bring the immediate prosperity it had promised. In California, the arrival of the transcontinental railroad coincided with a severe economic downturn in 1875.[54] Even in better times farmers and merchants commonly complained that railroad business practices denied them the profit they thought they were due. Possibly they were just greedy, but many people thought the railroad was getting more than its fair share.

Historian William Deverell points out that the railroad was disruptive in ways that are often overlooked. It changed the social environment and even the geography of the quaint rural and small-town landscape it crossed. Far from being the romantic influence we envision today, noisy, smelly, smoky trains were "an apt symbol of the blunt and violent 'civilizing' process of westward expansion."[55] The railroad's presence changed the traditional methods of doing business, the relationship between city and town, even conceptions of time and space. Many people profited by the changes, others were unwilling to adjust, and still others felt they simply had been steamrolled by developments over which they had little control.

Some of the Central Pacific's earliest opponents viewed the company as a threat to their liberty. Albertus Meyer of Oakland worried that the growth the railroad promised would destroy a relatively egalitarian society that had developed during the gold rush. Henry George, a more prominent critic, agreed. In an 1868 article, "What the Railroad Will Bring Us," George predicted that completion of the railroad would cause wages to fall and land values to rise, thus creating a permanent underclass. The railroad, he maintained, would become an overwhelming political force that would threaten the independence of working Californians.[56] Meyer and George were at first among a small minority, however.

It did not take long for the railroad to become enough of a powerful political and economic force in California that a sizable portion of the population considered it threatening. Even before they completed the transcontinental road, the Big Four began to buy up shorter lines within the state. Eventually they controlled over 85 percent of the track in California.

They also built a second transcontinental route and purchased interests in steamer lines in order to stymie competition for interstate trade. By 1871, when most of their operations were consolidated under the umbrella of the Southern Pacific Railroad Company, the partners had a stranglehold on transportation in California.[57] As Charles Francis Adams, Jr., put it, the railroad had usurped the function of the highway.[58] And in California it had a virtual monopoly. Furthermore, the Southern Pacific had become the state's largest employer and one of the state's largest landholders.[59] Its influence spread well beyond the transportation business into most facets of California's economic and social life. Eventually, critics would liken the Southern Pacific to an octopus, with Crocker and Stanford as its eyes, its tentacles crushing everything from competing stage, shipping, and telegraph lines to farmers, miners, and workers.[60]

The first organized opposition to the railroad attacked the practice of subsidizing the railroad with public funds. From the beginning of the project, the railroad sought and received local subsidies in addition to the grants from the federal government. It was fairly standard practice throughout the nation for communities to make contributions to a railroad in order to encourage its growth in their direction. Stuart Daggett's description of an 1872 agreement between Los Angeles and the Southern Pacific is illustrative. To ensure that the railroad would build trunk lines in its direction, the fledgling city of 6,000 people donated to the Southern Pacific more than $600,000 in cash, stocks, and land, more than $100 per capita.[61] The city would pay for the gift primarily by issuing bonds, that is, by putting itself into debt. Although the arrangement would later come under attack, it had significant support among the general population. The bond issue was, after all, approved by popular vote.

Nevertheless, many people thought that railroad subsidies constituted an unfair tax imposed on common citizens for the benefit of an already wealthy company. The railroad, they believed, played on the community's fear of being passed by. And reformers' suspicions that they were being blackmailed grew as the Southern Pacific's partners became stronger. Harris Newmark, a prominent Los Angeles merchant and farmer, recalled an incident that illustrated the railroad's power. After the Southern Pacific's line to Los Angeles was completed, some citizens became dissatisfied with the company's rates and fares and they invited Charles Crocker to a meeting to discuss the matter. Speaking to the assembly, Crocker explained that the company had invested a great deal of money building the line to the city and that the rates were set by the need to realize a profit on its investment. Then one of the spectators rose to tell "a little story"—a joke that played on the railroad magnate's plea of impoverishment. The audience had a good laugh at Crocker's expense, Newmark reported. Then Crocker made a memorable threat. "If this be the spirit in which Los Angeles proposes to deal with the railroad upon which the town's very vitality must depend, *I will make grass to grow in the streets of your city!*"[62]

Newmark's recollection of the meeting might have grown more dramatic with the passing of years, but his story provides a sense of how strong the belief was that the railroad had become too powerful. By the early 1870s politicians such as Democratic governor Henry H. Haight and Republican Newton Booth were trying to outdo each other in singing reformer Henry George's tune. Both men opposed the practice of subsidizing the railroads with public funds and feared that the Southern Pacific's growing strength would soon allow it to monopolize transportation. Echoing George, Booth warned that the Southern Pacific's overwhelming power "threatened the independence and liberty of every Californian."[63]

Complaints soon turned from the issue of subsidies to the railroad's rates and business practices. The Southern Pacific partners, as it turned out, were in the subsidy business themselves. When they thought encouraging a particular business would provide long-term benefit to the interest of the railroad, they gave that business favorable rates for shipping. When the interests of a brewer, a sugar refinery, or any other business coincided with the railroad's desire to increase profit by increasing the amount of freight traffic on its lines, the company quoted a favorable rate.[64] Shippers who were not so favored often complained that rates were set at the whim of the company managers. Some customers even claimed that company managers set rates that ensured farmers and merchants would get only a small profit from their products by determining what they were likely to be paid for their products at the market and then setting the rate as a percentage of that amount.[65]

Some historians have argued that, even if these types of business practices were common, the railroad's policies were not necessarily harmful to the public good. On the contrary, Richard J. Orsi points out, the railroad in many ways linked its own interest with the progress of the state and often used its power to strengthen and diversify California's economy and further the welfare of its citizens.[66] Still, the railroad clearly had almost unlimited leeway in setting its rates, and many of the people of California were dissatisfied with the arrangement.

Railroad opponents knew that acting as individuals they had no hope of influencing company policies. Their best chance lay in government regulation. But reformers who wanted the state government to bring fairness and control to railroad policies faced two disabilities, the railroad's power and their own inexperience.

The Southern Pacific's mark was plainly imprinted on the state political scene. Although the railroad may not have been the domineering monolith some of its critics made it out to be, it clearly wielded extensive power. There is no doubt that the railroad controlled some politicians who protected its interests in the halls of government. It also bought or controlled newspapers to protect its image in the arena of public opinion. Such tactics, along with a singleness of purpose in its own self-preservation, gave the railroad political influence that no other single force in California could match.[67]

Although Americans were used to seeing government regulate businesses, the railroad and other large multifaceted corporations presented a new situation. Most early nineteenth-century regulations were directed at specific types of businesses. Corporations that existed for a single purpose, to operate a bridge or a toll road, were subject to regulation as were companies that provided a public service, such as a slaughterhouse or a public market. Beyond that, regulations were usually aimed at a particular trade, such as lawyers or doctors, or at a particular product like tobacco or bread. Californians, and Americans in general, had little experience and were ill-prepared for using government to regulate corporate conglomerates the size and complexity of the Southern Pacific.[68] Perhaps this inexperience, even more than the company's power, explains why California's first attempts to regulate the railroad were unequivocal failures.

The idea of setting maximum rates first reached the floor of the state legislature in 1874, where the proposal died. A maximum-rates proposal failed again two years later, but this time the legislature created a State Board of Transportation Commissioners with the duty to supervise railroads and prevent extortion and unjust discrimination. Without a means of enforcing its orders the transportation board proved completely ineffective—the railroad simply ignored it. In 1878 the legislature replaced the board with a single transportation commissioner who was equally ineffective.[69]

The ineffectiveness of these first attempts notwithstanding, in California it was obvious that what had begun as a vague disillusionment with the railroad had grown into widespread opposition as the decade of the 1870s progressed. By the time Californians gathered in 1879 to revise their constitution, opposition to the railroad, and to corporations in general, had become a major issue in state politics.

The antirailroad sentiment in California was only a small part of a nationwide trend in the 1870s. Feelings against the railroads ran particularly strong in the Midwest where, by 1874, Minnesota, Iowa, Wisconsin, and Illinois had enacted extensive regulatory legislation. Collectively named the Granger laws, these statutes set rate schedules for railroads and grain elevators, outlawed unreasonable rate discrimination, and created regulatory commissions to enforce their objectives. The Granger laws were destined to become the battleground for a major conflict over the constitutionality of economic regulations.

Reformers won a partial victory in 1877 when the Supreme Court decided *Munn v. Illinois* and a group of related cases that have come to be called the Granger cases. The Court's majority ruled in these cases that states could regulate "businesses affected with public interest." But *Munn* and the other Granger cases were not unanimous. Writing one of his most well-known dissents, Stephen Field disagreed. With Field's dissent, *Munn* became the medium for a grand debate about the extent of the Constitution's protection of property rights and the limits of government power. Even more important, it was a debate that accentuated the differences between the reformer's and the conservative's vision of liberty. It demonstrated how wide the split in antebellum traditions had become. Field's dissent also set the tone for his future opinions regarding liberty, especially in cases that involved liberty, property, and the limits of government regulation. Before turning to the details of *Munn*, however, it is necessary to describe the background of the case and explain the clash of ideals and interests that led to it.

The terms Granger and Grange were the popular name for the Patrons of Husbandry, a farmers' alliance that came into being in 1867. The idea of the Grange was innocuous enough. The brainchild of a clerk in the U.S. Agricultural Bureau, it was organized for the purpose of improving the farmers' lot through education and cooperation. The Grange encouraged social interaction among farmers and taught business and agricultural skills. Local chapters purchased or built grain elevators or warehouses, which they operated as cooperatives. Some alliances even had success in lowering the price they paid for farming implements by organizing and purchasing supplies collectively.[70]

The most striking aspect about the Grange was how fast it grew. After struggling for its first four years, the organization's membership exploded in 1872 and 1873. Before that the number of local chapters affiliated with the Grange was measured in the hundreds, but 1,150 locals were organized in 1872. By 1873 the Grange counted more than 3,000 local chapters and had established a presence in all but a few states.[71]

Although the promise of improving rural life through education and cooperation may have had great appeal, the Grange's meteoric growth was more likely a symptom of discontent among the nation's farmers. Perhaps it was inevitable that the Grange would move from its original ideals to political action. Grange leaders adamantly professed to be nonpolitical, stating in the Declaration of Purposes adopted in 1874, "We emphatically and sincerely assert . . . that the Grange . . . is not a political or party organization." Yet almost without pause, the same declaration reminded members that by becoming Grangers they did not give up their right and duty to take a proper interest in the politics of the country. On the contrary, it pointed out, "It is right for every member to do all in his power legitimately to influence for good any political party to which he belongs."[72]

Members, particularly in the Midwest, were already following this course of action. In 1873 farmers who were sympathetic to the Grange organized into State Farmers' Associations. In Illinois, Iowa, Minnesota, and Wisconsin they successfully pressed for the defeat of unreceptive political candidates. Within a year Farmers' Associations became political parties. Joining with the Democratic party, they had significant success in the elections of 1874. Their political success was not long-lasting, however; before the decade ended, the farmers' political movement had fizzled.[73]

The Grange unquestionably was involved in politics, but there is a tendency to give the organization more than its share of the credit for the railroad regulations enacted in the 1870s. The so-called Granger laws were actually the product of cooperation between farmers and small-town merchants.[74] Merchants, in fact, were the first to press for laws regulating railroad and grain elevator rates. Beginning in early 1867 their representatives in midwestern state legislatures introduced a dozen bills to outlaw rate discrimination and regulate rates. The merchants had minimal success until farmers joined their cause. Together, the two interest groups had enough power to force rate regulations through the state legislatures. But the most significant of the laws were enacted before the Grange's astounding growth in 1872–1873.[75] Rather than being a cause of change, then, the Grange may have been just as much a product of some general discontent as the statutes themselves. Nevertheless, the Grange clearly represented ideals popular among the community of farmers, and its rise was undoubtedly an outgrowth of business conditions that many farmers found intolerable.

The business of transportation in the Midwest was quite different from

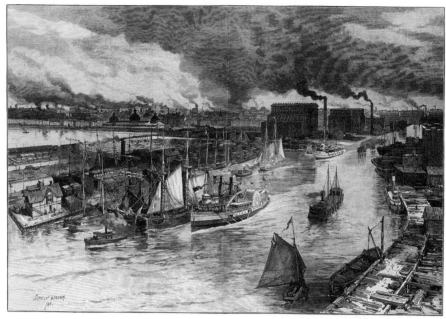

"VIEW OF CHICAGO FROM THE TOP OF THE LIGHTHOUSE." Shell & Graham lithograph showing the bottleneck in the flow of commerce at the mouth of the Chicago River. (Chicago Historical Society)

that in California. Few railroads in the nation had as much success as the Southern Pacific in avoiding competition and dominating transportation. Although it was popular for reformers to complain about monopolies, the concept of monopoly did not fully explain railroad policies. Neither did the concept of competition. A peculiar aspect of the railroad industry was that the business of any one railroad company might be characterized by both complete monopoly and cut-throat competition. The degree of competition it faced on any one route depended on geography and circumstances. Where a railroad controlled a strategic position like a mountain pass, valley, or river crossing, it might be able to set rates at will. Where it was the only line serving an area, a railroad's policies might in fact have been monopolistic. Where there was a competing line, however, or any reasonable alternative means of transportation, a railroad's freedom to control fares and set policy was severely inhibited.

Because railroad managers believed that the most satisfactory prices could be achieved where there was little or no competition, they did as much as they could to place their company into such a position. A company might try undercutting the fares of a competitor. It might provide special fares to larger customers or for a particular type of product. It might enter into pooling arrangements in which it agreed with other railroads to share freight and charge a fixed price.[76] Some economists, both contemporary and modern, have argued that considerations such as economies of scale justified these practices. The actual cost of providing service to a larger customer, for a single product, or from a particular place, they say, justified charging lower than usual rates. This observation may have been accurate, but railroad critics of the era saw another picture. Charles Francis Adams, Jr., observed that, while the usual result of competition generally was to reduce and equalize prices, railroad competition "led directly to systematic discriminations and wild fluctuations, and the more active the competition was, the more oppressive the discriminations became and the less possible was it to estimate the fluctuations."[77] Customers who were not among the privileged harbored a reasonable belief that the railroads compensated for lower rates in competitive markets by charging higher fares to them.

Railroad management was obviously more complex, but the important point is each side's perception of the controversy. Railroad managers saw competition and were driven by a desire to avoid it. Reformers saw monopoly, or more precisely, discrimination and favoritism. They talked about excessive rates but what they really meant was excessive rates for themselves. Except for the few people who favored government ownership of the railroads, nobody denied the companies' right to make a profit. It was not the aggregate amount of rates but rather rate discrimination that was the target of the attacks. Reformers denied that the company had the right to set rates arbitrarily and without regard to fairness.[78]

The railroads' practice of charging low rates for a long haul and high rates for a short haul came to symbolize rate discrimination. The favorable long-haul rates applied to shipments from one terminal city to another terminal city. Shippers from towns along the same line were charged the higher short-haul rate. It is easy to see why this practice became a symbol; it pitted rural shippers against the urban and small against the large. The rates for the shorter distance were usually set proportionally higher but were sometimes even absolutely higher than the rates the railroads charged for hauling goods for the longer distance. In other words the shorter haul might cost not only more dollars per mile but more dollars total. To the extent this policy produced unfair results, it was a kind of unfair practice that people found easy to grasp.

Small-town shippers may have had less cause to be upset than they thought. According to some economists, the price discrimination between long and short hauls was justifiable for two interrelated reasons. First, they say it was fair. Because the expense the railroad incurred for hauling from terminal point to terminal point was relatively lower, price discrimination roughly reflected the different cost of service for the two types of services. Second, they maintain that price discrimination actually resulted in cheaper rates for the small-town shippers because it tended to encourage the shipment of the greatest amount of goods. The increased volume caused overall prices to go down. Therefore, even those who paid the higher charges benefited.[79]

Railroads were transforming the country from a commercial system made up of regional and local economies to a system dominated by a national economy. Small-town farmers and merchants may have feared that trend as much as they feared the power railroads held. They were driven by a desire to take back some control from the companies. Antirailroad feelings combined elements of economic self-interest, republican virtue, and a particular form of regionalism.[80] The latter was not sectionalism in the antebellum sense but a vision of an economic system in which each region could develop its own resources and control its own economic destiny.[81]

This regional concern was certainly reflected in the Granger programs. Implying that the national market system smacked of colonialism, Granger leaders encouraged members to foster home manufacturing so as not to be "obliged to transport our raw material out and the manufactured article in." History "does not afford a single example of a country which has remained permanently prosperous by production and exportation of raw material," said Granger leader D. W. Adams; rather, those countries had always tended toward a condition of dependence and poverty.[82] Like the old Jacksonians, Grangers believed that both concentration of power and nationalization of the economy threatened their freedom. "We desire a proper equality, equity, and fairness; protection for the weak, restraint upon the strong; in short, justly distributed burdens and justly distributed power," Granger leaders declared. "These are American ideas, *the very essence of American independence.*"[83]

Unlike the old Jacksonians, however, Grangers and other reformers of the 1870s had come to believe that the only way to obtain this just distribution of burdens and power, and thus to ensure their freedom, was through government regulation of the transportation industry. D. W. Adams told his followers that against the railroads, "the people, in their individual capacity, are powerless and only through their united action as sovereigns can they obtain redress."[84] In the minds of these new reformers government alone could counterbalance the power and privilege of the railroad corporation. Adams's choice of words implies not only that he thought cooperative action was the one means by which people could control the railroads but also that it was a proper and natural consequence of democracy.

The Granger laws were a product of the desire to take back some control from the companies and a hope that government regulation could do it. Although the statutes of various states differed in many respects, four enacted in Illinois were typical.[85] One attempted to prevent "unjust discriminations and extortions" by requiring uniform rates for any class of goods and by outlawing the practice of charging higher rates for a short haul. The penalty for willfully violating this act was forfeiture of the railroad's franchise, and evidence that a railroad had charged a larger sum for the same class or for the short haul was prima facia evidence of the company's willful violation. A second act created a Board of Railroad and Warehouse Commissioners, which was given the power to prescribe maximum rates. A third act set maximum rates for passenger service. The fourth, which was destined to become the subject of the United States Supreme Court's opinion in *Munn v. Illinois,* set a maximum rate that could be charged for storing grain in Chicago's giant elevators.[86]

Opposition to the proposed Granger laws came from a variety of sources, but railroad leaders and attorneys took the lead in the political debates.[87] The railroads and reformers disagreed on almost every level, even on the basic proposition of whether regulation was consistent with the American system of government. While the reformers emphasized principles of democracy, railroads stressed the principle of limited government. In passing such regulation, the latter's leaders argued, the states went far beyond their power to interfere with individual liberty. Charles B. Lawrence, attorney for the Chicago & Northwestern Railroad, later captured this theory in his brief to the U.S. Supreme Court. The idea that the legislature has a general power to set maximum rates, he warned, "is at war with every principle of free government, and with all those provisions of our American Constitution which were designed to protect the natural rights of man against legislative aggression."[88] Railroads argued that when a state regulated the prices a railroad could charge for its services, it was in essence confiscating the railroad's property. Another attorney for the Chicago & Northwestern, John Cary, warned that this sort of legislation amounted to communism pure and simple. If not checked, Cary argued, it would "ultimately overthrow not only the rights of property, but personal liberty and independence as well."[89]

Fairness was also an element of the railroads' argument. Opponents of regulation reminded listeners that the railroads operating in Illinois, Minnesota, Iowa, and Wisconsin operated under a franchise that was, in essence, a contract with the state. Under that contract, they argued, they had a right to operate their business at a reasonable profit. If the state interfered with this right by establishing maximum rates, they said, it would violate its contract with the companies. There was a practical side to the railroads' argument as well. The Granger regulations would not ensure fairness, they maintained, because under the proposed maximum rates railroads would be unable to meet their obligations to stock- and bondholders. Even where they could pay their obligations, it would reduce the money available to the railroads, making it impossible to raise the capital necessary to run and expand the railroad system.

Soon after the Granger laws were passed a writer for the *American Law Review* predicted in 1874 that "the extreme impolicy of frightening capital out of a new state by such legislation foreshadows an early death to these enactments." The author then added a prescient postscript to the warning: "But even if they die next winter, they will hold a famous place in American legal history, for they have given rise to litigation which involves the gravest constitutional questions, and the principles of ownership in all property, as well as the control of the state over the corporations it creates."[90]

With the Granger laws on the books, railroad lawyers steadfastly advised their clients that the new statutes would not pass constitutional muster. Their advice set off a flurry of lawsuits in both the state and the federal courts. The affected companies used two tactics to get the cases into court: they either ignored the Granger legislation, thus forcing the states to sue for enforcement, or they initiated a lawsuit challenging the validity of the legislation.[91]

The companies had the advice of the most distinguished lawyers in the nation. These lawyers must have realized that, under the law as it stood at the time, they really did not have a very good case. This was especially true with respect to their most important point, that these laws violated their clients' rights under the due process clause of the Fourteenth Amendment. The Court had strongly indicated in the *Slaughter-House Cases* that it would not use this provision to oversee state attempts to regulate business. Still, the companies pressed their case. Their attorneys understood that they were actually recommending a calculated campaign to change the status of the law. They wanted to establish a doctrine that the Constitution guaranteed a fundamental right to be free of the type of price regulations created in the Granger laws. Such a doctrine would remove the issue of regulation from the political process. If successful, their attempt would be worth the effort.

Eight Granger cases eventually made their way to the U.S. Supreme Court in 1877. Of these, the Court chose *Munn v. Illinois* for its lead opinion on the matter. *Munn* differed from the other cases in that it did not involve a railroad at all. It began when the partnership of Munn and Scott was convicted of violating an Illinois law that imposed maximum charges for storage and handling grain in Chicago's elevators. In most ways, however, the circumstances of *Munn* were similar to those of the Granger cases involving railroads.

The importance of the Chicago grain elevators cannot be overstated. By the 1870s farming had become an integral part of a market economy.[92] Most of the grain produced in the Midwest made its way to Chicago's waterfront. From there it was shipped through the Great Lakes via the St. Lawrence River to the East Coast and European markets. All of the grain that arrived at this gathering point was stored in fourteen immense elevators, or warehouses, owned by nine business firms. Cooperation among the firms allowed them to fix the prices they charged for storage. Like railroad passages through a mountain pass, river valley, or over an exclusive route, the Chicago harbor was a transportation bottleneck. Control of that bottleneck gave the owners of the Chicago grain elevators a vise grip on the flow of commerce.

Of course, the elevator companies did not view their status in quite that light. Rather than as a bottleneck in commerce, they saw themselves as an essential cog, a view that led them to a secondary argument in their case before the Supreme Court. William C. Goudy and John N. Jewett, Munn and Scott's attorneys, emphasized their clients' importance to the flow of grain when they argued that the Illinois maximum-rate law violated Article 1, section 8 of the constitution, which gives Congress the power to regulate interstate commerce. The Court rejected this commerce clause claim. But even if the companies had won on this point, their victory would have been only partial. The commerce clause argument assumed that regulation was legitimate. If accepted, the state laws would be invalid, but the door would be open for Congress to regulate. Of course the companies knew that Congress had not passed laws regulating the industry (it would not until it passed the Interstate Commerce Act in 1887). Even so, looking at it from hindsight, the commerce clause argument may have been Munn and Scott's most reasonable point. Modern scholars maintain that uniform federal law would have been a more appropriate method of regulating the transportation industry, especially railroads, than was scattered state regulation.[93]

Besides being about a regulation of grain elevators, the facts of *Munn v. Illinois* differed from the other Granger cases in one other respect. Munn and Scott was a partnership; the railroads involved in the other cases were corporations. Thus the railroads were able to raise another secondary argument that the Granger laws violated the Article 1, section 10 guarantee that "no state shall pass any law . . . impairing the obligation of contract." Before the Civil War, this section, the contract clause, had been the primary source of constitutional protection of property rights. In contract clause doctrine, franchises and acts of incorporation were considered a contract between the state and the corporation it had created. In theory, a subsequent law or regulation placing new conditions on the corporation would alter the terms of that contract. In the other Granger cases, railroads argued that rate-fixing laws violated their contract in this manner. But there were exceptions to the inviolability of the corporate franchise, the most important of which recognized the state's right to include a clause in the original act reserving to itself the power to later revise the contract. Since all the acts creating the railroads involved in the Granger cases included such reserve clauses, the railroads had little hope of winning under this contract clause theory. Still, they did not give up. A reserve clause gave the state the power to alter the franchise, they admitted. It might even give the state the right to repeal the franchise. But the Granger laws did neither. They did not affect the status of the franchise but rather simply took property belonging to the corporation. A reserve clause, they argued, did not give the state the right to confiscate corporate property.[94]

Although it failed as a legal argument, the railroads' contract clause claim made a significant theoretical link to future theories regarding constitutional protection of property. It was an accepted premise of nineteenth-century liberalism that the rights and obligations relating to property are not bestowed from the state but rather flow from agreements made between parties. Freedom to make such agreements was thought to be an essential element of both private property and liberty. Like the "right to choose a calling," which guided Stephen Field's dissent in the *Slaughter-House Cases,* this idea was a predecessor of the later doctrine of liberty of contract.

The underlying premise of this theory was not entirely accurate, especially with respect to railroads. As a practical matter it was difficult to maintain that railroads created their property purely through individual contract.[95] The most essential property of a railroad was the franchise it received from the state. Additionally, the state usually gave railroads the power of eminent domain. Although eminent domain required that railroads pay just compensation, it gave the companies the ability to take another person's property if it lay along the proposed route. Local, state, or the federal government often provided subsidies of cash or loans. State and federal governments also gave the railroads grants of public land. Regardless of the inconsistencies, by mixing contract clause argument with a claim that the Granger laws confiscated their property, railroad attorneys provided a subtle reinforcement to the most important argument in *Munn v. Illinois*.

The most important issue in *Munn* and the other Granger cases was whether the state regulations violated the Fourteenth Amendment guarantee that no state shall deprive any person of life, liberty, or property without due process of law. This theory gave the companies a means of directly attacking the states' authority to regulate rates and services. It was similar to the argument that Louisiana butchers had raised, and that the Supreme Court had rejected, in the *Slaughter-House Cases*. But the butchers had maintained that the Fourteenth Amendment, taken as a whole, gave the federal courts authority to protect individual liberty and individual property from arbitrary, partial, and unjust legislation of state governments. Taking a slightly different approach, company lawyers in *Munn* honed in on one clause of the amendment—the due process clause.

The concept of due process, sometimes referred to as the "law of the land," predates the Fourteenth Amendment. It is found in the Magna Carta, the Fifth Amendment, and most state constitutions. With few exceptions, it was assumed to mean that a person could not be deprived of life, liberty, or property without the benefit of proper judicial hearing and procedure. In *Munn*, however, company attorneys argued that due process promised more than trial according to some course of settled judicial procedure. The guarantee, they said, was also meant to protect private rights from arbitrary government interference.

This theory concentrated on the substance of legislation rather than on the procedure by which the law was enforced. Substantive due process, as it came to be called, would give the judiciary the authority to overrule legislation that interfered with individual rights. Certainly part of the American constitutional tradition condoned resisting arbitrary assertions of power that threatened individual liberty, but that does not necessarily mean the due process clause was written into the Constitution as the kind of guarantee company attorneys were proposing.[96] Attractive as this idea might have been to the legal mind, there was very little precedent to support it. Company attorneys pointed to Daniel Webster's famous statement in the *Dartmouth College* case of 1819. The meaning of due process, Webster reasoned, "is that every citizen shall hold his life, liberty, property, and immunities under the protection of the general rules which govern society. Everything which may pass under the form of [legislative] enactment is not to be considered the law of the land."[97] They referred the Court to Thomas

Cooley's treatise, *Constitutional Limitations,* which maintained that legislation could not interfere with vested rights beyond what was allowed by "settled maxims of law" and safeguards for the protection of individual rights.[98] They could draw upon a few cases from state courts to support their proposition, the most well known being *Wynehamer v. New York.*[99] Other than that, there was little support for the argument. The United States Supreme Court had applied the concept of substantive due process only once—applying it to the Fifth Amendment's due process clause in the infamous *Dred Scott* case.[100] Justice Bradley had adopted the theory in his 1873 *Slaughter-House* opinion, but Bradley's opinion was a dissent.[101] Justice Miller's opinion for the majority in the *Slaughter-House Cases* conspicuously ignored the substantive due process argument.

Weaknesses aside, Munn and Scott's attorneys, John N. Jewett and William C. Goudy, persisted with this line of argument. Protection of private rights is the predominant idea upon which this government of ours was established; they argued, "so much so, that any legislation which violates or infringes these rights, may fairly be said to be in hostility to the fundamental principles upon which that government rests."[102] It was easy enough for Jewett and Goudy to establish the general proposition that property rights fell among those liberties the Constitution was intended to protect. Nobody would disagree with this basic contention. The Fourteenth Amendment is explicit in its protection of property. The Fifth Amendment contains the same due process protection with the additional provision "nor shall private property be taken for public use without just compensation." Additionally, the contract clause was always understood as a provision to protect property rights. The task that would test the company attorneys' skill was to show that setting maximum rates for grain elevators and railroads constituted the type of government activity that violated their clients' property rights.

Jewett and Goudy went about it like chemists. Blending analogies with the base ingredient of property rights, they created a distinct formula. From a recent Fifth Amendment case in which a government-sponsored canal project had flooded an individual's land, they offered the principle that destroying the value of property constituted confiscation.[103] Rate regulation, they argued, had the same effect. Next, they appealed to the equal protection clause of the Fourteenth Amendment in order to add a measure of fairness to their formula. As Goudy put it, "To forbid to an individual or to a class the right to the acquisition or enjoyment of property in such manner as should be permitted to the community at large, would be to deprive them of *liberty.*"[104] Jewett added a measure of alarm to the formula. Rate regulation amounted to class legislation, he argued. It operated under a theory in which "private possessions would be at the mercy of the legislative power, which would be the sole judge of what constituted 'the greatest good to the greatest number.' "105 From these elements Jewett and Goudy concluded that "it is not merely the title and possession of property that the Constitution is designed to protect, but along with this, the control of the uses and income, the right of valuation and disposition, without which property ceases to be profitable, or even desirable."106

Jewett emphasized that the dispute was purely a question of government power. Legislation fixing prices represented arbitrary and irresponsible power, he said, a power practically to annihilate private property by destroying the value of its use.107 Even Jewett and Goudy were willing to admit that there was a range in which the states had authority to enact regulations that affected business. This authority, the police power of the states, had long been recognized as a normal function of government. The company attorneys simply viewed the police power as quite limited in scope.

Goudy set the tone for his treatment of the police power with a bold assertion: "For the first time since the Union of these States, a legislature of a State has attempted to control the property, capital and labor of a private individual, by fixing the prices he may receive from other private persons, who choose to deal with him."108 The great attorney and one-time president of the Illinois bar association was no doubt taking an advocate's license with the facts; for regulation of all kinds, including price regulation, was a common facet of economic life in his time. Government set prices for all kinds of franchises: bridges, ferries, and canals provided the most graphic examples. Perhaps this was Goudy's point; the regulation of a franchise was, in theory, based upon a contract between the company and the state. Illinois' regulation of his client's grain elevators did not have the same contractual basis. It was purely statutory—an enforcement of the state's police power. Even then, there were plenty of examples of government regulation. Usury laws, which limited the amount of interest banks could charge for loaning money, were common to most states. States commonly limited the rates that hackmen (cabdrivers) and draymen (freight haulers) could charge. They regulated public inns. In the early nineteenth century Virginia even regulated the amount of fees attorneys could charge for their services.109

Jewett dismissed these examples of price regulation as "relics and implements of a former system, carried along by sufferance and general acquiescence, while the system of which they were a constituent part has long since been displaced, and its principles discarded."110 This was, of course, totally inconsistent with Goudy's contention that price regulation was unheard of. Whether it was a small slip or intentional, Jewett's point made explicit what had been implied throughout his and Goudy's arguments. They were not urging the Court to recognize the police power of the states as it was but as they believed it ought to be.

Jewett's and Goudy's idea of the police power began with the maxim sic utere tuo ut alienum non ladas (enjoy your own property in such a manner as not to injure that of another). More than a guiding principle addressed to property owners, this maxim, they maintained, also defined the limits of state authority. Citing Cooley's *Constitutional Limitations,* Goudy insisted that the state's police power was limited to enacting laws to preserve public order, to prevent criminal offenses, and "to establish, for the intercourse of citizen with citizen, those rules of good manners and good neighborhood which are calculated to prevent a conflict of rights, and to insure to each the uninterrupted enjoyment of his own, so far as is reasonably consistent with a like enjoyment by others." The company lawyers envisioned only a few types of laws in this last category. Laws regulating business that endangered public health, offended the senses, or created other nuisances were legitimate exercises of the police power. Also considered legitimate were laws that promoted peace and good order, by which they meant laws that protected property and provided rules for settling disputes that were likely to arise in the conduct of business.[111]

Illinois Attorney General James K. Edsall defended his state's regulation of grain elevator and railroad rates with a variation of the same theme. Quoting Massachusetts Chief Justice Lemuel Shaw, Edsall maintained that private property was held under the limitation that its use "shall not be injurious to the equal enjoyment of others having equal right to the enjoyment of their property, nor injurious to the rights of the community."[112] He interpreted this last phrase to mean that the state could interfere with property rights for the purpose of furthering the common good and promoting the general welfare.

Neither the company's nor the state's definition of police power was very precise, but the difference in emphasis was obvious. The company's narrow view of state power emphasized individual rights; the state's broader view of that power stressed the general welfare or common good. Just by getting the case into the Supreme Court the companies had succeeded in moving the debate over the legitimacy of government regulation from the political arena to the judicial. Once they were there they had also succeeded in seizing the high ground. The political debate had revolved around differing views about the nature of liberty. It had asked legislatures to balance the liberty of business owners against the liberty of farmers and merchants. In the courts, company lawyers successfully transformed the debate into a contest that pitted the liberty of business owners against government power.

To the extent that they predicted the Court would reverse the position it had taken in the *Slaughter-House Cases* and invalidate the Granger laws, company attorneys had badly miscalculated. Writing for a 7-to-2 majority in *Munn v. Illinois*, Chief Justice Morrison Waite upheld the Illinois warehouse regulations. The Court also upheld the other Granger laws that had been challenged. Still, the Court had faced a barrage of legal argument from a force of the nation's most prominent attorneys. In the process of explaining why these regulations fell within the range of powers the Constitution left to the states, Chief Justice Waite made some concessions. The resulting opinion yielded some significant victories for opponents of regulation, who, despite having lost on the outcome, could take heart in concessions made to their theory of law.

It was a major concession to opponents of regulation that Waite did not deny the theory of substantive due process. Statutes regulating the use of private property do not necessarily deprive an owner of his property without due process of law, he wrote. "Under some circumstances they may, but not under all."[113] To determine which circumstance applied, he would look at the nature of the police power and the nature of the property. The chief justice admitted that the state has limited authority to interfere with property that is exclusively private. But when private property is "affected with a public interest," he continued, it ceases to be juris privati only and is thus subject to more extensive regulation for the promotion of the general welfare.

Waite's reasoning seemed sensible enough, and he had age-old legal authority to back it up. Authority for the proposition traced back to the seventeenth-century writings of British jurist Lord Chief Justice Hale:

> If the king or subject have a public wharf, unto which all persons who come to that port must come and unlade or lade their goods . . . because they are the wharves only licensed by the king, . . . or because there is no other wharf in that port, . . . in that case there can not be taken arbitrary and excessive duties for cranage, wharfage, pesage, &c., neither can they be enhanced to an immoderate rate; but the duties must be reasonable and moderate, though settled by the king's license or charter. For now the wharf and crane and other conveniences are affected with a public interest.[114]

Ferries and warehouses joined with wharves as examples of the type of property that Lord Hale said could be affected with public interest. Subsequent British and American cases applying the rule provided other examples of properties, such as mills, turnpikes, and roads, that could legitimately be subjected to regulation.

For Chief Justice Waite and six other members of the Court who voted to uphold the Illinois rate regulation it was clear that the Chicago elevators were businesses affected with public interest. Company lawyers must have been especially dismayed that Justice Bradley voted with the majority to uphold the regulations. In the past, Bradley had shown an inclination to vote against state regulation. He had joined Field and Strong dissenting in the *Slaughter-House Cases,* and his separate opinion in that case had done the most to articulate the idea that the due process clause of the Fourteenth Amendment gave the Court power to oversee the substance of state legislation. Now, in *Munn,* only Field and Strong dissented. Not only had Bradley switched his vote, as it turned out, he was the member of the Court most responsible for developing the theory under which the case was decided. In a memo, "Outline of my views on the subject of the Granger Cases," Bradley acquainted Chief Justice Waite with the works of Lord Hale and articulated the "business affected with public interest" theory.[115]

In the *Slaughter-House Cases* Bradley and Field had agreed that the Fourteenth Amendment's guarantee of liberty included a right to choose a trade or calling. They agreed that government regulation of business could infringe upon this right to a degree that it violated the Constitution. In the *Slaughter-House Cases* they had also agreed that monopoly posed a threat to individual liberty. The extent to which Bradley and Field had agreed in the earlier case indicated that they had a shared interest in protecting individual liberty from government regulation, which makes their disagreement in *Munn* even more enlightening. It illustrates not only how different elements of society viewed liberty but also how these different views of liberty evolved from a common root. By writing his memo to the chief justice, Bradley left an unusual source of his views. The debate in *Munn* can be understood, therefore, as a contrast between Waite's majority opinion and Bradley's memo, on the one hand, and Field's dissent on the other.

Much of the disagreement centered on defining "business affected with public interest." Field's concept of the phrase conformed to his belief that regulation was appropriate only for government-created monopolies. He pointed out that the writings of Lord Hale, and many of the cases that Waite and Bradley had used to support their theory, involved goverment regulation of companies that operated an exclusive franchise—either by prerogative of the king or by contract with a state. The elevators in *Munn,* he argued, were private companies with no such exclusive franchise.[116] Waite and Bradley, however, seemed to use these past examples of regulation merely as a starting point or as an inspiration for the "business affected with public interest" rule they had developed. The examples they drew from the writings of Lord Hale and earlier cases did not serve as the sole justification for that rule.

Even if this was true, Field's argument demonstrated that Waite and Bradley faced the problem of providing some rule to determine when a property becomes affected with public interest. Waite struggled to articulate a general rule. "Property does become clothed with a public interest when used in a manner to make it of public consequence, and affect the community at large," he wrote.[117] But Field was quick to point out that this definition was not very helpful. It simply said that property was affected with public interest when the public had an interest in it. "If this be sound law," Field warned, "if there be no protection, either in the principles upon which our republican government is founded, or in the prohibitions of the Constitution against such invasion of private rights, all property and all business in the State are held at the mercy of a majority of its legislature."[118]

Waite and Bradley's idea of a business affected with public interest was not quite as open-ended as Field suggested, however. Although they may have failed to articulate a precise general rule, on one point they were very clear. The Chicago elevators fell into the category of business affected with a public interest because they operated as a virtual monopoly. In this sense, the facts of *Munn v. Illinois* had much in common with the facts of the *Slaughter-House Cases*. In neither case did the company involved have an actual monopoly. In both cases, however, the company had a vise grip on some essential element of a particular business. All of the New Orleans butchers had to ply their trade in the Crescent City Company's slaughterhouse. Similarly, virtually all grain shipped through Chicago had to be stored in one of the fourteen immense elevators owned by nine firms that cooperated in fixing the price to be charged for storage.[119] The only significant difference between the two situations lay in the source of their privileged position. The New Orleans slaughterhouse attained its status by virtue of a government franchise; the Chicago elevators attained theirs through private ownership and cooperation. This factor made no difference to Waite and Bradley, however. Waite quoted both the company attorneys and Lord Hale to describe the public nature of Chicago's elevators:

They stand, to use again the language of their counsel, in the very "gateway of commerce," and take a toll from all who pass. Their business most certainly "tends to a common charge, and is become a thing of public interest and use." Every bushel of grain for its passage "pays a toll, which is a common charge," and, therefore, according to Lord Hale, every such warehouseman "ought to be under public regulation, viz., that he take but reasonable toll." Certainly, if any business can be clothed "with a public interest," and cease to be *juris privati* only, this has been.[120]

Likewise, for Bradley, the source of a monopoly was of little consequence. Power and privilege were the focus of his attention. The important issue for him was that the public could not stand on equal footing with companies such as railroads and the Chicago elevators.[121] Despite the company attorneys' success in positioning themselves as defenders of liberty against government oppression, Bradley did not forget that the heart of this dispute was a fundamental disagreement about the meaning of liberty. And, because he was writing a memorandum for his own use rather than as judicial opinion, Bradley did not have to mince words. "Unrestricted monopolies as to those things which the people must have and use, are a canker in any society, and have ever been the occasion of civil convulsions and revolutions," he wrote. "A people disposed for freedom will not tolerate this kind of oppression at the hands of private corporations or powerful citizens."[122]

Waite and Bradley also emphasized that the debate should be carried out in the political arena. Waite reasoned that the existence of the Illinois statute indicated that the size of the Chicago elevators had led Illinois voters to suppose that regulations "such as are usually employed to prevent abuses by virtual monopolies might not be inappropriate here."[123] The controlling factor for Waite was that the state had the power to regulate businesses affected with public interest. Whether the rates it set provided reasonable compensation was a question for the legislature, he said, and for protection against legislative abuses people must resort to the polls, not to the courts.[124] Bradley agreed: "The right to regulate the rates and to declare what are reasonable and what are not, must be regarded as reserved to the legislature." Any other rule, he said, "would be subversive of the authority which the people have confided to the legislature for their protection."[125]

Field was not inclined to pay any such deference to legislative authority. In his opinion, "The legislation in question is nothing less than a bold assertion of absolute power by the State to control at its discretion the property and business of a citizen, and fix the compensation he shall receive."[126] Field's opinion revealed that he seriously distrusted the democratic process. "Government can scarcely be deemed to be free where the rights of property are left solely dependent upon the will of a legislative body without any restraint," he warned.[127] And, in his mind, it was the Court's duty to ensure that this did not happen.

In some ways, Field's reasoning was close to that of the majority. Field was perhaps more forceful in insisting that the due process clause of the Fourteenth Amendment gave the Court power to oversee the substance of state legislation, but he did not suggest that the due process clause interfered with the state's right to exercise its legitimate police power. Rather, where the majority applied a broad definition of what police power encompassed, which included the power to protect the general welfare, Field suggested a much more narrow version. The police power, he said, applies to "whatever affects the peace, good order, morals, and health of the community."[128] He had in mind the same range of power that the company attorneys had suggested. The state's power to interfere with property was limited to enacting laws to provide rules governing disputes, protecting community morality, and abating nuisance.

Field understood that the majority's test of "business affected with public interest" extended the police power to another level. He worried that if a business fell within the category, the state had authority to regulate that business for the broad purpose of promoting the general welfare. For Field this view was far too open-ended. Legislative power, he believed, should be more limited. Early in his dissent Field argued that Lord Hale's rule, and the other precedent upon which the majority had relied, applied only to government-granted franchises. As his dissent gathered steam it became clear that his argument was more than a fine point of law or a technicality. He stated explicitly that this distinction lay at the heart of his thinking: "It is only where some right or privilege is conferred by the government or municipality upon the owner, which he can use in connection with his property, or by means of which the use of his property is rendered more valuable to him, or he hereby enjoys an advantage over others, that the compensation to be received by him becomes a legitimate matter of regulation."[129] According to Field, if the state's authority to regulate business expanded beyond the narrow police power he envisioned, it was only because a particular company had submitted to regulation as an implied condition of its grant. The source of this added legislative authority was, in other words, contract.[130]

The extent to which Field would actually limit regulation became more clear in the other Granger cases. Those cases involved railroads—the type of corporate franchises that clearly fell into the category that even Field agreed could be subjected to extensive legislative authority. As corporate franchises, railroads had entered into a contract with the state. What is more, most had benefited from substantial government subsidies. Yet Field, if given the opportunity, would have invalidated the state regulation of rail-road rates as well. Railroad attorneys had argued that the existence of a reserve clause in the corporate charter did not give the state a right to de-stroy entirely the business of the corporation. Field apparently agreed. Dis-senting in *Stone v. Wisconsin,* another one of the Granger cases, he chided the majority for failing to seize this opportunity to expand the reaches of the contract clause. This was, for him, a way to place a limit on govern-ment's authority to regulate corporations.[131]

The conflict between Field and Bradley, formerly colleagues in dissent, reflected their different views of liberty. The two justices had started from the same point in the *Slaughter-House Cases,* where both displayed Jack-sonian and free-labor roots. They shared a concern for liberty and a dislike of privilege. Their differences remained hidden until *Munn v. Illinois.* Ulti-mately, Bradley emphasized a distrust of privilege, whatever its source, and retained an admiration for democracy. Field emphasized a distrust of gov-ernment, a deep, ardent concern for property rights, and an abiding confi-dence in the judiciary. This divergence, in turn, led them to their different conclusions about the nature of the state's power.

For years, *Munn v. Illinois* would stand for the proposition that a state had the authority to protect the general welfare by regulating businesses affected with a public interest. Although they had made some inroads in pressing their theories relating to substantive due process and property rights, company attorneys had failed to establish an unequivocal right to be free of government regulation. John Jewett reacted by warning that the *Munn* opinion "has sent a chill of apprehension through the very heart of the business enterprises of the nation."[132] Jewett exaggerated the reaction of the business community, but there was no doubt about the importance of the Court's decision. In the decade that followed, reformers would time and again turn to the opinion as constitutional sanction for their efforts to regulate and control corporate power.[133] Despite its obvious significance, however, legal scholar Thomas Cooley worried that "the subject has an im-portance which I fear is not appreciated by everyone; the case has certainly attracted less attention than it deserves."[134] The reason for Cooley's concern was that the Court's announcement of the *Munn* decision on March 1, 1877, was swallowed up in a political and constitutional crises taking place at the very same time.

The 1876 presidential contest between Rutherford B. Hayes and Samuel Tilden was the closest race in years. For the first time since the Civil War, Democrats believed they had a viable chance to win. So close was the popu-lar vote that on November 8, the day after the election, some Democratic papers announced "Tilden Elected!" But a Democratic victory was not to be. The closeness of the popular vote quickly produced a dispute over the vote of the electoral college. Republicans and Democrats both claimed to have won the popular vote in Florida, Louisiana, and South Carolina. Both parties thus maintained that the electoral colleges from those states should be made up of their nominees. In addition, the Oregon electoral college vote was left hanging when one elector was declared ineligible.

Constitutional order hung in the balance while the affected states and Congress tried to decide which group of electors should be recognized.[135] It is difficult today to appreciate the intensity of the conflict that stewed while Congress debated the issue. Sensing that victory was slipping from their grip, some Democrats even urged Tilden to take, by force if necessary, "his rightful place as president." One supporter urged Tilden to resign as governor of New York and then let the lieutenant governor call out the state militia. Another offered 10,000 men-at-arms from Georgia.[136]

The presidential election remained undecided for more than two months before Congress acted. On January 29, 1877, realizing that it had to come up with some plan for a peaceful selection of the president, Congress created an Electoral Commission composed of five senators, five representatives, and five justices of the Supreme Court. The members of Congress selected to the commission were split evenly as to party. Of the five Supreme Court justices selected, Miller and Strong were known as Republicans, Field and Clifford as Democrats. Bradley, a Republican, was thought to be the most open-minded of the justices, but his selection still gave Republicans one more member than Democrats had on the commission.

During winter 1876–1877, both the Court and the nation were understandably preoccupied with the presidential dispute. After more than a month of deliberation, the Electoral Commission's vote ended up strictly following party lines. As a result, Congress recognized the Republican electors from the disputed states. On March 5, 1877, four days after the Court announced *Munn*, Rutherford B. Hayes was inaugurated as president of the United States.

Like the rest of the justices on the commission, Stephen Field remained true to his old party ties.[137] The Electoral Commission of 1877 was his first public foray into partisan politics since his years on the California Supreme Court. Field had undoubtedly kept his finger on the nation's political pulse, but up to this time, his involvement was private and behind the scenes.[138] Interestingly, the justice's brother, David Dudley Field, also played a key role in the election dispute. In January 1877, with Tilden's support, David Dudley was elected to fill a vacancy as representative of the seventh Congressional District of New York City. In Congress, David Dudley returned the favor by serving as Tilden's advocate during the course of the election dispute.[139] The experience must have whetted the Field brothers' appetites. Within the next few years they came to believe that they could win the prize that Tilden had lost: the presidency for the Democratic party and for Stephen J. Field.

6

SOUND IN DOCTRINE, BRAVE IN DEED

As the nation began to speculate about the 1880 presidential race, few people were likely to be thinking of Stephen J. Field. He had won a few state elections and had undoubtedly gained some notoriety for his role in the disputed election of 1876. But he had been out of active politics since his appointment to the Supreme Court in 1863.

Besides, the most renowned political celebrity of the time was a Republican. Former president Ulysses S. Grant was undoubtedly the media favorite; the event of the year had been his trip around the world. Grant had been out of office for more than three years, replaced by fellow Republican Rutherford B. Hayes. Although Grant's two terms as president were marred by corruption, this hero of the Civil War still held a secure place in the hearts of many Americans. Admirers tended to excuse Grant from the excesses of his administration and preferred to regard him as a good-hearted leader misdirected by corrupt advisers. Many Republicans were disgusted with Hayes's patronage policy; for some, a third term for Grant seemed an attractive proposition. Grant denied wanting the nomination, but his cause was taken up by the "Stalwart" wing of the Republican party led by New York senator Roscoe Conkling. Grant's popularity was undeniable, but he faced strong opposition within his party. His greatest challenger was "The Plumed Knight," James G. Blaine. Blaine, formerly Speaker of the House and now senator from Maine, led the rival "Half Breed" faction of the party. In the early stages the battle for the Republican nomination thus appeared to be between the forces of Conkling and the forces of Blaine. It pitted two strong personalities and two powerful organizations in a struggle to represent the party that had been in power since the Civil War.

Other potential candidates muddled the Republican picture somewhat. Mugwumps favored Sen. George Franklin Edmunds. John Sherman, who had support from President Hayes, entered the race as well. James A. Garfield was a dark horse candidate, but when the Republican convention deadlocked, delegates turned to him. Garfield was a member of Congress from Mentor, Ohio, whose interest in education and scientific farming earned him the nickname "the sage of Mentor." Chester Arthur, a member of Conkling's Stalwart wing, was named for the vice-presidency. They campaigned for moderate tariff protection, sound money, pensions for veterans, a new Chinese treaty, and civil service reform.[1] On that platform, they ultimately won the general election.

It would be hard to imagine Field jumping into the ring had he been a Republican, but circumstances were different among the Democrats. Where the Republican battle apparently was shaping up as a clash of titans, the Democrats seemed to be in a race to fill a void. Still, party leaders sensed that their chances for victory were good. In 1876 their candidate, Samuel Tilden, thought he had won the popular vote only to lose the election in a disputed electoral count. The popularity of the party seemed to be on the rise; it lacked only a dynamic standard-bearer.

Early attention centered on Tilden. The former New York governor was a bundle of contradictions. Because of his business acumen and his tendency to engage in cut-throat business tactics some people called Tilden "the great forecloser." Yet his crusade against New York's political machine, Tammany Hall, and the shady investment practices and political manipulations of the Canal Ring gave him a reputation as a reformer and another title, "the sage of Gramercy Park." The disappointment of his losing the electoral college count after winning the popular vote in 1876 left many of the party faithful believing Tilden had not fought hard enough to secure the victory. Many supporters believed he had let them down, yet others thought he was the strongest candidate and that somehow he was owed the presidency. How better to capitalize on the "great fraud," the theory ran, than to run with the "great defrauded"?[2] By 1880, ill health and a mild stroke had left Tilden weak; nevertheless, he was unanimously regarded as the Democrat's frontrunner. Each of the other hopefuls saw the contest as being against Tilden.

The other Democratic hopefuls were not a particularly celebrated lot. Thomas A. Hendricks of Indiana had been Tilden's running mate in 1876. Horatio Seymour, a former governor of New York and the party's presidential candidate in 1868, was considered a possibility although he steadfastly denied any desire for the nomination. Pennsylvania senator Thomas Francis Bayard, a proponent of states' rights, sound currency, and tariff reform, had strong appeal in the South. Speaker of the House Samuel Jackson Randall, also of Pennsylvania, thought of himself as Tilden's heir apparent. The party's eventual nominee was Gen. Winfield Scott Hancock. Known as "Hancock the Superb," the hero of Gettysburg, he was admired in the North for performance on the field of battle and in the South for his fair enforcement of martial law after the war. But he had neither political experience nor a political reputation. A favorite cartoon of the election showed him asking an adviser, "Who is Tariff and why is he for revenue only?"[3]

Given the state of the party, Stephen Field may have felt he had a good chance for the nomination even though he did not have many of the essentials for a successful run. He certainly did not have a powerful organization. A colorful nom de plume seemed to work for some candidates, but he did not have that either. A title would go far toward satisfying the second need, though: General was good; Judge might work. And possession of that title might have been just enough to inspire Field, whose ego was certainly up to the task. Although he never stated explicitly why he decided to seek the Democratic nomination, Field left plenty of fodder for speculation.[4]

Some observers have speculated that Field was dissatisfied with life on the high court during the six years since Chief Justice Morrison Waite had been appointed. Finding himself more in the minority, the theory goes, Field was unwilling to limit his views to dissenting opinions.[5] It is true that Field's personality did not appear especially compatible with being on the losing end of the collegial decisionmaking process of an appellate court. But he clearly saw the advantages of being a justice of the Supreme Court of the United States. To a friend's early musing about the possibility of his nomination, Field responded coyly:

You say my name is being mentioned in connection with the presidency. I suppose you smiled at that, as I have; and would smile even more if I should be generally taken up as a candidate. But there is little probability of that—not one chance in a thousand. Therefore I do not give any thought to the subject nor allow it to disturb my sleep or trouble my digestion. Seriously, I would not give up the independence of thought and action I enjoy for the presidency for life.[6]

A second idea is that Field's run for the presidency was the product of a family grudge against Democratic front-runner Samuel Tilden.[7] Indeed, two of Field's older brothers, David Dudley and Cyrus, had had conflicts with Tilden. The Field brothers were close, ambitious, and cohesive; and they could be vindictive.

David Dudley's rivalry with Tilden was personal and political. Their relationship started amicably enough in 1844, when they joined a faction of the New York Democratic party—the Hunkers—supporting Martin Van Buren for president. Four years later the same ward of New York City sent both men as delegates to the state's Free-Soil League convention.[8] As governor, Tilden even appointed David Dudley to Congress to fill a vacancy. But tension eventually developed between them.

It began when Tilden led a campaign against Tammany Hall, which in 1875 ended in successful criminal and civil proceedings against Boss William M. Tweed. David Dudley, who had already made a reputation for defending the Canal Ring, was Tweed's chief defense counsel. This position did not put him into direct conflict with Tilden except for a period of time during Tweed's trial when David Dudley tenaciously cross-examined the governor.[9] The sides of the battle were clearly drawn, however. And, both in the trial and in the press, the conflict was sometimes vicious and sometimes personal. Prosecuting attorney Charles O'Connor, a Tilden ally, dubbed David Dudley "attorney general for rascals."[10] The reform press joined in, delighting in disparaging the character not only of defendant Tweed but of his attorney as well. As if to give special emphasis to what it viewed as his jaded defense of political scoundrels, the *New York Times* ended 1876 with a New Year's Eve article calling David Dudley a hypocrite. "He mourns . . . the hold which mercenaries and knaves have acquired in civic as well as national affairs," wrote the *Times,* "not dreaming, apparently, that the public will always associate him with the villainies of Tweed and the struggles of old Tammany to wiggle out of the grip of justice."[11]

The Tweed episode posed a threat to David Dudley Field's professional reputation. A second conflict in which Tilden played a role threatened the attorney's perception of his place in history. David Dudley was most proud of his role in law reform. Throughout his career he had crusaded to simplify the American version of English common law by organizing the rules of law into straightforward codes. That the crusade for codification had met with some success is evidenced by David Dudley Field's modest claim, "The sun does not shine in any of the twenty-four hours except upon some place in which the laws were written by me."[12] The state of New York adopted the Field Codes in 1848, but in 1876 and again in 1879 a state commission proposed changes. David Dudley fought the changes but only managed to secure a compromise in which the commission agreed to leave three of his most important codes in place. The compromise plan passed the legislature on April 25, 1879, only to be vetoed three days later by Tilden's successor and ally Gov. Lucius Robinson. Defeat seemed to increase David Dudley's obsession with codification. For more than a decade he continued to wage a futile crusade for adoption of the Field Codes. Although it is impossible to determine the extent to which David Dudley held Tilden responsible for the demise of his project, Tilden's role certainly must have been on his mind. Some indication of David Dudley's feelings showed in his recollection of the 1876 presidential contest between his party's candidate, Tilden, and the Republican, Hayes. "I liked neither candidate," he wrote, "and I do not remember that I even voted."[13]

Cyrus Field's conflict with Tilden was business related. In May 1877 Cyrus bought the floundering New York Elevated Railway Company. His interest in the rapid-transit system was said to have been sparked by his Gramercy Park neighbor, Samuel Tilden, who agreed to purchase a substantial bloc of stock to support the venture. The arrangement at first appeared to kindle a friendship. Cyrus arranged a trip to Europe for Tilden and introduced him to his British friends. Tilden in turn spoke at a dinner Cyrus hosted for one of those friends who later visited New York. Under Cyrus's guidance the condition of the New York Elevated improved so much that at the end of 1878 he claimed the company stock sold for five times as much as it cost when he purchased it.[14]

Good relations between the two men were not long-lasting, however. In summer 1879, when Cyrus was in London to raise capital for the company, Tilden sold all of his stock. The sale most likely yielded a handsome profit for Tilden, but it caused the value of New York Elevated stock to plummet. The company was wrecked, and Cyrus suffered a substantial loss. What followed was an unusually public display of bitterness. For much of July, August, and September 1879, New York City newspapers covered the incident as if it were a celebrity divorce. The *New York World,* favoring Field, and the *New York Times,* favoring Tilden, played dueling newspapers. Cyrus charged Tilden with treachery; Tilden responded in defense that he had done nothing wrong, that his sale of the stock was a normal business practice.[15]

Assuming he had been doublecrossed, Cyrus had reason to be angry. But his public outcry was suspicious. Cyrus Field was no innocent. He had made a fortune by financing the transatlantic cable, he had bought and sold railroads, he had done business with men such as Jim Fisk and Jay Gould. Yet his comments to the press sounded more like the lament of a lover scorned than a complaint about a business deal gone sour. Cyrus recounted Tilden's "treachery" in a letter to the *New York Tribune:*

It was reserved for Mr. Tilden to keep in the background with his intentions concealed; to take sweet counsel with his friend from whom he was about to part; to follow him to the ship, and bid him a tender adieu, lulling his suspicions . . . , and then hasten from the ship to his brokers to tell them to sell out as fast as possible.[16]

The letter then took a political turn. Recognizing that "men shrug their shoulders and say such things are done on Wall Street every day," Cyrus responded, "Yes, but they are not done by a president-elect of the United States." Although inaccurate, the title "president-elect" was a deliberate verbal slap. It questioned Tilden's character as a possible presidential candidate at the same time that it reminded the reader of his close defeat in 1876.

Tilden's confidants quickly realized that Cyrus Field's attack on Tilden was politically motivated. Ashley Cole warned Tilden that one of Cyrus's statements in the *World* and *Times* was printed in pamphlet form and would be disseminated nationwide.[17] Tilden wrote a careful reply calling on supporters to corroborate his recollection of the political events of 1876.[18] Cyrus's friends saw the political implications as well. Acquaintances wrote thanking him for "exposing the treacherous character of Tilden" and praising Cyrus for "dealing a fatal blow to Tilden's presidential aspirations."[19]

Although Stephen Field had not yet announced his intentions, Cyrus's persistent and deliberate attack on Tilden suggests that the decision to make a bid for the Democratic nomination had been made as early as summer 1879. That decision involved the entire Field family, including Cyrus, who until then had been an active Republican.

A seat on the nation's highest court gave Stephen Field the prestige some people might consider worthy of a presidential candidate. His family, along with wealthy friends, provided the money necessary to run a campaign. Yet Field lacked other political currency. First of all, his name recognition was negligible compared to the attention received by some other presidential hopefuls. From October 15 to 29, 1879, for example, California newspapers were preoccupied with Grant's visit to the Northwest. Grant's every move made the front pages; even the menus for his dinner receptions were printed in full. During that same week and a half the U.S. Supreme Court released opinions in one of the most important cases of the year. On October 22, the *Alta California* reported the *Sinking Fund Cases* on page 2 with the comment that the opinion was too complex to be discussed in full. Field's dissent merited about five lines.[20] Well into the first months of 1880 some newspaper accounts of the Democratic hopefuls did not even mention Field's name.[21] Nor did the supporters of other candidates view him as a threat.[22] Image-making would be one of the major challenges for the Field campaign.

Lack of an organization posed another problem for the Field campaign. While on the bench, the justice did keep his fingers in the mire of California politics. As one of the state's most prominent national figures he reigned at least as a figurehead over one wing of the Democratic party. But control of the California party, even if he had it, was not indicative of national power. New York would have seventy votes at the national convention;

Pennsylvania would have fifty-eight. California, in contrast, would send twelve delegates to the national convention in Cincinnati. The national party was not going to follow California's lead. Even more significantly, Field, unlike Grant, Blaine, or Tilden, could not count on a web of dedicated political operatives looking after his interests in the state parties throughout the nation. Field would eventually try to play this to some advantage by running as an outsider—a man identified with no faction and with no long record to defend. "He lacks political experience. So much the better," reasoned the *Memphis Daily Appeal*.[23]

Yet another problem for the Field campaign would be developing a platform. A political record did not flow naturally from his duties as a judge. The high court was an awkward place from which to take a stand on current issues, attack opponents, or try to fit into the popular mood. The peculiarities of legal disputes could make it difficult to avoid or deflect issues. The difficulties of campaigning from the bench were compounded by the fact that some people simply did not like the idea of a justice of the Supreme Court being actively involved in politics. Some critics thought it degrading—"in bad taste, and worse morals." Others argued that a judge should at least resign before running.[24]

It was not unheard of for a justice of the Supreme Court to run for political office, especially among the men who sat on the highly politicized Court of the Civil War and Reconstruction. Justice John McLean sought the presidential nomination from both the Whigs and Republicans in 1856 and 1860. In 1872, Justice David Davis was considered for the Liberal Republican nomination and was nominated by the Labor Reform party. Chief Justice Salmon P. Chase actively pursued the presidency.[25] Nevertheless, the sense of impropriety lingered, and it was employed against Field as the campaign progressed. "The fathers decided that it was wise to place one branch of the government above temptation and therefore made the tenure of office of the judges of the courts a life one," reasoned one convention delegate. "I am not in favor of changing that and giving the judges reason to expect political reward for their decisions."[26] Recognizing this sentiment, Field did not "announce" his candidacy. As one supporter pointed out, he could not prevent the use of his name. The Field campaign tried to turn the feeling around by presenting him as a Washington outsider with a clean slate and no political debts.[27]

The process of nominating a presidential candidate in the nineteenth century involved no primary elections, no thirty-second television spots, and no real direct appeal to the voting public. National conventions were not merely media shows. Candidates were actually chosen at the convention by delegates, who had earlier been chosen at state conventions. Most national conventions were what we would call brokered—that is, the choice of a candidate was worked out through political bargaining and votes of the delegates as the convention proceeded. Some delegates came "instructed" to vote for a particular candidate on the first ballot but most were uninstructed. Most delegates owed their presence at the convention to ties with local political organizations. The one desire they had in common was to be ultimately on the winning side. The challenge for Field and his backers was to build an image, organization, and platform that could convince the delegates that Field was a winner and to do so without an offensive breach of judicial decorum.

Some time after March 1880 the Field campaign published a pamphlet that plainly revealed their strategy. "JUDGE FIELD: Sound in Doctrine, Brave in Deed" first portrayed Field as a man of unwavering courage. After paying homage to Samuel Tilden, the party's standard-bearer of 1876, it launched an attack on Tilden's handling of the disputed election. "Mr. Tilden is an older and feebler man than he was then," the pamphlet observed. The party needed a candidate who "when elected, will defend the right of the people to have the president of their own choice, and will not cover his eyes before the drawn sword."[28]

The "sound doctrine" depicted in Field's campaign pamphlet represented a measured effort to convince each of the party faithful that Field had the support of the others. The pamphlet claimed he was acceptable to all factions in New York—a bold assertion considering its implication that Tilden was a coward. It also claimed that Field's judicial record as a defender of states' rights and as an opponent of centralization gave him the support of the South. Finally came the seemingly inescapable claim: being a Californian, Field would sweep the West.

"A Man of Pluck"

Democrats were frustrated when Hayes claimed the presidency for the Republican party in 1876. They referred to the episode as "the great fraud" or "the stolen presidency." Although many of the party faithful sympathized with Tilden, others blamed him for the loss, believing he had failed to stand up under pressure.[29] Field's campaign played to this latter feeling when it emphasized the judge's strength of character. Campaign literature aside, there is no telling what Field really thought of Tilden. But Field firmly believed himself to be a strong individual—"a man of pluck" as one newspaper headline put it.[30] His campaign played that theme to the hilt and in doing so, revealed something of the character of its candidate.

Creating this image posed the least of the problems faced by the Field campaign. In July 1877 Field dictated his *Personal Reminiscences of Early Days in California*.[31] Although Field claimed he published it for the benefit of a few friends, it had all the makings of a campaign biography. In it he took pains to address several apparent blots on his record of public service.[32] He also justified his unpopular positions in the California land dispute cases and noted his role as a legislator in passing homestead exemption laws and legislation that formalized customary mining law.[33]

What is most striking about *Personal Reminiscences*, however, is the number of tales of manliness and courage of convictions, peppered with pinches of wisdom and wiliness, that dominate Field's recollection of his early career. We find Field staring down Judge Turner, who tried to disbar Field and then threatened to "cut off his ear and shoot him down on the spot." We find him challenging a fellow state legislator, B. F. Moore, to a duel, averted only when Moore apologizes for his insults to Field. Field is saved from an unprovoked attack by Turner's brother. At a trial he exposes an attempt to bribe the jury, despite being threatened by "a general cocking of pistols." He faces down William T. Barbour, who backs out of a duel. Later when Barbour bushwhacks Field, catching him unarmed, Field recalls turning on him with the words, "You infernal scoundrel, you cowardly assassin—you come behind my back and put your revolver to my head and tell me to draw; you haven't the courage to shoot; shoot and be dammed." Obviously, he didn't. Even the impeachment proceedings against Field in 1868 were presented as an act of bravery. Field maintained they were a response to his stance in the *McCardle* case and were intended to intimidate and "act as a warning to all judges as to what might be expected if they presume to question the wisdom or validity of the Reconstruction measure of Congress." *Reminiscenses* was not the story of a man who would buckle under pressure or of a man who would let the presidency slip away when it was in his grasp.[34]

A more challenging task for the Field campaign would lie in publicizing the image his biography had created. The conventional method of the day involved setting up a "literary bureau" responsible both for directing the campaign and disseminating campaign propaganda. Describing "how presidents are nominated," the *Washington Post* reported that documents and directives that Blaine's literary bureau sent throughout the country "are to be measured by the ton."[35] Field's publicity campaign started in early spring. "It is apparent that friends of Judge Field . . . have started to increase activity," wrote a Tilden supporter. "The *Washington Post* of the 10th, with his coolie case dissenting opinion have come here to a large number and besides there are the published copies of that and other similar decisions."[36] By May 1880 it was widely known that Field had a well-organized literary bureau located in Washington, D.C., headed by L. Q. Washington.[37] The literary bureau also enlisted George C. Gorham to write letters for Field in the West.[38] By today's standards this was a late start, but in 1880 it was not unusual for publicity campaigns to begin in the winter before the party convention.[39]

Campaign advertising was nonexistent in those days. The chief methods employed by the literary bureaus involved persuading editors of local newspapers to support their candidate, feeding information to friendly newspapers, and planting stories in neutral or unfriendly papers.[40] L. Q. Washington's success in this regard is reflected in the *New Orleans Times-Picayune,* which constantly carried reports favoring Field or that were optimistic about his chances; many were signed L. Q. W.[41] Coverage in the *Atlanta Constitution, Memphis Daily Appeal,* and *Washington Post* also reflected L. Q. Washington's handiwork, as did the appearance of excerpts from *Personal Reminiscences of Early Days in California* in newspapers around the country.[42]

If friendly newspapers were unavailable it was possible to establish or buy one. On January 30, 1880, William S. Royall established the *Richmond Commonwealth,* an excessively pro-Field newspaper that went out of business soon after the Democratic National Convention in Cincinnati.[43] Field's rivals eyed the paper with suspicion. "I know well Royall," wrote a Tilden supporter, "and in my opinion he is the paid agent of Field's friends in Washington."[44] Similarly, in June 1880, Thomas Francis Bayard's supporters warned their candidate that Cyrus Field was going to purchase the *New York World* and use it as a campaign vehicle "for the Judge."[45] Their suspicions were soon realized. The *World* had been solidly and persistently anti-Tilden but had paid little attention to Field. Soon after the purchase, however, it ran a flattering piece on page 1 under the blaring headline, "Is It Likely to Be Field?"[46] The *World* backed Field from that time until it became obvious that his cause was lost.

The rapid organization of a literary bureau and the purchase of newspapers were indications that money would not be a problem for the Field campaign. A piece from his campaign literature actually boasted that the judge's brother would see to it that a very important ingredient in American politics—money—would not be lacking. As the June 1880 convention approached, it was said that a good deal was being spent in Field's behalf and that his campaign started off by depositing $14,000 to pay board bills in one Cincinnati hotel. There is no doubt that Field had the best organization of any of the aspirants, wrote the *Atlanta Constitution:* "Twelve million copies of his life have been circulated." Twelve million copies is hard to believe, but Field undoubtedly had the support of people such as Lloyd Tevis, president of Wells Fargo, and Leland Stanford of the Central Pacific, who were wealthy enough to carry off that feat.[47]

The money connection was sometimes used against Field as the convention progressed. Enemies charged that his campaign was being engineered by financier Jay Gould, who "wanted a man in the White House whom he could use for the benefit of his great corporations." With a less than subtle implication one newspaper reported that "a few scattered supporters are honestly for Field, but the majority of his supporters here are men who generally require the stimulus of another man's purse to make them a convert to any cause."[48]

A publicity blitz, no matter how well financed, was not likely to be enough to ensure Field's success. Because nineteenth-century candidates were actually chosen in the halls of the convention rather than in primary elections, political machines were vital. Successful candidates counted on a combination of a national organization loyal to them personally and widespread alliances with the leaders of local political machines. Field, a novice in running for national office, started out with neither. Furthermore, judicial decorum made it awkward for him to make direct pleas for support.

New York, New York

When an opportunity came to gain a political alliance and the support Field needed in New York, the task of seizing it fell to his brother David Dudley. Two factions, each a powerful political organization in its own right, coexisted in the New York Democratic party. Samuel Tilden held control of what was called the "regular Democratic organization." Its rival was New York City's Tammany Hall, led by John Kelly. Although Kelly supported Tilden in his 1876 presidential bid, a feud quickly developed between the two. In 1878 Tilden joined in an attempt to wrest control of Tammany from Kelly.[49] An editorial in the *Tribune* quickly recognized the national implications of this rift. The fight between Tilden and Kelly, it said, furnished the opportunity for those people bent on defeating Tilden's nomination.[50]

David Dudley had a reasonable link to Tammany, having represented

Kelly's predecessor, Boss Tweed, against corruption charges. As Tweed's attorney, David Dudley had never actually participated in the political activities of the organization, but by the time the fight between Kelly and Tilden came to a head, he had positioned himself in a prominent role. At the 1879 state Democratic convention, Kelly warned that Tammany Hall would not support the renomination of Lucius Robinson, Tilden's choice for governor. When the convention nominated Robinson anyway, Kelly and his followers stormed out of the hall and held a convention of their own. The chair of this rump convention was none other than David Dudley Field. Under his gavel, the Tammany group nominated Kelly for governor, making the gubernatorial election a three-way race.[51] With the Democrats split, Republican candidate Alonzo Cornell won.

Governor Robinson's defeat did not end the Kelly faction's activities. On January 22, 1880, the *Times* reported on a meeting of "bolting Democrats." The purpose of the meeting was to organize Tammany's efforts to place delegates to the upcoming national convention. Its most symbolic order of business was drafting a series of anti-Tilden resolutions, thinly disguised as a plea for party harmony. The resolutions were authored in a committee chaired by David Dudley Field.[52]

There is no evidence to show how successful David Dudley's efforts were to ingratiate himself with Tammany Hall. The *Times* speculated that, considering that he had served as Kelly's chief lieutenant, it was highly probable that Kelly might be induced to support Justice Stephen J. Field.[53] Kelly never committed himself to any candidate, however; his efforts in the 1880 campaign were aimed solely at destroying Tilden's chances. In any case, to some observers, it was apparent that he would not be successful in his efforts to control the state party. Late in January the *Times* reported that members of the Tammany group "were as melancholy a lot of people as the amiable eyes of David Dudley Field ever had the ill luck to smile upon." At the state convention in April, sixty of the seventy delegates chosen for the national convention were Tilden supporters. Kelly was resigned to sending an alternative delegation to Cincinnati.[54]

Some acquaintances thought Dudley's activism against Tilden would ultimately hurt his brother's chances.[55] The Field campaign surely recognized that possibility. Appearing on the same page of the *Times* that reported on Dudley's efforts for Kelly was an article in which the justice professed support and friendship for Tilden.[56] From that time on, Field would try to play both sides of the deck, continuing to claim he was acceptable to all the factions in New York.

Southern Exposure

Aside from New York, the most important region for aspiring Democratic candidates was the South. Another goal of the Field campaign, therefore, was to secure southern support and to convince potential delegates that its candidate was popular in the South. Field's credentials were good in this respect. With decisions in the *Test Oath Cases,* and his stance against the Radical Reform Congress in *McCardle,* Field could comfortably position himself as an opponent of growing centralization and a defender of states' rights. Those cases were twelve years old, however. Although symbolic to southerners of the excessiveness of Radical Reconstruction, they were hardly fresh on voters' minds. Furthermore, Field was not in a position to take to the stump to preach the gospel of states' rights or to rail against increased centralism. Deference to judicial decorum inhibited his ability to stir up southern sympathies in his favor.

Just as the campaign for his party's nomination was heating up, however, Field was presented with an opportunity to display his states' rights plumage from his seat on the bench. In March 1880 the Court ruled on a series of cases testing the validity of several statutes that had been motivated by Republicans' fear that state governments would fail to carry out their policies for Reconstruction. To combat state apathy or downright opposition, Congress had devised methods of overlaying state authority with the power of the federal government. The March 1880 cases involved two general concepts that Republicans employed to accomplish that task. First were the "enforcement statutes," so-called because they were intended to enforce the guarantees of the Thirteenth, Fourteenth, and Fifteenth Amendments. Enforcement laws defined as federal crimes certain activities usually thought of as being within state jurisdiction. The second concept was captured in the "removal laws." These provided that under certain circumstances cases could be removed—that is, transferred—from state courts to the federal courts. Cases involving the denial of civil rights created such a circumstance.

In *Ex parte Siebold* and *Ex parte Clark* the Supreme Court upheld the conviction of several state election officials for violating the Enforcement Acts of 1870 and 1871.[57] Both laws were aimed at practices that some officials in southern states employed to discourage blacks from voting or to dilute the impact of the black vote. The 1870 law made it a federal crime for state election judges to fail to perform their duty. The Supplementary Enforcement Act of 1871 provided for federal supervisors and deputy marshals to oversee elections and made it a federal crime to interfere with these officers or prevent them from performing their duty.

Along with the Ku Klux Klan Act of 1871, the Enforcement Acts of 1870 and 1871 were designed to give teeth to the Fifteenth Amendment's guarantee that newly freed black male citizens would have the right to vote. These laws were inspired by a three-year wave of Klan violence and intimidation in parts of the South. Blacks who had assumed any leadership role since emancipation were at risk.[58] Educated blacks were also singled out, such as Washington Eager, who was murdered because he could read and write. Blacks who asserted their rights were whipped, beaten, and even lynched. Whites who supported them were not immune, either. In North Carolina a farmer who had distributed his land to his former slaves was whipped. Attacks on and harassment of white teachers who taught blacks were not uncommon.[59] Led by men of the "aristocratic class" as well as poorer whites, the purpose of this intimidation was "to return to the old order of things."[60] These actions contained a social and an economic element that was aimed at indirectly destroying the independence of the freedmen. It also had a political element—to destroy the Republican party in the South. And it was fairly successful on all counts.

Democrats had substantial success in the 1870 elections. The Republican majority in the House was cut by sixty seats, and North Carolina sent a Democrat to the Senate.[61] Republicans were feeling their grip on the lever of government slipping, and federal enforcement of civil rights and voting rights in the South was one way by which they hoped it could be reestablished. Thus, an element of self-interest was behind the 1870 and 1871 enforcement laws. The partisan motive was inseparable from the more altruistic intentions, and as the most graphic instances of violence faded with time, the partisan motive stood out.

The charges that gave rise to *Ex parte Siebold* and *Ex parte Clark* did not stem from outbreaks of intimidation or violence. The officials involved were guilty of election fraud and stuffing the ballot box—activities as common in American politics as they are unsavory. The issue before the Court was whether the Enforcement Acts were a legitimate exercise of federal power. It really was not a difficult question. Article 1, section 4 of the Constitution provides that the decision of time, place, and manner of holding elections for U.S. senators and representatives rests with the states, but the same section expressly gives Congress the power to alter the state regulations. The federal laws under which Siebold and Clark were charged applied only to congressional elections. Admitting that regulation of House elections was within Congress' power, Siebold's attorney Bradley T. Johnson tried unsuccessfully to convince the Court that Congress had not implemented it properly. The regulatory power was an all-or-nothing proposition, he argued. Partial regulation of elections would interfere with regulation by the state and cause confusion. Congress had to run the elections completely or leave the states to their own devices. To this argument Justice Bradley curtly replied, "We are unable to see why it necessarily follows that, if Congress makes *any* regulations on the subject, it must assume exclusive control of the *whole* subject. The Constitution does not say so."[62]

If this first argument seems labored from a twentieth-century perspective, the second seems contrived and technical. To Democrats, southerners, and states' rights advocates in 1880, however, the issue was very real. And it provided Justice Stephen Field with an effective soap box. States' rights advocates were outraged that Congress neither passed an election law nor expressly adopted the state election laws. As they saw it, Congress had simply provided for federal enforcement of state laws. The Court's decision, they complained, had allowed Congress to define a new crime against the United States—the crime of disobeying a state law.[63]

Field agreed. Dissenting from the majority in both *Siebold* and *Clark* he argued that Congress had "asserted a power inconsistent with and destructive of the independence of the states."[64] Field's nineteen-page opinion warned that such a power would place every state under the control and dominion of the general government, even in the administration of its internal concerns. It would give the federal government the power to strip the states of the right to try in their own courts a violator of their laws and to punish a judicial officer of the state for the manner in which he discharged his duties. This approach represented a monumental change in our fundamental theory of government, Field continued. It was not a change contemplated by the Framers or by the people who had advocated the Civil War amendments or the states that had adopted them.[65] More than a legal opinion, Field's dissent was an impassioned play to a states' rights audience.

It played well. "Who made Congress a judge and a ruler over us?" asked the *Washington Post*. Under the approving headlines "JUDGE FIELD'S WARNING" and "An Absurd and Unconstitutional Law Dissected," the *Post* reprinted the dissent in full.[66] Other newspapers, especially in southern and border states, highlighted Field's opinion. The *New Orleans Times-Picayune* described it as "especially able." The *Cincinnati Enquirer* featured Field in a two-column piece covering "Clark's case." Two days later it echoed Field's states' rights complaint with a warning that "when the judiciary, the Supreme Court of the United States, surrenders to an heresy that seems to be all-pervading, and that is subversive of the letter and spirit of the Constitution, the friends of the Republic may well ask each other if they must begin to number its days." Field would not be a party to this destruction of the republic, the *Enquirer* concluded.[67]

These reactions to *Siebold* and *Clark* may have been exaggerated, but they were not fabricated. Advocates of states' rights truly believed these enforcement statutes intruded on state authority. More important, Democrats understood that these statutes were designed in part to protect Republican control of Congress.[68] The cases gave Field a timely opportunity to capitalize on these reactions. Another group of three cases decided just a few days earlier provided him even more opportunity to gain southern support.

State Action

Strauder v. West Virginia, Virginia v. Rives, and *Ex parte Virginia* involved state policies that excluded blacks from jury service. All of the cases occurred in March 1880, thus providing a timely opportunity for the Field campaign to appeal to local prejudice. Additionally, they provided a convenient target in the person of U.S. district court judge Alexander Rives.

In *Strauder v. West Virginia,* the first and most famous of this line of cases, a black man was tried and convicted of murder in the state court.[69] Before the trial began, Strauder petitioned that his case be removed to the federal court under a federal removal law, section 641 of the Revised Federal Statutes. Section 641 allowed removal of any case "against any person who is denied, or cannot enforce, in the judicial tribunals of the state . . . any right secured to him by any law providing for the equal civil rights of citizens of the United States or of all persons within the jurisdiction of the United States."[70] The equal right Strauder claimed to have been denied was a right to trial by jury impaneled without discrimination against his race. West Virginia law expressly limited jury service to "white male persons who are twenty-one years of age."[71]

If the state judge had granted the petition for removal, Strauder would have been tried in the federal court. Instead, he was tried and convicted in the state court. His only route to the federal court system was through the more arduous process of appeal. He would be required to appeal through the state appellate court system. Then, if his conviction was upheld and he could show that he had been denied rights to which he was entitled under the Constitution and laws of the United States, he could appeal to the U.S. Supreme Court. This course of events is exactly what happened, and the Supreme Court accepted Strauder's case.

Writing for the majority, Justice William Strong had little difficulty finding that the West Virginia statute was a denial of equal protection. That such a law constituted the type of discrimination prohibited by the Fourteenth Amendment "ought not to be doubted," he said. "Nor would it be if the persons excluded by it were white men." For him, the exclusion of blacks from jury duty amounted to an assertion of inferiority. It stimulated race prejudice and thus was "an impediment to securing to individuals of the race that equal justice which the law aims to secure to all others."[72]

Nor did Strong find much difficulty in deciding the removal law was within Congress' power. That issue had already been decided in *Tennessee v. Davis,* another decision he wrote on the same day, in which Strong addressed the claim that the removal law violated state sovereignty. "On the contrary," he replied, "a denial of the right of the general government to remove them, to take charge of and try any case arising under the Constitution or laws of the United States, is a denial of the conceded sovereignty of that government over a subject expressly committed to it."[73] In *Strauder,* as in *Tennessee v. Davis,* the power of Congress to authorize removal of criminal cases from state courts to the federal courts was upheld.

Read alone, the *Strauder* case seemed to promise that juries would be chosen without regard to race and seemed to indicate that the Court was inclined to take a broad view of the equal protection guarantee of the Fourteenth Amendment.[74] But the promise of *Strauder v. West Virginia* was short-lived. It began to lose its way on the day it was decided, when the Court delivered its opinions in the other two cases involving exclusion of blacks from jury service. *Virginia v. Rives* also stemmed from the trial of a black man, in this case two black men, for the murder of a white man.[75] Once again the jury was all white. Once again the accused petitioned for removal of their case to the federal court. The difference in the *Rives* case was that Virginia law did not expressly exclude blacks from jury service. Blacks were technically eligible, but the jury panels were actually chosen by county judges, and the defendants claimed that no one of their race had ever been allowed to serve.

Justice Strong, once again writing for the majority, avoided the question of whether this type of de facto discrimination was prohibited by the Fourteenth Amendment. But in a quick step backward from *Strauder,* he ruled that de facto discrimination did not trigger the removal right provided by federal statute. The statute provided for that right when persons could not enforce their equal rights in the state court, he reasoned. Since the county judge, not Virginia law, was the source of the racial discrimination, the defendants had an adequate state remedy. If they were not satisfied that the trial court had properly applied state law, they could appeal to higher state courts. And when they had exhausted their remedies in the state courts, they then might have a right to appeal to the U.S. Supreme Court.

There was technically another remedy available for blacks who had been convicted by an all-white jury. Continuing racial discrimination might give rise to criminal charges against the offending state official for violation of the Civil Rights Act of 1875. That was the issue in the third jury exclusion case, *Ex parte Virginia*. In this case Justice Strong upheld the conviction of Pittsylvania County judge J. D. Coles for systematically excluding black citizens from the jury list.[76]

Cold logic permeated these decisions. In a very technical sense they recognized a right and provided a remedy for varied acts of discrimination. But if one looks at them from the point of view of the people most directly affected, the recently freed black citizens, the remedy is so obviously defective that the right is almost nonexistent. To southern blacks, the enforcement, removal, and civil rights statutes represented a search for help from the federal government—what Eric Foner has called the power from without—to battle what they perceived to be entrenched local privilege.[77] The practical impact of the jury exclusion cases was to throw their legislative success back in their faces.

Ineffectiveness notwithstanding, Field dissented in *Strauder*, wrote a stinging dissent in *Ex parte Virginia,* and wrote a long separate opinion in *Rives.* His opinions argued forcefully against the constitutionality of the removal and enforcement statutes. Adopting a states' rights posture, he maintained that these statutes represented an unauthorized increase in the power of federal courts and an unwarranted federal interference with the states' authority to enforce their own criminal laws. He also used the cases to discuss the nature of civil rights and to develop the "state action" doctrine.

The idea of prosecuting criminal cases in the federal courts may not seem especially controversial to today's reader, who is accustomed to seeing mobsters prosecuted in federal courts on racketeering charges, murderers on conspiracy charges, abusive officials for civil rights violations, or cheats for mail fraud. In the 1870s, however, enforcement of criminal law was very much the province of the states. The Reconstruction Era removal acts rested on the assumption that prejudice might make it impossible for an individual to secure a fair trial in state courts. Removal of cases from the state to the federal courts was not unheard of, but before the Civil War, removal resulted primarily from diversity suits (civil suits involving parties from more than one state) and from cases involving customs and taxes.[78]

A states' rights tradition had thrived in the United States since the founding of the republic. The adherents to this tradition, who were testy with respect to any hint of encroachment on state authority, were always wary of the federal judiciary. Jefferson's followers, for example, proposed to weaken the authority of the U.S. Supreme Court and to dismantle lower federal courts. Taking the view that the Constitution was little more than a compact among the states, states' rights advocates often opposed the idea of judicial review in general. More specifically, they claimed that the federal courts did not have the power to review the constitutionality of state laws or of state court interpretations of the Constitution.[79] Although not limited to the South, the early tradition had strong southern and distinctly Virginian roots. It continued with Andrew Jackson, whose concern for states' rights and opposition to the federal judiciary came together in his 1832 veto of the Bank of the United States.[80] It was true that southerners were not averse to using the power of the federal courts to advance their causes. In 1855, for example, southern congressmen wanted federal courts to enforce fugitive slave laws.[81] But the particular expansion of judicial power that came into play in the jury exclusion cases was clearly aimed at the South. Thus, the states' rights tradition combined with circumstances to give Field a cause.

If the removal statute tested in *Rives* was not sufficient to raise southern ire certainly the circumstance of *Ex parte Virginia* was. By making those state officials who were responsible for selecting jurors—in this case county judges—liable under federal law, Congress essentially placed those officials under the supervision of the federal government. At least that was Field's view. "Nothing," he wrote, "could have a greater tendency to destroy the independence and autonomy of the States; reduce them to a humiliating and degrading dependence upon the central government, engender constant irritation; and destroy that domestic tranquillity which was one of the objects of the Constitution to insure."[82]

Where would it stop, Field asked; if blacks could demand representation on juries, why could not Chinese, or even more shockingly, women? If the federal government could interfere with a state's method of selecting jurors, it could also require conformity in the method of selecting judges. If it could so supervise the judicial branch of state government, it could interfere with the legislative and executive as well. In the end, Field warned, the state would sink to the level of a mere municipal corporation.[83]

Field's dissents culminated in a short, simplistic, yet eloquent essay on government. "The government created by the Constitution was not designed for the regulation of matters of purely local concern," he wrote. "The States required no aid from any external authority to manage their

domestic affairs." That the central government was created chiefly for matters of a general character, he reasoned, "is shown as much by the history
of its formation as by the express language of the Constitution."[84] For Field,
the Civil War amendments did not affect this balance. The Thirteenth,
Fourteenth, and Fifteenth Amendments did not make a change so radical in
the relation between federal and state authorities, he said. "The people in
adopting them did not suppose they were altering the fundamental theory
of their dual system of governments."[85]

Once again, Field's warning of centralization, his parade of horribles,
and his essay on government played well in the Democratic press. "MANIKIN
STATES" cried the headline of the *Washington Post,* which printed Field's
Ex parte Virginia dissent in full, as did other papers.[86] Throughout most of
March, newspapers carried articles and editorials that quoted liberally and
approvingly from his dissent. Linking Field's opinions to the states' rights
thinking of Thomas Jefferson, the *Post* described them as "like a bugle blast
of the Monticello statesman."[87] Others did not hesitate to connect them
to the upcoming election. "Democrats are delighted with the able and exhaustive opinions of Justices Field and Clifford," wrote the *Richmond State.*
"Several of the ablest lawyers in Congress tell me it sounds like the key-note
for the Democrats in the next presidential campaign and will give Judge
Field a tremendous boom for the presidency."[88]

Republican papers were less complimentary. Commenting on the cases,
the *New York Times* wrote, "If there were any suspicions of personal or
partisan bias it might most readily attach to the Justice who aspires to a
nomination for the Presidency, and whose judgment might unconsciously be
swayed by his ambition." Other Republican papers added that if the Democrats thought they could help their case, they should "accept Judge Field's
opinion as their platform in the coming campaign and go before the country on it." Nationwide reaction of the press indicated that the jury exclusion
cases received much attention. With his separate opinions, Field helped his
cause considerably in the South.[89]

Southern hostility toward the federal judiciary as a whole gave Field's
opinion a general appeal in that part of the country. Hostility toward the
federal judge who first ruled on the jury exclusion turned the episode
into an especially effective organizing tool in Virginia. *Virginia v. Rives* involved U.S. district judge Alexander Rives, who was old-stock Virginian.
His grandfather had been an officer in the Revolution, his father one of
the most wealthy and eminent merchants in the state. His older brother
William Cabell Rives had studied law under Jefferson and served as minister to France and as a U.S. senator before joining the Confederacy and serv-

ing in the Confederate Congress. In contrast, Alexander Rives might have seemed something of a disappointment to his neighbors in the Virginia Piedmont region. He bitterly opposed secession and, after the war, aligned first with the Conservative party and then with the Republicans. It was a Republican, President Grant, who appointed Rives to the federal court.[90]

Judge Rives began to attract attention in 1878 when he told a federal grand jury that state judges who systematically excluded blacks from jury service would be criminally liable for violations of the Civil Rights Act of 1875.[91] When Rives granted removal of the murder case against Lee and Burwell Reynolds, in effect ruling that Virginia's method of selecting jurors violated the Reynolds brothers' civil rights, it seemed that most of the white population of the state turned against the judge. In an extraordinary display of official animosity, the Virginia General Assembly passed a resolution censuring Rives and charging him with assumption and usurpation of judicial powers. As if to demonstrate solidarity, Virginia's Senator Edmunds and Congressman Cabell introduced similar resolutions in Washington.[92]

The Field campaign played on local animosity toward Judge Rives as it tried to secure Virginia as the first southern state to fall in line for their candidate. No sooner had Field's opinions been published than William Royall of the *Richmond Dispatch* went to work to capture the state's delegation. Although the outcome of his efforts were vague, Royall boldly declared victory at every opportunity. "Justice Field wins over the vote in Virginia," declared a March release from the *Dispatch*. The intention of the Field campaign was to create a self-feeding snowball. Claiming victory in Virginia, they hoped, would draw support in other southern states. Demonstrating support in those other states would in turn produce victory in Virginia. Thus even small victories were inflated. When Royall claimed that forty-eight of Richmond's seventy delegates to the state convention were for Field, for example, a New Orleans newspaper carried a front-page headline, "Field's Strength in Virginia."[93]

The problem with the plan was that the snowball was feeding mostly on air. Even the claim of victory in the city of Richmond was weak. A rival newspaper conducted a count of its own and concluded that "Richmond did not yesterday go for Judge Field by a two-thirds majority or by any other majority." A Tilden supporter who concurred that there was no particular preference for Field reported that "the dispatches sent from Richmond by L. Q. Washington were simply a falsehood. Field has no following except to the extent of the Commonwealth newspaper recently established by W. L. Royall (who I know well) and who in my opinion is the paid agent of Field's friends in Washington." In March the *Richmond State* had lauded

Field's opinions, but by late May it called his candidacy "little more than a joke." Despite these claims to the contrary, however, Field supporters continued until the first ballot of the national convention to count Virginia in their corner. As the campaign moved into June, Field's literary bureau also claimed Alabama, Tennessee, and Arkansas.[94]

Field's 1880 opinions definitely were intended to provide a boost to his political campaign. Whether they were merely a political expedient or part of a broader theory of jurisprudence is clouded by inconsistencies in his voting on similar issues. The enforcement and removal laws represented only one aspect of a broad expansion of the federal judiciary's power following the Civil War.[95] In the March 1880 cases, Field fostered the impression that he was not willing to join in that expansion, or to exalt federal judicial power against the states.[96] Yet he did not always vote that way. Both before and after 1880 he could be found voting in favor of the removal power, albeit in different circumstances. In an 1872 diversity case he wrote that the constitutionality of a removal law—the Prejudice and Local Influence Act of 1867—"can not be seriously questioned."[97] He also voted with the majority to expand the removal law in the 1885 *Pacific Railroad Removal Cases*.[98]

Furthermore, even his opinions in the jury exclusion cases of 1880 did not register disapproval of every form of expansion of federal judicial power. He disapproved only of expanding the *original jurisdiction* of the *lower* federal courts; these cases could still be appealed to the U.S. Supreme Court after they had run their course in the state judiciary. By insisting on a limited view of original jurisdiction for the lower federal courts and by allowing cases into federal court only on appeal, Field conveniently kept the power to review state legislation in his forum. Field argued in *Virginia v. Rives* that this was a matter of respect for state sovereignty built into the Constitution.[99] But in cases coming out of his own Ninth Circuit, Field seemed to have misplaced his respect for state sovereignty. Interference by lower federal courts in the policymaking of the western states became so great that by 1884 it was the object of a campaign against what *American Law Review* editor Seymour Thompson called "the law of the Ninth Circuit." The leading characteristic of this new law, Thompson complained, was unwarrantable enlargement of federal jurisdiction, the erection of general and irresponsible superintendency over the regulation of the states and over administration of their criminal laws.[100] Thompson's complaint about the Ninth Circuit echoed precisely Field's opinions in the jury exclusion cases. Nevertheless, there is little doubt that Field, the highest judicial officer in the Ninth Circuit, led the expansion of judicial power there.

It is tempting to attribute Field's apparent inconsistency regarding the use and extent of federal authority to nothing more than a grasp for power. That certainly would seem to fit his personality. Of course, nothing is quite that simple in law. An added element affecting Field's attitude was the nature of the right being claimed in any given dispute. He made this clear in *Virginia v. Rives* and *Ex parte Virginia*. The Thirteenth, Fourteenth, and Fifteenth Amendments gave Congress authority to pass legislation to protect civil rights, he would admit. But in his opinion selection for jury duty was not a civil right. It was a political right, and that category of rights, along with another class called social rights, was not protected by the Civil War amendments. A key, then, to finding some consistency in Field's view might be discovered by looking for a definition of civil rights.

Historians have made a number of attempts. Some say Field had in mind primarily economic liberties and property related rights.[101] Others maintain that Field's definition tracked the arguments of the Democratic and conservative Republican members of Congress who argued that the Fourteenth Amendment embodied the limited set of enumerated rights set forth in the Civil Rights Act of 1865.[102] Finally, it has been said that Field's concept of civil rights reflected a Jacksonian-inspired tradition of liberty.[103] A good argument can be made for any of these views, but in the jury exclusion cases, at least, Field did not say any of these things.

To be sure, Field gave examples of what he meant by civil rights. Borrowing a theme from his *Slaughter-House* dissent, he noted that the Thirteenth Amendment was intended to guarantee to every person a right to follow the ordinary pursuits of life without restrictions, other than are applied to all others, and to enjoy equally with them the earnings of his labor.[104] He finds in the Fourteenth Amendment procedural guarantees against arbitrary deprivation of life, liberty, and arbitrary spoliation of property.[105] That amendment, he said, also requires that the same rules of evidence and modes of judicial procedure be applied to all.[106] Regarding criminal law, he finds a guarantee that there shall be no different or greater punishment imposed for crimes.[107] Finally, he identifies substantive guarantees to make contracts, be a witness, acquire property, and pursue happiness.[108] But Field makes only one stab at a comprehensive definition. "Much confusion has arisen from the failure to distinguish between the civil and political rights of citizens," he notes in *Ex parte Virginia*. Then, as if to end the confusion, he continues:

Civil rights are absolute and personal. Political rights, on the other hand, are conditioned and dependent upon the discretion of the elective or appointing power, whether that be by the people acting through the ballot, or one of the departments of their government. The civil rights of the individual are never to be withheld, and may always be judicially enforced. The political rights he may enjoy, such as holding office and discharging a public trust, are qualified because their possession depends on his fitness, to be adjudged by those with whom society has clothed with the elective authority.[109]

What a careful reader finds in this statement is a system in which rights are defined as civil rights because they are absolute and that maintains that rights are absolute because they are civil rights. It is as circular and open-ended a concept as could be imagined.

Its open-endedness is dramatically apparent in the facts of *Virginia v. Rives.* The events leading to the trial of Lee and Burwell Reynolds for murdering Aaron Shelton began as a racially tinged conflict among schoolchildren. The incident started on a Tuesday, when Shelton's thirteen-year-old brother shouted epithets as he passed the county's black school. Some of the black students chased and caught young Shelton and "gave him a ducking." Seventeen-year-old Lee Reynolds, one of the accused brothers, was apparently among them. Later, young Shelton went back to the school, yelled again, and then ran off. The black students chased him again, but this time they ran into his twenty-three-year-old brother Aaron Shelton and his uncle, Asa Tuggle. Cussing the students, Aaron Shelton blamed Lee Reynolds for the dunking and threatened to get even.

On the evening of the same day, the bad blood shifted to another location. Driving up a side road near the school, Lee and Burwell Reynolds found their way blocked by a log Aaron Shelton had cut earlier. When they attempted to move it, Shelton came up and threatened to thrash them if they did. After arguments and threats from both sides, the brothers moved on. Two days later, the Reynolds brothers were pulling a slide up the same road. Burwell was driving; Lee walked in front carrying a gun and a stick. When they moved another log blocking the road, Asa Tuggle appeared and said, "Now boys you have moved that log and you must take the results." Shelton then drove up in his wagon. What happened next, as might be expected, was disputed. But Aaron Shelton's dying declaration captures the moment:

Lee Reynolds came up and I said to him, "I suppose you have threatened to take my life with that stick and gun?" and he said that he would kill me if I did not run; and if I ran that he would make his two dogs, then with him, catch me. I said to him, "Look here boy: do you know who you are talking to?" I was sitting on the wagon at this time. Just as I got off the wagon he cocked his gun, and I stepped up to him as quick as I could and jerked the stick from him and knocked him over the log we were going to load on the wagon. Just as he fell Burwell Reynolds ran up and stabbed me with a large knife in the back.

HIS

Aaron C.　×　Shelton

MARK[110]

History has left little evidence to indicate the kind of young men the Reynolds brothers were, whether they were hardworking and honest or the sort that looks for trouble. But we do know that they were caught up in an incident involving racial conflict, threats, intimidation, and finally death. Under the circumstances they had some cause to believe that as black men charged with murdering a white man they could not receive an impartial trial before a jury composed exclusively of whites.[111]

Fair process is what the Reynolds brothers sought, not the right to sit on a jury. If Stephen Field had been willing to look at the case from that perspective he would have seen that it fit cleanly into even his own narrow concept of civil rights. Field's own reasoning in *Ex parte Virginia* was that the equal protection clause of the Fourteenth Amendment "opens the courts of the country to every one, on the same terms, for the security of his person and property."[112] In terms of practical result, he was willing in *Rives* to compel a black man to stand trial before a jury from which his race had been systematically excluded.[113] In order to reach that result, Field conveniently had to miss the point that the *Rives* case was about fair process. He focused instead on an abstract right to participate in government. Choosing to ignore the realities of the case, Field, a champion of substantive due process, took a very narrow view of what the guarantee of fair procedure required in this case.

Open-ended though it might have been, Field's concept of civil rights had a particular leaning that reflected the grand debates of the time. One issue in these debates focused on the extent to which the Thirteenth, Fourteenth, and Fifteenth Amendments were intended to raise the former slaves to a level of equality with whites. In the jury exclusion cases the differences in opinion between Justices Strong and Field regarding this issue were unmistakable. "One great purpose of these [Civil War] amendments," wrote Strong, "was to raise the colored race from that condition of inferiority and servitude in which most of them had previously stood, into *perfect equality* of civil rights with all other persons within the jurisdiction of the States."[114]

If Strong meant that the goal of the amendments was to achieve total racial equality, that is not at all what Field envisioned by the term civil rights.
For him, the concept emphasized liberty rather than equality. Field believed
that the Civil War amendments simply enfranchised the former slaves with
a limited set of absolute rights—rights that were a necessary part of liberty.
These rights were derived primarily from natural law and consequently
were possessed equally by every person.[115] The amendments offered no further guarantee of equality.

A corollary to this line of thinking was that the Civil War amendments
guaranteed these rights only against the threat coming from government.
"There are many ways in which a person may be denied his rights," Field
observed. The denial may arise from government, and it may arise from
popular prejudice, passions, or excitement. Religious animosities, political
controversies, antagonisms of race, and a multitude of other causes will always operate to a greater or lesser degree, as impediments to the full enforcement of civil rights. With respect to the obstacles to the full enjoyment
of rights arising from these nongovernment sources, he continued, "persons
of the colored race must take their chances of removing or providing against
them with the rest of the community."[116] Never mind that social or economic forces might dispossess a significant number of people of these rights.
A crucial part of Field's notion of limited rights was that the law on this
constitutional plane protected individuals against government only.

The theory of the nature of civil rights to which Field subscribed meshed
rather neatly with the states' rights tradition to which he had aligned himself in the jury exclusion cases. They combined to form a legal guideline
that became known as the state action doctrine, the meaning of which was
the most conspicuous issue in *Virginia v. Rives.* In contrast to *Strauder,*
the exclusion of black jurors in *Rives* was not written into state law. It resulted from the way an otherwise satisfactory law was implemented. That
outcome raised a question of whether the Fourteenth Amendment imposed
on the states any positive duty to protect individual rights. District court
judge Rives delivered the argument that it did. The Fourteenth Amendment
guarantees that no state shall deny to any person within its jurisdiction the
equal protection of laws, Rives observed. "It matters not whether it be done
by the state by commission or omission, by law or want of law, by administration of its executive or judicial departments, the mischief is equal and
the remedy much needed."[117] Field disagreed. Emphasizing the prohibitory
language *no state shall* abridge privileges and immunities, deprive any person of life, liberty, or property without due process, or deny to any person
equal protection of the law, he maintained that the Fourteenth Amendment

was proscriptive only. It did not impose on the states any duty to guarantee rights; it simply prohibited states from passing and enforcing laws that were designed to accomplish the ends forbidden by the amendment.[118] In this respect, his opinion echoed the position Democratic members of Congress took in debates surrounding the enactment of the Fourteenth Amendment and other Reconstruction legislation.[119]

Field took the state action doctrine further than he had to in *Rives*. It certainly would not have been unreasonable to maintain that the actions of the county judge—an agent of the state—constituted state action in this instance. But Field would hear nothing of it. When an officer of the state "exercises power with which he is not invested by law, and does unauthorized acts," he observed, "the State is not responsible for them."[120] In other words, informal acts by the state's agent would not be enough to impute state action. In this instance, Field was simply not willing to look beyond the language of the statute to see its true impact.

The Court's majority in the jury exclusion cases did not disagree with Field that the Fourteenth Amendment applied to state action only.[121] They did disagree about—more precisely they were unclear about—the meaning of the phrase "state action."[122] But only three years later, in the *Civil Rights Cases,* the majority adopted Field's stance on state action. Overruling a provision of the Civil Rights Act of 1875 that provided equal access to inns, theaters, and public conveyances, it reasoned that only state action of a particular character was prohibited by the Fourteenth Amendment: "Individual invasion of individual rights is not the subject matter of the amendment."[123]

Historians have pointed out that judicial application of the state action doctrine did not produce a straight line of opinions.[124] State action, they say, was part of a complex interplay of social, political, and economic demands—a subtle dialectic—that changed as the nation adjusted to emancipation.[125] One of those complex considerations was an inherent tension between a desire to guarantee freedom for the former slaves and to preserve traditional notions of federalism.[126]

For Field, however, the subject was uncomplicated. To him the state action doctrine was not primarily a matter of federalism. Nothing could have been more fatal to his vision of liberty—a vision that saw government alone as the threat to individual liberty—than using government to protect rights against the acts of private individuals. *lib + anti-gov*

Although Field used the jury exclusion cases as a platform to gain southern support, it is doubtful that he altered his views to fit the cases into his presidential campaign plans. His opinions may have been written with more spirit than would have otherwise been the case, however. They thus provide a candid look into Field's political philosophy, specifically into what the concept of liberty meant to him. At the very minimum it meant not freedom to participate in the governance of society but rather freedom from governance. Even more, Field's opinions reflected a radical form of individualism that refused to recognize that government was not the only source of threats to liberty and that rejected demands for government to protect liberty against other private threats. For Field, the state action doctrine was more than a legal rule. It represented a fundamental part of his thinking about liberty, privilege, and civil rights.

Field's campaign literature tried to fit him into a tradition of states' rights that ran from Jefferson through Jackson. It was a tradition not only jealous of federal intrusions on state power but also particularly wary of the federal judiciary's involvement in state affairs. Field's opinions in the cases relating to his southern strategy conformed well to that tradition. But another prong of his campaign promised he would sweep the West. The cases there that would have an impact on the election involved discriminatory legislation against Chinese and business regulation. When Field moved into these subjects, a states' rights posture did not always yield the result he wanted. And when it did not, his allegiance to the tradition disintegrated.

7

THE PACIFIC CLUB SET

name for rr s.h. who supported friends w/ Field

The whole Pacific Coast was enthusiastic for Field, reported several Democratic papers. "Judge Field can carry California by ten thousand majority against any candidate the Republicans can name." "California is Democratic when the party is united, and it will be united with a will on Field." That is what the Field campaign wanted delegates to the national convention to believe. If true, it would remedy one weakness the Democrats had displayed in the 1876 presidential contest, when they had lost California by a narrow margin.[1]

From appearances, Field seemed to be a natural to place a lock on the western vote. Campaign literature described him as "the most Western of Western men." He was, after all, occupant of the most prestigious national office any westerner had obtained. He also had some history of success in California politics, having been elected to the state legislature and state supreme court. In 1857, the year of the famous battle between Gwin and Broderick, he had also been in the running for election to the U.S. Senate.[2] California Democrats also showed their support for Field in 1868 by nominating him as a favorite-son candidate at the national convention.[3]

The boasts of Field's literary bureau that the West was solidly behind its candidate seemed to have some effect. In early May a Bayard supporter predicted that Field was likely to get the twelve votes from California and the six from Oregon.[4] But some political insiders realized that making good on these promises would be difficult for Field. Its ink laced with sarcasm, the *New York Times* appraised his chances. "It is thought that the warm, magnetic, and jovial manner of Mr. Justice Field, and his judicial decisions upsetting the anti-Chinese legislation of the Pacific States would carry his nomination and election like wildfire through California, Oregon, Nevada, and Colorado. It does not matter that those states are naturally Republican, and that Democrats gnash their teeth at the mere mention of the name FIELD."[5] California journalist James O'Meara concurred. As early as December 1879 he advised Tilden's forces in the East that "Field has no chance in California."[6]

In truth, Field's claim to have the West in his pocket glossed over the complexities of California politics. California in 1880 was no longer the frontier in which Field had won political office. Explorers and prospectors were replaced by laborers and farmers. With completion of the transcontinental railroad in 1869 the state's urban centers grew in culture as well as in size, and markets opened for its produce. Completion of the railroad also dumped thousands of unemployed workers into the market and made the state more susceptible to a nationwide depression that began in 1873 and lasted for the remainder of the decade. Drought in 1877 intensified the hardships experienced by some Californians. Throughout the decade, economic grievances dominated the political scene. Much of the dissatisfaction—labeled "antimonopoly"—was aimed at the Central Pacific Railroad. But it spilled over into a hatred of Chinese immigrant labor. The railroad, once a symbol of growth and prosperity, became a symbol of oppression. The Chinese, who were already the target of prejudice, became despised, both as a competitor and as a reflection of the future of the labor force.

Much of this early antimonopoly sentiment found a place among the Democrats, splitting the party into two bitterly opposed factions. With the formation of the Workingmen's party in 1877, however, anti-Chinese and antirailroad feelings developed into its own political movement. Led by the incendiary Denis Kearney, the new party quickly became a force on the California political scene. In 1878 it elected one-third of the delegates to a convention that had been called to revise the state's constitution.[7] In state-wide elections a year later Workingmen elected six justices to the supreme court, one railroad commissioner, eleven state senators, and sixteen assemblymen.[8] Possibly of even more significance, Workingmen elected most municipal officials of San Francisco, including their mayoral candidate Isaac S. Kalloch.[9]

Workingmen's success came primarily at the expense of the Democrats. Kalloch's election virtually demolished the Democratic organization in San Francisco. In the 1879 gubernatorial election Democrats won only 30 percent of the vote, an outcome that stood in stark contrast to the prior election in which they had polled 50 percent. Republicans won most state offices. Even worse for the Democrats, Workingmen won more seats than the former did in the legislature. Establishment of a fourth party, the New Constitution party, drew from the Democratic ranks as well. By 1879 Democratic fortunes had sunk so low that they nominated for governor Hugh J. Glenn, who was already the candidate of the New Constitution party.[10]

The swell of public opinion in California was undoubtedly running against politicians who, like Field, called themselves conservatives and tended to support the state's major business enterprises. Within the Democratic party that remained after the split, however, the success of the anti-monopoly movement may have offered an opportunity for conservatives to take control. Those Democrats who bolted to the Workingmen's party or the New Constitution party were drawn from the antimonopoly ranks. Given the absence of some of their rivals, Field's supporters may have felt confident as 1880 began that they could control the county and state nominating conventions. Conservatives might be able to capture the remaining party loyalists, even as they appeared to be losing support among the population as a whole.

If that was indeed their plan, events of the year set them off course. In a February 1880 election of the San Francisco Board of Supervisors, the Democrats and Republicans joining as a fusion ticket soundly defeated the Workingmen.[11] Mayor Kalloch's popularity began to slip as he became involved in a feud with *San Francisco Chronicle* editor Michael DeYoung. The feud ended when Kalloch's son killed DeYoung. The new Board of Supervisors attempted several times to impeach Kalloch. Although he survived the impeachment attempts, his political career ended after one term in office. The statewide Workingmen's party, which started to chafe under the leadership of Denis Kearney, began to fall apart. The New Constitution party disbanded after the constitution was ratified. The effect of these developments was that absent Democrats began returning to the party. Thus, one historian writes that the nomination convention held in May 1880 was an occasion favorable to conciliation of recalcitrant members.[12] That might have been so, but the recalcitrant members brought along the antimonopoly spirit that had led to the success of the Workingmen's party. Their return intensified a rift that already existed.

That antimonopoly spirit was prevalent in the premier political event of the period, the California Constitutional Convention of 1878–1879. Despite their amazing success in electing delegates to the convention, Workingmen made up only one-third of the delegates. Alone, they were far from being a majority, but Workingmen acting in concert with delegates from the agrarian districts possessed the ability to control the convention. Some contemporary observers and historians believe that the Workingmen and farmers failed to take advantage of their strength. With that coalition outwitted by wily lawyer-delegates of a conservative stripe, they conclude, the constitutional convention actually produced a rather conservative document.[13] It may be that, when the smoke cleared, Workingmen had failed to accomplish all the goals they had hoped for at the convention. Nevertheless, there is little doubt that an antimonopolist agenda, with a focus on Chinese, corporations, and tax reform, dominated the proceedings. The constitution, ratified on May 7, 1879, clearly reflected the demands of dissatisfied laborers and farmers.[14]

The Chinese

An early order of business of the constitutional convention was to appoint a standing committee on the Chinese. There is some question about the extent to which the convention was committed to the anti-Chinese movement. One historian maintains that "able lawyers who were the employees of corporations such as the railroads, which had prospered through the employment of cheap Chinese labor, saw the situation as much less of an evil, and were in no great hurry to remedy it."[15] But another points out that only one delegate came out boldly in defense of Chinese immigration.[16] Furthermore, the delegates enthusiastically supported two anti-Chinese propositions. One was a petition asking Congress to take action to halt Chinese immigration. The other was a provision granting the legislature authority to "protect the state and local communities from aliens, vagrants, paupers, mendicants, criminals, and persons afflicted with contagious or infectious diseases, or who might be in any way dangerous to the state, and to provide for their removal from the state in case they refuse to comply."[17] The great support for these provisions indicated that at least publicly the vast majority of delegates agreed that Chinese labor and Chinese immigration were a problem. They disagreed over whether the state or the federal government had the power to remedy it. They also disagreed about solutions and the limits of government power in general. This disagreement would eventually play an important role in Stephen Field's campaign for the presidency.

One option the committee explored was to prohibit all future Chinese immigration into the state. The trouble with this approach was the likelihood that it would run into a wall of unconstitutionality. In the *Passenger Cases* of 1849, a split U.S. Supreme Court ruled that a state's attempt to regulate immigration through landing fees ran afoul of the commerce clause. The Court's ruling implied that under the Constitution the power to restrict immigration was granted exclusively to Congress.[18]

Nothing could have more exasperated anti-Chinese zealots. The court's interpretation of the commerce clause took from them the most direct and effective action they could employ against the Chinese. They complained that the power to prohibit immigration was placed in the hands of the distant federal government and easterners. Those delegates who favored a law excluding Chinese from the state did not give up, however. As N. G. Wayatt, a Workingmen's lawyer, pointed out, the constitutionality of a law could not always be determined in advance.[19] James J. Ayers, a delegate from Los Angeles and editor of the *Los Angeles Express,* also continued to maintain that the power to regulate foreign commerce was not the exclusive province of the federal government. He pointed to an earlier case, *New York v. Miln,* in which the Court upheld state regulations that a shipmaster post a bond for immigrants brought into the city. Such regulations, it held, were passed in the exercise of the normal police power of the states.[20] Besides, Ayers reminded the convention, the *Passenger Cases* were not unanimous. Chief Justice Taney had argued in dissent that the power to determine who is or is not dangerous to the interests and well-being of the state—to decide who should or should not be admitted to reside among its citizens—should lie with the state. Taney worried that if the federal government had the exclusive power over immigration Congress would be able to pass laws giving free blacks from places like the West Indies an absolute right to reside and trade in the southern states in spite of any state law to the contrary.[21] Noting that Ayers had quoted at length from Taney's dissent, another delegate, C. V. Stuart, warned, "I remember when Taney made another decision. Do you know what became of it? I remember the Dred Scott decision, . . . and I remember what that led to, and I think you do too."[22]

Another weakness of Ayers's argument was that the commerce clause was not the only provision of the Constitution that might affect the state's efforts to hinder Chinese immigration. The Supreme Court had recently invalidated a California law that had some of the same characteristics of the statute upheld in *Miln.* The California statute tested in *Chy Lung v. Freeman* allowed the commissioner of immigration to board a vessel, determine if any of its foreign passengers were lunatic, idiotic, deaf, dumb, blind, crippled, infirm, or in any way likely to become a public charge. For these passengers, or any who were convicted criminals or "lewd or debauched women," the commissioner was authorized to require the master of the vessel to post a bond of $500 in gold.[23] Chy Lung, one of a group of twenty-two Chinese women denied entry under the statute, sought a writ of habeas corpus in the state courts. When refused, she appealed to the U.S. Supreme Court.

The ostensible purpose of the statute was to protect the morals and health of the state's population. Prostitution was a problem in Chinatown. Furthermore, it was exacerbated by a shortage of Chinese women, the activities of underworld figures, and police corruption.[24] But prejudice exaggerated this reality to produce a fear that Chinese immigrants carried a particularly dreadful disease. "Chinese syphilis," for example, was said to be more potent, ravaging, and impervious to treatment than the Caucasian variety.[25] For Justice Miller, however, the statute's objectives merely provided a ruse. "It is hardly possible to conceive a statute more skillfully framed, to place in the hands of a single man the power to prevent entirely vessels engaged in a foreign trade, say with China, from carrying passengers, or to compel them to submit to systematic extortion of the grossest kind."[26] This was an exclusion law, Miller concluded. "The passage of laws which concern the admission of citizens and subjects of foreign nations to our shores belongs to Congress, and not to the states."[27] Miller did not mention the Burlingame Treaty with China, but he was expressly concerned that a state had intruded into the national government's power regarding international relations.

Stephen Field agreed. In another case, he more clearly connected California's attempt to exclude Chinese to the federal treaty. The case involved Chy Lung's twenty-one female companions on the voyage, who chose to follow a slightly different legal route. They began their case with a writ of habeas corpus in the Ninth Circuit, where the case came before Field. "The state has a right of self-defense," Field observed in *In re Ah Fong*, but this statute went beyond that right and encroached on the federal government's treatymaking power as well as its power to regulate commerce with foreign nations.[28] Besides, in practice it clearly discriminated against Chinese. It is certainly desirable that prostitution be suppressed, wrote Field, "but I have little respect for that discriminating virtue which is shocked when a frail child of China is landed on our shores, and yet allows the bedizened and painted harlot of other countries to parade our streets and open her hells in broad day, without molestation and without censure."[29]

Using the opportunity to lecture anyone who might chance to read his opinion, Field attempted to explain his position on the Chinese problem, parts of which he would repeat as the campaign for his party's presidential nomination progressed.

I am aware of the very general feeling prevailing in this State against the Chinese, and in opposition to the extension of any encouragement to their immigration hither. It is felt that the dissimilarities in physical characteristics, in language, in manners, religion and habits, will always prevent any possible assimilation of them with our people. Admitting that there is ground for this feeling, it does not justify any legislation for their exclusion, which might not be adopted against the inhabitants of the most favored nations of the Caucasian race, and of Christian faith. If their further immigration is to be stopped, recourse must be had to the federal government, where the whole power over this subject lies.[30]

Field may have believed he could convince fellow westerners of the logic of his position, but it was unlikely to endear him to the fervent anti-Chinese element in his home state.

Ah Fong and *Chy Lung* did not foreclose the possibilities for legislation discriminating against Chinese. Justices Field and Miller stated only that they would not allow states to completely prohibit immigration through laws dressed in the guise of legitimate regulations. The cases did not place any new limits on the police power of the states, a power that, according to Field, embraced regulations affecting health, good order, morals, peace, and public safety.[31] Both justices simply had concluded that the California law went beyond the scope of measures necessary and appropriate for those purposes and thus crossed into the federal sphere of authority.[32]

These decisions may have had an effect on the constitutional convention, for ultimately the delegates rejected the proposal to prohibit all further immigration of Chinese into the state.[33] Other proposals that would have barred Chinese from suing and being sued, fishing in public waters, and receiving licenses to carry on certain businesses were defeated as well.[34] But the convention delegates did adopt a number of anti-Chinese provisions that, presumably, they believed fell more squarely within the state's police power.

Four of these provisions became Article 19 of the new constitution. Section 1 empowered the legislature to pass regulations for the protection of the state from the "burdens and evils arising from the presence of aliens who are or may become vagrants, paupers, mendicants, criminals, . . . or invalids afflicted with contagious or infectious disease." Section 2 forbade corporations formed under the laws of the state from employing Chinese in any capacity.[35] Section 3 prohibited employment of Chinese in public works. Section 4 appeared to be primarily a statement of anti-Chinese feelings, declaring the presence of "foreigners ineligible to become citizens" dangerous and directing the legislature to do all within its power to discourage immigration. Calling "Asiatic coolieism" a form of human slavery, it further declared all contracts for coolie labor void and directed the legislature to provide punishment for companies importing such labor. It also delegated to municipalities the power to remove Chinese or limit their presence to certain areas in the city.[36] Two other provisions of the new constitution resulted in significant discrimination against Chinese. Article 1, Section 17 conspicuously omitted Chinese from a guarantee that gave foreigners of the white race or of African descent the same property rights as native born citizens. Finally, Article 2, section 1 listed natives of China along with idiots, insane persons, and persons convicted of infamous crimes among those individuals who would not be allowed to vote. Such was the mood of the convention.[37] And it carried over into the ratification debate, the legislative session, and the elections that followed.

Two months after Californians ratified the new constitution, a case came before the federal courts that would more directly test the limits of state power than did *Ah Fong* and *Chy Lung*. Perhaps more than any other factor the case of *Ah Kow v. Nunan* reinforced Stephen Field's reputation in California as a protector of the Chinese.[38] Also known as the *Queue Case*, it was actually the product of two statutes. In 1870 the California legislature passed a law requiring every lodging house to provide at least 500 cubic feet of air per inhabitant. Any person found sleeping in a lodging that violated this law would be liable for a fine of up to fifty dollars or imprisonment. Although general in its terms, the provision was probably aimed at overcrowding in San Francisco's Chinatown and motivated by a desire to harass Chinese. It certainly was enforced solely against the Chinese who, for the most part, frustrated the policy by refusing to pay fines and accepting short jail terms.[39] To give the statute more effect, the San Francisco Board of Supervisors passed an ordinance directing jailers to crop the hair of every male prisoner to a uniform length of one inch. They knew that for the Chinese, wearing their hair in a braided queue had spiritual meaning, and they undoubtedly acted either out of spite or in the hope that the threat of losing their queues would intimidate most Chinese into paying the fine.

In April 1878 Ho Ah Kow was convicted of violating the cubic-air statute. He defaulted on his fine and was sent to city jail where, following the San Francisco ordinance, the sheriff cut his queue. Relying on an 1870 federal civil rights statute, Ah Kow then sued the sheriff. When the case came before the circuit court, Field was absolutely indignant. To him the queue-cutting ordinance was nothing but a ruse.

Besides, we cannot shut our eyes to matters of public notoriety and general cognizance. When we take our seats on the bench we are not struck with blindness, and forbidden to know as judges what we see as men; . . . We may take notice of the limitation given to the general terms of an ordinance by its practical construction as a fact in its history. . . . If this were not so, the most important provisions of the constitution, intended for the security of personal rights, would, by the general terms of an enactment, often be evaded and practically annulled.[40]

This statement was from a man who, just a few months later in the jury exclusion cases, would be quite unwilling to look beyond the language of a statute to see its true impact and intent.

"Hostile and spiteful," Field called the queue ordinance, "legislation which is unworthy of a brave and manly people."[41] But was it unconstitutional? Field thought so, and to support his conclusion he employed several innovations in constitutional doctrine. Although at the time the Bill of Rights was not thought to be applicable to the states, he reasoned that this state ordinance amounted to cruel and unusual punishment. He borrowed from his *Slaughter-House* dissent the notion that the guarantees of the Fourteenth Amendment apply to the substance of laws as well as to the procedure for enforcing them. Perhaps he captured this idea of substantive equal protection better in an earlier case involving anti-Chinese legislation: "Equality of protection implies not only equal accessibility to the courts for the prevention or redress of wrongs, and the enforcement of rights, but equal exemption with others of the same class from all charges and burdens of every kind."[42]

From a hodgepodge of rationale, however, two primary reasons emerged for Field's opposition to the queue-cutting ordinance. First, it encroached upon the federal sphere of authority by interfering with the Burlingame Treaty between China and the United States. This theme was most prominent in Field's campaign literature. "I have always regarded the immigration of the Chinese in large numbers into our state as a serious evil, and likely to cause great injury to the morals of our people, as well as their industrial interests," he wrote. With words that might just as well have come from the mouth of Denis Kearney he added, "It is our duty to preserve this land for our people and their posterity forever; to protect and defend American institutions and republican government from the oriental gangrene."[43] But Field maintained that "no good can come of a resort to small vexations against the Chinese." The problem could not be solved by state law or municipal ordinance; it was a national question. Making perfect political sense, he argued that modification of the treaty was the only solution. President Hayes and the Republican party were to blame for the Chinese problem.[44]

To Field's critics the existence of the Burlingame Treaty and the administration's position on immigration made little difference. They recognized that the president and the Senate could modify or abrogate the treaty yet still blamed Field for the invalidation of the queue ordinance and accused him of being an advocate for the Chinese. "There is no real occasion for a Chinaman to employ counsel in any case where Mr. Justice Field sits as the Judge," chided the *San Francisco Examiner.* "No advocate, ardent in the cause of his client, could more adroitly plead . . . the cause of Ho Ah Kow."[45]

The second major reason Field gave for overturning the queue ordinance was that it amounted to discriminating legislation *by a state* against a class or sect of persons and thus was forbidden by the Fourteenth Amendment.[46] I emphasize "by a state" because, given Field's interpretation of the state action doctrine in the jury exclusion cases, it seems unlikely that he would have reached the same result had the sheriff shorn Ah Kow's queue without the express authority of legislation. Discriminatory legislation, not the discrimination itself, was the focus of Field's ire. "Class legislation" is the term he gave it. In the *Queue Case* Field demonstrated that he was willing to look deeper into the purpose and effect of the law when he sensed the state was overstepping the bounds of its authority and thereby encroaching upon a fundamental right. The class character of this legislation is nonetheless manifest because of the general terms in which it is expressed, he observed. "If this were not so, the most important provisions of the Constitution, intended for the security of personal rights, would, by the general terms of an enactment, often be evaded and practically annulled."[47]

Once again the anti-Chinese element was not impressed. To them Field's opinion was a product of unfounded assumptions and legal fiction. The *San Francisco Examiner* vehemently criticized the decision. "As a judge [Field] did what no judge has a right to do—he departed from the record, assumed as facts things which were not facts, and which were the exact reverse of what he stated as facts."[48] Insisting that the queue ordinance was written to have a general application, the *Examiner* somewhat overdramatically summarized the decision's impact:

The shears of the jailer may with impunity, and must, under the statute law, clip the ambrosial locks of the loftiest citizen of rank and fortune, if he shall become subject to discipline by crime, conviction and sentence. Yet all the might, power and majesty of the law of the general government must be interpreted to save the queue of the vilest coolie wretch who pollutes the land and disgraces our civilization.

Mongolians, it concluded, are henceforth to be viewed as a preferred race.[49]

Obviously, not everyone thought the outcome of the *Queue Case* was wrong. The conservative *Alta California* called the case "conclusive and [leaving] not the least room for doubt of its soundness."[50] Nevertheless, within a month of the decision, Field's campaign attempted to minimize any negative impact the case did have. His literary bureau published and distributed a pamphlet that included the opinion itself, accompanied by a "History of the Queue Cutting Ordinance."[51] The appended history was intended to demonstrate that Field was not mistaken in his assumption that San Francisco supervisors enacted the ordinance to harass Chinese. In

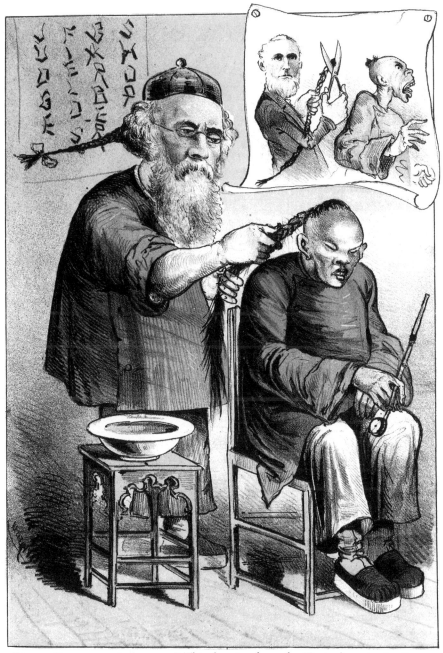

"Judge Righteous Judgment." This drawing from the *Wasp*, August 16, 1879, illustrates a critic's reaction to Stephen Field's decision in the *Queue Case*. (Courtesy Bancroft Library)

another pamphlet, "A Possible Solution of the Chinese Problem," Field charged that the treaty with China was one-sided. American laborers, merchants, and entrepreneurs were not afforded the same rights and opportunities in China as Chinese nationals were given here, he said. Laying the blame for the situation on the administration, he proposed a plan to get rid of the Chinese in America or to open up China for American industry.[52]

Both critics and supporters agreed upon one issue: despite the talk about treaties, vexations, and discrimination, this dispute was really about the limits of state power. Field's friend, Prof. John Norton Pomeroy, made this point soon after the decision was announced. "[Field's] opinion reiterates the doctrine, which has often been affirmed by the Courts, and which every student of Constitutional law knows to be elementary," Pomeroy observed, "that the powers of the individual States to deal with the matter, by virtue of their so-called police authority, is extremely narrow and imperfect, utterly incompetent to cope with the subject in all its relations."[53]

This was precisely the point that concerned the anti-Chinese forces. Not only did they despise the federal government's interference but more particularly the interference of the federal courts. Fearing Field's decisions in *Ah Fong* and *Ah Kow* would render the state powerless to "protect itself from the curse of coolie importation," the *Examiner* called for reorganization of the federal judiciary as well as election of a Congress that would put the matter beyond the reach of the judiciary.[54] The *Examiner*'s whining was certainly shrill, but its concern that judicial power tended to be arbitrary proved to have some basis. A sample of Field's later decisions regarding anti-Chinese legislation demonstrated the subjectiveness of his concept of "police power of the states." It is especially evident in a series of cases involving ordinances that regulated San Francisco laundries. In 1882 Field invalidated an ordinance requiring that laundry operators get a license and that, in order to do so, they obtain written approval from twelve citizens living in near proximity.[55] Field reasoned that this regulation was not aimed at the method of conducting the laundry business but at the business itself. Some businesses might be injurious to the public morals, offensive to the senses, or dangerous to the public health and safety, and therefore subject to the police power. For Field selling intoxicating liquors was one such business.[56] But the laundry business was not, and the ordinance was therefore outside the police power. This victory for Chinese launderers was not longlasting, however. In 1885 Field ruled that ordinances restricting the hours of operation for laundries were a proper exercise of the police power. In contrast to *Ah Kow v. Nunan,* he ignored claims that the general language of the regulations was a mere subterfuge for attempts to drive the Chinese out of the laundry business. Considering that the most salient fact in each of these cases was that local authorities were attempting to hinder the Chinese in their right to labor, the distinction Field made in these groups of cases was not extremely convincing.[57]

Several months after the *Queue Cases,* a case came before the federal courts that did directly test a provision of the new constitution. Article 19, section 9, prohibited corporations from employing in any capacity "any Chinese or Mongolian" and directed the legislature to enact laws to enforce the mandate.[58] In February 1880 the legislature responded by adding to the state penal code a section that made any corporate officers subject to criminal penalties and imprisonment for the offense of hiring Chinese. When Tiburcio Parrott, president and director of the Sulfur Springs Quicksilver Mining Company, was jailed for violating the act, he petitioned for a writ of habeas corpus to the U.S. Circuit Court for the District of California. Parrott claimed that both the statute and the state constitution were unconstitutional.

Parrott case

Timing made Tiburcio Parrott's appeal important to Field's campaign and significant for understanding Field's conception of civil rights. Filed in San Francisco in late February 1880, the case immediately became part of heated anti-Chinese agitation. On March 1 the San Francisco Committee on Health and Police condemned Chinatown "for sanitary reasons." Governor Perkins issued a proclamation making March 4 a holiday "for the purpose of giving our citizens a chance to express their sentiments on the growing evil of Chinese immigration."[59] When hearings in the *Parrott* case began that week anti-Chinese leader Denis Kearney incited a rally of unemployed workers, saying, "I will accept no decision but that of the people, and they say the Chinese must go."[60] As a precaution, National Guard troops moved into the city, where the *New York Sun* speculated they would stay "at least until the question of constitutionality of a law forbidding corporations to employ Chinese is decided by the United States Courts and the question of condemnation of Chinatown settled."[61] The federal courtroom was packed when hearings before Judges Ogden Hoffman and Lorenzo Sawyer began. Every San Francisco newspaper kept a daily tab on the developments, some recounting in detail the arguments of each side.[62]

Judges Sawyer and Hoffman agreed with Parrott's lawyers and ruled that California's prohibition against hiring Chinese labor was unconstitutional. Although he served as circuit justice for the Ninth Circuit, Field did not participate in the Tiburcio Parrott case. At the very time it was being argued he was in Washington, where the Supreme Court was announcing its opinions in *Ex parte Virginia* and *Virginia v. Rives.* Yet Field had imposed his personality and will over the federal courts in California to such an extent that critics of the case were likely to blame him for the outcome. Christian Fritz has pointed out that Field wished to be "the judge" of California and that Sawyer and Hoffman had come to experience his domineering presence and his expectation that they would give allegiance to his views.[63] Field's exercise of authority over the other judges came partly from stature and partly from statute. Federal law gave Field the power to overrule the opinion of a majority of the subordinate judges in cases over which he presided.[64] And it was possible for him to manipulate the docket so as to preside over cases he wanted.[65] Any outcome in *Parrott* to which Field was fundamentally opposed would have been unlikely. The contrast between it and Field's opinions in the jury exclusion cases is therefore stark.

Seymour D. Thompson, editor of the *American Law Review* in the mid-1880s, warned that Parrott's case represented an unauthorized expansion of federal judicial power.[66] It clearly was an interference with the normal prosecution of state criminal law: the same kind of interference Field was complaining about almost simultaneously in *Ex parte Virginia* and *Virginia v. Rives*. Why then was Field willing to acquiesce in the outcome? The answer seems to be that Field did not see an inconsistency at all. For him there were two differences between these sets of cases. One difference he found related to the nature of the discrimination and the scope of government authority. The other difference was the nature of the right.

With respect to the nature of the discrimination, the most obvious difference in these cases was its target. Chinese residents had some success in asserting constitutional rights when virtually all the nineteenth-century civil rights cases involving recently freed blacks resulted in setbacks. The situation of the Chinese in America may help to explain their successes. The broad implication of Chinese victories in civil rights cases was tempered by their status as resident aliens with no right to obtain citizenship. Black civil rights, by contrast, may have posed more of a long-term political threat. "Blacks . . . wanted more than free entry and a chance to labor for low wages at long hours in the hopes of turning merchant and sailing home rich, what they wanted was a due measure of control over their state governments."[67]

As important as this observation may be to understanding nineteenth-century views of civil rights, it does not fully explain the pattern of Stephen Field's opinions. First, Field's record on civil rights cases does not reflect a consistent difference in his treatment of the two races. Although it is true that he usually voted against black civil rights, his record as a protector of Chinese rights is erratic. Second, Field's record on civil rights appears inconsistent only when one focuses on race alone. The difference that mattered most to Field, however, was not race but the source of the discrimination. For him, discrimination coming from the state posed the only serious threat to liberty. Recall that, as Field interpreted them, the discrimination in *Virginia v. Rives* and *Ex parte Virginia* resulted from the actions of a private individual. The state was not the source. The discrimination in *Parrott*, by contrast, was written expressly into both state statute and the state constitution; there was no question of state action.

It may be that cases like *Strauder, Virginia v. Rives,* and *Ex parte Virginia* reflected black citizens' desire for a measure of control over their state governments. But the desire for such control was present in the Chinese cases as well. Chinese were the victims of discrimination in *Tiburcio Parrott*, but the direct targets of the laws overruled in that case were California's corporations. The beneficiaries of those laws were white laborers (antimonopolists or sandlotters) who were also seeking a degree of control over the social order and who were intent on using state government to accomplish their purpose. *Tiburcio Parrott* and the jury exclusion cases had this in common. Both represented an attempt to use government to control the practices, duties, or social behavior of a privileged class. In one case it was the state government being used, in the other it was the federal. Field would have nothing of either.

Of course, Field was not suggesting that government should be powerless. Rather, he believed that liberty would be best protected by confining government to a limited set of powers authorized by the Constitution. Federalism came into play in this respect. Field's theory of limited government confined the legislative activity of the states to their sphere of authority and federal activity to its sphere, not allowing one to entrench on the other. The state sphere of authority, known as the police power of the states, was limited to protecting health, safety, morals, and peace and good order. The federal sphere of authority was confined to the powers enumerated in or implied by the Constitution.

Field's opinions in cases involving Chinese and blacks thus reflect the interplay of three concepts: that protecting individual liberty is not a function of government, that government should be of limited power, and that the federal government alone has the power to carry on relations with foreign nations. Thus in *Ah Fong* Field was probably not consumed with a concern for the future of the twenty-one Chinese women who had been denied entry into the country. He overruled the California statute under which they had been denied entry because he believed the state had encroached on the federal treatymaking power. The outcome of that case favored the Chinese. But Field felt strongly that Chinese immigration should stop. The Chinese will never assimilate with "our people," he told John Norton Pomeroy; their presence causes conflicts between the races, disturbs the public order, and mars the progress of the country. "You know I belong to the class, who repudiate the doctrine that this country was made for the people of *all* races," he continued. "On the contrary, I think it is for our race—the Caucasian race."[68] Field tended to overrule discriminatory legislation only when it threatened his greater understanding of liberty.[69]

Some of the confusion regarding Field's race-related opinions in 1879 and 1880 might be explained by looking at his later opinions. When cases tested federal legislation to exclude Chinese immigrants, Field found it easier to rule against the Chinese. His attention turned to the federal government's treatymaking power and its power to regulate relations with foreign nations. In *Chew Heong v. United States* (1884), for example, he maintained that Congress had the right to change immigration laws even if those changes resulted in unfair treatment of people trying to get into the United States. Interestingly, Field carved a lonely path in *Chew Heong*. The issue there was whether an amendment to the Chinese Exclusion Act of 1882 should be applied retroactively. The 1882 law prohibited new Chinese immigration but allowed Chinese who had already established residence in the United States, but who had left the country for some reason, to return. Although Congress also required resident Chinese to obtain a certificate of registration, under court interpretations of the statute the lack of a registration card was not conclusive evidence that a person had never been a resident. Chinese who were denied entry into the United States could use all relevant evidence of their prior residence, including oral testimony, to establish the right to be readmitted. The 1884 amendment made the registration card the only allowable evidence of prior residence.[70]

In the circuit court, Judges Sawyer, Hoffman, and Sabin believed that equity required that the law in effect when Chinese left the country should apply when they sought to return. As circuit judge, Field had the power to disregard the opinion of all three, and he did. Since Chew Heong did not have a certificate, Field ordered him deported. Chew Heong appealed to the Supreme Court, which reversed Field's decision. The Supreme Court's majority reasoned that the treaty between the United States and China gave Chinese certain rights. Congress could withdraw those rights, they admitted. But, in the interest of equity, the Court would not retroactively apply that change unless Congress had provided clear evidence of its intent to do so. Field dissented. Congress has the power to alter immigration laws, he said, and the Court should not attempt to change it "by ingenious reasoning or fanciful notions of a purpose not declared on its face."[71]

Chae Chan Ping v. United States (the Chinese exclusion case of 1889) involved new federal legislation that excluded Chinese from the country and prohibited those Chinese residents who left the country from returning. This time the Supreme Court ruled that Congress had the power to exclude Chinese altogether and that the exclusion law could be applied retroactively. Field, speaking for a majority, flatly rejected the argument that Chinese who had left the country before the new restrictions were enacted had a vested right to return. The power to exclude foreigners is an attribute of sovereignty and cannot be delegated or given away, he said. The previous immigration acts gave Chinese laborers a license to enter the country and nothing more. That license, he concluded, is held at the will of the government and revocable at any time, at its pleasure.[72]

In cases involving exclusion of people who were seeking entry into the country, Field appeared to take a hard-line stance against the Chinese. His attitude changed dramatically, however, when deportation of Chinese who were already in the country was at issue. *Fong Yue Ting v. United States* (1893) tested the validity of a law known as the Geary Act. This statute prohibited all Chinese immigration, including the reentry of people who had once been residents, and required that Chinese then in the country apply for a certificate of residence. Chinese found without the certificate were thereafter presumed to be in the country unlawfully and subject to immediate arrest. They would then be deported unless they could prove, by testimony of a white witness, that they had good cause for not having the certificate. The Supreme Court upheld the legislation. The power to expel or deport foreigners rested on the same foundation as the power to exclude, reasoned Justice Gray. It was an attribute of national sovereignty and could be changed at will. Registration and identification were a natural extension of that power.[73]

Although it sounded much like Field's own language in the Chinese exclusion case, the majority's reasoning sent Field into a rage. The opinion bothered him so much that he suggested to his friend Don Dickinson that Congress should force the Court to decide on the issue again and that the Court should be increased in size to ensure a "proper" outcome. "Surely the American people are not to submit to such doctrines as have been announced in this case—which is nothing less than that the safeguards of the Constitution for life, liberty, and property can be suspended by Congress, with reference to any class, at its pleasure," he wrote.[74] For Field, deportation had nothing to do with the relations with foreign countries. It was an exercise of government power over individuals. The aspect that bothered him was not the deportation itself but the procedure under which it would take place. Field worried that under the majority's interpretation Chinese laborers could be deprived of their rights without a judicial trial.[75] It did not matter that the law applied only to foreign residents who were not citizens. Once they had gained the status of residents of the country, Field reasoned, Chinese were entitled to the same rights as citizens. By violating those rights Congress had exceeded its power: "Arbitrary and despotic power can no more be exercised over [Chinese residents], with reference to their persons and property, than over the persons and property of native-born citizens."[76]

This particular conception of governmental authority also guided Field's votes in cases that tested laws passed to protect civil rights. In *United States v. Cruikshank* (1876), Field voted with the majority to overrule the Enforcement Act of 1870.[77] Aimed at Ku Klux Klan activity, this law made it a federal crime to engage in private conspiracies to deprive black citizens of their civil rights or equal protection of the laws. When participants in a bloody racial attack called the Colfax massacre were indicted under the Enforcement Act, the Court overturned their convictions. The Fourteenth Amendment was intended to protect individuals from discriminatory actions of the state, wrote Chief Justice Waite; it does not say anything about the rights of one citizen against another. The Court employed this same reasoning seven years later in *United States v. Harris* (1883) when it overturned the convictions of several whites for assaulting and beating a group of blacks.[78] *Harris* involved a statute similar to the Enforcement Act. Section 5519 of the Revised Statutes of 1874 made it a federal crime for two or more persons to conspire to deprive a person of equal protection of the law. Once again the Court ruled the law unconstitutional because it extended to the acts of private individuals rather than the state; once again Field voted with the majority.

Section 5519 came into play again in *Baldwin v. Franks* (1887).[79] That case began in Nicolaus, California, when a band of white men raided Chinese living quarters, dragged the Chinese workers down to the Feather River, and drove them out of town on a barge. Once again the Court ruled the federal law that punished this activity was invalid. This time, however, Field dissented. Although his dissent seems inconsistent with his vote in *Harris*, Field saw a different angle in this case. A separate part of the 1874 law, section 5536, made it a crime to "conspire to prevent, hinder or delay the execution of any law of the United States." For Field this reference meant treaty as well. To him this case did not so much represent a conspiracy against Chinese as it represented a conspiracy against the execution of a law of the United States.[80] Congress, he reasoned, clearly has the power to pass laws ensuring compliance with its treaties.

The Chinese exclusion case, the Chinese deportation case, and *Baldwin v. Franks* came years after *Tiburcio Parrott*. Yet they demonstrate how the distinction between state and private action played into Field's thinking. They also demonstrated that Field could be flexible in applying his own ideas about the proper scope of government. Thus they help explain the apparent inconsistency between his attitude in *Tiburcio Parrott* and his vote in the jury exclusion cases. Recall, however, that there was another difference he saw between the two sets of cases: the difference in the nature of the right. The jury exclusion cases involved a dispute over the right to fair legal process, but the underlying principle of the *Parrott* decision was the right to labor.

"You might as well take the clothes from a Chinaman's back, or take his luggage from his hand, when he lands in this country as to take the sacred right to labor from him," argued T. I. Bergin, one of Parrott's attorneys.[81] With an excess of commas but little pause, Judge Sawyer agreed: "The right to labor is, of all others, after the right to live, the fundamental, inalienable right of man, wherever he may be permitted to be, of which he cannot be deprived, either under the guise of law or otherwise, except by usurpation and force."[82] From where was the right derived? For Sawyer its source was an apple. "Man ate and died," he wrote. "When God drove him forth from the Garden of Eden . . . , he invested him with an inalienable right to labor in order that he might again eat and live."[83] A link to the Constitution was provided by Field's and Bradley's dissents in the *Slaughter-House Cases,* both of which maintained the Fourteenth Amendment protected the right of any person to choose any lawful employment.[84] But these opinions too were founded primarily upon a theory of the natural rights of man.

In re Tiburcio Parrott was undoubtedly a case involving discrimination against Chinese. It was the Chinese right to labor that was being limited and the Chinese right to choose a lawful employment that was being inhibited. The law being challenged was intended to drive Chinese labor from the state. But neither the constitution nor the statute was directed toward the Chinese; each targeted the state's corporations. Thus *Parrott* provides a nice illustration of the broader implications of the natural rights theories so prevalent among judges and lawyers of the time and gives additional clues to Field's notion of liberty and his attitude toward privilege.

"In this city alone there are 8,397 corporations and they represent considerably more than one-half of the wealth of the city," lawyer Bergen argued. "They possess a constitutional *right to employ just whom they choose.*"[85] Judge Hoffman picked up this theme, maintaining that corporations possessed a fundamental right to utilize their property by employing such laborers as they chose and with such wages as might be agreed.[86] Using language that would become more common as the century progressed, he warned that upholding these regulations would amount to a declaration that corporations and their stockholders hold their property at the mercy of state legislatures.[87]

Field could be confident that, left to Hoffman and Sawyer, the *Tiburcio Parrott* case would reach the proper result. It was an easy case for all of them. The dichotomy between personal liberty and economic rights, which is very much a part of today's constitutional thinking, simply was not present. So extreme was the state's threat to both that even usually antirailroad and anti-Chinese newspapers thought the outcome of the case was correct.[88] The case is easy for historians, too. In it there is fodder for competing theories about the nature of nineteenth-century constitutional jurisprudence. Charles McCurdy might easily find in its language the free-labor ideology that he believes to be the foundation of Stephen Field's constitutional doctrine. Howard Graham and Robert McCloskey could have just as easily used it to support their belief that Field's doctrine was an extension of laissez-faire economics and Social Darwinism.

The federal court's ruling on *Parrott* came just two months before the California Democratic Convention. Field may have made a deliberate decision not to participate, but he did not alter his views to accommodate his presidential aspirations. Indeed, it is just as likely that he believed his position on the Chinese question actually strengthened his image, at least among "reasonable men." Judge Matthew Deady certainly thought so. Eight months earlier Field had upheld Judge Deady's decision in *Baker v. Portland,* which held an Oregon law prohibiting employment of Chinese labor in public works projects to be in conflict with the Burlingame Treaty.[89] That week Deady wrote in his diary, "[Field] affirmed my Chinese labor case upon rehearing and agreed with my opinion throughout—which was well for a candidate for the presidency."[90]

Deady's opinion notwithstanding, it is commonly thought that Field's Chinese decisions doomed his bid for the presidency. Brother Cyrus's biographer, for example, concluded that California turned against Field for his defense of the rights of Chinese immigrants.[91] No doubt some Democrats opposed Field for his stance on this issue. In some counties of the western states, for example, Democratic conventions expressed thinly veiled opposition to Field with resolutions to oppose "any judicial candidate for the presidency and anyone whose views on the Chinese question are not in accord with the peoples of the Pacific coast."[92] The *Tiburcio Parrott* case demonstrated, however, that both in politics and in law the matter was not so simple. Even the rabid anti-Chinese *San Francisco Examiner* was not outraged by the opinion. Calling the decision "expected by every intelligent citizen," the *Examiner* reasoned that no other outcome was possible under the law as declared by Mr. Justice Field and the Supreme Court of the United States. Then, as if it had been reading Field's campaign literature, the paper advised that people ought to cease agitating for these obstructive statutes and seek instead to organize to elect a president and members of Congress who would oppose Chinese immigration.[93]

The Railroad

Even this mellowing by those individuals who criticized Field for his Chinese decisions was unlikely to save his candidacy, however. The Chinese issue was important in California, but it was only part of a more general feeling of frustration. Many Californians sensed that they were losing control over their own lives and destiny to the power and privilege controlled by great corporations.[94] The *Examiner* unwittingly illustrated the link in an editorial on the "Chinese problem." The Burlingame Treaty should be modified or abrogated, it said, "and there ought to be such change or reconstruction in the Judiciary Department as will place on the bench judges who will not, in every case between the rich and the poor, and between large corporations and the people, so interpret and declare the law that the poor and the people are almost invariably cast and held to be in the wrong."[95] Most California antimonopolists perceived that their struggle depended upon establishing a measure of control over the state's dominant corporations.

This concern about corporate power dominated the constitutional convention of 1878–1879. In the early stages of the convention twenty-seven bills relating to corporations were introduced and directed to a Committee on Corporations. The convention's delegates considered virtually no other topic from November 12, the day that committee's report was read on the convention floor, until December 9.[96] Every day for almost a month the convention dedicated itself to discussing the committee's report, section by section. The report contained twenty-three sections, eight of them directed explicitly at railroads.[97] Some proposals were aimed at specific abuses. For example, one section, inspired by the Crédit Mobilier scandal, prohibited railroad officers from being involved with companies that furnished materi-

als and supplies to the railroad. Another section addressed a common lob-
bying abuse by outlawing the practice of granting free passes to public officials. There was an attempt to make directors and shareholders personally
liable for their share of a corporation's debt. A proposed amendment to another section attacked a standard strategy employed by railroads to establish control in a particular market. It provided that a railroad that reduced
its rates to compete with another line could not raise them from the reduced
standard once the competitor was destroyed.[98] Perhaps the tenor of the report was best captured by the first section on railroads, the opening line of
which declared, "All railroads, canals, and transportation companies shall
be common carriers and subject to legislative control."[99]

Control was the operative thought throughout the month-long debate.
While introducing the committee's report, Chair Morris M. Estee recounted
the words of a much-mentioned British member of Parliament: "Gentlemen, the state must control the railroads or the railroads will control the
state."[100] Though recognizing that the railroad provided a great service to
the state, Estee warned of the danger in this power. Single men have controlled hundreds of miles of railway, thousands of men, tens of millions of
revenue, and hundreds of millions of capital, Estee estimated. He emphasized that they wielded this enormous power "in practical independence of
the control of governments and individuals much as petty German des-
pots might have governed their little principalities a century or two ago."[101]
Volney E. Howard, of Los Angeles, echoed Estee's concerns: "Have the community no power to defend themselves?" he asked. "If not, then we had
better turn this government over to the Central Pacific Railroad Company,
if they are willing to pay the expense, for it is the practical government of
the state, and this country, and the most grasping unprincipled government
at that."[102]

Antimonopolists, of course, believed the state did have the power to control the railroads and other corporations. Corporations were creatures of
the state, they reasoned. And, in theory, the community gave corporations
extraordinary rights and allowed them to use powers of the state, like eminent domain, primarily to benefit the public good. Finding encouragement
in *Munn v. Illinois,* antimonopolists proposed a railroad commission with
the power to set rates and charges for the transportation of passengers and
freights.[103]

Although less dramatic in their arguments regarding the limits of state
authority, conservatives tended to be more polished. Both economic law and
past experience demonstrate that regulation would be ineffective and ineffi-
cient, they argued. Government interference violated universal principles of

business and must inevitably be destructive, Henry Edgerton explained to the convention. Conservatives emphasized that, despite incessant cries of the antimonopolists, the railroads had provided a great benefit to the state. "The corporations have jerked this state a hundred years ahead of the point of progress at which it would have stood without them," Edgerton observed, "Management of the railroad system . . . for many years past . . . has been eminently satisfactory to a large class of people."[104]

Munn notwithstanding, conservatives argued that most of the proposed regulations violated the underlying principles of American government. The railroad commission plan, Edgerton maintained, was contrary to the separation of powers.[105] But more important, these regulations were said to interfere with the right of private property and to violate due process of law. On November 22, in a rare display of emotion, Edgerton concluded a two-hour speech with a warning: "We are daily wandering further and further from the great organic principles which alone ought to engage our attention," he said; "a torrent of radicalism has set upon us which threatens to overwhelm our work."[106]

As debate on corporations progressed, it sometimes broke down into heated exchange. On November 21, William P. Grace, a Workingmen's delegate and carpenter from San Francisco, charged that some members of the convention were corporate lawyers who received retainer fees to "gag down and defeat the will of the people to compel the railroads to do a legitimate, square, honest business." Conservative delegate H. C. Wilson decided not to take this abuse quietly. Rising before the convention he mocked Grace's Irish brogue. "When we were discussing questions upon the Bill of Rights and questions which underlie constitutional government, a voice shrill and harsh went up, KAR-R-R-PARATION LIAYERR! An unfeathered biped shook his head and seemed to pride itself that it had said something intelligent, and had participated in the debate which was going on."[107] For the better part of that afternoon charges of "crook" and "Communist" were slung across the convention floor, each side demanding the other produce proof of its allegations.

In the end the unfeathered biped appeared to have won a slim victory. The section on corporations in the new constitution was hardly radical. Many Workingmen opposed it for not going far enough.[108] But the document included many of the measures the Committee on Corporations had proposed, including an elected railroad commission with the power to set rates.[109] Most important, the debates at the constitutional convention reflected what must have already been obvious to astute political observers. The one issue that overshadowed all others in California politics was the power, whether real or imagined, of the Southern Pacific and Central Pacific Railroads.[110]

At about the time the power of the Central Pacific and the method of regulation were being debated in California, Ohio senator Allen G. Thurman introduced into Congress a bill that tested corporate power and privilege in another way. The Thurman bill was intended to ensure the Pacific railroads would repay the debt that they owed to the federal government for financing construction of the transcontinental railroad. In 1862 Congress had created the Union Pacific, granted it the franchise to build westward, and provided a right-of-way. The Central Pacific, already incorporated in California, was given the right to build eastward under the same terms. In addition, the federal government raised capital for the railroads by issuing bonds as the companies completed laying sections of track. These bonds were, in effect, a loan with quite favorable terms to the companies. They were payable with 6 percent simple interest thirty years after the date they were issued. The companies were not required to make cash payments on the principle or the interest until the date of maturity, which would be sometime between 1895 and 1899. However, the 1862 law did provide that compensation the government owed to the railroads for transportation they provided, such as carrying troops and mail, would annually be applied toward the debt. Each year 5 percent of the net earnings of the companies was also to be applied to repayment.

Congress reserved the right to alter, amend, or repeal the Act of 1862. Two years later it did so, making the terms even more favorable to the companies. The Act of 1864 reduced the amount of annual payment of the debt to one-half of the money the railroads earned for services rendered to the government. It also allowed the companies to issue private bonds and made the lien of the government subordinate to that of the new private lenders.

Favored treatment of the Pacific railroads changed rather abruptly in the 1870s as public officials began to worry that the government's arrangement with the railroads did not adequately ensure repayment. Calling for change, Senator Thurman predicted that the railroads' annual payments under the 1864 law would yield $15 million. The problem he saw was that the amount remaining unpaid when the loan became due would be more than $119 million. In the meantime, the companies were paying out huge dividends and diverting money to trust companies. Thurman feared that when the debt came due the companies would be unable to meet their obligation.[111] The Crédit Mobilier scandal of 1872 did not help the companies' image. Nor was the railroad's image improved when officers declared a generous dividend to their stockholders. Public perception was that fortunes were being shifted into the pockets of a few men while the debt to the government languished. C. P. Huntington seemed well aware of the dangers this image posed both in political forums and financial markets. Upset about the company's decision in 1877 to give sizable dividends to its shareholders instead of repaying part of its debt, he scolded David Colton. "Nearly every road in the country is under a cloud, the Central Pacific not excepted," he said; "it always looks bad when the company is carrying a large floating debt."[112]

Senator Thurman proposed amending the 1864 law so that once again all the money that the railroads earned from providing services to the government would be withheld for payment of the debt. The difference between his bill and the original 1862 law was that only one-half the amount would be applied directly to the outstanding debt; the other half would be paid into a sinking fund. In other words, it would be put into an account, maintained in trust by the U.S. Treasurer, to be used to pay the debt when it came due.[113]

The railroads pulled out all stops to fight Thurman's bill. Yet railroad leaders were not completely opposed to the idea of a sinking fund. C. P. Huntington offered an alternative piece of legislation that would set up a sinking fund in exchange for an extension of the time at which the bonds would be due. For Huntington this conflict was a matter of power, politics, and profit. Privately, he said that Thurman was a demagogue and a liar who was simply playing on the issue to gain support in his bid for the presidency. Publicly, he called the Thurman plan unprovoked, impolitic, and unjust. But Huntington did not oppose the Thurman bill because he thought the sinking fund plan violated any fundamental right. He opposed it because this particular scheme for a sinking fund was not favorable enough to the company.[114]

If Thurman was a demagogue, at least he had good timing. Sensing the popular mood against the railroads, Congress passed his bill with relative ease, and it became law in May 1878. Almost immediately the railroads instigated lawsuits to challenge the act. The legal fireworks began when Albert Gallatin, a shareholder of the Central Pacific, sued the company in the Federal District Court of California.[115] Within a short time the Union Pacific brought a suit against the government in the U.S. Court of Claims. Combined when they were appealed to the Supreme Court, these two lawsuits became the *Sinking Fund Cases*. The Supreme Court heard arguments on March 19 to 21, 1879. A month and a half later, on May 5, 1879, it announced its opinion upholding the Thurman Act. Field, Strong, and Bradley read dissenting opinions as well. The written opinions were not delivered until October 20, 1879, however, close enough to the 1880 conventions to affect Field's chances.

Sinking fund cases

Chief Justice Waite's careful opinion for the majority hinged on one factor. In both the 1862 and the 1864 statutes Congress had reserved to itself the right to alter, amend, or repeal the law. Waite admitted that any changes Congress might impose must be reasonable, but he concluded that in this case they were. Turning his attention to policy, Waite noted that in less than twenty years a debt in the amount of $80 million would be due. The companies, he observed, were paying interest on their own bonds and dividing earnings among their stockholders without laying aside any funds to meet this enormous debt. In Waite's view, stockholders of the present were thus receiving, in the form of dividends, that which stockholders of the future might be compelled to lose. The Thurman Act made it a duty of the company to lay aside a portion of its net income to meet its debt when it came due.

F's dissent

The dissenters were as imaginative and forceful as Waite had been careful. They accused the government of mixing its role of sovereign with that of creditor. This dispute was a matter of contract, Field reasoned: "And when the government of the United States entered into that contract, it laid aside its sovereignty and put itself on terms of equality with its contractor."[116] As a party to the contract it could not simply change the terms of the agreement to suit itself. Convincing as this argument may have seemed, it ignored one major point. As Waite pointed out, the federal government is a sovereign. As such it has responsibilities to its citizens and taxpayers that could not be ignored.[117]

Unlike Waite, who had avoided great constitutional questions, Field and Bradley reveled in them. A contract is property, they reasoned. By destroying that property, the Thurman Act violated the Fifth Amendment guarantee that property shall not be taken without just compensation.[118] The act, they continued, also circumvented the judicial process and thus deprived the companies of due process of law, also guaranteed by the Fifth Amendment.

The dissenters' reasoning also drew analogies from contract clause doctrine. Article I, section 10 provides that no state shall pass any law impairing the obligation of contract. The fact that the contract clause expressly applies only to states did not deter the dissenters from claiming that the Thurman Act, a federal statute, violated the Constitution in this respect. Bradley spoke for all of the dissenters in maintaining that even though the contract clause was not directly applicable, "Congress may not pass arbitrary and despotic laws with regard to contracts any more than with regard to any other subject matter of legislation."[119] Nor did it matter to the dissenters that the 1862 and 1864 statutes both expressly reserved to Congress the right to amend the law if it saw fit to do so. Ignoring this, the dissenters applied a subtle presumption that, when it came to economic matters, a power not expressly granted to the federal government was denied. Strong captured the idea most vividly. "I search in vain for any express or implied grant of power to add new terms to any existing contracts made by or with the government, or any grant of power to destroy vested rights."[120]

While other dissenters would apply the contract clause to the federal government by analogy, Field took a slightly different approach. To allow the federal government the power to impair contracts, he maintained, would violate one of the great objects of the Constitution. The great object to which he referred was "the establishment of justice." He found it not in the body of the Constitution but in the preamble.[121] As he had done in the *Slaughter-House Cases,* Field looked to general principles of justice to find support for an unprecedented expansion of judicial authority. Taken to its limits, his argument implied that the Court could oversee any federal legislation that it thought might be unjust or unfair.

Field had a penchant for sweeping language and visionary reasoning. It is therefore difficult to say where in the *Sinking Fund Cases* his judging may have ended and his campaigning begun. Nevertheless, several long paragraphs at the end of his dissent bore the markings of a campaign speech.[122] Field first emphasized that the sanctity of contracts was essential to liberty. If government will not abide by its agreements, if it can change its contracts by legislation, then all property will be insecure, he warned. And where the rights of property are insecure the rights of person are insecure as well.

Turning to the issue at hand, Field admitted that there was a general feeling against the Pacific railroad companies, an attitude that the railroads had become so powerful that they should "be brought by strongest measures into subjection to the state." But Field argued that the power and influence of the railroads furnished no justification for the government's evasion of its contracts. There was a general principle involved here, he warned: "The law that protects the wealth of the most powerful, protects also the earnings of the most humble; and the law which would confiscate the property of the one would in the end take the earnings of the other." Field tried valiantly to link the interest of common wage earners to that of the railroads. Liberty meant the same to both, he reasoned. It did not matter that the companies were corporations. The nature of their rights were the same.[123]

Sound though this logic may have seemed to a sympathetic listener, it was unlikely to convince the Workingmen and farmers who had participated in the California constitutional convention. The contrast between their values and Field's could not be more glaring. While Field's concern was corporate liberty, they were concerned about corporate power. They wanted government to stand as a sovereign, to regulate and control the corporations, and to confront the threat that corporate power posed to their liberty.

As if he realized this, Field made an even more strained pitch to antimonopolists. He tried to tie the philosophy of states' rights to the regulatory spirit of the new California constitution. The Central Pacific is a creature of California, he said, and it is controlled by the state. "Under the [U.S.] Constitution the management of local affairs is left chiefly to the States, and it never entered into the conception of its framers that under it the creations of the states could be taken from their control."[124] The power to regulate railroads, Field told his readers, vested not in the federal government but in the states. He neglected to remind them of his dissent in *Munn v. Illinois,* an opinion in which he expressed a vision of very limited state authority.

Although the main thrust of his argument was aimed at the situation in California, Field did not ignore pure states' rights advocates. The majority opinion, he said, "had gone farther than any had even thought possible in the history of this country, to destroy the independence of the states and establish their helplessness even in matters of local concern, as against the will of Congress." The opinion Field delivered from the bench was slightly different from his official written opinion, and it was roundly reported in the press. The oral delivery ended with a sharp rebuke: "He must be dull indeed who does not see that under the legislation and the course of decision of late years, our government is fast drifting from its ancient moorings, from the system established by our fathers into a vast centralized and consolidated government."[125]

Accusing his Supreme Court brethren of being dullards seemed a serious breach of tradition. Certainly critics thought so. Rumors circulated that Field's zeal had caused the Supreme Court to consider a rule requiring minority justices to submit their opinions for approval.[126] Ultimately, the final written version of Field's dissent was somewhat toned down. On his main point, however, he remained firm. The Thurman Act interfered with the sanctity of contract and, in doing so, threatened the liberty of all. With respect to the Central Pacific, it violated the principles of states' rights.

No one seemed especially impressed with Field's states' rights reasoning, except Field himself. Writing to Matthew Deady about his still-forthcoming opinion, he proudly reported, "If there is any constitutional law acceptable to the profession generally throughout the country, it will be found there."[127] As Chief Justice Waite pointed out, however, California had never objected to Congress' action.[128] Even the conservative *Alta California* imagined that neither the people nor the officials of California would take offense at the federal law.[129] It was possibly more indicative of the state's mood that California Democrats were able to reconcile the Thurman Act with their desire to regulate corporations. At the state convention of July 1879, Democrats called for state regulation of railroad rates in the same breath in which they passed a resolution supporting the Thurman Act.[130] Newspapers from around the country joined the *New York Sun* in reporting that Field had made a great mistake in raising the states' rights issue against the Thurman bill.[131] The *San Francisco Examiner* exposed what many surely thought was Field's motive, "to give the judgment to the companies and the sop of states' rights to supporters of the Thurman Act."[132]

Critics complained that Field had introduced a campaign speech into the body of a judicial opinion, a claim that was later borne out in his campaign literature.[133] Many people were offended by the judge's political aspirations, and some went so far as to propose that the Supreme Court adopt a rule forbidding its members to become candidates for the presidency.[134] Leading the criticism was the *San Francisco Examiner*, in which the *Sinking Fund Case* triggered a month-long tirade against Field.[135] Charging that Field's "violent outbursts" were motivated by his desire to enhance a presidential boom on his behalf, the *Examiner*'s editors came close to calling for his resignation. "The prurient desire for the presidency is a bee in a bonnet, and wildly afflicts the head it attacks. No man who aspires to the exalted station ought ever to be upon the Supreme Bench."[136]

This idea of a conflict of interest was only a minor aspect of the attack against Field, however. Critics were really disturbed about what the *Examiner* called "his ardor to serve the great corporations." Not that they were accusing him of unethical behavior. Critics simply believed that Field's sympathy was with the corporations and that his legal philosophy favored the powerful. In the words of the *Examiner*, "In any case wherein the people or the state, or a private citizen, has been a party on one side, and a rich corporation the opposing party, [Field] has invariably pronounced opinion or given judgment in favor of the corporation." So intense was the *Examiner*'s feeling, that it found fault in even obscure cases. With the glaring headline, "Always on the Side of the Corporations," the newspaper took Field to task for an opinion favoring a railroad in a dispute over a Russian countess's lost baggage.[137]

Condemnation in the press certainly was not universal, but it was widespread.[138] Newspapers from the East Coast and the heartland as well as others in the West joined the *Examiner* in charging that Field was a favorite of the corporate and railroad interests.[139] Nor was this image of Field limited to the press; political insiders and rivals took the same view. One of Tilden's supporters from California noted that "it is more than suspected that the Central Pacific Railroad is for him" but advised the Tilden leadership that Field was not a favorite in California because of his decisions in favor of the corporations.[140] Bayard supporters thought the same. Perry Belmont commented that he had the same feeling about Field that he had about another candidate, former Erie Railroad president Hugh J. Jewett, "although Field's connection with the railroads is not quite as evident."[141]

Even fellow jurists were sensitive to Field's reputation. In the earlier Crédit Mobilier case Chief Justice Waite had refused to assign Field the task of writing the majority opinion because he thought it best to let someone not so closely identified with the railroad announce the decision.[142] Field's friend Judge Matthew Deady corroborated the belief by noting that Field was happy to find a case that would soften his image. In 1884, when Field was contemplating yet another sojourn into politics, Deady wrote in his diary: "We heard the Express Company case, which [Field] has taken to [San Francisco] with him to write a little opinion. It gives him an opportunity to say something not on the side of the Railways which I think he is rather pleased with than otherwise."[143]

Railroad leaders knew they could depend on Field. Planning strategy in the *Sinking Fund Cases,* David Colton wrote, "Judge Field will not sit in the Gallatin Case [in the U.S. district court], but instead will reserve his best efforts (I have no doubt) for the final termination of the case at Washington before the full bench."[144] Field's best efforts were not quite good enough, but "moneyed men" clearly preferred his opinion in the *Sinking Fund Cases* to that of the majority. Eastern tycoons such as Jay Gould, John D. Rockefeller, and Chauncey Depew assumed that the next president would have an opportunity to reshape the Court and wanted someone who would appoint men who sympathized "with the general view of the law taken by Judge Field and his associates in the minority" in the *Sinking Fund* and *Granger* cases.[145]

Field's informal links with the business elite were strong. He socialized with the Leland Stanford family and interceded in business affairs involving his brother Cyrus and C. P. Huntington. The people most active in his campaign were connected to the corporate elite as well. Lloyd Tevis, president of Wells Fargo, spent effort and money in his behalf. Former senator William Gwin, a mainstay in the Field campaign, was also quietly looking after the interests of the Central Pacific in Washington.[146] Many of these

"THE RAILROAD ROBBERS' WARNING." A drawing from the *Wasp,* April 5, 1884, just before the California Democratic Convention of 1894, shows Field (seated at the table, second from the left) at a Roman orgy with the railroad barons. (Courtesy Bancroft Library)

men were members of San Francisco's elite clubs, where they socialized, and some lived, in luxury.[147] There was no evidence of impropriety in these relationships, but evidence of a nefarious plot was unnecessary to turn California's antimonopolists against Field. James O'Meara summed up their feelings in a report to the Tilden campaign: "Field . . . has no following in this state beyond a comparatively few, and these are not of the class who mold popular opinion in the party ranks or conduct the canvass in times of organized action. We designate them the Pacific Club Set."[148]

On to Cincinnati

As late as May 14, 1880, friends predicted California would send a "straightout Field delegation" to the national convention in Cincinnati.[149] Events would soon prove, however, that the Pacific Club Set sorely overestimated the antimonopolists' resolve and organization. The miscalculation became evident from the opening of the California Democratic Convention on May 19. The first day was uneventful, but the second featured a roll-call vote to determine the delegates' preference for presidential candidate. The result was Thurman, 133; Tilden, 97; Seymour, 95; Field, 2; Hancock, 2; Hendricks, 1.[150] Field won only 2 out of 330 votes! It must have been a shocking setback for the Field troops, but all was not lost. This was only a preference vote and was not binding. The real work of the convention was in selecting delegates to the national convention.

That work was carried out on the third day, with results that were less clear. Of the twelve delegates selected, only two, J. E. McElrath and Jesse D. Carr, were unqualified Field supporters.[151] However, the delegates were officially sent to Cincinnati uninstructed.[152] Between May 21 and the start of the national convention on June 22 there was still room for the Field forces to line up the delegates necessary to win California's vote.

It would not be an easy task. The motivation driving the great majority of California Democrats became obvious in their preference for a presidential candidate. Thurman, seen as the man who sought to bring the Pacific railroads under federal control, received 40 percent of the vote. Tilden, who ranked second, received only 29 percent. The vote for Field, who sought to strike down the Thurman bill, was minuscule. Nevertheless, Senator Gwin immediately went to work on support for Field although he apparently did not have much luck while the delegation remained in California.[153] The campaign's best hope, therefore, was to wait until the delegates arrived in Cincinnati where Field's forces might be able to convince some delegates to switch their allegiance.

The even larger problem for Field was the blow to his nationwide image. As in California, most state conventions took place in late May or early June, and most delegations went to the convention uninstructed. June was the month in which they could be won over. Field's campaign rested heavily on the claim that he would unite the California party, carry the West, and thus secure victory for the Democrats. The California convention indicated that he could win only a small percentage of his own party in his home state. Naturally, reports of Field's political demise spread quickly among political activists. Eugene Casserly assessed the California results in a letter to another presidential hopeful, Thomas Francis Bayard: "If your friends here have not done all they could to insist for you, they left the 'Field boom' in a very bad condition. In truth there was nothing of it visible to the naked eye after the convention had adjourned."[154]

Reports in the national press were equally damaging. The *New York Herald* claimed victory for Tilden and reported, "The Field boom is collapsed and dead." The *Atlanta Constitution,* which had earlier shown some support for Field, was more restrained in reporting that his "little boom . . . is in a damaged and dwarfed condition." Newspapers from other parts of the country followed suit. The *New York Times* was particularly vicious. Its editorial, sarcastically titled THE UNAPPRECIATED FIELD, chided the Field family for having "all the talents, except that of winning popularity."[155]

Field's literary bureau reacted quickly and valiantly. Employing a nineteenth-century version of what we call spin-doctoring, L. Q. Washington spread reports that the news of Field's defeat was "wildly false" and that the majority of California delegates were actually in his corner. His efforts had some impact. In the following weeks, papers in cities such as New Orleans, Washington, and Atlanta reported that Field had the support of up to nine of the state's delegates.[156] Whether this publicity would cause delegates to come over to Field remained to be seen. One California delegate who was loyal to Bayard smugly observed the process: "I see that our friend Stephen J. Field and his friends are at work restoring—if they can—his shattered fortunes."[157]

Field's campaign claimed strong support in other states as well. In the West, Colorado, Oregon, and Nevada were said to be lined up. When the Nevada delegation declared for Tilden, the Field literary bureau put together another media blitz claiming four of the state's six candidates were for Field. In the South, Field claimed Alabama, Arkansas, and Virginia. His forces also claimed support in several midwestern states.[158]

It was part of the nature of nineteenth-century politics that most claims of support would be disputed until the national convention was under way. Even the candidates could not be certain that they had an accurate count. A Tilden supporter, for example, reported that although Field's friends persistently claimed Arkansas the delegation there was for Tilden. Another reported that the Missouri delegation was anti-Tilden, but he could not discern a preference for any other candidate.[159] This uncertainty made it even more important to maintain the image of a winner. Endorsements helped, and the Field campaign reported receiving them from local newspapers and politicians, Washington insiders, even Democratic opponents and Republicans.[160]

It was looking like the most important endorsement might be Tilden's. To some insiders the "Grand Old War-horse" seemed more old than grand. Many people believed he would drop out of the running. Yet rivals knew Tilden still commanded formidable support, so they cautiously began to position themselves as his heir.[161] Given the recent history of conflict between Field's brothers and Tilden, it would take incredible audacity for the Field campaign to claim heirship for their candidate. Besides, Field had subtly snubbed an overture from Tilden and actively worked against him.[162] Nevertheless, toward the end of May and in early June the Field literary bureau began to spread the word that Field was Tilden's favorite, or at least that he was not objectionable to Tilden.[163]

In case some individuals were skeptical, as even some supporters were inclined to be, the Field campaign sent Senator Gwin to talk with Tilden. After a short meeting, Gwin issued a press release. I had a long talk with Mr. Tilden, Gwin reported, "He says that . . . as far as he is concerned Judge Field has no brothers and that this little personal matter would not stand in the way with him if Field is likely to be nominated." The ploy backfired when Tilden's nephew, who was present at the meeting, forced Gwin to admit he lied about Tilden's statement.[164] Henry Tilden's action had its intended effect. The next day the *New York Tribune* predicted that Tilden would not let a member of the Field family carry off the prize. And the *San Francisco Examiner* delighted in pointing out that Gwin, having been implicated in one lie, could not be trusted to predict the sentiment of the California delegation.[165] After this episode Field's literary bureau initiated a backup tactic, emphasizing that their candidate was objectionable to no one and was everyone's second choice.[166]

Despite their travails, Field's forces exhibited supreme confidence when they arrived in Cincinnati, projecting 130 to 200 votes for their candidate on the first ballot. Their confidence was complemented by a lavish display of what one contemporary newspaper called "special effects." By all accounts the Field campaign spent money more freely than most. They took one hundred fifty rooms, three parlors, and a suite at the Gibson House Hotel. The day before the convention a large, decorated bandwagon drawn by six white horses paraded through the streets to the tune of victory for Field. Unlikely friends joined in spreading the word of Field's strength. The front page of one local newspaper, owned by a Republican friend of Cyrus Field, greeted newly arrived delegates with generous talk about Field's prospects. Among other reports, it carried Field's biographical sketch and his speech on the Chinese question. Despite his inability to win the New York slots, John Kelly sent an alternate delegation to Cincinnati. The Tammany men were reported to be "shouting for Field" and circulating the *New York Sun*, loaded with Field literature.[167]

With his campaign continuing to press states' rights and strength in the West, Field's candidacy at first excited substantial interest at the convention. Attacks on Field indicated that rivals were taking him seriously. He was reproached for dissenting in the *Sinking Fund Cases.* In an attempt to weaken Field's states' rights record, someone misrepresented his strong states' rights opinion in the Missouri *Test Oath Cases*. Field was damned with praise in a report that he was being considered for the vice-presidency. He was reported to have lost the support of the Virginia delegation and rumored to have dropped out of the race altogether. A more sober report in the *Atlanta Constitution* noted that the weak point of the Field movement was the inability of his managers to get a foothold in the New York delegation.[168]

Most of the convention's drama centered not on Field and California but on New York. Even more specifically it centered on the question of whether Tilden would stay in the race. If he did, New York's vote was likely to be split, and Field hoped to capture some of the delegates. On June 18 Tilden wrote a vague letter to the New York delegation indicating that he was withdrawing.[169] Field's forces were probably dismayed by events that took place five days later. David Dudley Field, in particular, had worked hard to secure the support of Tammany Hall. His plan failed on June 23 when, adopting a report of the credentials committee, the convention refused to grant any seats to the Tammany alternate delegation.[170] No one knows what actual effect these two events had on Field's chances, but with Tilden out of the race and Tammany rejected, New York's seventy votes went to Payne.[171]

The Field campaign's confidence and enthusiasm turned out to be mostly bluster. Once the convention came to order its high point may have been J. E. McElrath's speech nominating Field, which was rather sappy even for the oratory of the 1880s. McElrath promised that "if nominated by this convention [Field] will sweep California like the winds that blow through her golden gates." But California opponents cackled at McElrath's suggestion that Field was a protector of the miner and the homesteader, a founder of the West, and a savior of Virginia.[172] Field had promised his popularity in the West would draw votes from any Republican candidate, but he received only six of California's twelve votes. Although he had made some gains since the state convention, it was not a convincing demonstration of support from his home state. Having lost support in Virginia and other states as well, Field received only 65 of the 738 votes on the first ballot. It was far off his prediction and a distant fourth to the leader Hancock's 171 votes. Yet all was not lost at that point. To secure the nomination a candidate would need 492 votes. Deadlock was a possibility, and Field could still slip in as a compromise candidate. However, a rush to Hancock the next day destroyed any hope the Field forces might have had. Hancock won the nomination on the second ballot.[173]

Judging Field's Campaign

Charles Fairman calls Field's pursuit of the presidency a "short-lived ab-erration."[174] His use of that term raises two complementary questions with respect to Field's decisions during the course of the year. First, how well did Field's legal opinions serve as a campaign strategy, and how effective were they as a political device? In other words, was the strategy viable? Second, how did the political campaign affect Field's opinions from the bench?

Regarding the first question, Field probably had little chance of winning the nomination, but the campaign itself was not an aberration. His efforts produced the desired effect, just not enough of it. Although his states' rights posture was essential for victory at the Democratic convention, Field was competing with several other candidates for the same delegates on the same issue. On the convention's first ballot Field received only 40 of a possible 205 southern votes, but that was 40 of his total of 65 votes, and he lost the Virginia delegation at the last minute. He did not capture enough southern support even to come close to victory, but most of the support he did receive at the convention was garnered from the southern states. The situation in the West presented Field with different problems. The Chinese issue clouded his predictions of capturing the region. As the campaign progressed, it be-came obvious the fervent antimonopoly spirit in the West was detrimental to Field's plans. Despite these complications, Field won fourteen of thirty possible votes, almost half the western delegates.[175] Field was a distant fourth after the first ballot, but his southern and western support at least put him into a position to move forward had the convention deadlocked.

Regarding the second question, Fairman may have used "aberration" to convey a belief that it is a bad idea for a justice of the Supreme Court to run for elected office. In this respect, Fairman's concerns were well founded. Field's campaign efforts undoubtedly had a long-term effect on constitu-tional law. The state action doctrine, which played into his southern strat-egy, had been part of the debate over the Civil Rights Act of 1866 and the Fourteenth Amendment. In the early stages of Reconstruction it represented an interpretation that Democrats and Conservative Republicans would have attached to these laws.[176] By 1880, with Americans tiring of Reconstruc-tion, it may even have come to reflect the position of an emerging majority. But the interpretation was a matter of political debate. Field's individual opinions in the jury exclusion cases connected the political argument to the body of constitutional law.

The effect of Field's western campaign was even more glaring. The aver-sion to class legislation expressed in his Chinese cases was part of the *of class leg*

American psyche well before 1880. But Field used the concept to create a broader limitation on government authority than had ever before been imagined. It defined both class and privilege in a new way that eventually would give federal courts oversight of most types of legislation. His *Sinking Fund Cases* opinion—with its emphasis on economic rights, the limits of state power, and an introduction of the notion that corporations had the same rights as persons—gave some sense of the direction judicial oversight of economic regulation would take. Whether these ideas would have eventually become constitutional doctrine in any event is impossible to tell. There is, however, little question that Field at least sped the process.

Field's reaction to defeat and a glimpse at his personality were revealed in an incident two months after the convention. An article in the *New York Herald*, sizing up the state of the Democratic party, noted the turmoil and rivalry in California. Former Senator Gwin, Field's point man, was a tool of the railroads, the newspaper charged. At the convention he and the Field organization attempted to win control of the California party through promises of patronage. The Field managers had spent money lavishly in Cincinnati, the article alleged. Although most California support was pledged to other candidates, Field's managers turned some delegates to their candidate by paying their way to the convention.[177]

On the very day the article appeared, Field wrote to his brother Cyrus in New York. Recounting the contents of the article, he expressed dismay at its "bitter and malicious spirit." Field speculated that the correspondent must have been bribed by rivals or was "some old enemy whom I have probably given a just judgment." Then he requested his brother take action.

I wish you would call upon the editor of the *Herald* and ask him to give you the name of the writer of the article in question. My impression is that the writer is a miserable scalawag in California and, if I am correct, it would be a very easy thing for me to have his political head decapitated or his political nose sufficiently pulled to make him hereafter politically silent.

Cyrus evidently had no success, for three days later Field wrote a second letter to his brother. Denying he had promised any appointment, paid any money, or knew of any such payment in exchange for votes, Field wrote, "If there is anything in the world that I would value it would be that whatever support was given to me was given freely without consideration. The office itself would be to me of no value if it were obtained any other way." Demanding "personal satisfaction" and warning that he "would not be trifled with" Field again demanded to know the writer's identity. "I say to you that if they do not give me the name of the man who wrote that article it will be the saddest day for Mr. Bennett [of the *Herald*] that ever has been in his life, and those very men who refuse will before the month goes around, regret it bitterly."[178]

A few days after the *New York Herald* incident brother David Dudley Field intervened to calm his brother down. Once again Field wrote to Cyrus:

I have told [David Dudley] that I shall carry no enmities with me to California and shall utter no angry words towards those who have acted ungenerously towards me this last year. . . . Politics I put behind me, and in my present temper I never wish any more to hear of the subject.

Field also wrote to his friend Matthew Deady expressing relief that his 1880 presidential campaign was over and that he would "not be blamed for all the crimes on earth."[179] The judge did not predict his future very well, however. He would not cease to utter angry words toward his enemies; nor would he cease to be blamed "for all the crimes on earth." And, in 1884, he would make one more foray into presidential politics before turning his full attention to the power he might wield from the bench. In 1884, however, with antimonopolists in control of the party, Field's presidential aspirations were resoundingly crushed before his campaign even left California. In early June of that year the state Democratic convention, now dominated by the antimonopoly wing of the party, expressly resolved to oppose Field's nomination.[180]

The article that caused the exchange of letters among the Field brothers was buried on page 10 of an unfriendly newspaper. If Field's response seemed extreme, ill-tempered, self-righteous, and vindictive, perhaps it reflected not only his nature but that of the political rivalry in his home state and the intensity of the conflicting visions of liberty behind that rivalry. Antimonopolists and Field were speaking the same language: liberty, privilege, and abuse of power. But they could not make sense of one another's meanings. Antimonopolists hated Field because he symbolized a trend that they believed threatened their liberty. Field could not understand why he was so despised because he believed in his version of liberty and believed his vision was best for all.

Such passions are often dangerous enough in politics. Field's run for the presidency demonstrated that they could boil over into the realm of law. It is unlikely that the justice changed any of his votes to enhance his prospects. That would have been out of character. What he did do was use the bench to proselytize: to try to convince others that his interpretation of the concept of liberty was right and universal. His efforts left a residue in the body of constitutional law. That residue contained the seeds of the state action doctrine, the idea of a corporate person and corporate equal protection, and the concept of class legislation. It harbored the core of a highly disputed view of what liberty entails.

Field displayed remarkable creative powers in molding legal doctrine to fit his ideal of liberty. Yet he could not have been completely satisfied. Up to this time, some of his most important innovations had been raised in his dissenting or individual opinions. He must have realized that his influence would be fleeting unless a majority of the Court came to think as he did.

8

CLASS LEGISLATION

As America moved through the 1880s the issues of slavery, war, and reconstruction retreated more and more into the past. It was the beginning of the Gilded Age, a time in which political issues tended to be more concerned about encouraging economic and technical progress and dealing with the social and economic effects of industrialization. In this atmosphere, Stephen Field made unmistakable his ideas about the role of government, the nature of liberty, and protection of property.

Early in the decade, with the presidency still on his mind, Field once again stretched the limits of judicial interpretation. Between 1882 and 1884, he produced three sets of remarkably bold opinions. First, in the *Railroad Tax Cases* of 1882 and 1883, Field introduced a new theory of corporate equal protection that emphasized his belief in the neutral state and his notions about the limits of government power. Then, in *Butchers' Union v. Crescent City Livestock Company,* he restated his theory that the concept of liberty included a right to pursue a lawful calling and emphasized the role that this doctrine played in protecting entrepreneurial liberty. Finally, in *Spring Valley Water Works v. Schottler,* Field stressed the idea that regulation could amount to confiscation and thus deny a company its property without due process of law.

As bold, straightforward, and unabashed as these opinions may have been, they were not particularly successful either as judicial lawmaking or as a political strategy. None of them represented the views of the majority of the Supreme Court. Field's *Railroad Tax Cases* opinions came from the Ninth Circuit. In the other two cases his were separate opinions, one in dissent and one concurring. If the opinions had any effect on his political campaign in 1884, it was to increase the fervor of antimonopolist opposition and contribute to his quick defeat.

Political ambition seemed to have brought out the fighter in Field; defeat seemed to bring out the good lawyer. By the mid-1880s his opinions became more subtle, less confrontational, and less direct. That shift did not mean he had changed his mind, however. Corporate equal protection, entrepreneurial liberty, and relating regulation to confiscation reflected an ideal. Field's tactics for achieving that ideal evolved, but his commitment to it did not waiver. Neither did his definition of liberty, his ideas about the limits of government, or his commitment to property rights.

Corporate Equal Protection

When California changed its property tax law in 1879 the state presented Stephen Field with an ideal opportunity to announce a novel theory of corporate equal protection. The *Railroad Tax Cases* focused upon the part of the new property tax law that created the formula for assessing property values. Under this formula, taxes for most kinds of property were based upon the property's actual value less the amount of any mortgages held against the property. Railroads "and other quasi public corporations" were the exception. Their property taxes would be based upon the actual value of their property—without any deduction for the amount of mortgages. There was absolutely no doubt that California's scheme of property taxation treated railroad property differently from the property owned by other individuals or companies. As Field pointed out, a private person who owned land valued at $100,000 but encumbered with a mortgage of $80,000 would be assessed at $20,000. If the tax were 2 percent that person would pay $400 in taxes. A railroad owning adjoining property worth $100,000 but encumbered with a mortgage of $80,000 would be assessed at the full $100,000 and pay $2,000 in taxes. The discrimination, he concluded, was "too palpable and gross to be questioned."[1]

So glaring was the unequal treatment of railroads that this tax law seemed custom-made for a lawsuit in Field's court. Some reformers actually suspected the new tax law was designed to be a failure and was written in a way that would make it susceptible to a legal challenge.[2] But the peculiarities of California's tax scheme were really a product of the circumstances under which it was created. Passed as part of the constitution of 1880, the new tax law was inspired by two separate and competing desires.

The state's farmers were driven by a desire to be relieved of a system that they thought resulted in unfair double taxation on their land. Under old law, the state had assessed all property at its full actual value with no deduction for the mortgages. The mortgage itself, although less tangible than land or equipment, was also deemed to be a form of taxable property. Therefore, at the same time the state was taxing landowners for the full value of their property, it was also taxing lenders on the value of the mortgages they held against that same land. As part of the loan contract, lenders typically required the landowner to pay the taxes assessed on the value of the mortgage. Reasoning that they actually paid once for the value of their property including the amount of the mortgage against it and then again for the value of the mortgage, farmers and landowners believed they were the victim of double taxation. They thus pushed hard for a provision in the new constitution that would assess property at actual value less the amount of their mortgages.[3]

Although antimonopolists at the convention were sympathetic to the farmers' and landowners' plight, they were driven by a distinct desire to ensure that railroads did not escape their "fair share" of taxation. Most people believed that the railroads were mortgaged to the hilt and would pay little in taxes if allowed to deduct the value of their mortgages. They also suspected that, because lenders from out of state held many of the mortgages, California would not be able to collect taxes on the mortgages. Intuitively, antimonopolists thought the railroad mortgages were a breed of credit quite different from mortgages held against a farm. Even some tax experts agreed, noting that railroad mortgages were not only loans but a way of raising operating capital. Although the antimonopolists did not oppose reducing the assessed value of farms and other individual property, they did not want that reduction to apply to railroad property. Thus they pushed for a provision in the new constitution providing that the franchise, roadway, roadbed, and rolling stock of all railroads in the state be assessed at their actual value.[4]

Predictably dissatisfied with the new tax scheme, the railroads withheld their 1880–1881 taxes and sued in the state courts to test the validity of the law. These first legal sorties resulted in victory for the state when the California Supreme Court rejected the railroad's petitions to invalidate the assessment formula.[5] The railroads were not through, however. By continuing to withhold payment they forced various counties to institute suits in the state courts to enforce the higher court's order and recover the delinquent taxes. The railroads, having lost once in the state forum, now preferred to have the issue decided in the federal courts. When San Mateo County sued to recover back taxes from the Southern Pacific Railroad, the company filed a petition asking that the case be removed to the circuit court for the district of California—the court over which Justice Stephen Field presided when he rode circuit.

Southern Pacific's petition for removal represented the same kind of interference with state authority that Field had so strenuously opposed in *Strauder v. West Virginia*, *Tennessee v. Davis*, and *Virginia v. Rives*.[6] Among other things, the Jurisdiction and Removal Act of 1875 permitted removal to federal courts in all suits arising under the U.S. Constitution, federal laws, or treaties.[7] The state valiantly argued that the act meant that a suit could be removed only when it was brought on the basis of a federal question, not when a federal question was raised in defense as it had been here. But Field protested that his hands were tied: "If we were at liberty to give our view of its meaning, we should not hesitate to limit the authority to remove suits of a civil nature from a state court to a federal court," he wrote. "[But] the Supreme Court has already passed upon the meaning of the act, and held in express terms against the view suggested."[8]

On that note, Field accepted jurisdiction in the *San Mateo* case. And with that, he opened the door for all of the railroad tax disputes to be settled in the federal courts. Facing the prospect of deciding numerous cases involving most of the counties in the state, Field and Judge Lorenzo Sawyer chose to focus on two cases, *San Mateo v. Southern Pacific Railroad Company* (1882) and *Santa Clara v. Southern Pacific Railroad Company* (1883). The matter dominated his attention when he rode circuit in 1883. Explaining to Judge Matthew Deady that the tax cases had delayed his departure from San Francisco, Field lamented,

I have never, since I have been on the Coast, been punished as I have this Summer; and it looks very much as though I shall be deprived of my contemplated visit to Japan. I had hoped to get away from the very sight of lawbooks, and make this trip and thus secure the rest which I so much need. I fear I shall get back to Washington a much wearied man, poorly fitted for the fatigues of the long session of our Court.[9]

Field's presence must have worried supporters of the new tax about their prospects for winning in the federal courts. His reputation alone was cause enough for concern. Besides, at the time he took jurisdiction, Field had strongly hinted what the outcome would be. Lecturing the parties about the issues to be decided in the upcoming case, he advised them to prepare to address the question of whether the Fourteenth Amendment applies to corporations as well as to natural persons. If so, he said, the case would turn on the meaning of the equal protection clause. That clause, Field said "was designed to cover all cases of possible discriminating and partial legislation against any class."[10]

Lined up among the battery of lawyers for the railroad was the justice's close friend Hastings Law School professor John Norton Pomeroy. There is some reason to believe that Field used Pomeroy to influence the way in which the company presented its cases in the court. Whether the two simply

shared information or actively planned a strategy, they undoubtedly cooperated in the cases. In the time between the *San Mateo* and *Santa Clara*
cases, Field wrote to Pomeroy from Washington:

Some weeks ago, I wrote to you with reference to the San Mateo tax case
[then on appeal to the Supreme Court] telling you that its decision would
not be made until the next term, and enclosing you also certain memoranda
which had been handed me by two of the judges. Have you ever received
these? They were, of course, intended only for your eye, and I should be
glad to know that they have come to your hands.

I shall leave here for San Francisco about the first of June. I may perhaps
stop at Carson City on the way, to hold Court for a few days there.

I shall be ready to take up any new tax cases as soon as I arrive, and I
hope in whatever case is tried all the facts relating to the mortgage upon the
property of the Railroad Company will be shown and also the extent to
which its property has been subjected to taxation throughout the State.[11]

As usual, the justice did not disappoint. In both cases he and Judge Sawyer agreed that the state's method of assessing value was unconstitutional.
"Whatever the state may do," Field reasoned, "it cannot deprive any one
within its jurisdiction of the equal protection of the laws." Field emphasized
that this meant more than providing an equal access to the institutions of
the law; it also meant that the state cannot impose on one individual "any
greater burdens or charges than such as are equally imposed upon all others
under like circumstances." And what more obvious burden or charge could
there be than taxation? None, reasoned Field. "It is not possible to conceive
of equal protection under any system of laws where arbitrary and unequal
taxation is permissible."[12]

Field agreed with the state's argument that it was permissible to classify
property and tax different types of property at different rates. But that was
not the issue here, he reasoned. The tax law did not classify property; it
taxed all property at the same rate. The ground for complaint in these cases
was that the rule used to ascertain the value of railroad property for tax
purposes was different from the rule used to ascertain the value of property
belonging to natural persons. This, he concluded, was not providing for a
different rate of taxation for different kinds of property but for unequal
taxation according to the character of the owner.[13]

Implicit in the state's argument was that the very character of the
owner—that is, its corporate status—gave the state the right to treat it differently. That raised the most visible question presented in these cases:
whether corporations were persons for purposes of the equal protection

clause. Field decided that they were. It is true that corporations are artificial persons, he reasoned. But they consist of aggregations of individuals united for some legitimate business purpose. "It would be a most singular result if a constitutional provision intended for the protection of every person against partial and discriminating legislation by the states, should cease to exert such protection the moment the person becomes a member of a corporation. We cannot accept such a conclusion."[14]

Field reminded his readers of the role corporations had come to play in late nineteenth-century society. They engage in manufacture and commerce, build ships, construct houses, bring the products of earth and sea to market, build railroads, and carry water to our cities, he observed. They also erect colleges, churches, and theaters. "Indeed," he continued, "there is nothing which is lawful to be done to feed and clothe our people, to beautify and adorn their dwellings, to relieve the sick, to help the needy, and to enrich and ennoble humanity, which is not to a great extent done through the instrumentalities of corporations."[15]

When antimonopolists looked at the corporation they did not see this same altruistic instrumentality. They saw a threatening power—a power strong enough to bring the state to its knees by refusing to pay taxes. Equal protection and liberty had a different meaning when viewed from their perspective. As one antimonopolist leader put it, they thought of themselves as "the front rank of the battle now waging between the people on one side and aggregated capital on the other; between the equal rights of all on one side and the exclusive and oppressive privileges of the favored few on the other."[16]

Still, even Field's opponents had to admit he had made a good point regarding the importance of corporations, which had become ubiquitous in American society of the 1880s. Since it would be impossible to function without them, the law would have to accommodate them. Drawing analogies between corporations and persons for legal reasons was already a common practice. In order to determine the proper jurisdiction of a lawsuit, for example, the law recognized corporations as "citizens" of the state in which they were incorporated.[17] But Field's opinions in the *Railroad Tax Cases* were not about drawing analogies or tinkering with legal procedure; they were about fundamental rights. It was one thing to classify corporations as persons for a particular purpose. It was quite another to give an artificial entity—a form of business association—all the rights of a natural person. None but the most extreme among antimonopolists proposed to eliminate corporations; they wanted to establish the states' power over them. For antimonopolists, Field's notion of fundamental rights raised one *anti-monopolists arg* (handwritten margin note)

particularly troubling question: <u>Didn't the state have authority</u> to control the artificial entity it <u>had created?</u>

Turning to an established principle of constitutional law, the state's lawyers tried to make this very point. For most of the century, the state's power to control corporations fell under the umbrella of Article 1, section 10 of the Constitution, which guarantees that no state shall impair the obligation of contracts. In the *Dartmouth College* case the Supreme Court ruled that corporate charters constituted a contract that could not be impaired.[18] Regulations that changed the terms of the charter were therefore invalid unless the charter itself reserved to the state the power later to alter and amend the charter. This was a significant "unless" because states thereafter made it a standard practice to include reserve clauses both in specific corporate charters and in passing general laws governing the formation of corporations. In this vein the state argued that under such a reserve clause the state retained the power to change the manner of taxation by applying a new method for assessing taxable value.

Field was not swayed. The reserve clause gives the state power over the corporation's franchise but it does not give the state power over the corporation's property, he reasoned. The state can retain power only over that which it grants. It grants the franchise, but it does not grant the cars on the track or the engines that move them. "The property of the corporation, acquired in the exercise of its faculties, is held independently of such reserve power," Field concluded, "and the state can only exercise over it the control which it exercises over the property of individuals engaged in similar business."[19]

If Field's interpretation of the contract clause had subsequently been adopted by the majority of the Supreme Court, it would have taken constitutional law in a drastically new direction. From the time of John Marshall, the Court had insisted that tax exemptions in a corporate charter be narrowly construed.[20] Field had previously followed that reasoning. Writing for the Court in *Tomlinson v. Jessup* (1872) he expressly ruled that a reserve clause in a corporate charter allowed the state to change the terms of a charter and tax a railroad.[21] Now he was saying that, reserve clause notwithstanding, a state could not change its tax law with respect to corporate property without running a risk of violating the corporation's rights. A reserve clause, he reasoned, does not give the state power to withdraw from corporations the guarantees of the Constitution.[22] Finding the applicable guarantee in the Fourteenth Amendment's equal protection clause, Field seemed willing to use it to circumvent nearly a century of precedent under the contract clause.

For Field, California's tax scheme represented a type of class legislation that was "the very essence of tyranny."[23] "When burdens are placed upon particular classes or individuals, while the majority of the people are exempted, . . . oppression becomes possible and lasting," he warned.[24] The Fourteenth Amendment was intended to avoid that kind of oppression. "It stands in the constitution as a perpetual shield against all unequal and partial legislation by the states, and the injustice which follows from it, whether directed against the most humble or the most powerful; against the despised laborer from China, or the most envied master of millions."[25] While this ideal sounded benign enough in the abstract, it was obvious that the practical effect of Field's railroad tax decision was to provide a constitutional shield for the envied master of millions. And it would be impossible to convince Field's enemies that this was not always his intention.

The *Railroad Tax Cases* played an important role in Field's second run at the Democratic presidential nomination. Taxation of railroads was the one issue, more than any other, that solidified political opposition against him in California. As R. Hal Williams points out, the tax question went right to the heart of the antimonopolists' struggle to establish the supremacy of the state over corporations.[26] With the antimonopolists gaining control of the Democratic party in 1884, county convention after county convention passed resolutions expressly opposing Field's candidacy.[27] By the time the party gathered in Stockton on June 10, 1884, the mood had turned decidedly against Field. In one resolution, delegates condemned the federal judiciary for interfering with the state's collection of taxes on railroad property. Then, in a mortal setback for Field's friends, the convention passed its final resolution: "That the democracy of California unanimously repudiates the presidential aspirations of Stephen J. Field, and that we hereby pledge ourselves to vote for no man as delegate to the national convention of July 8, 1884, who will not before this convention pledge himself to use his earnest endeavors to defeat these aspirations."[28] The extent of feelings against Field was reemphasized when a motion to strike this resolution was defeated by a vote of 453 to 19. Savoring their victory, antimonopolists boasted that each delegate to the upcoming national convention thereby pledged himself for "Tilden first, Thurman second and for Field never."[29]

Reflecting on "the very strange action in California," Field wrote to John Norton Pomeroy: "Had I received the cordial support, instead of opposition of that state my candidacy, according to the judgment of my friends, would have stood great chances of success."[30] He complained to fellow conservative John DeBarth Shorb that "words of praise, nay even of consideration, have so seldom been spoken of me or of my work." But he

"THE RETURN OF THE PRODIGAL." The *Wasp* of July 11, 1885, during the time the railroad tax cases were pending, depicts Field groveling before Leland Stanford. (Courtesy Bancroft Library)

continued his letter to Shorb in a more philosophical vein: "I have long since ceased to expect [words of praise], feeling confident that at some future day my services in support of order, for the security of rights of person and of property, and of the great institutions of society, will be recognized and appreciated."[31]

On another level, Field took the defeat personally. When the presidential election of 1884 put a Democrat, Grover Cleveland, in the White House, Field became deeply involved in the struggle to control federal patronage in his home state. He attacked his old enemies personally and with a vengeance. Years later, upset that William English was to be appointed collector of the Port of San Francisco, Field called the antimonopolist leader "one of the most offensive, cowardly and base opponents I ever had in California."[32]

Field never gained Cleveland's confidence. By 1886 he was genuinely frustrated by the president's failure to listen to his recommendations.[33] But in earlier letters to Cleveland and his advisers, Field wrote that patronage should be reserved for "conservative men, . . . who believe in order, in law, in property, and the great institutions of society." Field's letters contained one persistent theme. The antimonopolists' views were "agrarian and communistic," he warned, and they represented nothing more than a desire "to break down all associated capital by loading it with unequal and oppressive burdens."[34]

Field's letters reinforced the perception that the *Railroad Tax Cases* had already made clearer than ever: a certain class consciousness permeated Field's doctrine. The opinions demonstrated how his version of the neutral state would turn on its head the old Jacksonian ideal upon which Field was weaned. They offered a different kind of government neutrality that, instead of ensuring that government did not create a powerful elite, would ensure that it did not interfere with the powerful elite.

As a practical matter, the *Railroad Tax Cases* resulted in an astounding victory for the Southern Pacific. The state of California joined the counties in appealing the cases to the Supreme Court, but while the appeal was pending, the validity of the assessment method was uncertain. State and county governments had no means of determining the amount of tax and thus no authority to collect back taxes from the railroads. In the wake of Field's decision, therefore, the Southern Pacific was able to force the state into settlement and essentially dictate the terms of its own taxation. The cases were a depressing setback for reformers. For the people who had hoped to find in the government an ally in their struggle against the railroad, "there could be no more forceful illustration of the fact that a power had grown up in the State greater than the State itself."[35]

The impact of Field's opinions on constitutional doctrine, however, was limited. When *Santa Clara* was appealed to the Supreme Court, Chief Justice Waite told the attorneys, "The court does not wish to hear argument on the question whether the provision in the Fourteenth Amendment to the Constitution, which forbids a State to deny to any person within its jurisdiction the equal protection of the laws, applies to corporations. We are all of the opinion that it does."[36] Field's colleagues on the bench were ready to recognize the principle of a corporate person, but that was only a partial victory for Field. The far more important point of Field's opinion was his theory that a corporation was a unique class of person that under the equal protection clause was entitled to protection against discrimination. The Supreme Court majority made it just as certain that they were unwilling to adopt that theory. Ultimately, the full Court did confirm the result of Field's circuit court ruling, but it did so on the basis of a peculiarity in the California law, ignoring the sweeping constitutional theories upon which Field had based his circuit court opinions.

Field's theory of corporate equal protection was a grand experiment that failed. The Supreme Court ignored it, and Field himself soon abandoned it. Never again did he attempt to employ the equal protection clause to invalidate a tax on corporations. Later, he wrote opinions upholding a tax on the corporate franchise, a tax dedicated to paying the salaries of railroad commissioners, and even upholding a law that treated one type of company differently from others in the way taxes were computed.[37]

The corporate equal protection theory also lost its allure for Field in cases involving regulation rather than taxation. In 1888, for example, Field ruled that equal protection did not prohibit a state from imposing special regulations on foreign corporations.[38] That same year he explained that "specific regulations for one kind of business, which may be necessary for the protection of the public, can never be just ground of [an equal protection] complaint, because like restrictions are not imposed upon businesses of a different kind."[39] Field's abandonment of corporate equal protection did not signal that he was giving up, however. All the while he was looking to other legal devices that would accomplish the same goals.

Entrepreneurial Liberty and the Police Power

A decade had passed since Stephen Field had first suggested in the *Slaughter-House Cases* that liberty under the Fourteenth Amendment included a right to pursue a lawful calling. New Orleans butchers again were going to provide the opportunity for him to expand on that idea. The

Slaughter-House Cases had upheld the Louisiana legislature's decision in 1869 to grant to Crescent City Livestock Company a twenty-five-year exclusive right to operate a slaughterhouse in New Orleans. In 1879, a new Louisiana constitution gave cities, rather than the state, the power to regulate slaughtering within their respective limits. The same section of the new constitution also included the provisos that no monopoly or exclusive privilege could exist and that the slaughtering business could not be restricted to the land or houses of one company. A separate section abolished "the monopoly features" in any existing charters, except those of railroads. Given this new authority, the city of New Orleans quickly enacted an ordinance that opened the slaughtering business in the city to general competition. Pouncing on the opportunity, the Butchers' Union Company opened a competing slaughterhouse.

The ongoing battle of New Orleans butchers became a constitutional issue once again when the Crescent City Company successfully turned to the federal circuit court for an injunction to prohibit its rival from continuing in business. The Butchers' Union Company appealed to the Supreme Court, which decided the case in early May 1884, about a month before the California Democratic Convention. *Butchers' Union Co. v. Crescent City Co.* was, in the main, a contract clause case. Everyone agreed that the 1869 Louisiana legislature had given Crescent City Company an exclusive right. The issue was whether a later legislature could repeal that right without violating the prohibition of Article 1, section 10 of the U.S. Constitution that "no state shall pass any law . . . impairing the obligation of contract." A unanimous Supreme Court decided that it could.[40]

Writing for the Court, Justice Miller recognized that the state legislature could grant an exclusive right. In granting an exclusive right to a private corporation it could not, however, bargain away the powers required for it to perform its function as a government. These were referred to as the police power of the states. This was not new doctrine. Miller pointed to numerous opinions, including Field's opinion in *Boyd v. Alabama,* to support the proposition that one legislature could not agree to a contract that would restrain the power of a subsequent legislature to legislate for the public welfare.[41] The only question thus was whether the provisions of the new Louisiana constitution at issue in this case constituted an exercise of the police power. Miller described the police power as "well known but undefined." Attempting to fill in a definition, Miller noted that the term referred to laws "indispensable to the public welfare" and at least included "laws to protect public health and public morals." The regulation of slaughterhouses, he concluded, was a matter of public health.[42]

Although he agreed with the result, Stephen Field thought the original act was invalid for another reason. By giving an exclusive right to the Crescent City Company, Field reasoned, the Louisiana legislature had taken from other butchers the right to pursue a lawful calling. Essentially repeating his argument from the *Slaughter-House Cases*, Field maintained that monopolies such as the one in question were prohibited by common law, destroyed freedom of trade, discouraged labor and industry, and allowed grantees to enhance the price of commodities. They were also void because they interfered with an individual's liberty to pursue a lawful calling, he reasoned. Just as he had done a decade earlier, Field found this right to pursue a lawful calling in natural rights and in the Declaration of Independence. He also found support in the economic thinking of his day. Quoting from Adam Smith's *Wealth of Nations*, Book 1, chapter 10, Field wrote:

The property which every man has is his own labor, as it is the original foundation of all other property, so it is the most sacred and inviolable. The patrimony of the poor man lies in the strength and dexterity of his own hands, and to hinder his employing this strength and dexterity in what manner he thinks proper, without injury to his neighbor, is a plain violation of this most sacred property. It is a manifest encroachment upon the just liberty both of the workman and of those who might be disposed to employ him. As it hinders the one from working at what he thinks proper, so it hinders the others from employing whom they think proper.

Field made the same connection to the Constitution as he had done in the *Slaughter-House Cases*. Melding the concepts of due process of law, equal protection, and privileges and immunities of citizens, he reasoned that the Fourteenth Amendment guaranteed the right to pursue a calling.[43]

In a separate concurring opinion Justice Bradley agreed with Field that the Fourteenth Amendment guarantees what he called "the liberty of pursuit." He also agreed that the original law was void because it created a monopoly. But Bradley, who described monopolies as "the bane of our body politic," had already demonstrated that he had a much broader view of what constituted a monopoly.[44] He would apply the term to any business that had a vise grip on a commodity or on the flow of commerce, which included monopolies created by private means as well as those granted by government.

Bradley opposed Crescent City's monopoly for its own sake, but Field opposed it only because the state's grant of exclusive privilege restricted any other individual's pursuit of ordinary employment and business.[45] Monopoly was, in this sense, the ultimate form of regulation. Perhaps Field's nephew, Justice David Brewer, best explained the difference between Field's and Bradley's view of monopoly. Dissenting in *Budd v. New York* (1892) Brewer argued that there are two types of monopoly, one of law and the other of fact. A monopoly of law exists when exclusive privileges are granted from the state, he said. Because the law creates it, the law alone can break it, and being a creation of the law it is the legitimate subject of legislative regulation. A monopoly of fact, he reasoned, exists where anyone by his money and labor furnishes facilities for business that no one else has. The existence of a monopoly of fact does not justify regulation, he concluded. Because no exclusive privilege exists, anyone can break a monopoly of fact.[46]

With a concern about monopoly as he defined it combined with a distrust of government, Field's opinion in *Butchers' Union v. Crescent City* reflected elements of several traditions and political or economic theories. He attacked government-granted monopolies in a manner that would have brought a smile to the face of any old Jacksonian. His glorification of the right to pursue a calling satisfied the ideals of free labor. His opposition to regulation and admiration of Adam Smith reflected the influence of laissez-faire economics. The case was easy for him, however, because he believed the original Louisiana slaughterhouse statute had created a monopoly of law.

Understanding Field's conception of monopoly also helps to explain some apparent inconsistencies in his opinions. Despite his reputation as a champion of big business, for example, Field wrote an 1892 opinion that thwarted the Illinois Central Railroad's scheme to control Chicago's lakefront. His opinion in *Illinois Central Railroad v. Illinois* invalidated a state law granting to the Illinois Central perpetual use of the submerged land running along almost the entire Chicago waterfront. Field then turned to the public trust doctrine he and Judge Baldwin had developed thirty-two years earlier while on the California Supreme Court. The grant to Illinois Central amounted to an abdication of the state's control of the harbor, he observed, and such an abdication was not consistent with the exercise of the public trust, which requires government to preserve those waters for use of the public. The state can no more abdicate its trust over the property in which the whole people are interested, he said, than it can abdicate its police powers in the administration of government and the preservation of the peace. Public trust was not, however, the only consideration underlying Field's opinion. Field was outraged that the Illinois law would transfer the "management and entire commerce of the harbor of a great city" from the state to the absolute control of one private corporation.[47] The thought of a state granting such control over the stream of commerce once again brought out Field's opposition to monopolies of law, to monopoly as an inhibition on the individual's right to pursue a calling, and to monopoly as the ultimate form of regulation.

To the extent that it dealt with the nature of monopoly, Field's opinion in *Butchers' Union v. Crescent City* did little more than embellish his dissent in the *Slaughter-House Cases*. But the new case highlighted another concept that was even more important to Field and presented him an opportunity to refine more clearly his ideas about limitations on state authority. That concept was the police power of the states.

Field had always agreed with the majority's general proposition that the police power could not be granted away. The idea that disturbed him was the majority's implication that the notion of police power was merely a means of describing a vast range of state authority. The police power, Miller had noted, was a term that referred to "laws indispensable to the public welfare." This was the traditional view. John Marshall simply used the term to distinguish the functions of state government from the functions of the federal government.[48] Chief Justice Roger Taney later described the police power as "nothing more or less than the power of government inherent in every sovereignty to the extent of its dominion, the power to govern men and things."[49] Field, however, intended to show that the concept of police power also played a role in defining the limits of government.

The limitation was found in his definition of police power. The traditional definition recognized that there were limits to a state's authority under the police power. A state could not pass legislation that conflicted with a provision of the Constitution or that inhibited individual liberties that the Constitution guaranteed. Field agreed with that, but added that police power was, in any case, limited to a particular set of functions. So long as regulations do not conflict with any constitutional inhibition or natural right, he maintained, no one disagrees that the states possess the power to prescribe regulations affecting the morals, health and safety, and peace and good order of society.[50] Combined, these three categories represented expansive boundaries for state authority. But boundaries they were, nevertheless.

Field's record regarding the public morals category of the police power was the most clear-cut. He believed the state had a right and a duty to promote Protestant or Victorian morality. From his earliest days in California, he had voted to uphold Sunday closing laws.[51] He consistently upheld laws to control gambling and lotteries.[52] In *Ex parte Jackson*, after a long discourse on the importance of mail service to a free press, he upheld a law that prohibited sending obscene, lewd, or lascivious material through the mail.[53] In *Crowley v. Christensen* Field followed his long-established pattern of upholding laws regulating the sale of alcoholic beverages. "By the general concurrence of opinion of every civilized and Christian community, there are few sources of crime and misery to society equal to the dram shop," he wrote. "The sale of liquor has been, at all times, considered the proper subject of legislation."[54] Still, Field had reservations when the Court upheld a Kansas law that declared all bars and breweries to be common nuisances and authorized officials to seize them and destroy all the liquor and property located on the premises. "[I cannot] see how the protection of the health and morals of the people of the State can require the destruction of property like bottles, glasses, and other utensils, which may be used for many lawful purposes," he wrote. Worried that the destruction of private property had been taken beyond a legitimate purpose, Field maintained that this law had "crossed the line which separates regulation from confiscation."[55]

Field's record with respect to the health and safety category of the police power was more complex. He undeniably recognized that states had the authority to protect its citizens from disease and hazards. When California assessed landowners to pay for swamp-reclamation projects, Field found the state's desire to "drain milarious districts" to be a legitimate health and safety concern.[56] He was even willing to admit that this authority extended to state laws regulating medical practice. Noting that medicine is a profession that must "deal with all those subtle and mysterious influences upon which health and life depend," he upheld a West Virginia law that required physicians to obtain a license.[57]

Yet in other cases where the state appeared to be interested in protecting public health and safety, Field ruled against the legislation. He reasoned, for example, that a state law requiring inspection of cattle at the border to be a burden on interstate commerce and that a law prohibiting the sale of oleomargarine was not a health law at all.[58] Similarly, in *Butchers' Union v. Crescent City*, he disagreed with the majority's contention that the state was relinquishing its authority to protect public health. Thus health and safety proved to be a concept that allowed Field flexibility in applying his police power doctrine. This was nowhere more evident than in the Chinese laundry ordinance cases, in which Field overruled a law requiring the licensing of laundries but upheld laws limiting the hours of operation and the hours of labor in laundries.[59]

The health and safety component mixed with the peace and good order component in cases involving laws abolishing the fellow servant doctrine. This doctrine was a nineteenth-century court-made rule that relieved employers of liability for on-the-job injuries to their workers whenever the injury was caused in part by a co-worker. In the 1880s, Kansas, Minnesota, and other states enacted legislation to abolish the fellow servant doctrine in cases involving railroads. The railroads complained that, by imposing liability where there had been none before, the new laws deprived them of property without due process. They also argued that because the change was directed only at railroads it deprived them of equal protection of law. Writing for the Court, Field rejected both claims on the basis that "the hazardous character of the business of operating a railway would seem to call for special legislation with respect to all railroad corporations, having for its object the protection of their employees as well as the safety of the public."[60]

By peace and good order, Field meant laws that provided for the settlement of disputes and laws intended to smooth the flow of commerce. The fellow servant doctrine was just one of many rules courts used to govern legal disputes. These doctrines were not based on a constitutional right; they did not take property or limit its use. They were simply judicially created rules that made presumptions and assigned burdens of proof to be applied in a particular dispute. Field generally agreed that it was well within the states' police power to pass statutes changing the burdens and presumptions. On this basis, he also upheld other changes in the rules governing disputes. He wrote opinions that upheld so-called fencing laws, for example. Although there were variations, these laws applied when a railroad had failed to maintain fences or refused to settle disputes with farmers whose stock had been injured by a train. Usually the law provided double damages to the farmers.[61]

As with the health and safety component, this concept of peace and good order provided a good deal of flexibility. In *Gulf, Colorado and Santa Fe Co. v. Ellis,* for example, Field joined in an opinion invalidating a Texas law that required railroads to pay attorneys' fees and court costs to a plaintiff who won a suit against them.[62] He upheld an Illinois law that required railroads to assume the cost of constructing crossing facilities and maintaining flagmen along their routes.[63] Illinois might have been motivated by the desire to protect public safety and the desire to smooth the flow of commerce in that case. But Field agreed with the majority of the Court that there was no public factor in a Nebraska law requiring railroads to erect grain elevators along their lines. The Court found the Nebraska statute unconstitutional.[64]

These cases involved a subtle interplay between the nature of the po-

lice power and the intensity of the individual right that was supposed to
have been violated. Although the outcome of various cases was sometimes
confusing, the elements of Field's police power jurisprudence were taking
shape. First, it was clear that the concept of police power was for Field not
just a description of government authority but also a limit on government
power. Second, even when state legislation was within the boundaries of
the police power, it had to conform to Field's notion of individual liberty.
This included Field's idea that the guarantee of liberty in the due process
clause included the right to pursue a lawful calling and his belief that the
equal protection clause prohibited partial and discriminating "class legislation." Finally, and perhaps most important, was Field's insistence that the
power to determine whether a statute fell within the boundaries of the police power or violated an individual right rested with the courts, not with
the legislature.

This last aspect of Field's police power jurisprudence was the prominent
feature in the 1888 case *Powell v. Pennsylvania*. The law in question prohibited the sale and manufacture of oleomargarine as a substitute for butter.
Charged with selling two cases of oleomargarine, Powell maintained in his
defense that oleomargarine was not a threat to public heath. The statute, he
argued, was therefore not a lawful exercise of the police power.

John Harlan, who wrote the majority opinion, summarized Powell's
constitutional claim this way: the defendant claimed that the Pennsylvania
law deprived him of his "enjoyment upon terms of equality with all others
in similar circumstances of the privilege of pursuing an ordinary calling
or trade, and of acquiring, holding, and selling property" and that this
right "is an essential part of his rights of liberty and property as guaranteed
by the Fourteenth Amendment."[65] Here was a statement that should have
made Stephen Field proud; with just a few words it captured most of the
ideas about liberty that he had been preaching for decades.

But Harlan was not willing to declare the Pennsylvania law unconstitutional. "Every possible presumption . . . is in favor of the validity of a statute," he wrote, and "this continues until the contrary is shown beyond a
rational doubt."[66] To Harlan, this presumption was a matter of separation
of powers. The prohibition of oleomargarine may have seemed silly to him.
It certainly must be surprising to most of us—a generation eating "I Can't
Believe It's Not Butter—Light." But in Harlan's opinion questions of fact
and of public policy belonged to the legislature. "If all that can be said
of this legislation is that it is unwise, or unnecessarily oppressive to those
manufacturing or selling wholesome oleomargarine as an article of food,

their appeal must be to the legislature, or to the ballot-box, not to the judiciary," he said. "The latter cannot interfere without usurping powers committed to another department of government."[67]

That Field disagreed with this presumption was evident from the way he described the issue before the Court. The question distinctly presented, he said, is "whether a state can lawfully prohibit the manufacture of a healthy and nutritious article of food designed to take the place of butter."[68] Field was outraged. The discovery of a new article of food, equally healthy and nutritious and less expensive than butter, should be a matter for congratulations, not for prohibition, he said. The Fourteenth Amendment guarantees the right to pursue a lawful calling and equal protection of the law, he reminded his readers. "Who will have the temerity to say that these constitutional principles are not violated by an enactment which absolutely prohibits an important branch of industry for the sole reason that it competes with another, and may reduce the price of an article of food for the human race?"[69]

Although he was willing to admit that the state had the power to pass regulations to protect public health, Field argued that the state must show that the regulations it does enact have a reasonable relationship to this legitimate end. A mere declaration by the state that a statute relates to health is not enough, he reasoned. "The court must be able to see that [the law] has in fact some relation to the public health, that the public health is the end aimed at, and that [the law] is appropriate and adapted to that end."[70] Disagreeing with Harlan about the relative powers of the branches of government, Field argued that it is up to the courts to determine whether the facts support the state's claim and to enforce the Constitution.

Forceful though Field's opinion might have been, in 1888 he was still writing in dissent. By the mid-1890s, however, the Court was beginning to turn to his way of thinking. Before Field resigned from the bench, a new majority on the Supreme Court would expand upon his theory that the Fourteenth Amendment guaranteed a right to pursue a lawful trade or calling. Furthermore, it would adopt his belief that the Court should stand as a watchdog guarding against state intrusions on entrepreneurial liberty.[71]

Justice Rufus Peckham, who joined the Court in December 1895, was one new member who was destined to carry on where Field had left off. In the 1897 case of *Allgeyer v. Louisiana*, Peckham wrote an opinion that expanded even further Field's ideas of entrepreneurial liberty. "In the privilege of pursuing an ordinary calling or trade, and of acquiring, holding and selling property must be embraced the right to make all proper contracts in relation thereto," he wrote.[72] The right to pursue an ordinary calling was thus transformed into "liberty of contract." The theory was already familiar in scholarly writings and had been applied in lower court cases.[73] But *Allgeyer* marked the first time that it was recognized in the Supreme Court of the United States. Now the nation's highest court was willing to rule that the Fourteenth Amendment guaranteed a fundamental right to enter into any agreement without interference from the state.

Of course, liberty of contract could not be absolute. As one particularly plainspoken critic put it, "The spectacle of a government that cannot prohibit a contract merely because two grown persons desire to make it, is so utterly absurd as to be beyond the region of discussion if government of any kind is to continue."[74] Liberty of contract would still be subject to a legitimate exercise of the police power. And there were all kinds of government restrictions on what people could or could not agree to. But the Court would soon grant to itself the authority to determine the proper balance. In 1905 a 5 to 4 majority in *Lochner v. New York* relied on liberty of contract to invalidate a New York law limiting the hours of work in bakeries. Field had died by this time, but his influence was perhaps stronger than ever.

The opinions in *Lochner v. New York* bore an eerie resemblance to those in *Powell v. Pennsylvania*. Justice Harlan, who had written the majority opinion in *Powell,* was still on the Court. Harlan admitted in *Lochner* that liberty of contract was among the rights envisioned in the Fourteenth Amendment's guarantee that no person could be deprived of life, liberty, and property without due process of law. He agreed that laws infringing upon liberty of contract could be justified only if they were legitimate exercises of the state's police power. He thus agreed that a law limiting bakers' hours could be justified only as a health measure. But in Harlan's opinion, "When the validity of a statute is questioned, the burden of proof, so to speak, is upon those who assert it to be unconstitutional."[75] He went further to provide a measure of that burden: "The state is not amenable to the judiciary, in respect of its legislative enactments, unless such enactments are plainly, palpably, beyond all question, inconsistent with the Constitution of the United States."[76]

Harlan's opinion in *Lochner* was a virtual photocopy of his opinion in *Powell v. Pennsylvania.* This time, however, he was in the minority. As if standing in for Stephen Field, Peckham wrote a majority opinion that placed a heavy burden on the state to prove the legitimacy of its legislation. "The mere assertion that the subject relates, though but in a remote degree, to the public health, does not necessarily render the enactment valid," he wrote. "The act must have a more direct relation, as a means to an end, and the end itself must be appropriate and legitimate."[77] Six years after Field's death, the transformation to his way of thinking on the matter of entrepreneurial liberty was complete.

Confiscation

Complementing Field's notions about entrepreneurial liberty was the idea that government regulation of economic matters could constitute confiscation of private property. Field illustrated the link in *Mugler v. Kansas* by implying that a state regulation on the sale and manufacture of alcoholic beverages would be illegitimate if it deprived brewers of their property without just compensation.[78] He made his point more boldly in an opinion he wrote just prior to the California Democrats' 1884 nominating convention in Stockton. That case involved Spring Valley Water Works, a company formed in 1858 to supply water to the city of San Francisco. Under the original law governing the company, a board of commissioners set the rates for water. The board comprised four members, two chosen by the city and two by the company. If unable to agree, the four members themselves chose a fifth. The constitution of 1879 changed this method for rate-making. Under the new constitution San Francisco's board of supervisors (city council) had the sole authority to fix the rates for water supplied to the city.

Spring Valley Water Works claimed that this change in the method of setting rates violated the contract clause of the U.S. Constitution. The company's case made its way to the Supreme Court where a majority, noting that the original rate-setting law was subject to a reserve clause, rejected the company's claim.[79] This relatively mundane case would have given little cause for attention had it not been for Stephen Field's dissent.

Borrowing from his *Railroad Tax Cases* opinion, Field argued that the reserve clause applied only to the corporation's franchise, not to the property it subsequently acquired. Because it had harnessed the water, Field reasoned, the company had a property interest in the water. "Indeed," he wrote, "it is a general principle of law, both natural and positive, that where a subject . . . which otherwise could not be brought under the control or use of man, is reduced to such control or use by individual labor a right of property in it is acquired by such labor."[80]

Field's reasoning subtly shifted between a discussion of constitutional doctrine under the contract clause to the theory of contract in common law. The purpose of the original contract was to create an impartial body to determine rates, he reasoned. "From the very nature of its creation and its relation to others, the board of supervisors, an elective body, cannot be impartial."[81] Besides, Field maintained, the city is a party to the contract. By upholding the new law that gave city authorities full control over rate-making, the Court had allowed the state to break a vital provision of the original agreement. In this sense, he complained, the majority sanctioned the idea that a contract made between an agency of state government and a corporation is binding only on the corporation.

Viewing the original law strictly as a contract allowed Field conveniently to ignore that in passing laws to create and govern corporations the state was acting not only as a party to a contract but also as sovereign. Chief Justice Waite addressed this point indirectly when he noted that the majority had no doubt that it is within the power of government to regulate the prices at which water is sold by one who enjoys a virtual monopoly. That question, he said, was settled in *Munn v. Illinois*.[82]

The power of the sovereign to protect the interests of the people was not Field's concern, however. Rather, in this case he was undoubtedly driven by the thought of the sovereign as a threat to the interest and liberty of a business. In language extraordinarily frank for a judicial opinion, he left no doubt that his dissent was inspired by a deep distrust of the democratic process:

There will always be . . . a great pressure upon the board by the people electing it to regulate the price of water in their interest, without regard to that of the company. The influence thus exerted to warp the judgment of the members and change the character of the body from that of an impartial tribunal to one acting in the interest of its constituents, every practical man dealing with the corporation would appreciate and act upon. All the influences usually brought to bear at elections to secure the choice of those who will carry out the wishes of the voters, we should expect to see applied to secure the election of candidates thus empowered to fix the price of the article which the voters daily consume.

It was difficult for him to conceive of any tribunal more liable to be controlled by external influences against the interests of the company.[83]

Field's emphasis that the company did not have the benefit of an impartial tribunal fit neatly into his belief that rate-making was a judicial rather than a legislative question. Allowing a legislative body to act as the rate-making tribunal, he argued, would be equivalent to allowing the legislature to take the company's property on its own terms.[84] It would, in other words, amount to confiscation.

The conflict between Field and Waite in the *Spring Valley Water Works* case was, in many ways, a continuation of their earlier disagreements regarding rate regulation. For seven years Field had been waging battle against the *Munn* doctrine, and the Court still did not appear to be moving in his direction.[85] On the surface, the *Railroad Commission Cases* of 1886 extended the pattern.[86] These cases challenged a Mississippi law that began by declaring railroad tracks to be public highways, prohibited discrimination in rates and fares, and created a railroad commission to regulate the roads. Mississippi did not simply authorize the commission to set maximum rates. It created a detailed regulatory scheme under which the commission had power to set railroad rates, supervise railroad policies, and, in the mind of the companies, virtually micromanage railroad operations in the state.

John A. Campbell and E. L. Watson represented the railroad interests in the most important of the *Railroad Commission Cases*. Campbell's innovative argument in the *Slaughter-House Cases* had first linked the Fourteenth Amendment guarantees of due process and equal protection to the Jacksonian distaste for government-granted monopoly and the ideals of free labor. Now he moved beyond those concepts and into the realm of general economic theory. Railing against Socialist writers, Campbell and Watson classified the Mississippi legislation as one of those "new schemes for readjusting the relations of society" by which "land and instruments of production were to be made the collective property of all." "This can never be attained," they reasoned. "Individual effort is necessary for the creation of property. The right of free competition to buy, to sell, to dispose of property, is essential to our civilization and habits of life. The law imposes few limits on it except for the protection of good morals. Out of this freedom spring contracts and the security afforded to property and personal liberty."[87]

Campbell's and Watson's warnings of impending doom did not sway a majority of the Supreme Court. Treating the Mississippi law as an ordinary regulation, Chief Justice Waite once again emphasized that *Munn* was settled doctrine. Arguments for the railroad's interest did draw one concession from Waite, however. Although reaffirming the proposition that general statutes regulating the use of railroads and fixing maximum rates do not necessarily deprive the owners of due process of law, he admitted that the power of regulation is not without limit. "Under pretense of regulating fairs and freights, the state cannot require a railroad corporation to carry persons or property without reward; neither can it do that which in law amounts to a taking of private property for public use without just compensation."[88] Those claims were not at issue in this case, he said, because the commission had yet to set any rates.

Waite's concession provided Field with just the kind of wedge he could use. What does "without reward" mean, he asked. At the very least it meant that the companies should recover the cost of providing the service. To that much Waite had agreed. But who should make that determination, Field asked. Should it be a government commission "appointed by the legislature, not interested in the property, nor required to possess any knowledge of the intricacies and difficulties of the business"? Does anybody believe that companies would have undertaken the work to build or improve railroads had they been informed that such a commission would allow them to recover a return on their investment that represented less than the cost of the undertaking?[89]

Letting the questions answer themselves, Field turned his attention to the antidiscrimination provision of the Mississippi law. The success of a railroad business depended upon its ability to make reasonable discriminations in its charges, Field explained. Discrimination in rates and charges based on the amount of business done, the character of the material transported, the existence of competitive lines, differences in bulk and weight, or likelihood of breakage and decay are an indispensable part of the business. They are also the type of considerations that influence stockholders.

Strictly as a matter of practical business sense, Field's argument against the antidiscrimination provision of Mississippi's law was a good point. But when he attempted to explain what the nature of a reasonable discrimination was, Field let slip one assault on the majority opinion that highlighted the difference between his outlook and the concerns of antirailroad reformers. With biting sarcasm, Field offered a dim view of the practical result of the majority opinion. "If [a railroad] attempts to encourage the cultivation of fruits, or the manufacture of cotton, woollen or silken fabrics, or any other industry along its line of road by a reduction of rates until the business is established, it makes a discrimination," he chided, "and, if higher rates are charged to others, the exaction of the difference is to them extortion."[90] Reformers might have used the same words but with a drastically different tone of voice; for what Field admired as private enterprise and initiative with the potential to do great good, reformers feared as incredible power in the hands of private corporations over which they had no control.

Taken to its logical conclusion, Field's argument meant that any interference with a business's practices could constitute confiscation of that business's property. Although not clear about which provisions of the Constitution might come into play, he implied that any such confiscation would violate fundamental law. Attractive as these theories may have been to those businesses, they were not yet firmly entrenched in law. The general ideas to which Field subscribed were gaining popularity in some segments of the legal profession, in some law journals, and in some state and lower federal courts, but they had not yet captured the Supreme Court of the United States.

That was the status of law in March 1888 when Chief Justice Morrison Waite, who had authored *Munn* and often served as Field's adversary, died suddenly after contracting pneumonia. Field, who had already been a member of the Court for twenty-five years, aspired to the chief justiceship and had the support of Justices Bradley and Matthews. But President Cleveland decided to look outside the Court for his new chief justice and chose Melville W. Fuller, a Chicago attorney supported by railroad lawyer William C. Goudy.[91]

The first major test of state rate-making authority under Fuller's leadership came two years later in *Chicago, Milwaukee and St. Paul Railway Company v. Minnesota,* often referred to as the *Minnesota Milk Rate Case.*[92] In the meantime there had been another significant change on the Court. On January 6, 1890, Field's nephew David Brewer was sworn in to replace Stanley Matthews. As a federal circuit judge, Brewer had developed a reputation similar to that of his uncle's. He distinguished himself, according to one observer, as the first federal judge to break with the precedent of *Munn* and to assert that the reasonableness of railroad rates was properly a subject of judicial determination.[93] In an Iowa case he had ruled that the notion of just compensation implied three things: "Payment of the cost of service, interest on bonds, and then some dividend."[94]

Perhaps sensing an opportunity, railroad attorney John Cary, who represented the Chicago, Milwaukee and St. Paul Railroad, took the idea of confiscation to its extreme. Arguing that the Minnesota Railroad and Warehouse Commission had set unreasonably low rates for shipping milk, Cary maintained that the state's rate-making law "violated the natural right which belongs to every one to fix the price of his services and of his property or its use."[95]

The Court overruled the Minnesota law, but on a much narrower point. Writing for the majority, Justice Samuel Blatchford ruled that Minnesota's statutory scheme violated the company's right to due process because it did not provide for appeal from the commission's decision. Blatchford's seemingly narrow opinion in the *Minnesota Milk Rate Case* included more than a guarantee of judicial procedure, however. It also contained one significant concession to those individuals who opposed government regulation. "The question of the reasonableness of a rate of charge for transportation by a railroad company," he wrote, "is eminently a question for judicial investigation."[96]

That statement led Justice Bradley to complain, "I cannot agree to the decision of the court in this case. It practically overrules *Munn v. Illinois.*"[97] The governing principle of *Munn,* he reminded his readers, was that regulation of railroads and other businesses affected with public interest is a legislative prerogative and not a judicial one.

In his dissent, Bradley did not let Cary's claim that the railroad had a natural right to fix the price of its services slip by. The railroad's argument implied that Minnesota's rates violated a constitutional prohibition that no *state* could take private property for public use without just compensation, he observed; "but there is no such clause in the Constitution of the United States." The takings clause, Bradley pointed out, is found in the Fifth Amendment, which is "prohibitory upon the federal government only, and not upon the state governments."[98] Besides, Bradley continued, "There was, in truth, no deprivation of property in these cases at all. There was merely a regulation as to the enjoyment of property, made by a strictly competent authority, in a matter entirely within its jurisdiction."[99] This last point was the most important, for it highlighted and simplified the differences between Bradley, on one side, and Field and Brewer on the other. Bradley was issuing a warning. Although the Court had not come close to adopting the Field and Brewer position in this case, he seemed to sense that it was on the verge of doing so.

Surely, the court seemed to be moving away from *Munn.* But Bradley had overreacted to the impact of the *Milk Rate Case.* The railroad had not established that they had been required to do business without just compensation or that the commission's rates had confiscated their property. Blatchford had written a careful opinion for a 6-to-3 majority. Miller had voted with the majority but emphasized in his concurring opinion that state authority was limited only by extreme misuse.[100] Even Bradley agreed with that point. "I do not mean to say the legislature or its constituted board of commissioners . . . may not so act as to deprive parties of their property without due process of law," he admitted. But in the spirit of John Harlan's opinion in *Powell v. Pennsylvania,* he emphasized that the Court should presume that the legislature acted in good faith.[101]

Two years later Field and Brewer were still in the minority. But, dissenting in *Budd v. New York,* Brewer stated more clearly than ever the idea that any government regulation interfering with a company's ability to make a profit could constitute an act of confiscation of the company's property. *Budd* involved warehouse rates in the Port of New York. Fearing that warehouse owners could skirt the state's maximum rate for storing grain by overcharging customers for mechanically shoveling the grain between ships

Justice Field on his eightieth birthday. (C. M. Bell, Collection of the Supreme Court of the United States)

and barges and the warehouse, the state enacted a regulation that a warehouse could charge customers only for the actual cost of providing that service. Ignoring that this shoveling was only part of a larger profitmaking process, Brewer maintained that the regulation required service without profit and was thus confiscation plain and simple. New York's law specifies that the proprietor of the warehouse can charge only that which he pays out—the actual cost, Brewer complained: "I had supposed that no man could be required to render any service to another individual without some compensation."[102]

In winter 1896 Justice Field began to show signs of age. He was eighty years old and had sat on the high bench for almost thirty-four years. He had been in poor physical health for some time. Knee pain and gout made it difficult for him to walk and even assume his seat on the bench. His mind was becoming noticeably weaker. Colleagues observed that he had difficulty following arguments and that he voted on cases and then forgot how he had voted. There is an old story—a myth, some would call it—that fellow justices selected John Harlan to approach Field with the suggestion that he resign. Searching for a way to broach the topic, someone recalled that Justice Field had been part of a committee that had performed a similar task when in 1870 Justice Grier had become mentally feeble. Harlan, it is said, went over to Field who was sitting alone in the cloakroom. Gingerly raising the subject, Harlan asked Field if he recalled how anxious the Court had become with respect to Justice Grier's condition and the feeling of the other justices that in his own interest and that of the Court he should give up his work. Harlan then asked Field if he remembered what had been said to Justice Grier on that occasion. The old man listened, the story goes; gradually he became alert, and finally, his eyes blazing with the old fire of youth, he burst out, "Yes! And a dirtier day's work I never did in my life!"[103]

Regardless of the story's authenticity, Field was not about to resign in 1896. He was closing in on the record for tenure held by Chief Justice John Marshall. More important, his resignation in that year would give an appointment to Grover Cleveland—and Field still carried a grudge against the president from the 1884–1885 struggle to control patronage in California. He had indicated this attitude during Cleveland's campaign when he told Matthew Deady that, should the Democrats succeed, he would "find some difficulty in selecting one of that political faith to recommend" as his replacement. When Cleveland did win the election in 1892, Field's friends indicated that they were well aware of the justice's dislike for the president. "Judge Field, I feel certain, does not intend to resign," wrote Sen. Joseph M. Dolph. "I guess he has repeatedly said that Mr. Cleveland should never appoint his successor, but I think he has now concluded to outlive the next administration."[104] Four years later, William McKinley's election to the presidency opened the door for Field's resignation. The president-elect chose Californian Joseph McKenna to be his attorney general with the understanding that McKenna would be in line for Field's seat. Quietly, Field sent a letter of resignation to the president. It took effect on December 1, 1897.[105]

In March 1898, some three months after Field's resignation, the Court came as close as it would ever come to adopting his ideas regarding confiscation. In *Smyth v. Ames* it ruled that the due process and equal protection clauses of the Fourteenth Amendment guaranteed that regulated businesses receive a fair return upon the value of the property it employs for the public convenience.[106] Even more significantly, the Court decided that determining what was a fair rate of return was a matter for the judiciary. And, surprisingly, it was John Harlan who wrote the opinion. *Smyth v. Ames* involved a Nebraska regulation on rates charged by the Union Pacific and other affiliated railroads. Harlan's opinion depended heavily upon the finding that, although the company's overall profits were high when interstate rates were factored in, the state had set rates for intrastate service at a price that was lower than the company's cost of operation. To reach that point, however, Harlan had to wade through a mass of conflicting financial data and charts. In other words, he had to become a rate-making board.

Emphasizing that regulating rates that railroads charged within a state was normally a function for state legislatures, Harlan reasoned it was nevertheless up to the judiciary to determine if those regulations went so far as to deprive the companies of their property without just compensation and due process of law.[107] He thus rationalized that the Court was not usurping the legislative function. The legacy of *Smyth v. Ames* proved to be otherwise. For the next forty years the Court became rate-maker and accountant.[108] Yet an even greater significance to the case was captured in a report from the board of secretaries of the Nebraska Board of Transportation, which was made part of the record. The report frankly explained that

the present controversy between the people and the railroads of this state originally grew out of the question, not of rates or reduction of rates, but of control. The people, recognizing the railroads as common carriers, not entitled, under the state constitution, to the same broad liberty of action in business that the individual citizen has, wanted to control the roads. The roads, impatient of interference, wanted to control themselves, and manage their business in their own way.[109]

Smyth v. Ames did not guarantee that companies would be able to manage their own business in their own way. It did mean, however, that if a state intended to regulate business it could do so only under the scrutiny of the Supreme Court of the United States and within the constraints created by the Court's interpretation of the Fourteenth Amendment.

Dreams of Field

No one knows whether Stephen Field paid much attention to the proceedings in *Smyth v. Ames*. He was eighty-two years old and had shown signs of mental feebleness even before he resigned. He died on April 9, 1899, just a few months after the Court had delivered its opinion. Nevertheless, Stephen Field had lived to see his years of persistence bear fruit.

For thirty-four years Field had championed a vision of liberty that revered property, elevated freedom of exchange to a constitutional right, rejected government interference in business matters, and reflected an admiration for power and privilege. It was by no means the vision of liberty all Americans shared. For most of Field's career, it was not even a vision most members of the Supreme Court shared. By the time of Field's death, however, the Court was polishing liberty of contract doctrine into a tool that protected entrepreneurial liberty. It was moving toward a definition of police power that restricted state authority to enact economic regulation. It was defining the commerce clause in a way that limited Congress' power to interfere with business. And it had already made itself the final arbiter of the validity of rate regulations.

Surely Justice Field would have taken delight in the years that followed. For nearly four decades, a narrow majority of the Supreme Court vigorously applied most of the legal doctrine he had pioneered. Field's vision of liberty would dominate constitutional doctrine until its clash with Franklin Delano Roosevelt's New Deal produced a backlash in 1937.[110]

his legacy in SC ↑

9

STEPHEN FIELD'S LEGACY

When America celebrated the centennial of the Constitution in 1887, Stephen Field had already been a member of the Supreme Court for almost a quarter of a century. He had, in other words, played a key role in interpreting the Constitution for almost one-fourth of the republic's existence. Still, his reputation as one of the most important justices to have sat on the Court was not secure. Undoubtedly he had been a forceful advocate on the Court. He had championed the theories of substantive due process and the right to choose a trade or profession. He had authored hundreds of opinions, many of which had a significant impact on how the law would respond to advances in technology and changes in society. But when the Court faced controversial and fundamental questions, questions about how to define the nature of liberty and the power of government, Field usually had found himself in the minority. If the Court had not subsequently adopted his way of thinking, Stephen Field would have been just another minor character in history. But the Court did adopt his way of thinking. Between the late 1800s and 1937, a period usually referred to as the laissez-faire era, Field's idea of liberty served as the underlying premise for much of the Supreme Court's decisionmaking. Indeed, Field did not stand alone. Many legal scholars and prominent members of the bar as well as judges of lower federal courts and state appellate courts shared his views. Field's status as justice of the U.S. Supreme Court is what made him stand out.

As senior justice, Field was given the honor of presenting the keynote address at the New York State Bar Association's celebration of the centennial of the Constitution. Throughout most of his talk he praised the Court's role as a check upon the excesses of the political branches of government. Toward the end of his speech, however, Field's praise evolved into a warning and a frank assessment of the problems that characterized society,

as population and wealth increase—as the inequalities in the conditions of men become more and more marked and disturbing—as the enormous aggregation of wealth possessed by some corporations excites uneasiness lest their power should become dominating in the legislation of the country, and thus encroach upon the rights or crush out the business of individuals of small means.[1]

266

[handwritten margin: reag prob of w/ aggreg of wealth + power]

Field's words demonstrated that he understood and recognized the problems that industrialization, urbanization, and the economic developments of the last half of the century had brought to American society. Further, they showed that he understood the concerns expressed by reformers of his time—that the enormous aggregation of wealth posed a threat to individual liberty. Yet as Field continued, his emphasis on the protection of property and the Constitution as a restraint on government power just as clearly *[margin: but]* demonstrated his belief that an even greater danger to American society lay in the reformers' solution—government regulation.

As population in some quarters presses upon the means of subsistence, and angry menaces against order find vent in loud denunciations—it becomes more and more the imperative duty of the court to enforce with a firm hand all the guarantees of the Constitution. Every decision weakening their restraining power is a blow to the peace of society and to its progress and improvement. It should never be forgotten that protection of property and to person cannot be separated. Where property is insecure, the rights of persons are unsafe. Protection to the one goes with protection to the other; and there can be neither prosperity nor progress where either is uncertain.[2]

Field believed regulation was appropriate to protect the public health and safety, to enhance its morals, and to preserve order. But he refused to accept the reformers' proposition that government regulation could be used to balance disparities in economic and political power and thus preserve individual liberty.

Field denounced such efforts as "class legislation." He had used the term as early as 1885 when he said, "Class legislation, discriminating against some and favoring others, is prohibited."[3] As time passed, however, the meaning of Field's references to class legislation became more clear. In 1895 he voted with the majority of the Court to overrule the new federal income tax. Writing a separate opinion Field reasoned that, "whenever a distinction is made in the burdens a law imposes or in the benefits it confers on any citizens by reason of their birth, or *wealth,* or religion, it is class legislation."[4] For Field, the income tax had the earmarks of class warfare and an attack on wealth. "The present assault upon capital is but the beginning," he wrote. "It will be but the stepping-stone to others, larger and more sweeping, till our political contests will become a war of the poor against the rich; a war constantly growing in intensity and bitterness."[5]

There may have been some justification for Field's concern about class warfare. The early 1890s were not the best of times for those people who would put their entire fate in the hands of the market economy. The panic of 1893 had thrown the country into the worst depression it had ever experienced. Labor unrest was growing and it had taken a violent turn in the Homestead strike of 1892 and the Pullman strike of 1893. The market economy was also coming under more serious theoretical attacks than ever before, ranging from the radical assaults of Marxism to criticism from the more mainstream scholars of the New School of Economics.

In the crisis, the Supreme Court assumed the role of a bastion of conservatism and protector of property rights. It strove to limit or reduce the impact of government regulations that interfered with business freedom. Besides overruling the income tax the court substantially weakened two important pieces of federal regulatory legislation, the Sherman Antitrust Act and the Interstate Commerce Commission Act.[6] It also did its part to prevent labor organizations from interfering with business freedom. In 1895, the same year that it overruled the income tax and weakened the antitrust act, the Court gave its blessing to the anti-union device of the labor injunction.[7]

As the years passed, Field and other conservative men had grown more emphatic in their charges that certain economic regulations were objectionable as "class legislation" driven by "communistic and agrarian tendencies."[8] This type of language led historian Howard Jay Graham to write in the 1950s that underlying Field's legal doctrine was a fear of class conflict.[9] Graham was expanding on a traditional interpretation that grew from the Progressive Era. According to this interpretation, the Court of the early twentieth century used the vague language of the Fourteenth Amendment and an imaginative interpretation of the commerce clause to fashion a doctrine that created a constitutional barrier to reform. This doctrine was not based on the text of the Constitution; rather, it found its inspiration in the precepts of laissez-faire economics. Conservative judges, according to this interpretation, were attempting to attach laissez-faire economics to the Constitution.

It is easy to see the connection. The constitutional doctrine of the beginning of the twentieth century was characterized by a jealous protection of property consistent with one precept of laissez-faire—the natural right of property. Liberty of contract doctrine fostered free exchange, another natural right under laissez-faire theory. In addition, the police power jurisprudence of the era reflected laissez-faire's distrust of government and the desire to rely instead on the free play of the market.

Traditional historians saw Stephen Field as a forefather of this laissez-faire constitutionalism. Carl Brent Swisher noted that "Field sought to read into the Constitution . . . a laissez-faire order in which he believed with all the depths of his being."[10] Similarly, Robert Green McCloskey maintained that the opinions of the late nineteenth-century Supreme Court and of Field in particular "became representative of conservative political theory in this period." Field, he concluded, was a key player in reshaping the Constitution to conform to the requirements of laissez-faire, Social Darwinism, and the gospel of wealth.[11]

Revisionist historians have disagreed that laissez-faire economics and Field's jurisprudence were "cut from the same bolt of cloth." Charles McCurdy argues that Field's jurisprudence left room for government's legitimate role in American life. The final product of Field's jurisprudence, he says, "was an extraordinarily consistent body of immutable rules designed to separate the public and private sectors into fixed and inviolable spheres."[12] Although McCurdy's observation is undoubtedly true, it comes closer to describing a method than a philosophy. It leaves open the most important questions, such as a definition of the immutable rules and of the authority that is to be assigned to the public sphere. Field addressed those questions with legal opinions that glorified entrepreneurial liberty and tended to equate economic regulation with confiscation of property. He originated the doctrine that liberty in the Fourteenth Amendment guaranteed a right to choose a trade or calling. Then he helped transform that relatively benign idea into the doctrine of liberty of contract, which elevated entrepreneurial liberty to a fundamental right. Regardless of whether his ideas were adapted from laissez-faire economics, they undoubtedly represented a radical form of individualism. Most important, Field subscribed to a vision of liberty that a substantial portion of the American people in his day and in the Progressive and New Deal eras did not share.

Still, McCurdy maintains that Stephen Field's legal doctrine and the doctrine of the laissez-faire era were not the result of judges simply attaching an economic theory to the Constitution. They were, in his words, the product of habits of thought that were deeply imbedded in the American consciousness well before the liberty of contract doctrine entered American law.[13]

Some writers, McCurdy, Michael Les Benedict, Howard Gillman, and Alan Jones among them, maintain that some of these habits of thought come from Jacksonian Democracy.[14] They tend to see the connection between Jacksonian Democracy and laissez-faire constitutionalism as having two related prongs. First, they point out that an antigovernment theme permeates both philosophies. Second, and perhaps more important, they presume that Field's aversion to class legislation bears a resemblance to the Jacksonian opposition to special legislation. As David M. Gold put it, the force driving the judicial doctrine of the laissez-faire era was not a wish to protect business from government but an animus against "special" or "class" legislation.[15]

Gold's comment is enlightening because it expressly intermingles the concepts of special privilege and class legislation. Although the two phrases sound much alike, they are not identical. Class legislation did not have the same meaning to late nineteenth-century opponents of government regulation as special privilege had for Jacksonians. When Stephen Field and other judges and lawyers attacked economic regulation as class legislation, they meant laws that benefited one segment of society at the expense of another.[16] They were attacking a general theory of government that would use the state's power to equalize distribution of wealth by placing heavier burdens on one economic group—the wealthy.[17] The Jacksonian idea of special privilege was not so broad. It referred to the practice of granting specific government favors that resulted in profit for a particular individual or group of individuals.

Although laissez-faire constitutionalism and Jacksonian Democracy no doubt shared the ideals of a commitment to liberty, equality under the law, and government neutrality, the meaning of liberty and the reason for neutrality were not the same. Whereas Field and other late nineteenth-century opponents of class legislation were motivated by fear of democracy, Jacksonians were motivated by a desire for democracy. Jacksonians opposed special privilege because it resulted in artificial inequalities of wealth. They feared it because it tended to concentrate power. To Jacksonians, government's doling out of special privilege created a vicious cycle that threatened both liberty and democracy. Artificial inequalities of wealth gave the people with the most money the means with which to influence government, which in turn resulted in these same people receiving more special privilege. Jacksonians worried that this cycle of privilege allowed the rich and powerful to bend government to their own purposes. Their response was to favor limiting the power of government.[18]

It is important to emphasize that the Jacksonians' distrust of government stemmed primarily from their fear of special privilege and artificial inequalities of wealth. Corporations and special privilege put too much power in the hands of too few individuals. In the Jacksonian mind, the source of that power was government. We may find in Field's theories of limited government statements that sound like Jacksonian slogans, but the link is misleading. Jacksonians were not thinking in terms of government as a regulator; they wanted to limit government in order to limit the power of moneyed interests.

Failure to recognize this distinction confuses any interpretation of Field's legal doctrine. Historian Morton Keller, for example, argues that "Field adhered to old American values of private right and individual freedom that led him to be as ill at ease with corporate power as he was with legislative activism."[19] But Field's reaction to the disputes that swirled around him in the last half of the nineteenth century graphically demonstrates that he was not the least bit ill at ease with corporate power. What did make him ill at ease was corporate power that originated with government, power that fell within the old-style Jacksonian definition of monopoly. Thus he opposed corporate privilege in the *Slaughter-House Cases* and in *Illinois Central Railroad v. Illinois*. When government was removed as the direct source, however, when the power and privilege of corporations appeared to have grown from individual effort, Field was often unwilling to allow government to enact legislation to curb the excesses of corporate power. He made this point in *Munn* and in his many opinions in cases involving economic regulation.

Although Field and the later opponents of regulation may have been true to some aspects of the Jacksonian tradition, their opposition to class legislation turned the tradition on its head. Implicit in their charges of class legislation was the idea that wage earners, farmers, artisans, and laborers represented the entrenched forces of political privilege and that corporations and powerful business interests were the oppressed.

McCurdy and other scholars also find the roots of laissez-faire–era constitutionalism in another "deeply imbedded habit of thought"—antebellum free-labor thinking. When they point to Justice Stephen Field's idea of the right to choose a lawful profession it is easy to see the connection. A laborer's right to agree to the terms of employment appears linked to free-labor thinking in its rawest form—as a contrast to indentured servitude. Field's view thus appears not as a reflection of laissez-faire thinking but as an instance of justices steeped in free-labor ideology resisting the very idea of unfree labor contracts.[20]

As the century progressed and the legal theory of a right to choose a lawful profession evolved into freedom of contract, the goals and ideals of free labor became more complex. Free labor was initially a response to traditions that gave employers legal control over an employee's labor. Slavery and indentured servitude provide the obvious examples, but legal control existed even where the laborer had entered into the employment agreement voluntarily. By the mid-nineteenth century most of these forms of legal compulsion had disappeared. But there were deeper reasons for free labor's opposition to indentured servitude and legal compulsions. The free-labor ide-

ology was driven by a desire for economic independence and by an ideal
that some individuals referred to as the dignity of labor. To most proponents, free labor meant labor with economic choices and with the opportunity to quit the wage-earning class.[21] Later nineteenth-century wage earners
found that the repeal of legal compulsions did not ensure that their hopes
for independence, choice, and opportunity would be achieved. In a world
where concentrated corporate power was becoming more predominant,
economic compulsion could just as effectively threaten their liberty. Placed
in this world, wage earners and reformers began to turn to government for
help, and they did so in the name of free labor.[22]

Freedom to choose a profession and liberty of contract may have been
appropriate ideals in any criticism of slavery, indentured servitude, or situations where labor was made unfree because of legal compulsion. These
theories unquestionably reflected free-labor ideals in the elementary sense.
But given the goals of free labor and the changes in social and economic
conditions, it is just as clear that liberty of contract doctrine did not capture
the essence of the free-labor tradition as it had developed by the turn of the
century. It ignored the disparities of bargaining power between workers and
employers and the realities of the labor market. It did little to foster the
independence and dignity of common workers or to provide them with economic choices.[23] It mattered not to reformers whether liberty of contract
doctrine was rooted in laissez-faire economics or in an outdated version of
free-labor ideology. They saw only a policy that denied many Americans any
real liberty and that failed to help solve the problems of an industrialized
society.

Revisionist historians have demonstrated that Stephen Field and his successors did not simply pull *Wealth of Nations* from their bookshelves and
attach it as an addendum to the Constitution. By reaching a bit farther into
history, they have correctly identified a link to older American traditions. In
the process they have illustrated the complexity of constitutional development and proven that late nineteenth- and early twentieth-century doctrine
was not, as some of the traditional interpretations implied, simply the product of a conspiracy to attach a particular economic theory to the Constitution.[24] Nevertheless, the implications of their discovery can be exaggerated
and misconstrued.

It would be a mistake to presume that laissez-faire constitutionalism was
an inevitable outgrowth of those old traditions. Michael Les Benedict, who
observes that there was a symbiotic relationship between the laissez-faire
concept of liberty and the Jacksonian heritage of hostility toward special
legislation, concludes that it was inevitable that the two merged.[25] Similarly,

Herbert Hovenkamp implies that the merger was inevitable when he explains that economists and judges of the late nineteenth century operated in the same uniquely American "market" for ideas.[26] Perhaps neither Benedict nor Hovenkamp means that the old Jacksonian and free-labor traditions inevitably led to laissez-faire constitutionalism in the precise form it came to take, but that is certainly an implication that can be drawn from their statements. The story of Stephen Field and the conflicts in which he was embroiled demonstrate that the only inevitability was that judges and lawyers who favored laissez-faire policy would find and exploit the link to those traditions.

Field's critics and opponents—whether settlers seeking land or farmers and businesses seeking railroad regulation—certainly did not see anything inevitable about the judge's theory of liberty. Nor were most of these people "communistic and agrarian." They did not oppose property; they wanted property. They did not oppose profit; they wanted profit. They did not think they were rejecting the ideals of Jacksonian Democracy and free labor; they were searching for policies that would allow them to realize those ideals. Even anti-Chinese zealots, racist and misguided as they were, were driven in part by old free-labor ideals.

The story of Stephen Field's career demonstrates that as the century passed, both the Jacksonian and free-labor traditions splintered, sending out shoots in different directions.[27] Each shoot professed an interest in liberty, each claimed to foster equality. But each offered different views about what liberty and equality meant, and different ideas about the role of government and the value of democracy. If the judiciary was influenced by these traditions, it also was faced with competing theories of government that reflected a schism in the traditions. Although the direction taken by the Court as the century progressed undoubtedly had a basis in the Jacksonian and free-labor traditions, it was not the only path that would have been consistent with those traditions. Nor was it necessarily the best route available.

A tendency to depict the traditions of free labor and Jacksonian Democracy running in a single straight line through Stephen Field's opinions to the constitutional doctrine of the laissez-faire era exaggerates the implications of the revisionists' discoveries. Proof that late nineteenth-century constitutional doctrine has roots in Jacksonian Democracy and free-labor theory does not mean that the matured doctrine embodies these ideals in anything like their antebellum form. It does not disprove the likelihood that laissez-faire economics had a significant impact on Stephen Field's thinking and significantly altered the direction of constitutional law.[28] Furthermore, the tendency to depict laissez-faire constitutionalism as sole heir to the free-labor and Jacksonian traditions has an unfortunate side effect. Intended or not, it gives to that doctrine a sense of democracy and egalitarianism that is not justified.

The extent to which laissez-faire jurisprudence was an inevitable out-growth of antebellum American traditions is not just an inconsequential scholarly debate. It has important implications for the development of constitutional law today. A number of recent cases suggest that the Supreme Court may be moving into a new era of judicial oversight of economic regu-lation predicated upon many of the same ideas that Field championed.[29] Where Field found the source of economic liberty in the Fourteenth Amendment's due process clause; these cases find it in the Fifth Amendment guarantee that property shall not be taken for public use without just com-pensation. Nevertheless, the underlying theory of liberty and of the limits of government power is the same. In many respects this trend is a new form of radical individualism, which, like Field's view, sees the protection of property as a central objective of the constitutional scheme. It views govern-ment as the most serious threat to individual liberty. In arguing that any regulation may constitute a "taking" of the value of one's property, this ap-proach tends to equate regulation with confiscation. Its objection that most regulation involves "rent seeking"—that is, a transfer of property from one individual or group to another—bears a close similarity to Field's complaint against class legislation.

Not all revisionist historians are interested in attaching economic in-dividualism to the Constitution.[30] Nevertheless, the revisionist discovery could be viewed as legitimizing a return to laissez-faire–style jurisprudence. The advocates of new economic individualism point to tradition to support their ideas. They would like to see a direct line of tradition running from Jacksonian Democracy and free labor to their theories. They would like to stake an exclusive claim on the traditional meaning of liberty. Stephen Field's story, however, demonstrates that neither the straight line of tradi-tion nor the exclusive claim on the meaning of liberty is found there.

Throughout his life, Stephen Field was a magnet for criticism. Few jus-tices of the Supreme Court have incited such intense feelings among the American public. Not all the attention was negative. Field was the object of admiration just as strong as the criticism to which he was subjected. He could be admired as a protector of liberty, and there is no reason to doubt that his devotion to individual liberty was genuine. But it was his defini-tion of liberty that brought him into conflict with reformers. Whether Cali-fornia settlers, homesteaders, antimonopolists, or Grangers, nineteenth-century reformers shared a view of liberty quite different from Field's. To them, Field's opinions threatened to define liberty in such a way that it snatched real liberty from the average individual. In this regard Field was a symbol not only of the conflicts but also of the questions facing late nineteenth-century America.

Field has also been admired for his legal skills, both in his own time and by historians. Charles McCurdy makes a good case for his observation that Field produced "a remarkably consistent" body of legal doctrine. Looking at it in a broad sense, there is little doubt that Field did develop a consistent doctrine, but it was so open-ended a doctrine that it allowed him the flexibility to pursue a personal agenda. The result was an interpretation that could help release the forces of economic development in the last part of the nineteenth century. At the same time, it was an interpretation of the Constitution that could be used to justify greed and foster the concentration of economic power. Stephen Field's story also demonstrates how, with luck, longevity, and persistence, judges might impose their own will upon the development of constitutional doctrine. Field did possess impressive legal skills. He used those skills, however, not only to interpret the Constitution but also to mold the constitutional doctrine into a form that suited his own beliefs.

The Terry Incident

Nearly 100 years after Field's death, it is impossible to say with certainty where his beliefs came from or what motivated him. Swisher implies they derived from reading laissez-faire economists. Graham claims they were the product of Field's fear of radicalism. Modern revisionists maintain they evolved from the political ideals that were dominant during his youth. Some of his contemporaries charged that Field's judging was the product of his desire to protect railroads and other powerful interests.

It is not an extreme indulgence in postmortem psychoanalysis, however, to believe that the adventures of Field's early adulthood—adventures of which most people could only dream—had an indelible impact on his beliefs regarding liberty, privilege, and government power. Stephen Field's rise to prominence began in the chaos of early California. He witnessed the process of turning that rugged country into a great state, and he had been an important part of the transformation. From his vantage point, the transformation of California was accomplished through the individual effort of ambitious and farsighted men. No doubt, he truly believed himself to be one of them. Field's record indicates that he admired individualism, he admired ambition, and he admired power. He had great confidence in his own ability, and he was quick to seize control of an issue. Perhaps those qualities explain why Field seemed to become entangled in chaotic disputes throughout his career on the bench.

There is no proof that Field remained attached to the ideas he developed in his early adulthood, but one episode toward the end of his career certainly demonstrated that he maintained old rivalries. It also revealed that decades of sitting on the Supreme Court had not softened him. He was still willing to take charge of a problem in order to ensure that the final outcome was one that he preferred. And he was willing to approach the task in much the same way as he had done in the chaos of early California. This particular episode occurred when Field was in his seventies, decades removed from the gold rush. It involved famous personalities, incredible wealth, shocking discoveries, sex, and greed. The incident, which ended with the death of Field's old nemesis David Terry, is a story that no treatment of Stephen Field can do without.[31]

It began with the not-so-chance meeting of William Sharon and Sarah Althea Hill. Sharon, who had just completed a term as U.S. senator from Nevada, was one of the wealthiest men in the West. He had made his fortune in the silver mines of Nevada, but the sixty-year-old gentleman had, for years, made his home in California. As owner of the luxurious Palace Hotel and other enterprises, he was a well-connected pillar of San Francisco society. Sharon did have his faults. Some critics claimed his success was in no small part the result of salting mines and cheating partners, but that could have been envy speaking. Yet even friends agreed on one weakness in his character. In the carefully chosen words of Judge Matthew Deady, "In [Sharon's] composition there appears to be a vein of sentiment and love of pleasure that has led into illicit relations with the other sex, and given him the reputation of a libertine."[32]

Although Sarah Althea Hill claimed it was business that first brought them together, business may not have been uppermost in Sharon's mind when he arranged a meeting with the twenty-seven-year-old beauty in summer 1880. By all accounts, Sarah Althea was as vivacious and energetic as she was beautiful. The young woman, who claimed to be from an important Missouri family, came to California in 1871 with little money. Sarah Althea's occupation remains open to speculation. Some writers describe her as a prostitute; others only imply that that was her profession. Everybody agrees, however, that she had some kind of relationship with a woman called Mammy Pleasant—the proprietress of one of the classiest bordellos in the city. Whatever her profession, Sarah Althea was outspoken and had a tendency to flout convention—a tendency that would later turn into a violent streak.

If passion was not on William Sharon's mind at their first meeting, it soon turned in that direction. Within weeks he arranged for Sarah Althea to live in the Grand Hotel. A convenient walkway between the Grand and the Palace hotels allowed her to join Sharon for regular visits in his quarters. Both parties could agree on one rudimentary point: the arrangement involved sex. Beyond that, they had substantially different stories about the nature of their relationship. Sharon maintained that Sarah Althea had agreed to become his mistress and that he in turn had agreed to pay her expenses at the Grand plus about $400 per month. Sarah Althea said that Sharon had indeed made such an offer but that she had refused it. She had resisted the senator's advances, she said, until after Sharon had proposed, and the two had entered into a contract of marriage on August 25, 1879, a contract that she agreed to keep secret for two years.

The two apparently lived in bliss for a little more than a year. Then in November 1881, Sharon decided to end the relationship. He offered Sarah Althea a severance package worth $7,500. She would not be satisfied with that sum, however. Kicked out of the suite in the Grand Hotel with her dignity and security badly bruised, she set her sights on a greater share of Sharon's millions.

Sharon was alerted to Sarah Althea's plans when, two years later in September 1883, a "concerned citizen" named William Neilson tried to have the senator arrested for adultery. Neilson subsequently published a copy of the alleged marriage contract and a series of letters from Sharon to Sarah Althea that became known as the "Dear Wife letters." By revealing the existence of this marriage contract, Sarah Althea set off a race for the courthouse. Sharon filed a suit in the U.S. circuit court asking that the document be declared a forgery and fraud and that Sarah Althea be enjoined from using it for any purpose. Later, Sarah Althea's supporters would charge that Sharon brought his suit in the federal court "at the instigation and advice of Stephen Field." "Don't forget what I have told you," Field supposedly told Sharon, "bring your suit in our court and you will be all right."[33] The charges against Field were hearsay, and they were also self-serving. There is no evidence that Field instigated the federal suit. But the idea that he gave Sharon some advice is not out of the question. The two men traveled in the same social circles. Field regularly stayed at Sharon's Palace Hotel when he was in San Francisco. Although Field did not participate in all the hearings surrounding this dispute, he regularly discussed the case with Judges Deady and Sawyer.[34]

Shortly after Sharon filed his case in the federal court, Sarah Althea filed for divorce in the state court.[35] Few observers at the time doubted that Mammy Pleasant was behind the divorce suit from the beginning. The old woman testified that she had made Sarah Althea's fight her own. She advanced $5,000 for prosecution of the suit, and she hired George Washington Tyler, a rough-and-tumble trial attorney, to be Sarah Althea's lawyer. Early in the trial Tyler made one decision that would influence the turn of events indelibly: he added David Terry to Sarah Althea's legal team. Terry, the former judge of the California Supreme Court, was best known as the man who had killed David Broderick in a duel. He had since fought in the Civil War, reestablished his reputation in law and politics, and often could be found cast in opposition to Stephen Field.

Once the state divorce trial was under way the press was treated to months of Sarah Althea's antics. While lawyers fought the legal skirmishes, her purpose, it seemed, was to keep the trial in the public eye. She was a master at it. Early in the trial, the press reported her every move, from her daily grand entrances to her outbursts in the courtroom. She taunted and threatened witnesses and provided testimony titillating enough to keep daily readers glued to their newspapers. At one point she tried to turn the trial into a testimonial to nineteenth-century female virtue. When Judge Sullivan ordered her to give up the purported marriage contract for inspection, Sarah Althea dramatically held it to her bosom, saying that she would not let anybody take the document that was the only evidence of her honor.

Exciting as the case was, the outcome turned on a somewhat dull issue—whether the marriage contract was genuine. Judge Sullivan concluded that it was. On Christmas Eve, 1884, he issued a preliminary order giving Sarah Althea $2,500 per month alimony and $60,000 in attorney fees. Two months later he granted her divorce. Senator Sharon, as would be expected, appealed and requested a new trial.

The state trial had ended before hearings in the federal case had even begun, but Sharon's appeal kept the state case open. In the meantime, his attorneys were finally making progress in the federal court. Sharon's right to go to federal court hinged on diversity of citizenship. Sarah Althea was a citizen of California; he claimed to be a citizen of Nevada. To the lay public this may have seemed ridiculous, since Sharon had lived in San Francisco for years. But as Judge Lorenzo Sawyer accurately pointed out, citizenship and residency are not the same thing. Sharon had recently served as senator from Nevada, and he had never stated any intent to change his citizenship. On October 16, 1884, and again in March and April 1885, Sawyer ruled that the federal courts did indeed have jurisdiction.[36]

On December 26, 1885, one year and two days after the state court had granted Sarah Althea a divorce, the federal court ruled that the marriage contract was a forgery. Judge Matthew Deady saw no logic in Sarah Althea's story and thought the relationship she described ran against human nature. Deady viewed the trial as little more than a parade of perjurers, some of whom changed their story in the middle of the trial and others who admitted having been paid or given a financial interest in the outcome. The judge implied that the case ultimately came down to whom he believed. And he was willing to place his faith in the belief that wealth and power were purveyors of the truth. "It must also be remembered that [Sharon] is a person of long standing and commanding position in this community, of large fortune and manifold business and social relations, and is therefore so far, and by all that these imply, specially bound to speak the truth," Deady wrote. Sarah Althea, in contrast, was a "comparatively obscure and unimportant person, without property or position in the world" and thus, he presumed, without incentive to speak the truth.[37]

A short time after the federal court's decision that the marriage contract was a forgery, there was another startling development. On January 7, 1887, Sarah Althea and her lawyer, David Terry, were married. When their romantic involvement began is impossible to say, but from the time of their marriage, Terry assumed an even more vigorous role in protecting Sarah Althea's interests.

At the time, the parties were at an apparent stalemate. The state court had granted Sarah Althea's divorce, but the federal court had determined that her marriage had never existed. The state court's decision was pending appeal. The federal court's decision would not be final until the time to file an appeal had passed. Senator Sharon died in November 1885, but his son Frederick Sharon and son-in-law Francis G. Newlands carried on the effort. Sharon's heirs waited for two years until the time for Sarah Althea to appeal the federal case had passed. Then they instituted a motion to revival—a legal strategy that would have the effect of making Judge Deady's decision final and enforceable.

Shortly before the hearing on this motion, the Terrys boarded a train to San Francisco. As they moved through the cars, they came upon Judge Lorenzo Sawyer. Sarah Althea walked up and down the aisle leering at the judge. Suddenly she stopped, took hold of his hair, and shook his head. Terry, it is said, made little effort to intervene. Some accounts even claim he laughed or threatened Sawyer as he led his wife away. Although stories differ on the point of how vigorously Sarah Althea assaulted Sawyer, it makes little difference; such a brazen attack on a federal judge had to be considered a serious matter. It was only a precursor of things to come.

Sitting as circuit judge, Field took over the hearing on the motion for revival. With Judges Sawyer and Sabin sitting beside him Field began to read the court's ruling.[38] As soon as Sarah Althea realized that Field was going to order her to give up the marriage contract she suddenly jumped up and screamed at Field, "Judge, are you going to take the responsibility of ordering me to deliver up that marriage contract?" When Field told her to take her seat, she became even more incensed. "You have been paid for this decision," she yelled; "how much did Newlands pay you?" Field ordered that she be removed from the courtroom, but when Marshal J. C. Franks approached her she slapped him in the face. That caused David Terry to act. At six feet, three inches and nearly 250 pounds, Terry was a formidable man, but he was also sixty-six years old. "Don't touch my wife," he warned. When Franks continued to try to escort Sarah Althea from the room, Terry punched him in the face. Other deputies jumped into the fray. As they wrestled, the old lawyer tried to pull out a knife, but he was finally subdued and led into custody in the marshal's office.

At first, Terry did not take his confinement too seriously. "Tell that old bald-headed son of a bitch, Field, that I want to go to lunch," he said as time waned. More than the lunch hour would pass before Terry was released, however. After some deliberation Field and his colleagues sentenced the lawyer to six months in jail and his wife to three months for contempt of court. When Terry petitioned for early release, Field denied his plea. Although the conditions of his imprisonment were not uncomfortable, Terry served the entire sentence. He used the time to write bitter diatribes against Field. In the meantime, Sarah Althea's threats became even more audacious. In the aftermath of her outburst she boasted that she could have killed Field from where she stood in the courtroom but that she was not yet ready to kill the old villain.[39]

Even though the seriousness of Sarah Althea's threats may have been in doubt, it was not unreasonable for U.S. government officials to be concerned about Field's safety. When the judge returned to California in summer 1889 they appointed David Neagle as his bodyguard. Neagle was said to be the stuff of old westerns—a small man who, in his early days in Tombstone, Arizona, had built a big reputation as a quick gun. On August 13 he accompanied Field on the train from Los Angeles to San Francisco. Keeping an eye out, he noticed that the Terrys boarded the train in their hometown, Fresno.

The next morning, the train came to its usual stop in Lathrop, where its schedule allowed passengers to get off for breakfast in the stationhouse. Field was suffering with knee pain but with Neagle's help made his way to a front table and ordered their food. In a short time, Terry came in, walked past Field, and sat at a second table. Sarah Althea apparently saw Field, turned around, and rushed back out the door. What happened next is the subject of dispute. Field and Neagle say that when Terry noticed Field, he got up, walked over to the table, and struck Judge Field "a violent blow in the face, followed instantaneously by another blow." Hotelman F. J. Lincoln swore that Terry merely brushed Field with an open hand, as if to insult him.[40] Whatever happened, Neagle did not waste any time. The body-guard drew his gun and shot Terry twice. One bullet lodged in Terry's spine, quickly killing him.

Neagle later swore that he thought Terry was reaching for a knife, but no knife was ever found. When Sarah Althea came back into the restaurant and realized what had happened, she draped herself over her husband's dead body. "If my husband had killed Justice Field the crowd would have lynched him," she screamed to shocked onlookers, "and now, . . . you will not help me punish the murderers of my husband."[41] The tension was high, but dur-ing the commotion Neagle had quickly moved Field to the railroad car. If Field and Neagle were in danger, they were safe when the train moved out. But the drama was not yet over.

During the last few years of his life, David Terry had acted as if he had misplaced his better judgment. Still, he was a prominent man, a distin-guished lawyer, and had been a respected public servant. Over the course of his career, Terry had grown popular with miners, settlers, and Californians of antimonopolist sentiment. Now he lay dead on the Lathrop stationhouse floor. Naturally, many people believed there should be an inquiry; some even thought that the men responsible should stand trial for homicide.

A county sheriff, who had also boarded the train after the shooting, im-mediately arrested Neagle and took him to the Stockton jail; Field contin-ued to San Francisco alone. A few days later, the county sheriff from Stock-ton traveled to San Francisco to serve an arrest warrant on Field. Joined by friends at his room at the Palace Hotel, the justice made a great show of submitting to the sheriff's authority. "You are but doing your plain duty,

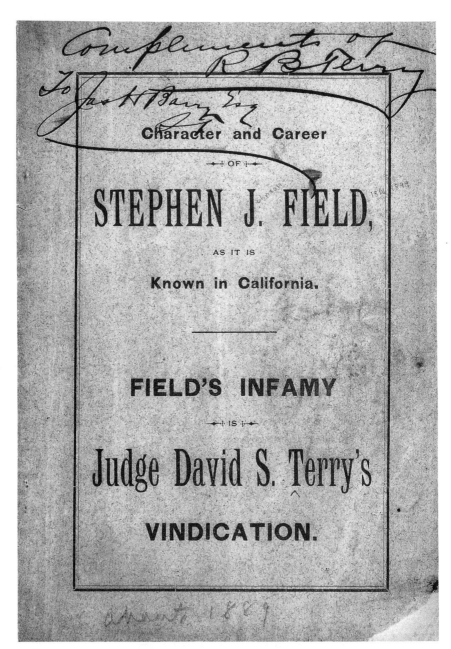

Character and Career

⊹ OF ⊹

STEPHEN J. FIELD,

AS IT IS

Known in California.

FIELD'S INFAMY

⊹ IS ⊹

Judge David S. Terry's

VINDICATION.

Some of Field's battles precipitated a "war of pamphlets." This pro–David Terry publication was typical. (Courtesy Huntington Library) and I mine in submitting to arrest," he told the officer.[42] But adroit legal maneuvering kept Field out of custody, and the charges against him were quickly dropped.

David Neagle's situation was more complicated. Some people believed that Field was implicated in the incident, but there was no strong sentiment that he should be punished for Terry's death.[43] People had less sympathy for Neagle, however. Many believed that the man who had pulled the trigger should at least be tried for Terry's death. Fearing the possibility that Neagle would be convicted of homicide in a state court or perhaps even lynched while in the Stockton jail, federal officials petitioned to the federal court for a writ of habeas corpus. They argued that Neagle was an official of the U.S. government, had been carrying out his duty, and was therefore immune from state prosecution. Neagle found a friendly ear in the U.S. circuit court, where Judge Sawyer quickly granted the writ, releasing Neagle from custody. The state appealed to the U.S. Supreme Court, which voted 6 to 2 to uphold Sawyer's ruling. Justice Lamar and Chief Justice Fuller dissented on the grounds that Neagle's appointment as deputy marshal had been informal and that he was not carrying out a duty explicitly created by federal law. Field, displaying a rare concern for conflict of interest, did not participate.[44]

David Terry's death in 1889 ended a feud that had started when he and Field served together on the California Supreme Court. Although more than a quarter of a century had passed, both Field and Terry reacted to this conflict in much the same way as they had reacted to conflicts in their early days on the California frontier. Misguided by a peculiar sense of honor that was based on chivalry, Terry resorted to bullying, threats, and violence. A cunning Field also seemed to spoil for a fight. Field, however, placed his trust in the institutions of the law—so long as he controlled them.

Activist Judge

The Terry incident brings to mind one other aspect of Stephen Field's legacy: his judicial activism. Throughout his career, Field was a vigorous proponent of a strong judiciary. For him, however, the idea of expanding the Court's authority was sometimes more than a matter of philosophy of government. It was also a matter of personal power. Field was eager to assume jurisdiction in order to take control of political disputes, especially in his home state. The Terry incident, the *Biddle Boggs* case, the San Francisco land conflict, and the *Railroad Tax Cases* were simply the most obvious examples of his manipulation of the legal process for that purpose.

The Court provided Field with a base of power, and he guarded it jealously. Examples occurred throughout his career. When he was still on the state court, Field refused to obey a writ of error from the U.S. Supreme Court that would have taken the San Francisco land case, *Hart v. Burnett,* out of his control. After he was elevated to the United States Supreme Court, Field joined with Justice Grier's objection in *Ex parte McCardle* when Congress reduced the high court's power to issue writs of habeas corpus.

Field's use of that power made him a prototype for the activist judge. An able lawyer, Field knew well how to mold precedent to support groundbreaking ideas, and he made every effort to get those ideas on record. When he could not sway a majority of the Court, he was quick to publish his own opinions. More than any previous judge, Field used dissenting, concurring, and separate opinions to advance his theories. Riding circuit on the Pacific Coast, Field tried to create his own body of law, one that critics called "ninth circuit law." He even encouraged academic friends to write on subjects in which he was interested.

Even while he guarded his own forum, Field was not beyond dabbling with the jurisdiction or makeup of the courts if it suited his purpose. Early in his career on the federal bench Field enlisted the aid of Senator Conness in order to shift the San Francisco land cases from Judge Hoffman's federal district court to his own circuit court. Later, he was willing to change the makeup of the Supreme Court in order to reach the result he wanted. In a revealing letter to Don Dickinson in 1893, Field complained that the outcome of what he called "the Chinese deportation case" had affected him "very unpleasantly." To reverse the outcome, Field suggested his own version of court-packing. It might be possible to increase the size of the bench, he confided to Dickinson. "As a general rule it would be dangerous to increase the size of the bench for the purpose of correcting a bad decision," he admitted, "but where that decision goes to the very essentials of Constitutional Government, the question of an increase of the bench may be considered and acted upon."[45]

Field had proposed a Court reorganization earlier. In the early 1880s he began to talk about a plan to increase the Supreme Court to twenty-one justices and divide it into three sections. One section would take equity cases, the second would hear common law cases, and the third would take patent and admiralty cases. Constitutional questions and cases construing treaties, he said, could be turned over to the full bench. Even then, however, he hoped the reorganization would accomplish a particular purpose. "We would thus have one court for the decisions of constitutional questions and questions arising upon treaties," he told his friend Judge Matthew Deady, "and what would be equivalent to three courts for hearing of all questions affecting . . . property rights."[46] If given his way, Field would have filled the courts with "able and conservative men."[47]

Although Field's ideas about dabbling with the Court's makeup may raise questions about his regard for the institution, they never had any impact on constitutional history. Yet there is no doubt that Field himself did have a substantial impact. His influence on constitutional doctrine did not result from his plans to reorganize the judiciary. Nor did it come from a position of leadership within the Court. Field coveted, but never attained, the office of chief justice. In relations with his colleagues he tended to be a maverick. Over the course of his long career he never led a long-running majority coalition. Undoubtedly, Field's influence was the result of his tenacious sense of purpose and his perseverance.

Stephen Field acted and wrote as if he believed himself to be the one person destined to lead his fellow citizens into the future. With characteristic confidence, he told Matthew Deady, "The good people of California generally are furious the first year at my decisions and about the third year afterwards begin to approve of them."[48] This sense of destiny may have come from the experience of his early years, when he sorted through the chaos of gold rush California to rise to the top of the state and national judicial systems. Chaos seemed to suit Field. Certainly his experience must have left him with some belief that the gold rush provided the opportunity for farsighted, strong-willed individuals to achieve greatness. A lifetime of perseverance and tenacity paid off handsomely for Field. He left a legacy that only a handful of other public figures of his day could match.

NOTES

Introduction

1. Victor M. Berthold, *The Pioneer Steamer California: 1848-1849* (Boston: Houghton Mifflin, 1932), 65.

2. *Cummings v. Missouri,* 71 U.S. (4 Wall.) 277 (1867); *Ex parte Garlans,* 71 U.S. (4 Wall.) 333 (1867).

3. Francis Wayland, *Elements of Political Economy* (Boston: Gould, Kendall, and Lincoln, 1945), 118-21, 151-52.

4. *Lochner v. New York,* 198 U.S. 45, 75-76 (1905), Holmes dissenting.

5. Theodore Roosevelt, "Judges and Progress," *Outlook,* January 6, 1912, 42.

6. Bernard Schwartz, *A History of the Supreme Court* (New York: Oxford University Press, 1993), 174-75.

7. Charles W. McCurdy, "The Roots of 'Liberty of Contract' Reconsidered: Major Premises in the Law of Employment, 1867-1937," *Yearbook of the Supreme Court Historical Society* (1984): 24.

8. Michael Les Benedict, "Laissez-Faire and Liberty: A Reevaluation of the Meaning and Origin of Laissez-Faire Constitutionalism," *Law and History Review* 3 (Fall 1985): 293; Howard Gillman, *The Constitution Besieged: The Rise and Demise of Lochner Era Police Powers Jurisprudence* (Durham, N.C.: Duke University Press, 1993); David M. Gold, *The Shaping of Nineteenth-Century Law: John Appleton and Responsible Individualism* (Westport, Conn.: Greenwood Press, 1990).

9. Gillman, *Constitution Besieged,* 13.

10. McCurdy, "Roots of 'Liberty of Contract,' " 33.

11. William Wiecek, *Liberty Under Law: The Supreme Court in American Life* (Baltimore: Johns Hopkins University Press, 1988), 17.

12. Robert J. Steinfeld, *The Invention of Free Labor: The Employment Relation in English and American Law and Culture, 1350-1870* (Chapel Hill: University of North Carolina Press, 1991), 187, describes this evolution: "As the nineteenth century wore on, wage workers complained more and more bitterly that the power of property was making them slaves to their employers. And they could appeal to deeply entrenched American attitudes for support for their claims. But their argument was now more difficult and more contradictory."

1. A Forty-niner, Not a Miner

1. These population estimates are very rough; I have derived them from a variety of sources. See John S. Hittell, *The History of the City of San Francisco* (San Francisco: A. L. Bancroft, 1878), 117, 133, 429.

2. For background on Field's early life, see Carl Brent Swisher, *Stephen J. Field: Craftsman of the Law* (1930; rpt., Hamden, Conn.: Archon Books, 1963).

3. See Peter R. Decker, *Fortunes and Failures: White-Collar Mobility in Nineteenth-Century San Francisco* (Cambridge: Harvard University Press, 1978), 1-59.

4. Stephen J. Field, *Personal Reminiscences of Early Days in California* (1877; rpt., New York: Da Capo Press, 1968), 6 (hereafter PR).

5. Robert Glass Cleland, ed., *Apron Full of Gold: The Letters of Mary Jane Megquier from San Francisco, 1849-1856* (San Marino, Calif.: Huntington Library, 1949), 24-25; Carolyn Hale Russ, ed., *The Log of a Forty-Niner* (Boston: B. J. Brimmer, 1923), 64-65.

6. Robert M. Senkewicz, S.J., *Vigilantes in Gold Rush San Francisco* (Stanford, Calif.: Stanford University Press, 1985), 15.

7. Lula May Garrett, "San Francisco in 1851 as Described by Eyewitnesses," *California Historical Society* 22 (September 1943): 256.

8. Charles Ross Parke, *Dreams to Dust: A Diary of the California Gold Rush*, ed. James E. Davis (Lincoln: University of Nebraska Press, 1989), 103.

9. Cleland, ed., *Apron Full of Gold*, 39; see also Garrett, "San Francisco in 1851 as Described by Eyewitnesses," 258.

10. Roger W. Lotchin, *San Francisco, 1846-1856: From Hamlet to City* (New York: Oxford University Press, 1974), 174.

11. Ibid., 174-78.

12. Cleland, ed., *Apron Full of Gold*, 33.

13. John Walton Caughey, *Gold Is the Cornerstone* (Berkeley: University of California Press, 1948), 91, 214-15.

14. PR, 6.

15. Ibid., 8-11.

16. Hubert Howe Bancroft, *The History of California*, vol. 6, *1848-1859*, in *The Works of Hubert Howe Bancroft*, vol. 23 (San Francisco: History Company, 1888), 146.

17. For a discussion of the use of law on the route to California, see John Phillip Reid, *Law for the Elephant: Property and Social Behavior on the Overland Trail* (San Marino, Calif.: Huntington Library, 1980).

18. David Alan Johnson, *Founding the Far West: California, Oregon, and Nevada 1840-1890* (Berkeley: University of California Press, 1992), 43.

19. Bancroft, *History of California*, 6: 133-34.

20. Cleland, ed., *Apron Full of Gold*, 10-22.

21. Caughey, *Gold Is the Cornerstone*, 68.

22. Bancroft, *History of California*, 6: 136.

23. PR, 4-5.

24. John Haskell Kembell, *The Panama Route, 1848-1869*, University of California Publications in History, vol. 29 (Berkeley: University of California Press, 1943), 31-58, and appendix; PR, 3-5; Cleland, ed., *Apron Full of Gold*, 10-22; Oscar Lewis, *Sea Routes to the Gold Fields: The Migration by Water to California in 1849-1852* (New York: Alfred A. Knopf, 1949), 163-223; Bancroft, *History of California*, 6: 126-42; Ernest A. Wiltsee; *Gold Rush Steamers of the Pacific* (1938; rpt., Lawrence, Mass.: Quarterman Publications, 1976).

25. Kevin Starr, *Americans and the California Dream, 1850-1915* (New York:

Oxford University Press, 1986), 63–64. Reid, *Law for the Elephant,* 30, notes that some sought a change of scenery, not a change of society.

26. Cleland, ed., *Apron Full of Gold,* 30.

27. Parke, *Dreams to Dust,* xix, citing Charles A. Kirkpatrick Diary, June 23, 1849–1850.

28. J. S. Holliday, *The World Rushed In: The California Gold Rush Experience* (New York: Simon and Schuster, 1981), 376. Holliday edits the letters of William Swain, who also said that other classes of arrivals were gamblers who enjoyed the excitement, individuals of vicious temperament who enjoyed lawlessness, and a better class of people who had been decoyed by specious hopes.

29. Ibid., 116.

30. Jo Ann Levy, *They Saw the Elephant: Women and the California Gold Rush* (Hamden, Conn: Archon Books, 1990), 108–25. See Paula Mitchell Marks, *Precious Dust: The American Gold Rush Era, 1848–1900* (New York: William Morrow, 1994), 337–66; Parke, *Dreams to Dust,* xiii; and Walker D. Wyman, ed., *California Emigrant Letters* (New York: Bookman Associates, 1952), 168–69.

31. Bancroft, *History of California,* 6: 227.

32. Wyman, ed., *California Emigrant Letters,* 29, letter signed VJF, April 6, 1849.

33. Ibid., 78, letter signed W. B. Royall, October 26, 1849.

34. Rodman W. Paul, *California Gold: The Beginning of Mining in the Far West* (Lincoln: University of Nebraska Press, 1947), 175.

35. See Reid, *Law for the Elephant.*

36. Holliday, *The World Rushed In,* 58–59; William Henry Ellison, *A Self-Governing Dominion: California, 1849–1860* (Berkeley: University of California Press, 1950), 23, 279.

37. PR, 2.

38. Ibid., 11–13.

39. Sister M. Benilda Desmond, O.P., "The History of the City of Marysville" (Master's thesis, Catholic University of America, 1962), 56. Note that the Yuba River was said to have produced more gold than any other river in the United States (J. Chester Merriam, *The Bars of the Yuba River* [N.p., 1951]).

40. Earl Ramey, "The Beginnings of Marysville," part 1, *California Historical Quarterly* 14 (September 1935): 206. This is the first of a three-part article, which is also available as a book: Earl Ramey, *The Beginnings of Marysville* (San Francisco: California Historical Society, 1936).

41. PR, 14.

42. Ibid., 15–19.

43. Giving the organization an American twist, Marysville residents also elected a town marshal.

44. W. H. Parks to Judge Stephen J. Field, May 10, 1880, California Room, Marysville City Library. Field alludes to this story, minus some of the color, in PR. The letter is one of a number that Field solicited when he dictated the book.

45. Ibid. Parks's account was slightly inaccurate. There were at least two other women in the general area: Mrs. Covillaud was a survivor of the Donner party; Covillaud's partners William Foster and Michael Nye were married to two other survivors (Ramey, "Beginnings of Marysville," part 1, 205–6).

46. Field apparently received his appointment as justice of the peace from Peter H. Burnett, who was elected governor December 10, 1849, at the same time the constitution was ratified.

47. William Schuyler Moses. Contempt of court and how the Judge purged the attorney guilty of it: A mining incident on the Yuba in 1850. Typescript (carbon), 4 l., (BANC MSS C-D 5154). The Bancroft Library, University of California, Berkeley. Transcript (n.d., carbon copy), "Recollections of an Incident Involving Stephen J. Field," Bancroft Library, University of California, Berkeley. Moses later was a carpenter and millwright. He is remembered as a lifelong member of the Masonic Order. Since he describes Field as the late chief justice, I assume it was written in the late 1890s, forty to fifty years after the incident supposedly took place. Moses mistakenly referred to Field as chief justice; although on the Supreme Court for more than thirty years, Field never served as chief justice. See also Edwin Sherman, ed., *Fifty Years of Masonry in California,* supplement (n.p.: n.d.), 166.

48. There was a higher court, the Court of First Instance, in Sacramento, and its judge apparently rode circuit occasionally, but the alcalde was fully in charge of the justice system day to day. See Ramey, "Beginnings of Marysville," part 1, 222. For Field's account of his experience as alcalde, see PR, 18–32. A good general description of the office of alcalde in California is found in Charles Howard Shinn, *Mining Camps: A Study in American Frontier Government* (New York: Alfred A. Knopf, 1948), 78–98, 143, and 172.

49. Ramey, "Beginnings of Marysville," part 1, 223, citing Register of Suits before the first alcalde of Marysville in the county clerk's office, 150.

50. PR, 26.

51. Ibid., 27.

52. Ramey, "Beginnings of Marysville," part 1, 213.

53. PR, 28.

54. Court reorganization is detailed in Ellison, *A Self-Governing Dominion,* 67–68. I use the term "state" loosely since California, though organized as a state through its new constitution, was not yet admitted to the Union.

55. Earl Ramey, "The Beginnings of Marysville," part 2, *California Historical Society Quarterly* 14 (December 1935): 376–77, notes that Field was defeated by an able opponent, Henry Peter Haun, who was later a U.S. senator.

56. W. T. Ellis, *Memories of My Seventy-Two Years in the Romantic County of Yuba, California* (Eugene: University of Oregon Press, 1939), 2.

57. PR, 30. Field was a reluctant taxpayer, however. On November 21, 1850, the county's assessment set the value of his sixty-one lots at $33,550. Field disputed this figure and succeeded in reducing his property taxes by $115.50 (see Petition, Stephen Field to the Yuba County Court of Sessions, November 9, 1850, Bancroft Library, University of California, Berkeley). Regarding the city's social life, Field was a founder and an elder of the Presbyterian church (Earl Ramey, "The Beginnings of Marysville," part 3, *California Historical Society Quarterly* 15 [March 1936]: 43).

58. PR, 33–46; Ramey, "Beginnings of Marysville," part 2, 378–82; *People ex rel Mulford v. Turner,* 1 Cal. 143 (1850); *People ex rel Field v. Turner,* 1 Cal. 152 (1850); *Ex parte Field,* 1 Cal. 187 (1850); *People ex rel Field v. Turner,* 1

Cal. 188 (1850), motion for attachment (refused); *People ex rel Field v. Turner*, 1 Cal. 190 (1850), writ of mandamus.

59. PR, 43; William Turner, *Documents in Relation to Charges Preferred by Stephen J. Field and Others before the House of Assembly of the State of California Against Wm. R. Turner*, 2d ed. (San Francisco: Whittin Towne and Company, 1856), 24, 26.

60. PR, 44–45.

61. Ibid., 62–63.

62. Ibid., 41; *People v. Turner*, 1 Cal. 143, 150 (1850).

63. *Ex parte Robinson*, 86 U.S. (19 Wall.) 505, 512 (1873). Field was not fully committed to the right, however. In 1873 he concurred in a decision that allowed Illinois to refuse to admit women to the practice of law (*Bradwell v. Illinois*, 83 U.S. [16 Wall.] 130, 140 [1873]).

64. PR, 49. The brother in New York was David Dudley Field, an attorney and leader in the Free-Soil movement. The brother in Tennessee was probably Matthew Dickinson Field, an engineer.

65. *Marysville Herald*, September 20, 1850, 2–1; Field repeats this in PR, 49–50.

66. Ibid., September 24, 1850, 2–3.

67. Ramey, "Beginnings of Marysville," part 2, 391–92. The vote was 363 for McCarty to 255 for Field.

68. PR, 50–54.

69. John T. McCarty to William R. Turner, November 22, 1850, and William T. Barbour to William R. Turner, February 21, 1853. These letters are found in Turner, *Documents in Relation to Charges Preferred by Stephen J. Field and Others*, 6–7 and 28–29. See PR, 61.

70. Ramey, "Beginnings of Marysville," part 2, 389–90, quoting the *Marysville Herald*, August 13 and 23, 1850; see also August 6 and 27, 1850.

71. Bancroft, *History of California*, 6: 450–52.

72. Paul W. Gates, *Land and Law in California: Essays on Land Policies* (Ames: Iowa State University Press, 1991), 5. This book reprints a series of Gates's articles.

73. Gates, *Land and Law*, 5. Gates divided squatters into two groups, those who were unaware of an adverse claim to the property and those who, though aware of an adverse claim, settled anyway, hoping that the claim would be declared invalid and the land returned to the public domain (158).

74. See Josiah Royce, *Studies of Good and Evil* (1889; rpt., Hamden, Conn: Archon Books, 1964), 306–11.

75. Don W. Wilson, *Governor Charles Robinson of Kansas* (Lawrence: University Press of Kansas, 1975), 7.

76. Bancroft, *History of California*, 6: 454.

77. Royce, *Studies of Good and Evil*, 326–27.

78. Wilson, *Governor Charles Robinson of Kansas*, 7–8.

79. For description of the Sacramento Squatter Uprising I have relied upon W. W. Robinson, *Land in California* (Berkeley: 1948; rpt., University of California Press, 1979), 114–16; Royce, *Studies of Good and Evil*, 298–348; Wilson, *Governor Charles Robinson of Kansas*, 6–9.

80. Royce, *Studies of Good and Evil*, 346.

81. See Gates, *Land and Law in California,* 158.

82. Robinson, *Land in California,* 116; Gates, *Land and Law in California,* 159–80, 309–10.

83. Bancroft, *History of California,* 6: 463–64.

84. PR, 19–21.

85. The *Settlers' and Miners' Tribune* published Turner's pamphlet, *Documents in Relation to Charges Preferred by Stephen J. Field and Others;* see *Marysville Herald,* December 24, 1850, 2–1.

86. Ramey, "Beginnings of Marysville," part 2, 390–91.

87. PR, 62–65; John Norton Pomeroy, *Some Account of the Work of Stephen J. Field* (1881; rpt., Littleton, Colo.: Fred B. Rothman, 1986), 19–20. Field was also on the conference committee regarding the bill to reorganize the judiciary. He turned down an appointment to the Committee on Education. See *Journals of the Legislature of the State of California and Its Second Session* (Eugene Casserly, State Printer, 1851), 818, 843, 1591.

88. *Journals of the Legislature,* 836, 843, 950–56, 1434–49, 1495–98; PR, 72–74; Pomeroy, *Some Account of the Work of Stephen J. Field,* 21–22. It appears that Robinson took an extended leave of absence. I began to notice that toward the middle of the session he was continually listed as not present at the opening of the day.

89. Pomeroy, *Some Account of the Work of Stephen J. Field,* 15–19; PR, 74–75; *Journals of the Legislature,* 837.

90. PR, 75; *Journals of the Legislature,* 936, 948, 1442–43, 1452–53 (John Bigler, speaker of the assembly, sponsored the resolution to ban smoking).

91. This account is adapted from PR, 65–69. *Marysville Herald,* March 25, 1851, 2–5.

92. PR, 70–71.

2. California Dreaming

1. David Allan Johnson, *Founding the Far West: California, Oregon, and Nevada, 1840–1890* (Berkeley: University of California Press, 1992).

2. For background on Gwin, see William Henry Ellison, "Memoirs of Hon. William M. Gwin," *California Historical Society Quarterly,* 4 parts, 19 (1940): 1–26, 157–84, 256–77, 344–46; James O'Meara, *Broderick and Gwin* (San Francisco: Bacon, 1881); William Henry Ellison, *A Self-Governing Dominion: California, 1849–1860* (Berkeley: University of California Press, 1950), 22–101; Johnson, *Founding the Far West,* 117–20.

3. Ellison, "Memoirs of Hon. William M. Gwin," 3.

4. Johnson, *Founding the Far West,* 130–37.

5. Circumstances regarding California's admission are described in Ellison, *Self-Governing Dominion,* 74–101. The Compromise of 1850 is treated in Harold M. Hyman and William M. Wiecek, *Equal Justice Under Law: Constitutional Development, 1835–1875* (New York: Harper Torchbooks, 1982), 143–48. The Compromise of 1850 also settled the border between Texas and New Mexico.

6. For background on Broderick, see Jeremiah Lynch, *The Life of David C. Broderick: A Senator of the Fifties* (New York: Baker and Taylor, 1911); David A.

Williams, *David C. Broderick: A Political Portrait* (San Marino, Calif.: Huntington Library, 1969); O'Meara, *Broderick and Gwin;* Ellison, *Self-Governing Dominion,* 22–100.

7. Robert M. Senkewicz, S.J., *Vigilantes in Gold Rush San Francisco* (Stanford, Calif.: Stanford University Press, 1985); Christian G. Fritz, "Popular Sovereignty, Vigilantism, and the Constitutional Right of Revolution," *Pacific Historical Review* 63 (February 1994): 39–66, has noted that vigilantism had more idealistic links to nineteenth-century notions of popular sovereignty.

8. While reading California newspapers for other purposes, I noticed that before 1858–1859 issues relating to slavery seemed overshadowed by local issues such as homestead, use of swamp land, mining rights, and the Pacific railroad. Slavery received more attention in the political conventions. In 1858 California Democrats, like the rest of the nation, split on the issue of slavery in Kansas. That year the Democratic party held two separate conventions. One group cast its lot with the South, favoring the position that Kansas be admitted as a slave state under what was called the Lecompton Constitution. The other group—Anti-Lecompton forces within the party—opposed the extension of slavery into Kansas. See Winfield J. Davis, *History of Political Conventions in California, 1849–1892* (Sacramento: California State Library, 1893), 6–181.

9. Johnson, *Founding the Far West,* 125, notes that the convention's efforts to establish state boundaries were linked to the national debate over the extension of slavery, but the debates also testified to the delegates' ambivalence regarding the issue.

10. Ellison, *Self-Governing Dominion,* 30.

11. Ibid., 121.

12. Harry L. Watson, *Liberty and Power: The Politics of Jacksonian America* (New York: Noonday Press, 1992), 149–50. In this section I have relied heavily on Watson; Lawrence Frederick Kohl, *The Politics of Individualism: Parties and the American Character in the Jacksonian Era* (New York: Oxford University Press, 1989); Arthur M. Schlesinger, Jr., *The Age of Jackson* (Boston: Little, Brown, 1945); Marvin Meyers, *The Jacksonian Persuasion: Politics and Belief* (Stanford, Calif.: Stanford University Press, 1957); and Donald B. Cole, *The Presidency of Andrew Jackson* (Lawrence: University Press of Kansas, 1993).

13. Kohl, *Politics of Individualism,* 5, describes Jacksonians as people who were unsettled by America's movement from a society based on tradition to one based on individualistic social order.

14. Ibid., 29, quoting the *Congressional Globe,* January 10, 1844, and November 7, 1839; see also ibid., 22. Charles Sellers describes Jacksonians as people who were uncomfortable about the evolution from a subsistence to a market economy: "The two greatest bugaboos of the subsistence world were debt and taxes, through which the market world could seize the farmers' land to enforce its demands for money" (*The Market Revolution: Jacksonian America, 1815–1846* [New York: Oxford University Press, 1991], 15).

15. Kohl, *Politics of Individualism,* 112, 188, 208; Watson, *Liberty and Power,* 10–11; Hyman and Wiecek, *Equal Justice Under Law,* 9; Meyers, *Jacksonian Persuasion,* 167. Sellers, *Market Revolution,* generally describes the opposition to special privilege more as a matter of class struggle. See also Daniel Feller, *The Jack-*

sonian Promise in America, 1815–1840 (Baltimore: Johns Hopkins University Press, 1995), 169–75.

16. Kohl, *Politics of Individualism*, 193; Watson, *Liberty and Power*, 36, 131–39.

17. Kohl, *Politics of Individualism*, 207, 218–19; Watson, *Liberty and Power*, 146.

18. Kohl, *Politics of Individualism*, 104, 109, 188, 208; Watson, *Liberty and Power*, 170.

19. Watson, *Liberty and Power*, 170; Kohl, *Politics of Individualism*, 26–31, 57, 115, 203, 218.

20. Kohl, *Politics of Individualism*, 109–10, 166.

21. Johnson, *Founding the Far West*, 102.

22. Ibid., 122–25.

23. Ibid., 127–29. Johnson notes that some delegates to the constitutional convention of 1849 hoped to prohibit free blacks from the state because it was thought that they would undermine the equality of conditions that made California mining communities the epitome of free society. Some whites also feared that working side by side with blacks in the goldfields would denigrate the value of white free labor.

24. Charles Howard Shinn, *Mining Camps: A Study in American Frontier Government* (New York: Alfred A. Knopf, 1948), 226.

25. Shinn, *Mining Camps*, 239, reproduces the notice. It also appears on the cover page of John R. Umbeck, *A Theory of Property Rights: With Application to the California Gold Rush* (Ames: Iowa State University Press, 1981).

26. See John S. Hittell, *Resources of California* (San Francisco: A. Roman, 1863), 355–57; Rodman W. Paul, *California Gold: The Beginning of Mining in the Far West* (Lincoln: University of Nebraska Press, 1947), 210–39; Umbeck, *Theory of Property Rights*, 90–96; and Shinn, *Mining Camps*, 221–46.

27. Mark Wyman, *Hard Rock Epic: Western Miners and the Industrial Revolution, 1860–1910* (Berkeley: University of California Press, 1979), 6, provides a concise definition of the different mining methods as a prelude to his discussion of the industrialization of the mining industry.

28. Robert Kelley, *Battling the Inland Sea: American Political Culture, Public Policy, and the Sacramento Valley, 1850–1986* (Berkeley: University of California Press, 1989), discusses these conflicts and the environmental impact of hydraulic mining. Hydraulic mining created the conflict Justice Field addressed in *Johnson v. Kirk*, 98 U.S. (8 Otto.) 453 (1878).

29. Paul, *California Gold*, 217–27; Newell D. Chamberlain, *The Call of Gold: True Tales on the Gold Road to Yosemite* (Mariposa, Calif.: Gazette Press, 1936), 34; see Shinn, *Mining Camps*, 240, for an example of the type of regulations promulgated for the quartz industry.

30. *Statutes of California*, 2d sess., 1851, 149 (sec. 621 of the Civil Practice Act). See Paul, *California Gold*, 221–22; PR, 73–74; and John Norton Pomeroy, *Some Account of the Work of Stephen J. Field* (1881; rpt., Littleton, Colo.: Fred B. Rothman, 1986), 17–19. California's courts, including the state supreme court, soon followed suit in recognizing the customary codes; see *Irwin v. Phillips*, 5 Cal. 140, 146 (1855).

31. See Richard Griswold del Castillo, *The Treaty of Guadalupe Hidalgo: A Legacy of Conflict* (Norman: University of Oklahoma Press, 1990), 180, 182, 190;

Charles I. Bevans, ed., *Treaties and Other International Agreements, 1776–1949* (Washington, D.C.: Department of State, 1972), 9: 791–806.

32. W. W. Robinson, *Land in California* (Berkeley: University of California Press, 1948), 34. Robinson notes that seven pueblos were recognized by the U.S. government in 1851: Sonoma, San Francisco, Monterey, San Jose, Santa Barbara, Los Angeles, and San Diego (60).

33. Ibid., 63.

34. This figure is based on the claims filed before the U.S. Land Commission according to the California Land Act of 1851. Paul Gates et al., *Four Persistent Issues: Essays on California's Land Ownership Concentration, Water Deficits, Sub-State Regionalism, and Congressional Leadership* (Institute of Governmental Studies, Berkeley: University of California Press, 1978), 7 (Gates uses this figure consistently in his other writings); see also Robinson, *Land in California*, 69–71.

35. The best concise description of the formal and informal procedure governing Mexican land grants I have found is in Christian Fritz, *Federal Justice in California: The Court of Ogden Hoffman, 1851–1891* (Lincoln: University of Nebraska Press, 1991), 141–46; see also Robinson, *Land in California*, 46–51, 66–69.

36. Paul Gates, *Land and Law in California: Essays on Land Policies* (Ames: Iowa State University Press, 1991), 5, 157, 186 (the book is a compilation of articles he wrote from the 1950s to the 1970s).

37. Ellison, *Self-Governing Dominion*, 106–7; Gates, *Land and Law in California*, 6–7.

38. Cole, *Presidency of Andrew Jackson*, 59–61.

39. See Gates, *Land and Law in California*, 64–93. For Frémont's interest in the Land Act of 1851, see *Congressional Globe*, 21–23, 31st Cong., 1–2d sess. (1849–1850).

40. Paul Gates has steadfastly defended the Land Act of 1851 even against these types of charges, maintaining that the act did little more than transfer final adjudication of claims from Congress to the courts. Delays and uncertainty were even more common under the old system. In any case, he argues, it was not the procedure of the act that should be blamed for delays but fraud. See Gates, *Land and Law in California*, 24–63.

41. An Act to Ascertain and Settle the Private Land Claims in the State of California, 9 Stat. 631 (March 3, 1851).

42. Josiah Royce, *Studies in Good and Evil* (Hamden, Conn.: Archon Books, 1964), 304, 325; Hittell, *Resources of California*, 453–61.

43. Ellison, "Memoirs of Hon. William M. Gwin," 158–59.

44. del Castillo, *Treaty of Guadalupe Hidalgo*, 73.

45. Robinson, *Land in California*, 31; Gates, *Land and Law in California*, 14, 26–27. Henry George adds that delays caused by legal proceedings hurt the squatters as well as the Californios and that only speculators gained (*Our Land and Land Policy* [1871; rpt., New York: Doubleday and McClure, 1902], 45). George's book is available on microfiche from Fred B. Rothman and Company. See Johnson, *Founding the Far West*, 240, for a measured treatment of the impact of the act on Californios; see Fritz, *Federal Justice in California*, 168–69, for a discussion of ethnic rivalries surrounding the land struggle.

46. *Congressional Globe*, January 15, 1851, 256.

47. Kevin Starr, *Americans and the California Dream, 1850–1915* (New York: Oxford University Press, 1986), 162.

48. *Congressional Globe,* January 27, 1851, 350.

49. Gates, *Land and Law in California,* 9, citing John Frémont to Able Stearns, October 26, 1847, December 12, 1851, and April 20 and October 3, 1854, Huntington Library.

50. Ellison, "Memoirs of Hon. William Gwin," 161; Sellers, *Market Revolution,* 10, points out the paradox of property. In his terms, "The capitalist doctrine of private property was the juridical foundation for both the market's expansion and the farmers' resistance."

51. George, *Our Land and Land Policy,* 99.

52. Daniel Feller, *The Public Lands in Jacksonian Politics* (Madison: University of Wisconsin Press, 1984), 17.

53. An Act to Appropriate the Proceeds of Public Lands, and to Grant Preemption Rights, 5 Stat. 567 (September 4, 1841). Roy M. Robbins, *Our Landed Heritage: The Public Domain, 1776–1970,* 2d ed. (Lincoln: University of Nebraska Press, 1976), and Feller, *Public Lands in Jacksonian Politics,* both follow this evolution in detail. Robbins emphasizes sectional conflict in the politics surrounding land reform. Feller persuasively points out that the tradition of treating this subject as a battle between settlers and speculators tends to oversimplify the issue. Johnson, *Founding the Far West,* 240–41, also points out that the crude procedures initiated under land reform afforded opportunity for fraud and abuse.

54. George W. Julian, *Speeches on Political Questions* (New York: Hurd and Houghton, 1872), 51. See Patrick W. Riddleberger, *George Washington Julian: Radical Republican* (Indiana Historical Bureau, 1966), 76–78, who points out that at the time of this speech Julian's cause was abolitionism; it was not until after the Civil War that he focused primarily on land reform.

55. Julian, *Speeches on Political Questions,* 51–52.

56. Ibid., 55.

57. George, "Our Land and Land Policy," 10.

58. Julian, *Speeches on Political Questions,* 50–66. Julian presented this speech, "The Homestead Bill," to the House of Representatives on January 29, 1851. Riddleberger, *George Washington Julian,* 76–77, 190, calls it one of the most important speeches in Julian's career (see Julian, *Speeches on Political Questions,* 60). Another Jacksonian theme, distrust of creditors and the banking system, appeared in the movement's efforts to make homesteads secure against creditors. The legacy of this aspect of the homestead movement survives at least in my home state of Texas; see Texas Constitution, Article 16, secs. 50, 51; Tex. Prop. Code, chapters 41, 42.

59. Julian, *Speeches on Political Questions,* 57.

60. Eric Foner, *Free Soil, Free Labor, Free Men: The Ideology of the Republican Party Before the Civil War* (New York: Oxford University Press, 1970), 28, 56.

61. Schlesinger, *Age of Jackson,* 451, 455. David Dudley Field introduced the Wilmot Proviso at the New York Democratic Convention on September 29, 1847. Daun van Ee, *David Dudley Field and the Reconstruction of the Law* (New York: Garland, 1986), 123–24.

62. Julian, *Speeches on Political Questions,* 56.

63. Ibid., 56.

64. Ibid., 59–60.

65. Robert J. Steinfeld, *The Invention of Free Labor: The Employment Relation in English and American Law and Culture, 1350–1870* (Chapel Hill: University of North Carolina Press, 1991).

66. Jonathan A. Glickstein, *Concepts of Free Labor in Antebellum America* (New Haven: Yale University Press, 1991), 2; see also Foner, *Free Soil, Free Labor, Free Men,* 40.

67. Foner, *Free Soil, Free Labor, Free Men,* 11, quoting speeches of Hon. Richard Yates, delivered at the Republican ratification meeting (Springfield, Ill., 1860), 6.

68. Glickstein, *Concepts of Free Labor in Antebellum America,* 12, 306; Eric Foner, "Abolitionism and the Labor Movement in Anti-Bellum America," in *Politics and Ideology in the Age of the Civil War,* ed. Eric Foner (New York: Oxford University Press, 1980), 59; Foner, *Free Soil, Free Labor, Free Men,* 16–17.

69. Some pre–Civil War land reformers were undoubtedly influenced by the Socialist and utopian ideas of Albert Brisbane, George Henry Evans, and Robert Owen. See Robbins, *Our Landed Heritage,* 97–104.

70. Johnson, *Founding the Far West,* 42, explains that much larger plots were available in 1850s Oregon. See Gates, *Land and Law in California,* 5.

71. Gates, *Land and Law in California,* 5.

72. Most commentators see the act as a victory for settlers. See Carl Swisher, *History of the Supreme Court of the United States: The Taney Period, 1836–1864,* vol. 5, *Oliver Wendell Holmes Devise History of the Supreme Court* (New York: Macmillan, 1974), 774; Lewis Grossman, "John C. Frémont, Mariposa, and the Collision of Mexican and American Law," *Western Legal History* 6 (Winter/Spring 1993): 18; Gates, *Land and Law in California,* 9–10 (although Gates argues that it only extended a well-tried system of land administration and adjudication to California).

73. An Act to Ascertain and Settle the Private Land Claims in the State of California, 9 Stat. 631 (March 3, 1851); Grossman, "John C. Frémont, Mariposa, and the Collision of Mexican and American Law," 18.

74. The estimate of 900 square miles is in *Frémont v. U.S.,* 58 U.S. (17 How.) 551, 570 (1854), Catron dissenting.

75. *Frémont v. U.S.,* 58 U.S., at 545–46; Grossman, "John C. Frémont, Mariposa, and the Collision of Mexican and American Law," 25–28.

76. Charles Gregory Crampton, "The Opening of the Mariposa Mining Region, 1849–1859, with Particular Reference to the Mexican Land Grant of John Charles Frémont," (Ph.D. diss., University of California, Berkeley, 1941), 38–41, 53–55, 207; Grossman, "John C. Frémont, Mariposa, and the Collision of Mexican and American Law," 30–31. Other business, a politically motivated court-martial, the state constitutional convention, and the U.S. Senate demanded Frémont's attention during this time.

77. Fritz, *Federal Justice in California,* 143–45.

78. Comments on Hoffman's opinion are found in Grossman, "John C. Frémont, Mariposa, and the Collision of Mexican and American Law," 51–53; Fritz, *Federal Justice in California,* 134, 146–49, 179; Crampton, "Opening of the Mariposa Mining Region," 214–20.

79. Swisher, *History of the Supreme Court,* 780.

80. *Frémont v. U.S.,* 58 U.S., at 557.

81. Ibid., at 569-70.

82. Ibid., at 571.

83. Ibid., at 572.

84. *Arguello v. U.S.,* 59 U.S. 539, 550 (1855).

85. Ibid., at 552. Fritz, *Federal Justice in California,* 151-52, points out that Daniel's opinion reflects little regard for Hispanic Californians. The main targets of Daniel's remarks, however, were monopolists and speculators.

86. See Gates, *Land and Law in California,* 13; Grossman, "John C. Frémont, Mariposa, and the Collision of Mexican and American Law," 21, 46.

87. Crampton, "Opening of the Mariposa Mining Region," 234.

3. Showdown at Las Mariposas

1. When suspicious claims threatened the ownership of valuable San Francisco lots, the Land Commission and the courts began to scrutinize grants more closely. Most commentators say the Limantour claim caused a shift in attitude. See Joseph Ellison, *California and the Nation, 1850-1869: A Study of the Relations of a Frontier Community with the Federal Government,* University of California Publications in History (Berkeley: University of California Press, 1927) 16: 22-24; Carl Swisher, *History of the Supreme Court of the United States: The Taney Period, 1836-1864,* vol. 5, *Oliver Wendell Holmes Devise History of the Supreme Court* (New York: Macmillan, 1974), 782; Christian Fritz, *Federal Justice in California: The Court of Ogden Hoffman, 1851-1891* (Lincoln: University of Nebraska Press, 1991), 165-73.

2. Ellison, *California and the Nation,* 20.

3. Paul Gates, *Land and Law in California: Essays on Land Policies* (Ames: Iowa State University Press, 1991), 169-72, points out that occupancy laws had long been in place in other states; citing *Billings v. Hall,* 7 Cal. 1 (1857).

4. *San Francisco Evening Bulletin,* July 13, 1858, 3-2.

5. For the story of the 1857 senate contest, I have relied upon William Henry Ellison, *A Self-Governing Dominion* (Berkeley: University of California Press, 1950), 284-93. See also David A. Williams, *David C. Broderick: A Political Portrait* (San Marino, Calif.: Huntington Library, 1969), 148-56; James O'Meara, *Broderick and Gwin* (San Francisco: Bacon and Company, 1881); Jeremiah Lynch, *The Life of David C. Broderick* (New York: Baker and Taylor, 1911), 141-58.

6. O'Meara, *Broderick and Gwin,* 160. It is fair to say that O'Meara did not have much use for Stephen Field, but his account of the events in 1857 makes reasonable sense. See also *San Francisco Evening Bulletin,* July 17, 1857, 2-7, expressing the belief that the Democratic nominations were prearranged as part of a compromise between Broderick and Gwin regarding the Senate contest.

7. O'Meara, *Broderick and Gwin,* 180.

8. PR, 71.

9. See O'Meara, *Broderick and Gwin,* 180-82.

10. PR, 71.

11. *Alta California,* July 14, 1857, 1-1; Winfield J. Davis, *History of Politi-*

cal *Conventions in California, 1849–1892* (Sacramento: California State Library, 1893), 77; *Sacramento Union*, July 16, 1857. The vote was Field, 185; Burnett, 121; McCune, 6.

12. *San Francisco Evening Bulletin*, July 15, 1857, 3-2.

13. *Alta California*, July 18, 1857, 2-1; *San Francisco Evening Bulletin*, July 15, 1857, 2-1, and July 21, 1857, 2-1.

14. *Sacramento Daily Bee*, July 27, 1857, 3-3.

15. *Sacramento Union*, August 29, 1857, 2-2; Davis, *History of Political Conventions in California*, 84. The returns for justice of the supreme court were Field, 55,216; Bennett, 18,944; Ralston, 19,068; see PR, 98–99.

16. Letter of Joseph G. Baldwin from the *Sacramento Union*, May 6, 1863, published in PR, 111–15.

17. These observations are based on a rough count of the cases in volumes 10 through 13 of the *California Reports*. The number of opinions in which Field was the author or concurring justice jumps dramatically from volume 13 through volume 21. Information regarding changes in the court's membership may be found on the cover pages of each volume. Notice of Field's absence is reported at 10 Cal. 581 (1859). See also J. Edward Johnson, *History of Supreme Court Justices of California, 1850–1900,* 2 vols. (San Francisco: Bender-Moss, 1963).

18. Charles W. McCurdy, "Stephen J. Field and Public Land Law Development in California, 1850–1866: A Case Study of Judicial Resource Allocation in Nineteenth-Century America," *Law and Society* 10 (Winter 1976): 265–66. Focusing on mining, land, and water law, McCurdy makes a strong case for his point.

19. See *Baldwin v. Simpson*, 12 Cal. 560 (1859), *Mott v. Hawthorn*, 17 Cal. 58 (1860), and *Hutton v. Schumaker*, 21 Cal. 453 (1863), for cases involving squatters; see McCurdy, "Stephen J. Field and Public Land Law Development in California," 240–46, for cases involving miners.

20. See *Martin & Davis v. Browner*, 11 Cal. 12 (1858). Christian G. Fritz, "Politics and the Courts: The Struggle Over Land in San Francisco, 1846–1866," *Santa Clara Law Review* 26 (1986): 127–64, illustrates the complexity of land disputes in California.

21. *Waterman v. Smith*, 13 Cal. 373 (1859), 21 Cal. 504 (1863).

22. *Rico v. Spence*, 21 Cal. 504 (1863), first to receive patent; PR, 128.

23. *Yount v. Howell*, 14 Cal. 465 (1859); *Ely v. Frisbie*, 17 Cal. 250 (1861).

24. *Lathrop v. Mills*, 19 Cal. 513 (1861); Baldwin wrote this opinion. He was undoubtedly influenced by the fact that this provision was part of a broader act that had already been overruled.

25. *Johnson v. Van Dyke*, 20 Cal. 225 (1862); the land in question fell within Frémont's Mariposa claim.

26. *Ferris v. Coover*, 10 Cal., at 622–29 (1858).

27. *Ferris v. Coover*, 10 Cal., at 621–22; see also *Cornwall v. Culver*, 16 Cal. 423 (1860); *Mahoney v. Van Winkle*, 21 Cal. 552 (1863).

28. *Ferris v. Coover*, 10 Cal. 588, 630; Field is quoting from Justice Grier in *United States v. Sutherland*, 60 U.S. (19 How.) 363, 364 (1856).

29. Both Mexican law and custom are discussed in *Mahoney v. Van Winkle*, 21 Cal., at 578–79.

30. Charles Gregory Crampton, "The Opening of the Mariposa Mining Region,

1849–1859, with Particular Reference to the Mexican Land Grant of John Charles Frémont" (Ph.D. diss., University of California, Berkeley, 1941), 172. See also Hubert Howe Bancroft, *History of California*, vol. 6, 1848–1859, in *The Works of Hubert Howe Bancroft*, vol. 23 (San Francisco: History Company, 1888), 416; Ira B. Cross, *Financing an Empire: History of Banking in California*, 4 vols. (Chicago: S. J. Clarke, 1927), 1: 131.

31. Crampton, "Opening of the Mariposa Mining Region, 1849–1859," 195. On quartz mining methods, see John S. Hittell, *Resources of California* (San Francisco: A. Roman, 1863), 273–86.

32. Crampton, "Opening of the Mariposa Mining Region, 1849–1859," 223, cites *Alta California*, April 11, 16, and May 3, 1855, noting complaints that investment was frozen. He discusses elsewhere the substantial investments that were made during the period.

33. *Frémont v. United States*, 58 U.S. (17 How.) 542, 565 (1854); see also Crampton, "Opening of the Mariposa Mining Region, 1849–1859," 224; *United States v. Frémont*, 59 U.S. (17 How.) 30, 31–34 (1855), which upholds the district court order of Judges Hall McAllister and Ogden Hoffman to carry out the ruling of *Frémont v. United States*.

34. Crampton, "Opening of the Mariposa Mining Region, 1849–1859," 231–34, explains Hays's rationale for removing the panhandle from the survey.

35. Ibid., 229–30, 212 (citing *San Francisco Herald*, June 25, 1852), 236–37 (citing *San Francisco Bulletin*, May 27, 1858); *Alta California*, March 24, 1858, 2–1; See also *San Francisco Evening Bulletin*, May 7, 1858, 2–1, and June 4, 1858, 3–3.

36. Royce D. Dalmatier, Clarence F. McIntosh, and Earl G. Waters, eds., *The Rumble of California Politics, 1848–1970* (New York: John Wiley and Sons, 1970), 44, 46, 48.

37. *Alta California*, August 2, 1858, 3–1. Boling was a member of the Central Committee of the Miners and Settlers Association of Mariposa; see *San Francisco Evening Bulletin*, June 4, 1858, 3–3.

38. *Merced Mining Company v. Frémont*, 7 Cal. 317 (1857); Terry concurred in the opinion, and Murray wrote a separate opinion. Merced's supporters also argued that the company's gold was being robbed; see *Alta California*, August 2, 1858, 3–1.

39. *Hicks v. Bell*, 3 Cal. 219 (1853).

40. John Raymond Howard, *Remembrance of Things Past* (New York: Thomas Y. Crowell, 1925), 81. Biddle Boggs is also described in Allan Nevins, *Frémont: Pathmarker of the West* (Lincoln: Bison Books, University of Nebraska Press, 1992), 460, and in Andrew Rolle, *John Charles Frémont* (Norman: University of Oklahoma Press, 1991), 180.

41. Newell Chamberlain, *The Call of Gold: True Tales on the Gold Road to Yosemite* (Mariposa, Calif.: Gazette Press, 1936), 64.

42. Crampton, "Opening of the Mariposa Mining Region, 1849–1859," 246.

43. *Biddle Boggs v. Merced Mining Company*, 14 Cal. 279, 289–91, arguments of Joseph Baldwin and S. Heydenfeldt, for respondent. Interestingly, *Biddle Boggs I* was not immediately published in the *California Reports* but is reported along with the later opinion in 1859. A reprint of the first opinion appeared in *Alta California*, March 19, 1858, 1–3.

44. Ibid., 14 Cal., at 305–7.

45. Ibid., 14 Cal., at 312-14.

46. Ibid., 14 Cal., at 314; for pro-Frémont editorials and letters, see *Alta California,* March 24, 1858, 1-5, 2-1, and May 24, 1858, 1-5.

47. Crampton, "Opening of the Mariposa Mining Region, 1849-1859," 249.

48. Ibid., 247-49, and *Alta California,* September 14, 1857, 1-2.

49. For the story of the siege of the Black Drift mine, I have relied upon Crampton, "Opening of the Mariposa Mining Region, 1849-1859," 250-53; Howard, *Remembrance of Things Past,* 84-87; Nevins, *Frémont,* 464-65; and Jessie Benton Frémont, *Far West Sketches* (Boston: D. Lothrop, 1890), 53-83.

50. Howard, *Remembrance of Things Past,* 86-87.

51. *San Francisco Evening Bulletin,* July 15, 1858, 2-3.

52. Both letters are reprinted in the *San Francisco Evening Bulletin,* July 15, 1858, 2-3. By this time, even the *Bulletin* considered the Merced group as aggressors.

53. Davis, *History of Political Conventions in California,* 90, 92, 94.

54. *Alta California,* August, 6, 1858, 2-1; August 29, 1858, 2-2; July 16, 1858, 2-1.

55. *San Francisco Evening Bulletin,* August 13, 1858, 2-1, and August 25, 1858, 2-1.

56. *Biddle Boggs,* 14 Cal., at 315, notes that a rehearing having been granted, the case was again argued at the July term, 1858. Baldwin's argument is summarized on 332-33.

57. *San Francisco Evening Bulletin,* June 4, 1858, 3-3.

58. *San Francisco Evening Bulletin,* August 7, 1858, 2-1; August 13, 1858, 2-1; August 25, 1858, 2-1; August 31, 1858, 2-1; June 10, 1858, 2-1.

59. Davis, *History of Political Conventions in California,* 95; Johnson, *History of Supreme Court Justices of California,* 77.

60. Field sat on a few cases to which he had been connected as an attorney. He even argued some cases before the supreme court after he had already been elected; see *People v. Barbour,* 9 Cal. 230 (1858). I have not found any cases in which he participated in the decision afterward, however.

61. A. Russell Buchanan, *David S. Terry of California: Dueling Judge* (San Marino, Calif.: Huntington Library, 1956), 94.

62. Buchanan, *David S. Terry of California,* 95-110; Williams, *David C. Broderick,* 230-61; Davis, *History of Political Conventions in California,* 104.

63. *Biddle Boggs v. Merced Mining Company,* 14 Cal. 279 (1859); the second opinion begins at 355. Cope concurred.

64. Ibid., at 357-66.

65. Ibid., at 366-73. Attempting to sway public sentiment, Frémont's attorneys argued that it was the government that insisted on the second survey; Frémont, they claimed, had never wanted it. *San Francisco Evening Bulletin,* June 8, 1858, 3-3.

66. *Alta California,* November 26, 1859, 1-3; this article may also be found in a scrapbook of newspaper clippings covering the *Biddle Boggs* case, which is held at the Huntington Library.

67. *Biddle Boggs,* 14 Cal., at 379; *Hicks v. Bell,* 3 Cal. 219 (1853).

68. *Biddle Boggs,* 14 Cal., at 375.

69. *Moore v. Smaw and Frémont v. Flower,* 17 Cal. 199 (1861).

70. *Hornsby v. United States,* 77 U.S. (10 Wall.) 224, 237 (1869); Field was citing the *Frémont* case.

71. *Moore v. Smaw and Frémont v. Flower,* 17 Cal. 199 (1861); for an admiring contemporary review, see *American Law Register* 10 (1862): 462.

72. See *Daubenspeck v. Grear,* 18 Cal. 443 (1861), for a case applying the doctrine to a small plot. *Sacramento Union,* November 26, 1859, 2–3.

73. *Sacramento Union,* December 15, 1859, 1–7.

74. Robert A. Burchell, "The Faded Dream: Inequality in Northern California in the 1860s and 1870s," *Journal of American Studies* 23 (August 1989): 216.

75. *Sacramento Union,* November 26, 1859, 2–3; November 25, 1859, 1–3; December 8, 1859, 2–3.

76. His memoirs, written years later, highlighted his accomplishments in this respect (PR 121–36); see also John Norton Pomeroy, *Some Account of the Work of Stephen J. Field* (1881; rpt., Littleton, Colo.: Fred B. Rothman, 1986), 20–30. On the basis of a Westlaw search, I estimate that Field wrote about sixty-five opinions in cases dealing with Mexican land grants. For an example of Field's later favoritism toward grant holders' opinions, see *Hornsby v. United States,* 77 U.S. (10 Wall.) 224 (1870). For his attitude regarding squatters, see *Van Reynegan v. Bolton,* 95 U.S. 33 (1877).

77. Pomeroy, *Some Account of the Work of Stephen J. Field,* 34, 29–35.

78. *Alta California,* December 24, 1859, 4–1; *Sacramento Union,* November 25, 1859, 1–3.

79. *Sacramento Union,* November 26, 1859, 2–3, reporting on *Biddle Boggs.*

80. Crampton, "Opening of the Mariposa Mining Region, 1849–1859," 263–65; Chamberlain, *Call of Gold,* 111, 112; *San Francisco Evening Bulletin,* December 15, 1859, 4–2.

81. Nevins, *Frémont,* 583–601; *The Great Libel Case: Opdyke vs. Weed* (New York: American News Company, 1865).

82. Frémont to David Dudley Field, September 26, 1878; Frémont to Stephen J. Field, September 27, 1878, Field-Musgrave Collection, Perkins Library, Special Collections, Duke University, Durham, N.C.

83. "The Gold Key Court or the Corruptions of a Majority of It," a copy of which is held at the Huntington Library, is signed "Ex-Supreme Court Broker" and has no date. It includes charges relating to a variety of other land cases, including the San Francisco cases (discussed in chapter 4).

84. PR, 108–9, Stephen J. Field to J. DeBarth Shorb, October 27, 1886, J. DeBarth Shorb Collection, Huntington Library.

85. During the same term in which they decided *Biddle Boggs,* the California justices tactfully ruled that mere entry upon a 500-acre tract of public mineral land did not give one person a right to exclusive occupancy. To hold otherwise, Baldwin wrote for the court, would mean that the whole mineral region might be monopolized by a few men—a doctrine that would in effect exclude the mass of people in the state from participation in the mines (*Burdge v. Smith,* 14 Cal. 381 [1859]). This was the kind of language miners liked to hear, but they knew it was not truly representative of the court's general attitude. As if to reinforce its anti-miner reputation, a year later the court invalidated a state statute that gave miners the right to go onto private land but required payment to the landowner for any damage done (*Gillan v.*

Hutchinson, 16 Cal. 153 [1860]). In another interesting case, *Norris v. Hoyt,* 18 Cal. 217 (1861). Field rejected the argument that a person who had purchased property secured by a patent could not own the property because he was a foreigner.

86. Davis, *History of Political Conventions in California,* 165–80, with respect to the nomination of justice of the supreme court, reports "W. C. Wallace over . . . J. J. Baldwin declining" (172). I have assumed that this means that Baldwin was nominated and declined. Norton, who was also the Settlers' party nominee, won the election (180). Field did not think much of Norton, whom he described as "not adapted for appellate work" (see Johnson, *History of Supreme Court Justices of California,* 85).

4. The Tenth Justice

1. Stanley I. Kutler, *Judicial Power and Reconstruction Politics* (Chicago: University of Chicago Press, 1968), 18–19. Usual accounts hold that the tenth seat was created as a result of a narrow decision in the *Prize Cases,* but Kutler disputes that there was a direct causal connection between the two events (for a full discussion of judicial reform in 1862 and 1863, see 12–30).

2. Ibid., 14.

3. See Eric Foner, *Free Soil, Free Labor, Free Men: The Ideology of the Republican Party Before the Civil War* (New York: Oxford University Press, 1970), 73–102, for a discussion of the slave power.

4. David M. Silver, *Lincoln's Supreme Court* (Urbana: University of Illinois Press, 1956), 87, quoting Wait Talcott to Lyman Trumbull, February 1, 1863, Trumbull Papers, Library of Congress.

5. An Act to Provide for the Circuit Courts for the Districts of California and Oregon, 12 Stat. 794 (March 3, 1863).

6. See Carl Swisher, *History of the Supreme Court of the United States: The Taney Period, 1836–1864,* vol. 5, *Oliver Wendell Holmes Devise History of the Supreme Court of the United States* (New York: Macmillan, 1974), 775–76, 805–6, 830–31. For some background on Judge McAllister, see John D. Gordon III, *Authorized by No Law: The San Francisco Committee of Vigilance of 1856 and the United States Circuit Court for the District of California* (San Francisco: Ninth Judicial Circuit Historical Society, 1987).

7. For detailed discussion of these appointments, see Silver, *Lincoln's Supreme Court,* 57–93.

8. Stephen J. Field to Abraham Lincoln, October 25, 1861, Lincoln Papers, Library of Congress; see also Silver, *Lincoln's Supreme Court,* 89; Milton H. Shutes, *Lincoln and California* (Stanford, Calif.: Stanford University Press, 1943), 144–45 (Governor-elect Leland Stanford and Horace Carpenter, president of the Overland Telegraph Company, sent the other messages).

9. The story originates in Henry M. Field, *The Life of David Dudley Field* (New York: Charles Scribner's Sons, 1898), 195–96. Henry, who appeared to be the designated family historian, also wrote a history of his brother Cyrus's exploits. Henry M. Field, *The Story of the Atlantic Telegraph* (New York: Charles Scribner's Sons, 1892).

10. Foner, *Free Soil, Free Labor, Free Men,* 152–53, 164, 177, 184; Daun van Ee, *David Dudley Field and the Reconstruction of the Law* (New York: Garland, 1986), 114–45.

11. Van Ee, *David Dudley Field and the Reconstruction of the Law,* 145, traces the relationship between David Dudley Field and Salmon P. Chase, expressing the belief that Field was instrumental not only in the appointment of his brother but also in the later appointment of Chase as chief justice. The fact that Stephen Field, then associate justice, wrote a letter recommending Chase for chief justice lends weight to van Ee's belief. See Stephen J. Field to Abraham Lincoln, October 16, 1864, Lincoln Papers. See also David Dudley Field to Abraham Lincoln, July 15, 19, 1863, Lincoln Papers; letters from David Dudley Field to Salmon P. Chase for the years 1861 to 1864, Chase Papers, Historical Society of Pennsylvania; David Dudley Field to Salmon P. Chase, March 11, 1864, Stephen J. Field Collection, Bancroft Library, University of California, Berkeley; Reverdy Johnson to David Dudley Field, February 25, 1863, Field Collection. See also Lyman Trumbull Papers, and Silver, *Lincoln's Supreme Court,* 89, n. 19.

12. PR, 115.

13. Ibid., 115–16; Silver, *Lincoln's Supreme Court,* 88–93; Swisher, *History of the Supreme Court,* 806–10. The Rare Book Collection of the Library of Congress holds a facsimile letter from California senators Milton S. Latham and J. A. McDougal and congressmen A. A. Sargent, F. F. Low, and T. W. Phelps to Lincoln, urging Field's appointment.

14. Later Field recalled that the presence of numerous California land and mining disputes on the Supreme Court's docket was one factor contributing to his appointment. Whether or not this was true, he did seem to write a disproportionate share of opinions in land dispute cases (PR, 116; Stephen J. Field to Don Dickinson, July 16, 1893, Dickinson Papers, Library of Congress).

15. *United States v. Augisola,* 68 U.S. (1 Wall.) 352 (1863).

16. *United States v. D'Aquirre,* 68 U.S. (1 Wall.) 311 (1863).

17. *Pico v. United States,* 69 U.S. (2 Wall.) 279 (1864); *Graham v. United States,* 71 U.S. (4 Wall.) 259 (1866).

18. *Malarin v. United States,* 68 U.S. (1 Wall.) 282 (1863).

19. *United States v. Yorba,* 68 U.S. (1 Wall.) 412 (1863).

20. *United States v. Halleck,* 68 U.S. (1 Wall.) 439 (1863).

21. Field's first significant opinion for the Supreme Court held that, prior to an 1860 act of Congress, the U.S. district court had no jurisdiction to correct surveys or to revise the action of the surveyor general (*United States v. Sepulveda,* 68 U.S. [1 Wall.] 104 [1863]). Following his California rule, he held that the issue of fraud could not be raised for the first time on appeal (*United States v. Augisola,* 68 U.S. [1 Wall.] 352 [1863]). Yet he was willing to allow the claimant of a grant to unite his claim for rents and damages to a suit for ejectment (*Beard v. Federy,* 70 U.S. [3 Wall.] 478 [1865]). Following another doctrine he had developed on the state court, he ruled that when boundaries designated in the grant contain more land than confirmed by the board, the grantee has the right to select the location of his land (*United States v. Pacheco,* 69 U.S. [2 Wall.] 587 [1864]).

22. *Hornsby v. United States,* 77 U.S. (10 Wall.) 224 (1867). Even in conflicts

among people claiming Mexican grants to the same land, he displayed a generous sense of equity (*United States v. Armijo,* 72 U.S. [5 Wall.] 444 [1866]).

23. *Frisbie v. Whitney,* 76 U.S. (9 Wall.) 187 (1869). *Frisbie* was not an especially good case by which to measure the Court's attitude toward homesteaders. It involved a conflict between speculators who purchased land from the holders of an invalid Mexican grant and opportunistic squatters who quickly settled the land after the grant was declared invalid. See Paul W. Gates, *Land and Law in California: Essays on Land Policies* (Ames: Iowa State University Press, 1991), 209–28.

24. *New York Times,* May 19, 1870.

25. *Yosemite Valley Case (Hutchings v. Low),* 82 U.S. (15 Wall.) 77 (1872); see Brief for the Plaintiff in Error, microfilm records.

26. *Yosemite Valley Case,* 82 U.S., at 87.

27. See chapter 2, notes 51–53 and accompanying text.

28. Paula Mitchell Marks, *Precious Dust: The American Gold Rush Era: 1848–1900* (New York: William Morrow, 1994), 187, quoting James L. Tyson, *Diary of a Physician in California* (Oakland, Calif.: Bio Books, 1955), 60.

29. For a more detailed treatment of the San Francisco pueblo cases, see Christian G. Fritz, *Federal Justice in California: The Court of Ogden Hoffman, 1851-1891* (Lincoln: University of Nebraska Press, 1991), 180–93; Roger W. Lotchin, *San Francisco, 1846-1856: From Hamlet to City* (New York: Oxford University Press, 1974), 143–49; Molly Selvin, *This Tender and Delicate Business: Public Trust Doctrine in American Law and Economic Policy, 1789-1920* (New York: Garland, 1987), 170–277; and Carl Swisher, *History of the Supreme Court of the United States,* 807–10. Field gives a clear if prejudiced account of the dispute in his memoirs (PR, 136–43).

30. *Hart v. Burnett,* 15 Cal. 530 (1860).

31. PR, 141–42. One of those anonymous circulars was "The Gold Key Court or the Corruptions of a Majority of It," a copy of which is held at the Huntington Library, signed "Ex-Supreme Court Broker," and which has no date.

32. *Hart v. Burnett,* 20 Cal. 169 (1862).

33. Fritz, *Federal Justice in California,* 196–209, provides the best treatment of this series of events. See also PR, 142–45; Hubert Howe Bancroft, *History of California,* vol. 7, 1860–1890, *The Works of Hubert Howe Bancroft,* vol. 24 (San Francisco: History Company, 1890), 230–31, and Swisher, *History of the Supreme Court,* 807–9.

34. Fritz, *Federal Justice in California,* 196, citing *Congressional Globe,* 38th Cong., 1st sess., 1863.

35. Ibid., 197–202; an Act to Expedite the Settlement of Titles to Lands in the State of California, 13 Stat. 332 (July 1, 1864).

36. *San Francisco v. United States,* 21 Fed. Cas. 365 (Cir. Ct.; N.D. Cal., 1864).

37. Fritz, *Federal Justice in California,* 201–5.

38. Both the judicial and legislative activities that followed *San Francisco v. United States* are reported along with the opinion (21 Fed. Cas., at 370–80; Field's negative remarks regarding Williams are found at 370–73).

39. *United States v. Circuit Judges,* 70 U.S. (3 Wall.) 673 (1865).

40. An Act to Quiet Title to Certain Lands Within the Corporate Limits of the

City of San Francisco, 14 Stat. 4 (March 8, 1866); see *Townsend v. Greeley,* 72 U.S. 337 (1866).

41. PR, 145–50.

42. *United States v. Greathouse,* 26 Fed. Cas. 18, 19–21 (1863), provides most of the details of this incident. See also Bancroft, *History of California,* 7: 287–88. For color, see William Martin Camp, *San Francisco: Port of Gold* (New York: Doubleday, 1947), 122–51; James H. Wilkins, ed., *The Great Diamond Hoax and Other Stirring Incidents in the Life of Asbury Harpending* (Norman: University of Oklahoma Press, 1958), 1–61.

43. J. Edward Johnson, *History of Supreme Court Justices of California, 1850–1900,* 2 vols. (San Francisco: Bender-Moss, 1963), 1: 79, maintains that Field used his influence to have charges against young Baldwin dropped. But Camp, *San Francisco: Port of Gold,* notes that charges against the sixteen others were dropped for lack of evidence (144).

44. The provision for capital punishment made the old statute unworkable in light of the potential number of people who could be charged with treason during the Civil War. Harold M. Hyman, *A More Perfect Union: The Impact of the Civil War and Reconstruction on the Constitution* (New York: Alfred A. Knopf, 1973), 95–98, points out a number of other reasons why the law of treason proved to be an ineffective weapon for the Union. See also J. G. Randall, *Constitutional Problems Under Lincoln* (Urbana: University of Illinois Press, 1951), 74–96.

45. Fritz, *Federal Justice in California,* 194–96, notes that the case marked the beginning of a long and tense relationship between the two federal judges and examines the relationship between Hoffman and Field in detail. Fritz is of the opinion that the *Greathouse* case caused Field to lose confidence in Hoffman and resulted directly in Field's efforts to remove the pueblo cases from Hoffman's court.

46. Samuel Klaus, ed., *The Milligan Case* (New York: Alfred A. Knopf, 1929), 7.

47. Ibid., 8–9.

48. A. P. Sprague, ed., *Speeches, Arguments, and Miscellaneous Papers of David Dudley Field,* 3 vols. (New York: D. Appleton, 1884), 1: 43.

49. See Klaus, *Milligan Case,* 22–25.

50. For the facts leading to *Ex parte Milligan,* see ibid., 33–47.

51. Sprague, *Speeches, Arguments, and Miscellaneous Papers of David Dudley Field,* 1: 42.

52. *Ex parte Milligan,* 71 U.S. (4 Wall.) 2 (1866).

53. Klaus, *Milligan Case,* 47–48; Mark E. Neely, Jr., *The Fate of Liberty: Abraham Lincoln and Civil Liberties* (New York: Oxford University Press, 1991), 175–84, disputes the importance of *Milligan* and points out that trial by military commission continued for years after the decision.

54. Kutler, *Judicial Power and Reconstruction Politics,* 65–71.

55. *Ex parte McCardle,* 73 U.S. (6 Wall.) 318 (1867), on motion to dismiss appeal for want of jurisdiction.

56. Kutler, *Judicial Power and Reconstruction Politics,* 79, quoting *Congressional Globe,* 40th Cong,. 2d sess., 1883–84 (March 14, 1868). For details of the events surrounding the case, see Charles Fairman, *Reconstruction and Reunion 1864–88,* in *Oliver Wendell Holmes Devise History of the Supreme Court of the United*

States (New York: Macmillan, 1971), 6: 433–514. U.S. Constitution, Article 3, sec. 2, gives Congress the power to regulate the Court's appellate jurisdiction.

57. *Ex parte McCardle,* 74 U.S. (7 Wall.) 506 (1869). Note that the Court may still have been able to claim jurisdiction under the Judiciary Act of 1789.

58. Fairman, *Reconstruction and Reunion, 1864–88,* 6: 473–74, notes that he was unable to find the original text of this memorandum. He relies on John Norton Pomeroy, *Some Account of the Work of Stephen J. Field* (1881; rpt., Littleton, Colo.: Fred B. Rothman, 1986), 49–50; the memo can also be found in PR, 173.

59. Chief Justice Chase pointed this out in his dissent by arguing that to deny the right of habeas corpus here was to deny the right to protect a large class of citizens against arbitrary imprisonment (*Tarble's Case,* 80 U.S. (13 Wall.) 397, 413 (1852).

60. Ibid., at 403.

61. For a full treatment of loyalty oaths during the Civil War and Reconstruction, see Harold Hyman, *Era of the Oath: Northern Loyalty Tests During the Civil War and Reconstruction* (Philadelphia: University of Pennsylvania Press, 1954).

62. Foner, *Free Soil, Free Labor, Free Men,* 92; see also 99.

63. An Act to Prescribe an Oath of Office, 12 Stat. 502–3 (July 2, 1862), reproduced in Hyman, *Era of the Oath,* 158–59.

64. *Cummings v. Missouri,* 71 U.S. (4 Wall.) 277, 279–81 (1867).

65. Van Ee, *David Dudley Field and the Reconstruction of the Law,* 179–80. Van Ee explores the political ramifications, noting that Democrats claimed that the loyalty test law would be overturned and so urged people to vote without taking the oath.

66. Sprague, *Speeches, Arguments, and Miscellaneous Papers of David Dudley Field,* 106.

67. Ibid., 108.

68. *Cummings v. Missouri,* 71 U.S., at 294, argument for the state.

69. Ibid., at 303, argument for the state.

70. Ibid., at 315–16, reply for Cummings.

71. Ibid., at 320.

72. *Ex parte Garland,* 71 U.S. (4 Wall.) 333, 379 (1867).

73. *Cummings v. Missouri,* 71 U.S., at 325. For reaction to the *Test Oath* decisions, see Hyman, *Era of the Oath,* 113–19; see also Fairman, *Reconstruction and Reunion, 1864–88,* 6: 240–248.

74. *Ex parte Garland,* 71 U.S., at 335, Miller dissenting.

75. Ibid., 71 U.S., at 392, Miller dissenting. Miller recognized in the *Test Oath Cases* an early version of what would later be called dual federalism. These elastic rules of construction, he complained, "cramp the powers of the Federal government when they are to be exercised in certain directions, and enlarges them when they are exercised in others." Van Ee, *David Dudley Field and the Reconstruction of the Law,* 178, makes this point as well.

76. Excellent recent works on the original purpose of the Fourteenth Amendment are Earl M. Maltz, *Civil Rights, the Constitution, and Congress, 1863–1869* (Lawrence, Kans.: University Press of Kansas, 1990); Michael Kent Curtis, *No State Shall Abridge: The Fourteenth Amendment and the Bill of Rights* (Durham, N.C.: Duke University Press, 1990); and William E. Nelson, *The Fourteenth Amendment:*

From *Political Principle to Judicial Doctrine* (Cambridge: Harvard University Press, 1988). References to the voluminous earlier works on the subject can be found in these books.

77. Ronald M. Labbé, "New Light on the Slaughterhouse Monopoly Act of 1869," in *Louisiana's Legal Heritage,* ed. Edward F. Haas (Pensacola, Fla.: Perdido Bay Press, 1983), 143 and 143–63; *Slaughter-House Cases,* 83 U.S. (16 Wall.) 36, 38 (1873).

78. Labbé, "New Light on the Slaughterhouse Monopoly Act of 1869," 151, quoting testimony of Dr. E. S. Lewis before the Louisiana House of Representatives, Special Committee on the Removal of the Slaughter Houses, *Minute Book* (1867). See Herbert Hovenkamp, *Enterprise and American Law, 1836–1937* (Cambridge: Harvard University Press, 1991), 118–20.

79. Labbé, "New Light on the Slaughterhouse Monopoly Act of 1869," 150.

80. Ibid., 152–54; *Slaughter-House Cases,* 83 U.S., at 38–41.

81. Labbé, "New Light on the Slaughterhouse Monopoly Act of 1869," 149, and Fairman, *Reconstruction and Reunion, 1864–88,* 6: 1322.

82. William J. Novak, "Public Economy and the Well-Ordered Market: Law and Economic Regulation in Nineteenth-Century America," *Law and Social Inquiry* 18 (Winter 1993): 20. See also William J. Novak, *The People's Welfare, Law and Regulation in Nineteenth-Century America* (Chapel Hill: University of North Carolina Press, 1996).

83. Novak, "Public Economy and the Well-Ordered Market," addresses the idea of a well-ordered market. I have addressed the constitutional aspects of early and mid-nineteenth-century regulation in "Liberty and the Public Ingredient of Private Property," *Review of Politics* (Winter 1993): 85–116.

84. Regarding charges of bribery, see Labbé, "New Light on the Slaughterhouse Monopoly Act of 1869," 155–56, and Fairman, *Reconstruction and Reunion, 1864–88,* 6: 1322–24. Hovenkamp, *Enterprise and American Law,* 122–24, disputes that bribery was involved.

85. Labbé, "New Light on the Slaughterhouse Monopoly Act of 1869," 154–55, notes that some of the investors had New Orleans connections. See also Fairman, *Reconstruction and Reunion, 1864–88,* 6: 1329.

86. Labbé, "New Light on the Slaughterhouse Monopoly Act of 1869," 145–47; Hovenkamp, *Enterprise and American Law,* 121.

87. Fairman, *Reconstruction and Reunion, 1864–88,* 6: 1324–27.

88. *Brown v. Maryland,* 25 U.S. (12 Wheat.) 419 (1827); *Willson v. Black-Bird Marsh Creek,* 27 U.S. (2 Pet.) 245 (1829).

89. *City of Chicago v. Rumpff,* 45 Ill. 90 (1867); although Stephen Field cites this case in his dissent to the *Slaughter-House Cases,* it provides only tangential support for his position (see 83 U.S., at 106–7).

90. Labbé, "New Light on the Slaughterhouse Monopoly Act of 1869," 149.

91. Benjamin R. Twiss, *Lawyers and the Constitution* (Princeton: Princeton University Press, 1942), 49.

92. *Slaughter-House Cases,* 83 U.S., at 62.

93. *Barron v. Baltimore,* 32 U.S. (7 Pet.) 243 (1833).

94. *Slaughter-House Cases,* 83 U.S., at 71.

95. Ibid., 83 U.S., at 72.

96. See Robert C. Palmer, "The Parameters of Constitutional Reconstruction: Slaughter-House, Cruikshank, and the Fourteenth Amendment," *University of Illinois Law Review* (1984): 739–70.

97. *Slaughter-House Cases,* 83 U.S., at 80.

98. Ibid., 83 U.S., at 96, Field dissenting.

99. Ibid., 83 U.S., at 88–89, Field dissenting.

100. Ibid., 83 U.S., at 86, Field dissenting. Michael Les Benedict, "Laissez-Faire and Liberty: A Reevaluation of the Meaning and Origins of Laissez-Faire Constitutionalism," *Law and History Review* 3 (Fall 1985): 327–28, maintains that although the slaughterhouse legislation was partly a legitimate health measure, it also transferred property or its benefits from one portion of the community to another.

101. *Slaughter-House Cases,* 83 U.S., at 108–9, Field dissenting.

102. Ibid., 83 U.S., at 97, Field dissenting (emphasis in original). Field used the words "natural" and "inalienable" three paragraphs earlier; I have added them for clarity and emphasis.

103. The legal precedent that Field offered to support his argument had significant weaknesses. He imputed the right to pursue a trade from broader language in Justice Bushrod Washington's circuit opinion in *Corfield v. Coryell.* He offered three state cases that only indirectly supported his proposition. The strongest authority in his support would have come from the *Test Oath Cases,* which he wrote. See *Slaughter-House Cases,* 83 U.S., at 97, 104–9, Field dissenting.

104. *Slaughter-House Cases,* 83 U.S., at 104, 105, 110, Field dissenting.

105. Ibid., 83 U.S., at 109, Field dissenting (emphasis added).

106. William E. Nelson, *The Fourteenth Amendment,* 8, 9, 64–90. Regarding the congressional debates, Nelson astutely makes the point that the framing generation understood constitutional politics as a rhetorical venture designed to persuade people to do good rather than as a bureaucratic venture intended to establish precise legal rules. My point is that the function of the judiciary should be to establish a precise and consistent set of rules.

107. *Slaughter-House Cases,* 83 U.S., at 78.

108. Ibid., 83 U.S., at 112, 114–16, Bradley dissenting.

109. Ibid., 83 U.S., at 120, Bradley dissenting.

110. See Jane M. Friedman, *America's First Woman Lawyer: The Biography of Myra Bradwell* (Buffalo, N.Y.: Prometheus Books, 1993).

111. *Bradwell v. Illinois,* 83 U.S. (16 Wall.) 130, 135, 133–37 (1873), argument for the plaintiff in error.

112. Ibid., at 139.

113. Ibid., U.S., at 141, emphasis added. It is interesting to note that Bradley professed sympathy with the movement to give women more rights. Also note that Chief Justice Chase dissented from the opinion of the Court.

114. *Bartemeyer v. Iowa,* 85 U.S. (18 Wall.) 129 (1874).

115. Emphasizing that he was not faced with the question of an outright prohibition of slaughtering, Field implied that such a law might pass constitutional muster (*Slaughter-House Cases,* 83 U.S., at 87–88, Field dissenting). Nelson, *Fourteenth Amendment,* 169, argues that Field's dissent in *Slaughter-House* simply was that the state could not permit some butchers to enjoy exclusive rights not granted to all butchers.

116. *Bartemeyer v. Iowa,* 85 U.S., at 138, Field dissenting; Nelson, *Fourteenth Amendment,* 158, maintains that Field's was a narrow interpretation of the Fourteenth Amendment in that it recognized that fundamental rights were subject to valid application of the police power.

117. See *Mugler v. Kansas,* 123 U.S. 623 (1887), and *Crowley v. Christensen,* 137 U.S. 86 (1890). Michael Les Benedict, "Victorian Moralism and Civil Liberty in the Nineteenth-Century United States," in *The Constitution, Law, and American Life: Critical Aspects of the Nineteenth-Century Experience,* ed. Donald G. Nieman (Athens: University of Georgia Press, 1992), 91–122, explores the relationship between economic liberty and Victorian morality and explains why most nineteenth-century jurists would probably have followed the same course as Field.

5. Vise Grip on the Flow of Commerce

1. J. D. B. Stillman, "The Last Tie," *Overland Monthly* 3 (1869): 77–84; William Deverell, *Railroad Crossing: Californians and the Railroad, 1850–1910* (Berkeley: University of California Press, 1994), 23; John Hoyt Williams, *A Great and Shining Road: The Epic Story of the Transcontinental Railroad* (New York: Times Books, 1988), 266; John P. Davis, *The Union Pacific Railway* (Chicago: S. C. Griggs, 1894), 155–57.

2. See Milton H. Shutes, *Lincoln and California* (Stanford, Calif.: Stanford University Press, 1943), 31–58.

3. For summaries of the bill, see Williams, *A Great and Shining Road,* 42–48, 78–79; Stuart Daggett, *Chapters in the History of the Southern Pacific* (New York: Ronald Press, 1922), 48–54; Charles Fairman, *Reconstruction and Reunion, 1864–88,* vol. 7, *Oliver Wendell Holmes Devise History of the Supreme Court of the United States* (New York: Macmillan, 1987), 589. The actual statutes are the Act to Aid in Construction of a Railroad, 12 Stat. 489 (July 1, 1862), and the Act to Aid in Construction of a Railroad, 13 Stat. 356 (July 2, 1864). I will treat the two bills as one, the form taken after amendment in 1864. Readers interested in the details should be aware that there are significant differences.

4. Williams, *A Great and Shining Road,* 9.

5. Tzu-Kuei Yen, "Chinese Workers and the First Transcontinental Railroad of the United States of America" (Ph.D. diss., St. John's University, N.Y. 1976), 128.

6. Williams, *A Great and Shining Road,* 143–44.

7. Davis, *Union Pacific Railway,* 139; Yen, "Chinese Workers and the First Transcontinental Railroad of the United States of America," 131.

8. Williams, *A Great and Shining Road,* 114.

9. Ibid., 90.

10. Ping Chiu, *Chinese Labor in California* (Madison: State Historical Society of Wisconsin, 1963), 42, 46.

11. Yen, "Chinese Workers and the First Transcontinental Railroad of the United States of America," 29–32.

12. Ibid., 137–38; Williams, *A Great and Shining Road,* 98.

13. Yen, "Chinese Workers and the First Transcontinental Railroad of the United States of America," 29–36, 38, 130; Chiu, *Chinese Labor in California,* 47; Williams,

A Great and Shining Road, 181. Chinese did walk off the job at least once, however. On June 24, 1867, they struck, demanding an eight-hour day and forty dollars a month.

14. Alexander Saxton, *The Indispensable Enemy: Labor and the Anti-Chinese Movement in California* (Berkeley: University of California Press, 1971), 63; Yen, "Chinese Workers and the First Transcontinental Railroad of the United States of America," 111.

15. Yen, "Chinese Workers and the First Transcontinental Railroad of the United States of America," 37; Chiu, *Chinese Labor in California,* 46.

16. Yen, "Chinese Workers and the First Transcontinental Railroad of the United States of America," 120; Shih-shan Henry Tsai, *The Chinese Experience in America* (Bloomington and Indianapolis: Indiana University Press, 1986), 17.

17. Williams, *A Great and Shining Road,* 143–44, 161; Yen, "Chinese Workers and the First Transcontinental Railroad of the United States of America," 129.

18. Charles J. McClain, *In Search of Equality: The Chinese Struggle Against Discrimination in Nineteenth-Century America* (Berkeley: University of California Press, 1994), 30, quoting the Burlingame Treaty, July 28, 1868, Art. 6, 16 Stat. 740.

19. John R. Wunder, "Anti-Chinese Violence in the American West, 1850–1910," in *Law for the Elephant, Law for the Beaver: Essays in Legal History of the North American West,* ed. John McLaren, Hamar Foster, and Chet Orloff (Pasadena, Calif.: Ninth Judicial Circuit Historical Society, 1992), 212–36; Tsai, *Chinese Experience in America,* 67–72; Elmer Clarence Sandmeyer, *The Anti-Chinese Movement in California* (Urbana: University of Illinois Press, 1939), 40–56.

20. *Lin Sing v. Washburn,* 20 Cal. 534, 582 (1862), Field dissenting.

21. *Ah Hee v. Crippen,* 19 Cal. 491 (1861); for more details of this case and *Lin Sing v. Washburn,* see McClain, *In Search of Equality,* 24–29.

22. *Ah Hee v. Crippen,* 19 Cal., at 496–97 (1861).

23. Sandmeyer, *Anti-Chinese Movement in California,* 25, quoting from the *Marin Journal,* March 30, 1876. This type of statement was common in the anti-Chinese publications of the day, and I chose this source for its convenience.

24. Williams, *A Great and Shining Road,* 117, 162–63.

25. Jonathan A. Glickstein, *Concepts of Free Labor in Antebellum America* (New Haven: Yale University Press, 1991), 2; Eric Foner, *Free Soil, Free Labor, Free Men: The Ideology of the Republican Party Before the Civil War* (New York: Oxford University Press, 1970), 59–60.

26. See Tsai, *Chinese Experience in America,* 3–10.

27. Ibid., 7, citing an Act to Prohibit the Coolie Trade by American Citizen in American Vessels, 11 Stat. 340 (1862).

28. Compare Tsai, *Chinese Experience in America,* 9, with Sandmeyer, *Anti-Chinese Movement in California,* 28.

29. For reference to whippings, see Yen, "Chinese Workers and the First Transcontinental Railroad of the United States of America," 38.

30. Ibid., 41–42.

31. Foner, *Free Soil, Free Labor, and Free Men,* 60–63.

32. Harold M. Hyman and William M. Wiecek, *Equal Justice Under Law: Constitutional Development, 1835–1875* (New York: Harper Torchbooks, 1982), 129–30, note that the Wilmot Proviso was defended in these terms.

33. See William Henry Ellison, *A Self-Governing Dominion: California, 1849–1860* (Berkeley: University of California Press, 1950), 58. Foner, *Free Soil, Free Labor, and Free Men,* 262, notes that racial prejudice was especially severe in the West.

34. Robert J. Steinfeld, *The Invention of Free Labor: The Employment Relation in English and American Law and Culture, 1350–1870* (Chapel Hill: University of North Carolina Press, 1991).

35. Ibid., 186–87.

36. Daggett, *Chapters in the History of the Southern Pacific,* 55–56, points out that this amount was theoretical. Intervening factors reduced the amount of land the railroads actually received.

37. W. H. Hutchinson, "Southern Pacific: Myth and Reality," *California Historical Quarterly* 48 (December 1969): 326.

38. For summaries of the bill, see Williams, *A Great and Shining Road,* 42–48; Daggett, *Chapters in the History of the Southern Pacific,* 54–56; and Fairman, *Reconstruction and Reunion,* 7: 589–90. The actual statutes are found at 12 Stat. 489 (1862) and 13 Stat. 356 (1864). The act of 1862 gave a 200-foot right-of-way and ten sections of land. As amended in 1864, it gave a 100-foot right-of-way and twenty sections of land.

39. Daggett, *Chapters in the History of the Southern Pacific,* 54–56.

40. Williams, *A Great and Shining Road,* 42–48; see also Daggett, *Chapters in the History of the Southern Pacific,* 3–20, and Oscar Lewis, *The Big Four* (New York: Alfred A. Knopf, 1938).

41. Williams, *A Great and Shining Road,* 84.

42. Charles Francis Adams, Jr., "Railroad Inflation," *North American Review* 108 (January 1869): 148.

43. Williams, *A Great and Shining Road,* 280.

44. Adams, "Railroad Inflation," 147; Sean Dennis Cashman, *America in the Gilded Age,* 2d ed. (New York: New York University Press, 1988), 32; for profits of the Crédit Mobilier, see also Davis, *Union Pacific Railway,* 170–71.

45. Williams, *A Great and Shining Road,* 183–84; Daggett, *Chapters in the History of the Southern Pacific,* 75–82.

46. Williams, *A Great and Shining Road,* 177, 281–83.

47. Fairman, *Reconstruction and Reunion,* 7: 599, Act of March 3, 1873, 17 Stat. 485 (1873).

48. *United States v. Union Pacific R.R.,* 91 U.S. 72 (1875).

49. *United States v. Union Pacific R.R.,* 98 U.S. 569 (1879). For a more detailed account of both Union Pacific cases, see Fairman, *Reconstruction and Reunion,* 7: 589–602.

50. C. Peter Magrath, *Morrison R. Waite: The Triumph of Character* (New York: Macmillan, 1963), 258–60, citing Waite to Field, November 7 and 10, 1875, Morrison R. Waite Papers, Library of Congress; the case was the first (*United States v. Union Pacific R.R. Co.,* 91 U.S. 72 [1875]). See also Fairman, *Reconstruction and Reunion,* 7: 593–95.

51. John G. Sproat, *The Best Men: Liberal Reformers in the Gilded Age* (New York: Oxford University Press, 1968), 173.

52. Deverell, *Railroad Crossing,* 34.

53. Albro Martin, *Railroads Triumphant: The Growth, Rejection, and Rebirth of*

a Vital American Force (New York: Oxford University Press, 1992); see especially 162–63.

54. Deverell, *Railroad Crossing*, 35.

55. Ibid., 25.

56. Ibid., 16–22. Carefully tracing the railroad's impact on California's social, political, and economic life, Deverell draws out the sources and intricacies of railroad opposition. Henry George, "What the Railroad Will Bring Us," *Overland Monthly* 1 (October 1868): 297–306.

57. Daggett, *Chapters in the History of the Southern Pacific*, 140–53, 222–36; Julius Grodinsky, *Transcontinental Railway Strategy, 1869–1893: A Study of Businessmen* (Philadelphia: University of Pennsylvania Press, 1962), 26.

58. Charles Francis Adams, Jr., *Railroads: Their Origin and Problems* (New York: G. P. Putnam's Sons, 1886), 81. Adams was speaking of railroads in general.

59. David Alan Johnson, *Founding the Far West: California, Oregon, and Nevada, 1840–1890* (Berkeley: University of California Press, 1992), 234–35, 241.

60. The depiction of the Southern Pacific as an octopus is usually attributed to Frank Norris's famous novel, *The Octopus* (New York: Doubleday, 1901), but the image was used earlier in critical publications such as the *San Francisco Wasp*.

61. Daggett, *Chapters in the History of the Southern Pacific*, 128–29.

62. Harris Newmark, *Sixty Years in Southern California, 1853–1913* (New York: Knickerbocker Press, 1916), 504–6.

63. Deverell, *Railroad Crossing*, 29–31.

64. Daggett, *Chapters in the History of the Southern Pacific*, 258–59.

65. Ibid., 257, n. 1; Newmark, *Sixty Years in Southern California*, 504.

66. Richard J. Orsi, "The *Octopus* Reconsidered: The Southern Pacific and Agricultural Modernization in California, 1865–1915," *California Historical Society Quarterly* 54 (1975): 197–220. For a defense of railroad policy generally, see Martin, *Railroads Triumphant*; for a more contemporary defense of the Southern Pacific, see John P. Irish, "California and the Railroad," *Overland Monthly* 25 (1895): 675–81.

67. Deverell, *Railroad Crossings*, traces the sources of discontent with the railroad and the weakness and strength of both the railroad and its opponents, providing a sophisticated and captivating account of the railroad's place in California's political and economic life.

68. Ibid., 27.

69. Daggett, *Chapters in the History of the Southern Pacific*, 183–84.

70. Solon Justus Buck, *The Granger Movement: A Study of Agricultural Organization and Its Political, Economic, and Social Manifestations, 1870–1880* (Lincoln: University of Nebraska Press, 1965), 238–301; Ezra Carr, *The Patrons of Husbandry on the Pacific Coast* (San Francisco: A. L. Bancroft, 1875), 301.

71. Buck, *Granger Movement*, 53, 62.

72. Carr, *Patrons of Husbandry on the Pacific Coast*, 109, reproduces the Declaration of Purposes of the National Grange, adopted in St. Louis, February 1874.

73. Buck, *Granger Movement*, 80–122.

74. Gerald Berk, *Alternative Tracks: The Constitution of American Industrial Order, 1865–1917* (Baltimore: Johns Hopkins University Press, 1994), 78. Charles Fairman, "The So-Called Granger Cases: Lord Hale and Justice Bradley," *Stan-*

ford Law Review 5 (1953): 587–678, observes that the term "granger case" was first used in Field's dissenting opinion to *Stone v. Wisconsin,* 94 U.S. 181, 183 (1877).

75. Fairman, "So-Called Granger Cases," 598–600.

76. See George H. Miller, *The Railroads and the Granger Laws* (Madison: University of Wisconsin Press, 1971), 17–23.

77. Adams, *Railroads,* 119–20.

78. See Miller, *Railroads and the Granger Laws,* 19.

79. Herbert Hovenkamp, *Enterprise and American Law, 1836–1937* (Cambridge: Harvard University Press, 1991), 153–56, clearly explains this reasoning.

80. Alan Jones, "Republicanism, Railroads, and Nineteenth-Century Midwestern Constitutionalism," in *Liberty, Property, and Government: Constitutional Interpretation Before the New Deal,* ed. Ellen Frankel Paul and Howard Dickman (Albany: State University of New York Press, 1989), 239–66, identifies the element of republican virtue; Berk, *Alternative Tracks,* notes the regionalism.

81. Berk, *Alternative Tracks,* 77–80, notes that merchants and farmers were not natural allies; farmers distrusted merchants, he observes. They thought of merchants as middlemen—parasites preying upon the toil of the producing classes.

82. Address of Worthy Master D. W. Adams, in Carr, *Patrons of Husbandry on the Pacific Coast,* 126.

83. Granger Declaration of Purposes, in ibid., 110 (emphasis added).

84. Annual Address of Worthy Master D. W. Adams, at the last session of the National Grange, held in Charleston, February 1875, in ibid., 125.

85. Fairman, "So-Called Granger Laws," 597–620, discusses these laws in some detail; Miller, *Railroads and the Granger Laws,* 59–87, discusses the politics leading to enactment of these laws.

86. The statute is reproduced in *Munn v. Illinois,* 94 U.S. 113, 114–17 (1877); Miller, *Railroads and the Granger Laws,* 79, notes that Chicago grain dealers were the principle victims of warehouse overcharging and that the Chicago Board of Trade was largely responsible for the enactment of this law.

87. Berk, *Alternative Tracks,* 85–86, points out that the railroad leaders were not unanimous in their opposition to the Granger laws. A. B. Stickney, president of the Chicago Great Western Railway, was sympathetic to some aspects of the legislation. Conversely, Ward M. McAffee, "Local Interests and Railroad Regulation in California During the Granger Decade," *Pacific Historical Review* 37 (February 1968): 51–66, points out that farmers and merchants were not uniformly opposed to railroad policies. McAffee maintains that those communities lacking railroad facilities generally were united in opposition to railroad regulation, fearing that it would slow construction to their locales.

88. Miller, *Railroads and the Granger Laws,* 185, citing C. B. Lawrence's argument in *Piek v. Chicago & North Western Rwy Co.,* 94 U.S. 164 (1877).

89. Miller, *Railroads and the Granger Laws,* 185, citing John Cary's argument in *Piek v, Chicago & North Western Rwy Co.,* 94 U.S. 164 (1877).

90. "The Wisconsin Railroad Acts," *American Law Review* 9 (1874): 51–60.

91. See Fairman, *Reconstruction and Reunion,* 7: 334–35; for more detail, see Miller, *Railroads and the Granger Laws.*

92. For background on the pre-Civil War evolution from a subsistance to a mar-

ket economy, see Charles Sellers, *The Market Revolution: Jacksonian America, 1815–1846* (New York: Oxford University Press, 1991).

93. Hovenkamp, *Enterprise and American Law,* 136–37, makes this point by maintaining that railroad regulation was a problem of federalism.

94. See *Peik v. Chicago & North Western Rwy.,* 94 U.S. 164, 175–76 (1877); the Court ruled that a corporation had no greater rights than did an individual, and therefore *Munn v. Illinois* actually settled this question. The railroads also argued that the Granger laws impaired the obligation of contracts made between the railroads and their bondholders. The Court rejected this argument, reasoning that the bondholders could acquire no greater rights than were granted to the corporation. See *Chicago, Burlington, and Quincy Railroad Co. v. Iowa,* 94 U.S. 155, 162 (1877).

95. Reuben M. Benjamin, a member of the Illinois constitutional convention of 1870, captured the inconsistency in the railroads' argument. "Whenever the public interests demand the construction of a railroad, the legislature without any hesitancy, authorizes the corporation to take private property—the very homestead—for that purpose. Whenever the same public interests require a limitation of the rates of railroad charges, the plea is set up that the legislature has no power, whatever, to act upon the matter" (Fairman, "So-Called Granger Cases," 595, citing Debates and Proceedings of the Constitutional Convention of the State of Illinois, 1637 [1870]).

96. For an example of this tradition, see John Phillip Reid, *In Defiance of the Law: The Standing Army Controversy, The Two Constitutions, and the Coming of the American Revolution* (Chapel Hill: University of North Carolina Press, 1981). Some scholars argue to the contrary that the due process limitation was understood at a much earlier time to encompass a substantive restraint on legislative authority. See Robert E. Riggs, "Substantive Due Process in 1791," *Wisconsin Law Review* (1990): 941–1003, and Edward Keynes, *Liberty, Property, and Privacy: Toward a Jurisprudence of Substantive Due Process* (University Park: Pennsylvania State University Press, 1996). Howard Gillman, *The Constitution Besieged: The Rise and Demise of Lochner Era Police Powers Jurisprudence* (Durham, N.C.: Duke University Press, 1993), 20–60.

97. See W. C. Goudy, "Brief for the Plaintiffs in Error, *Munn v. Illinois*," in *Landmark Briefs and Arguments of the Supreme Court of the United States: Constitutional Law,* ed. Philip B. Kurland and Gerhard Casper (Washington, D.C.: University Publications of America, 1975), 7: 511. Webster made this argument in *Dartmouth College v. Woodward,* 4 Wheaton 518 (1819). That case was decided upon contract-clause grounds; it did not deal with due process. See Wallace Mendelson, "A Missing Link in the Evolution of Due Process," *Vanderbilt Law Review* 10 (1956): 125, 128–29.

98. See, Goudy, "Brief," 512. Goudy cites Thomas M. Cooley, *Constitutional Limitations,* 351ff.

99. *Wynehamer v. New York,* 12 N.Y. 378 (1856).

100. *Dred Scott v. Sandford,* 60 U.S. (19 How.) 393, 450 (1857). Goudy did not make reference to *Dred Scott.*

101. The *Slaughter-House Cases,* 83 U.S. (16 Wall.) 36, 114–17 (1873), Bradley dissenting. Goudy also cited *Bartemeyer v. Iowa,* 85 U.S. (18 Wall.) 129, 133 (1874) in support of this proposition. Howard J. Graham notes that some corporate attorneys were apparently encouraged by Justice Miller's opinion for the majority in that

case (*Everyman's Constitution* [Madison: State Historical Society of Wisconsin, 1968], 121, n. 51). There was, however, little justification for their optimism. Miller's treatment of the due process clause was very narrow.

102. John N. Jewett, "Brief for Plaintiffs in Error," in Kurland and Casper, eds., *Landmark Briefs,* 548.

103. Goudy, "Brief," 515; Jewett, "Brief," 558, citing *Pumpelly v. Green Bay Company,* 80 U.S. (13 Wall.) 166 (1871).

104. Goudy, "Brief," 521.

105. Jewett, "Brief," 554–55. The idea that government regulation was a product of radicalism was apparently making its way into the realm of law. Later, Jewett would be more explicit, linking rate regulation to "communism, or, at least, the communistic spirit against which the prohibitions of the constitution were directed" (662).

106. Ibid., 557.

107. Ibid., 549.

108. Goudy, "Brief," 483.

109. See James K. Idsall, attorney general, "Brief for Defendants in Error, *Munn v. Illinois,*" in Kurland and Casper, eds., *Landmark Briefs,* 645–46, 653; William J. Novak, "Public Economy and the Well-Ordered Market: Law and Economic Regulation in Nineteenth-Century America," *Law and Social Inquiry* 18 (Winter 1993): 1–32; *A Collection of All Such Acts of the General Assembly of Virginia of a Public and Permanent Nature as Are Now in Force,* 2d ed. (Richmond: Samuel Pleasants, Printer, 1814), 356–83. Miller, *Railroads and the Granger Laws,* 31, points out that even railroad regulation was considered a normal practice. James Ely, Jr., *Guardian of Every Other Right: A Constitutional History of Property Rights* (New York: Oxford University Press, 1992), 62, maintains that regulations of the era were piecemeal and enforcement was lax.

110. Jewett, "Brief," 571.

111. Goudy, "Brief," 517, 519; Jewett, "Brief," 550. Goudy cites Cooley, *Constitutional Limitations,* for this proposition.

112. Edsall, "Brief," 650. Goudy, "Brief," 517, cites this same statement but chose to ignore the last phrase.

113. *Munn,* 94 U.S., at 125.

114. Ibid., at 127.

115. We have Charles Fairman to thank for bringing Bradley's "Outline of my views on the subject of the Granger Cases" to light. Fairman reproduces the Bradley memorandum in "So-Called Granger Cases," 670–79.

116. *Munn,* 94 U.S., at 139–41, Field dissenting.

117. Ibid., at 126. Waite, not known as a brilliant writer, once admitted to Field, "The difficulty with me is that I cannot give the reason as I wish I could" (Morrison Waite to S. J. Field, April 28, 1882, Field Collection, cited in Magrath, *Morrison R. Waite,* 185).

118. *Munn,* 94 U.S., at 140, Field dissenting.

119. Ibid., at 130–31. Waite pointed out that Munn and Scott's attorneys had themselves made this point when they emphasized the importance of the warehouses to the flow of commerce.

120. Ibid., at 132.

121. Bradley had expressed this view in an earlier case in which a railroad required its customers to agree to a contract that would reduce the railroad's liability from what it would be under common law (*New York Central Railroad Company v. Lockwood*, 84 U.S. [17 Wall.] 357, 379 [1873]). See also Bradley, "Outline of my views on the subject of the Granger Cases," 673.

122. Bradley, "Outline of my views on the subject of the Granger Cases," 670. Many commentators continue to treat *Munn* as a conflict between public power and private right; see Miller, *Railroads and the Granger Laws,* 172, 181; Berk, *Alternative Tracks,* 82; and Charles McCurdy, "Justice Field and the Jurisprudence of Government-Business Relations: Some Parameters of Laissez-Faire Constitutionalism, 1863–1897," *Journal of American History* 61 (March 1975): 970–1005.

123. *Munn,* 94 U.S., at 132.

124. Ibid., at 132–34.

125. Bradley, "Outline of my views on the subject of the Granger Cases," 677.

126. *Munn,* 94 U.S., at 148, Field dissenting.

127. Ibid.

128. Ibid., at 145, Field dissenting. William E. Nelson, *The Fourteenth Amendment: From Political Principle to Judicial Doctrine* (Cambridge: Harvard University Press, 1988), 158, 164, maintains that Field's position was moderate because it would protect only fundamental rights and it did not accord absolute protection for even those fundamental rights.

129. *Munn,* 94 U.S., at 146, Field dissenting.

130. Ibid., at 146–47, Field dissenting.

131. *Stone v. Wisconsin,* 94 U.S. (4 Otto.) 181, 183–85 (1877), Field dissenting.

132. Jewett, "Brief," 662. Summing up the impact of *Munn,* Richard C. Cortner says, "The judiciary was now unavailable as a forum in which business interests, including railroads, could attack the reasonableness of the regulations to which they were subjected by government" (*The Iron Horse and the Constitution: Railroads and the Transformation of the Fourteenth Amendment* [Westport, Conn: Greenwood Press, 1993], 8).

133. This subject will be treated in more detail in chapter 7.

134. Thomas M. Cooley to Stephen J. Field, January 8, 1878, Field Collection. The letter also thanks Field for sending a copy of his dissent and reports that Cooley is writing an article on the subject.

135. Charles Fairman, *Five Justices and the Electoral Commission of 1877* in *Oliver Wendell Holmes Devise History of the Supreme Court of the United States,* supp. to vol. 7 (New York: Macmillan, 1988); see 40–41 for newspaper headlines. Fairman, whose primary interest is in reassessing Justice Bradley's performance on the Electoral Commission, covers the election dispute in detail.

136. A. W. Grizzan to S. J. Tilden, December 1, 1876, and A. W. Robinson to S. J. Tilden, December 25, 1876, Tilden Papers, New York Public Library. There are more such letters in the Tilden Collection.

137. Field maintained that the state of Florida had clearly cast its vote for the Tilden electors. In true partisan fashion, he accused the Republicans of resorting to "technical subtleties and ingenious devices" to avoid looking at the evidence in the Florida election (Fairman, *Five Justices and the Electoral Commission of 1877,* supp. to vol. 7, 87–89).

138. Field kept his hand in California politics, and he corresponded with his friend Matthew Deady about the condition of the Democratic party; see for example, Field to Matthew Deady, February 11, 1876, Matthew Deady Collection, Oregon Historical Society.

139. See Daun van Ee, *David Dudley Field and the Reconstruction of the Law* (New York: Garland, 1986), 316–20, for details; for criticism of Field's election and his role as Tilden's lawyer, see *New York Times,* January 3, 1877, 4-1 and 8-4; January 17, 1877, 4-4; and February 4, 1877, 6-1.

6. Sound in Doctrine, Brave in Deed

1. For a treatment of the 1880 election, see H. Wayne Morgan, *From Hayes to McKinley: National Party Politics, 1877–1896* (Syracuse, N.Y.: Syracuse University Press, 1969), 1–101. For a description of the platform, see Herbert J. Clancy, *The Presidential Election of 1880* (Chicago: Loyola University Press, 1958), 95–96.

2. David M. Jordan, *Winfield Scott Hancock: A Soldier's Life* (Bloomington: Indiana University Press, 1988), 257.

3. The cartoon is from *Harper's Weekly,* November 13, 1880, and is reproduced in Morgan, *From Hayes to McKinley,* illustrations following 235.

4. Field had also been the favorite-son candidate of California in 1868. Charles Fairman, *Reconstruction and Reunion, 1864–88,* vol. 7, *Oliver Wendell Holmes Devise History of the Supreme Court of the United States* (New York: Macmillan, 1971), 545–46.

5. Howard Jay Graham, *Everyman's Constitution* (Madison: State Historical Society of Wisconsin, 1968), 134–40.

6. Stephen J. Field to Matthew Deady, May 31, 1879, Deady Collection.

7. Carl Brent Swisher, *Stephen J. Field: Craftsman of the Law* (1930; rpt., Hamden, Conn.: Archon Books: 1963), 283–84.

8. James K. McGuire, ed., *The Democratic Party of the State of New York,* 3 vols. (New York: U.S. History Company, 1905), 1: 222; Alexander C. Flick, *Samuel Jones Tilden: A Study in Political Sagacity* (1939; rpt., New York: Kennikat Press, 1963).

9. Undated transcript of Gov. Samuel Tilden's testimony, Box 23, Tilden Papers.

10. Daun van Ee, *David Dudley Field and the Reconstruction of the Law* (New York: Garland, 1986), 295.

11. *New York Times,* December 31, 1876, 6-1.

12. Van Ee, *David Dudley Field and the Reconstruction of the Law,* 331, citing New York Bar Association Reports 3 (1878): 135.

13. David Dudley Field, "Notes for My Autobiography," Field-Musgrave Collection. Van Ee, *David Dudley Field and the Reconstruction of the Law,* 316, citing Field's diary entry of November 7, 1876, reports that Field actually voted for Hayes. The diary is handwritten in pen and resembles the EKG of a person near death. I applaud van Ee's efforts in translating the diary but have chosen to rely on the typed notes.

14. Isabella Field Judson, ed., *Cyrus W. Field: His Life and His Work* (New York: Harper and Brothers, 1896), 296–98; see also Samuel Carter III, *Cyrus Field: Man of Two Worlds* (New York: G. P. Putnam's Sons, 1968).

15. *New York Herald,* July 8, 5-1, July 9, 5-4, July 13, 5-5, July 14, 10-1, July 28, 2-2; *New York World,* August 21, 1-2, August 22, 1-2 August 23, 1-2, August 24, 1-4, August 27, 1-2, August 28, 1-2, August 29, 1-2, September 6, 1-2; *New York Times,* August 22, 1-1, August 23, 1-1, August 28, 1-5; *New York Tribune,* August 2, 10-2, August 22, 8-6, September 8, 5-2, September 27, 10-1; all are from 1879.

16. *New York Tribune,* September 27, 1879, 10-1, "Replying to Mr. Tilden."

17. Ashley W. Cole to Samuel Tilden, September 6, 1879, Tilden Papers.

18. Tilden to Daniel Dows, September 15, 1879; see also numerous drafts of the reply, Tilden Papers.

19. See letters to Cyrus Field from W. G. Dix, June 6, 1879, G. A. Hollinger, June 6, 1879, Francis M. Weld, June 7, 1879, Jerome Hopkins, June 7, 1879, and E. M. Ames, June 7, 1879, Cyrus W. Field Papers, New York Public Library.

20. *Alta California,* October 22, 1879, 2-1; the *San Francisco Chronicle,* October 21, 1879, 3-7, October 22, 1879, 1-1, paid more attention to the case, but Grant's visit dominated its pages as well.

21. *New York Times,* February 18, 1880, 1-6; *Washington Post,* March 19, 1880, 1-1.

22. Correspondence from Bayard supporters is filled with concern about Tilden. Although they discuss the prospects, strengths, and weaknesses of other candidates, Field is not mentioned until May (August Belmont to John Hunter, February 9, 1880; Perry Belmont to Thomas Francis Bayard, April 23 and 24, 1880; John Hunter to Bayard, April 21, 1880; Sidney Webster to Bayard, April 27, 1880). Field is mentioned in Blanton Duncan to Bayard, May 4, 1880, and E. Casserly to Bayard, May 22, 1880, Thomas F. Bayard Collection, Library of Congress.

23. *Memphis Daily Appeal,* June 19, 1880, 2-4; see also *Cincinnati Commercial,* June 13, 1880, 2-1.

24. E. Casserly to Thomas Francis Bayard, June 12, 1880, Bayard Collection; *San Francisco Evening Bulletin,* December 22, 1879, 3-6; *Missouri Republican,* June 22, 1880, 4-2.

25. Fairman, *Reconstruction and Reunion,* 6: 23, 515-58, 1465-66, and 7: 485; Harold M. Hyman and William M. Wiecek, *Equal Justice Under Law: Constitutional Development, 1835–1875* (New York: Harper Torchbooks, 1982), 179.

26. *New York Tribune,* June 22, 1880, 1-1 (comment was by Congressman Whitthorne of Tennessee). The Eureka County Nevada Democratic Convention, for example, passed a resolution opposing "any judicial candidate for the presidency" (*San Francisco Chronicle,* May 24, 1880, 3-4).

27. *Missouri Republican,* June 22, 1880, 4-2; *Memphis Daily Appeal,* June 18, 1880, 2-4, June 20, 1880, 1-2; *Atlanta Constitution,* May 22, 1880, 1-5, June 11, 1880, 1-3; *Cincinnati Commercial,* June 13, 1880, 2-1.

28. "Judge Field: Sound in Doctrine, Brave in Deed," campaign pamphlet, Library of Congress call no. E664, f46J9.

29. One supporter, for example, suggested calling out the New York State militia (A. W. Grizzan to Samuel J. Tilden, December 17, 1876, Tilden Papers); there are numerous other examples in the collection.

30. *Atlanta Constitution,* June 12, 1880, 1-3.

31. PR was dictated to Theodore Hittle in July 1877, and some of the addendum was also dictated that year (see 194). Parts were used extensively in the campaign.

It was published in 1893, with an addendum by George Gorham. Hittle's notes are in the Sutro Branch of the California State Library in San Francisco.

32. An impeachment proceeding and two charges of misconduct are explained as conspiracies (PR, 153–97). Field calls the last two incidents "the Moulin vexation" and the "Hastings malignity."

33. Ibid., 121–24, 72–73. Field's memories are in many instances supported by letters of corroboration that appear in an appendix, a characteristic that seems odd for personal memoirs, especially given that the letters were solicited long after the events took place.

34. Ibid., 43–45, 66–69, 83, 90, 177.

35. *Washington Post*, May 10, 1880, 1–6, "How Presidents Are Nominated."

36. James O'Meara to Montgomery Blair, March 24, 1880, Tilden Papers.

37. *Chicago Tribune*, May 24, 1880, 1–4; *San Francisco Chronicle*, May 28, 1880, 3–4.

38. *New York Times*, May 20, 1880, 4–3.

39. In the *Washington Post*, May 10, 1880, 1–6, "How Presidents Are Nominated," the writer notes that both Blaine's and Sherman's bureaus began operating about that time.

40. For example, Charles Burton of the *Lynchburg Virginian* was reported to be for Field (*New York Times*, March 31, 1880, 1–5). As the convention began, the *Cincinnati Commercial*, owned by Cyrus Field's friend Murat Halstead, showed strong support for Field.

41. See *New Orleans Times-Picayune*, May 23, 2–1; June 1, 1–5; June 3, 1–3; June 5, 1–4; June 6, 1–5; June 18, 1–4; June 19, 1–4; June 21, 1–2, 1880. It was highly unusual for such articles to be signed.

42. *Cincinnati Commercial*, June 19, 1880, 1–1; *Atlanta Constitution*, June 12, 1880, 1–3; *New York Tribune*, May 23, 1880, 4–6.

43. Fairman, *Reconstruction and Reunion*, 7: 481–85.

44. William [name illegible] to Montgomery Blair, May 18, 1880, Tilden Papers. The writer was a former editor of the *Danville* (Va.) *News*, which he said was "recently closed."

45. [Name illegible] to Thomas Francis Bayard, June 12, 1880; E. Casserly to Thomas Francis Bayard, June 12, 1880, Bayard Collection. Cyrus Field also bought the *Mail and Express* in 1880 and held onto it until 1890. See the business papers in Box 3, Cyrus Field Papers.

46. *New York World*, June 11, 1880, 1–2, "Is It Likely to Be Field?"

47. *New Orleans Times-Picayune*, June 18, 1880; *St. Louis Globe Democrat*, June 22, 1880, 2–3 (a Republican paper); *Atlanta Constitution*, June 20, 1880, 1–1.

48. Morgan, *From Hayes to McKinley*, 79; *St. Louis Globe Democrat*, June 23, 1880, 1–5.

49. Clancy, *Presidential Election of 1880*, 61.

50. *New York Tribune*, August 5, 1879, 4–2, "Tilden Against the Field."

51. Flick, *Samuel Jones Tilden*, 445; McGuire, ed., *Democratic Party of the State of New York*, 2: 5–6.

52. *New York Times*, January 22, 1880, 1–2, "Kelly's Campaign Plans." After the January meeting, Dudley's connections with Tammany appear to have dropped off. See the *New York Times*, May 8, 1880, 1–3, reporting on Kelly's state committee; David Dudley Field is not listed.

53. *New York Times,* January 23, 1880, 4-4, "Mr. Kelly's Way." With its usual disdain for the Field family, the *Times* continued, "The country can never flourish thoroughly so long as one of the Field family does not govern it. In point of fact, the country was invented for the Field family, and the sooner we acknowledge it, the better for the country."

54. *New York Times,* February 2, 1880, 1-3; March 6, 1880, 1-1; January 28, 1880, 1-3, "The Democratic Split"; April 18, 1880, 1-1; April 19, 1880, 1-1; April 20, 1880, 1-1; April 21, 1880, 1-5, 4-2; April 22, 1880, 1-7, 4-1; April 23, 1880, 1-2; April 26, 1880, 1-1.

55. Lorenzo Sawyer to Matthew Deady, September 18, 1879, Deady Collection.

56. *New York Times,* January 22, 1880, 1-1, "The Democracy at Sea."

57. *Ex parte Siebold,* 100 U.S. 371 (1880); *Ex parte Clark,* 100 U.S. 399 (1880).

58. Eric Foner, *Reconstruction, 1763–1877: America's Unfinished Revolution* (New York: Harper and Row, 1988), 426. Foner tells us, for example, of Jack Dupree, president of a Republican club and a black man "who would speak his mind," who had his throat slit and was disemboweled within sight of his wife, who had just given birth to twins.

59. Ibid., 426-31.

60. Ibid., 431-33.

61. Ibid., 444; Fairman, *Reconstruction and Reunion,* 7: 149.

62. *Ex parte Siebold,* 100 U.S., at 383 (emphasis in original).

63. *Washington Post,* March 13, 1880, 2-1.

64. *Ex parte Clarke,* 100 U.S., at 409. Field wrote only one opinion but addressed it to issues in both cases.

65. Ibid., at 414.

66. *Washington Post,* March 13, 1880, 2-1, 2-3. As if to prove the righteousness of its case, the *Post* continued in biblical language, "Who art thou that judgest another man's servant—to his own master he standeth or falleth."

67. *New Orleans Times-Picayune,* March 9, 1880, 1-3; *Cincinnati Enquirer,* March 9, 1880, 1-3; March 11, 1880, 4-2; March 12, 1880, 4-2.

68. For example, the California Democratic Convention in 1879 passed a resolution decrying "federal efforts to interfere with elections through federal supervisors of elections and federal marshals" (Winfield J. Davis, *History of Political Conventions in California, 1849–1892* [Sacramento: California State Library, 1893], 415).

69. *Strauder v. West Virginia,* 100 U.S. 303 (1880).

70. Ibid., at 311.

71. Ibid., at 305; the statute included certain exceptions.

72. Ibid., at 308.

73. *Tennessee v. Davis,* 100 U.S. 259, 267 (1880). A federal revenue officer was charged with murder in a Tennessee court when a moonshiner was killed in a raid on an illegal still. Since section 643 of the Revised Statutes expressly provided for removal in such cases, the question of whether the statute violated the Constitution was clear. The Court upheld the statute; Field and Clifford dissented.

74. Benno Schmidt, Jr., wrote an article on the *Strauder* case, with a catchy subtitle: "Juries, Jurisdiction, and Race Discrimination: The Lost Promise of Strauder v. West Virginia," *Texas Law Review* 61 (May 1983): 1401-99.

75. *Virginia v. Rives,* 100 U.S. 313 (1880).

76. *Ex parte Virginia,* 100 U.S. 339 (1880).

77. Eric Foner, *Reconstruction, 1763–1877*, 444, 459.

78. William Wiecek, "The Reconstruction of Federal Judicial Power, 1863–1875," *American Journal of Legal History* 13 (October 1969): 336–40.

79. See Bernard Schwartz, *A History of the Supreme Court* (New York: Oxford University Press, 1993), 53–57.

80. See Donald B. Cole, *The Presidency of Andrew Jackson* (Lawrence: University Press of Kansas, 1993), 100–106, and Harry L. Watson, *Liberty and Power: The Politics of Jacksonian America* (New York: Noonday Press, 1990), 143–45.

81. Stanley Kutler, *Judicial Power and Reconstruction Politics* (Chicago: University of Chicago Press, 1968), 146.

82. *Ex parte Virginia*, 100 U.S., at 358; see also, *Rives*, 100 U.S., at 337, for similar language.

83. *Rives*, 100 U.S., at 335; *Ex parte Virginia*, 100 U.S., at 366, 370.

84. *Ex parte Virginia*, 100 U.S., at 354–55.

85. *Ex parte Virginia*, 100 U.S., at 363; *Rives*, 100 U.S., at 337–39.

86. *Washington Post*, March 9, 1880.

87. *Washington Post*, March 3, 1880, 1–4, 2–2; March 9, 1880, 2–2; March 22, 1880, 2–2. See also *New York World*, March 2, 1880, 8–1; *Nation*, March 4, 1880, 165–66; March 25, 1880, 227–28, and 265; April 8, 1880, 265; and April 22, 1880, 299; *Albany Law Journal* 21 (1880): 302, 341.

88. *Richmond State*, March 2, 1880, 4–2.

89. *New York Times*, March 8, 1880, 4–2; March 13, 1880, 4–3; *St. Louis Globe-Democrat*, March 3, 1880, 4–1; *Nation*, March 25, 1880, 227. The opinions received very little attention in California, however. See *San Francisco Chronicle*, March 2, 1880, 3–5; *San Francisco Evening Bulletin*, March 4, 1880, 3–5.

90. Raymond L. Dingledine, Jr., "The Political Career of William Cabell Rives" (Ph.D. diss., University of Virginia, 1947); Russell Stewart Wingfield, *William Cabell Rives: A Biography* (Richmond, Va.: Richmond College Historical Papers, 1915); *National Cyclopedia of American Biography*, 19: 111–12.

91. Fairman, *Reconstruction and Reunion*, 7: 445–46 (this would later be the issue in *Ex parte Virginia*).

92. Allan B. Magruder, "Removal of Suits from State to Federal Courts," *American Law Review* 13 (1879): 436–37; Fairman, *Reconstruction and Reunion*, 7: 442–48; Kutler, *Judicial Power and Reconstruction Politics*, 149.

93. *San Francisco Chronicle*, March 6, 1880, 3–3; *Richmond State*, May 14, 1880, 1–3; *New Orleans Times-Picayune*, May 15, 1880, 1–5.

94. *Richmond State*, May 14, 1880, 1–3 (the *State* was a pro-Seymour paper); William [name illegible] to Montgomery Blair, May 18, 1880, Tilden Papers (the author described himself as a former editor of the *Danville News*, which was "recently closed"); *Richmond State*, March 2, 1880, 4–2, and May 21, 1880, 2–1.

95. Wiecek, "Reconstruction of Federal Judicial Power, 1863–1875," 333–59, and Kutler, *Judicial Power and Reconstruction Politics*, 143–60.

96. Fairman, *Reconstruction and Reunion*, 7: 411.

97. *Railway Co. v. Whitton's Adm'r.*, 80 U.S. (13 Wall.) 270 (1872); Fairman, *Reconstruction and Reunion*, 7: 392–93.

98. *Pacific Railroad Removal Cases*, 115 U.S. 1 (1885). Fairman, *Reconstruction and Reunion*, 7: 433, maintains that Field originally intended to dissent; see also

Kutler, *Judicial Power and Reconstruction Politics*, 157; Peter Magrath, *Morrison R. Waite* (New York: Macmillan, 1963), 239–42.

99. *Rives*, 100 U.S., at 337.

100. Book Review, *American Law Review* 18 (1884): 535–36.

101. See Robert Green McCloskey, *American Conservatism in the Age of Enterprise, 1865–1910* (New York: Harper Torchbooks, 1951), 117–23.

102. See Schmidt, "Juries, Jurisdiction, and Race Discrimination," 1422–24, and Field, in *Ex parte Virginia*, 100 U.S., at 365.

103. See Charles W. McCurdy, "Justice Field and the Jurisprudence of Government-Business Relations: Some Parameters of Laissez-Faire Constitutionalism, 1863–1897," *Journal of American History* 61(1975): 970–81, and idem, "The Roots of 'Liberty of Contract' Reconsidered: Major Premises in the Law of Employment, 1867–1937," *Yearbook of the Supreme Court Historical Society* (1984): 20–33.

104. *Ex parte Virginia*, 100 U.S., at 363, Field dissenting.

105. Ibid., at 366.

106. Ibid., at 367.

107. Ibid.

108. *Rives*, 100 U.S., at 333; *Ex parte Virginia*, 100 U.S., at 367.

109. *Ex parte Virginia*, 100 U.S., at 369.

110. *Ex parte Virginia*, Record, at 6, Declaration of Aaron Shelton, from *Commonwealth v. Burwell and Lee Reynolds*, found in *United States Supreme Court Records and Briefs*, available on microfilm from Scholarly Resources, Wilmington, Delaware.

111. Ibid., at 7. This was the plea reflected in their petition for removal to the federal court.

112. *Ex parte Virginia*, 100 U.S., at 367.

113. It is a variation of Strong's theme in *Strauder*, 100 U.S., at 309.

114. *Ex parte Virginia*, 100 U.S., at 345–45 (emphasis added).

115. This conflict between total racial equality and limited absolute equality is developed in Earl M. Maltz, *Civil Rights, the Constitution, and Congress, 1863–1869* (Lawrence: University Press of Kansas, 1990). His argument that Democrats and conservative Republicans favored the latter adds support to Benno Schmidt's view that Field was rearguing the Democratic position in the debates over the Civil Rights Act of 1875.

116. *Rives*, 100 U.S., at 332–33.

117. *Virginia v. Rives* (answer of Judge Rives to the order to show cause why writ of mandamus should not issue, Record, at 21, para. 24).

118. *Rives*, 100 U.S., at 333–34. This was not the first time the Court employed the state action doctrine; see *United States v. Cruikshank*, 92 U.S. 542 (1876).

119. Maltz, *Civil Rights, the Constitution, and Congress, 1863–1869*, 70–78, 102.

120. *Rives*, 100 U.S., at 334.

121. Maltz, *Civil Rights, the Constitution, and Congress, 1863–1869*, 102, maintains that during the Reconstruction Era, no one suggested that private action per se could be a violation of the Fourteenth Amendment. Laurent B. Frantz, "Congressional Power to Enforce the Fourteenth Amendment Against Private Acts," *Yale*

Law Review 73 (1964): 1353–84, maintains that some people quickly saw a need to do so.

122. The majority conceded in *Strauder* that the language of the amendment is prohibitory but recognized that "every prohibition implies the existence of rights and immunities" (*Strauder*, 100 U.S., at 310). *Rives* is unclear on the state action doctrine because the decision is based on the specific language of the removal statute. In *Ex parte Virginia* the Court only refers to the state action doctrine in determining the liability of a public official.

123. *Civil Rights Cases*, 109 U.S. 3, 11 (1883).

124. Michael Les Benedict, "Preserving Federalism: Reconstruction and the Waite Court," *Supreme Court Review* 39 (1978): 65–69, citing Frantz, "Congressional Power to Enforce the Fourteenth Amendment Against Private Acts," *Yale Law Journal* 73 (1964): 1353.

125. Schmidt, "Juries, Jurisdiction, and Race Discrimination," 1490, citing Eric Foner, "Reconstruction Revisited," *Reviews in American History* (1982): 86.

126. Benedict, "Preserving Federalism," 47.

7. The Pacific Club Set

1. *Memphis Daily Appeal,* May 25, 1880, 1–1; *New Orleans Times-Picayune,* May 12, 1880, 1–5, "Hottest Telegraph—Washington," signed L. Q. W.

2. William Henry Ellison, *A Self-Governing Dominion: California, 1849–1860* (Berkeley: University of California Press, 1950), 288. Some observers believed Field parlayed his support in that contest into a seat on the nation's highest court (James O'Meara, *Broderick and Gwin* [San Francisco: Bacon, 1881], 160).

3. Charles Fairman, *Reconstruction and Reunion, 1864–88,* vol. 6, *Oliver Wendell Holmes Devise History of the Supreme Court of the United States* (New York: Macmillan, 1971), 545–46, citing *Official Proceedings of the Democratic National Convention of 1880* (Dayton, Ohio: Daily Journal Book and Job Rooms, 1882), 143 (hereafter *Official Proceedings*).

4. Blanton Duncan to Bayard, May 4, 1880, Bayard Collection.

5. *New York Times,* January 23, 1880, 4–4, "Mr. Kelly's Way."

6. James O'Meara to Montgomery Blair, December 15, 1879, Tilden Papers.

7. R. Hal Williams, *The Democratic Party and California Politics, 1880–1896* (Stanford, Calif.: Stanford University Press, 1973), 16; Elmer Clarence Sandmeyer, *The Anti-Chinese Movement in California* (Urbana: University of Illinois Press, 1939), 66; Winfield J. Davis, *History of Political Conventions in California, 1849–1892* (Sacramento: California State Library, 1893), 371–75; Carl Brent Swisher, *Motivation and Political Technique in the California Constitutional Convention, 1878–79* (Claremont, Calif.: Pomona College, 1930), 17–31.

8. Royce D. Dalmatier, Clarence F. McIntosh, Earl G. Waters, eds., *The Rumble of California Politics: 1848–1970* (New York: John Wiley and Sons, 1970), 89.

9. Williams, *Democratic Party and California Politics, 1880–1896,* 19.

10. Ibid.; Davis, *History of Political Conventions in California,* 413, 418; Edith Dobie, *The Political Career of Stephen Mallory White,* Stanford University Publications, History, Economics, and Political Science, vol. 2, no. 1 (Stanford, Calif.: Stan-

ford University Press, 1927), 28. At the Democratic convention, a resolution that no candidate would be eligible for the nomination of the convention who was affiliating with another party was defeated by a vote of 290 to 67 (Davis, *History of Political Conventions in California,* 417).

11. Sandmeyer, *Anti-Chinese Movement in California,* 75.

12. Dobie, *Political Career,* 28.

13. Swisher, *Motivation and Political Technique;* for other accounts of the constitutional convention, see Harry N. Scheiber, "Race, Radicalism, and Reform: Historical Perspective on the 1879 California Constitution," *Hastings Constitutional Law Quarterly* 17 (Fall 1989): 35–80; Gordon Morris Bakken, "California Constitutionalism: Politics, the Press and the Death of Fundamental Law," *Pacific Historian* 20 (1986): 5–17.

14. Williams, *Democratic Party and California Politics, 1880–1896,* 16.

15. Swisher, *Motivation and Political Technique,* 90.

16. Sandmeyer, *Anti-Chinese Movement in California,* 70.

17. *Debates and Proceedings of the Constitutional Convention of the State of California,* C. B. Willis and P. K. Stockton, official stenographers, 3 vols. (Sacramento, 1880), 1: 248, and 2: 677, 679, 739 (hereafter *Debates and Proceedings*); Swisher, *Motivation and Political Technique,* 91; Sandmeyer, *Anti-Chinese Movement in California,* 68.

18. *Passenger Cases,* 48 U.S. (7 How.) 283 (1849).

19. Swisher, *Motivation and Political Technique,* 90.

20. *Mayor of the City of New York v. Miln,* 36 U.S. (11 Pet.) 102 (1837).

21. *Passenger Cases,* 48 U.S., at 464 (1849), Taney dissenting.

22. *Debates and Proceedings,* 2: 642; Sandmeyer, *Anti-Chinese Movement in California,* 70.

23. *Chy Lung v. Freeman,* 92 U.S. 275, 277 (1875).

24. Shih-shan Henry Tsai, *The Chinese Experience in America* (Bloomington: Indiana University Press, 1986), 40–42.

25. Stuart Creighton Miller, *The Unwelcome Immigrant: The American Image of the Chinese, 1785–1882* (Berkeley: University of California Press, 1969), 164.

26. *Chy Lung,* 92 U.S., at 278.

27. Ibid., at 280.

28. *In re Ah Fong,* 1 F. Cas. 213, 216 (C.C.D. Cal., 1874).

29. Ibid., at 217.

30. Ibid. Christian Fritz, *Federal Justice in California: The Court of Ogden Hoffman, 1851–1891* (Lincoln: University of Nebraska Press, 1991), 121–32, suggests that the most important factor guiding federal judges in many of the cases involving discrimination against Chinese was the nation's obligations under the Burlingame Treaty.

31. *In re Ah Fong,* 1 F. Cas., at 216.

32. *Chy Lung,* 92 U.S., at 280.

33. *Debates and Proceedings,* 1: 248, Report of the Committee on Chinese, sec. 4.

34. Sandmeyer, *Anti-Chinese Movement in California,* 68–72; *Debates and Proceedings,* 1: 248.

35. As originally proposed, violation of this law would have resulted in forfeiture

of the corporate franchise. The penalty was dropped in the final version of the constitutional provision, and it was left up to the legislature to pass laws carrying out the provision. See Sandmeyer, *Anti-Chinese Movement in California,* 69.

36. Constitution of 1879, Art. 19; Sandmeyer, *Anti-Chinese Movement in California,* 69–72.

37. Sandmeyer, *Anti-Chinese Movement in California,* 65, concludes that Chinese labor was not the foremost concern, but it provided the emotional drive that could unite the working men of the state.

38. *Ah Kow v. Nunan,* 12 F. Cas. 252 (C.C.D. Cal., 1879).

39. Charles J. McClain and Laurene Wu McClain, "The Chinese Contribution to the Development of American Law," in *Entry Denied,* ed. Sucheng Chan (Philadelphia: Temple University Press, 1991), 8–12, make the point that by the 1870s many discriminatory statutes used general language.

40. *Ah Kow v. Nunan,* 12 F. Cas., at 255. Field's opinion was published in pamphlet form for the presidential campaign. It included an appendix that contained debate on the housing and queue ordinances and commentary from various newspapers (the pamphlet is in the General Collection, Library of Congress). See also *Cummings v. Missouri,* 71 U.S. (4 Wall.) 277, 325 (1866), which contains similar language.

41. *Ah Kow v. Nunan,* 12 F. Cas., at 256–57.

42. *In re Ah Fong,* 1 F. Cas., at 218.

43. *New York Tribune,* April 12, 1880, 2–5, reprint of a letter published in the *San Francisco Morning Call.*

44. This was Field's standard position found in a number of sources. It was part of a campaign pamphlet, "A Possible Solution of the Chinese Problem: Views of Mr. Justice Field, from the *San Francisco Argonaut,* of August 9, 1879" (Library of Congress, microfilm, call no. JV6875 1879 F5). See also *Cincinnati Enquirer,* June 12, 1880, 9–1, and *Deseret News* (Salt Lake City), June 23, 1880, 1–3.

45. *San Francisco Examiner,* July 8, 1879, 2–1; see also July 11, 1879, 2–1.

46. *Ah Kow v. Nunan,* 12 F. Cas., at 256.

47. Ibid.

48. *San Francisco Examiner,* July 11, 1879, 2–1.

49. Ibid., July 9, 1879, 2–1.

50. *Alta California,* July 8, 1879, 2–2.

51. "Invalidity of the Queue Ordinance," Library of Congress, microfilm, call no. F870. C5U5, 1879.

52. "A Possible Solution of the Chinese Problem"; this pamphlet is made up of an excerpt from the *Argonaut,* August 9, 1879, a letter from John Norton Pomeroy, and a communication between the U.S. minister to China and the State Department. A portion was repeated in a letter to the *San Francisco Morning Call* and printed in the *New York Tribune,* April 12, 1880, 2–5.

53. *San Francisco Evening Bulletin,* July 7, 1879, reprinted in "Possible Solution of the Chinese Problem."

54. *San Francisco Examiner,* July 8, 1879, 2–1; July 9, 1879, 2–4; July 11, 1879, 2–1.

55. *In re Quong Woo,* 13 Fed. 229 (C.C.D.Cal., 1882).

56. *Crowley v. Christensen,* 137 U.S. 86 (1890).

57. This was Judge Lorenzo Sawyer's view of the matter (see Linda C. A. Przy-byszewski, "Judge Lorenzo Sawyer and the Chinese: Civil Rights Decisions in the Ninth Circuit," *Western Legal History* [Winter/Spring 1988]: 38). Sawyer's view was eventually adopted by the Supreme Court in *Yick Wo v. Hopkins,* 118 U.S. 356 (1886).

58. The provision is reproduced along with several other anti-Chinese provisions in Sandmeyer, *Anti-Chinese Movement in California,* 71–72.

59. *Alta California,* March 3, 1880, 1–2; *San Francisco Evening Bulletin,* March 4, 1880, 2–2.

60. *Washington Post,* February 26, 1880, 1–7, "The Chinese Must Go."

61. *New York Sun,* March 9, 1880, 1–5, "Troops in San Francisco."

62. See *San Francisco Evening Bulletin,* March 6, 1880, 4–3; March 8, 1880, 1–3; March 9, 1880, 1–2; *San Francisco Chronicle,* March 7, 1880, 7–1.

63. Fritz, *Federal Justice in California,* 46, citing Henry W. Corbett to Matthew Deady, April 18, 1869, Deady Collection.

64. An act of June 1, 1872, 17 U.S. Stat. 196, provided that whenever a difference of opinion existed among judges sitting as a circuit court, the opinion of the presiding judge or presiding justice would prevail, and the case would be appealable to the Supreme Court. Cited in Fritz, *Federal Justice in California,* 31, n. 2. This is exactly what happened in the *Chew Heong* case, 21 F. 791, 112 U.S. 536 (see Fritz, *Federal Justice in California,* 238–41).

65. There is some evidence that Field decided not to sit in an important railroad case. See Carl Brent Swisher, *Stephen J. Field: Craftsman of the Law* (1930; rpt., Hamden, Conn: Archon Books, 1963), 247–48, and C. Peter Magrath, *Morrison R. Waite: The Triumph of Character* (New York: Macmillan, 1963), 231.

66. Seymour D. Thompson, "Abuses of the Writ of Habeas Corpus," *American Law Review* 18 (1884): 23. The expansion of "ninth circuit law" became something of a crusade for Thompson; see Howard J. Graham, *Everyman's Constitution* (Madison: State Historical Society of Wisconsin, 1968), 141–43.

67. Przybyszewski, "Judge Lorenzo Sawyer and the Chinese," 52; some people might not fully agree with the image this statement projects regarding Chinese aspirations. See Charles McClain, "The Chinese Struggle for Civil Rights in Nineteenth-Century America: The First Phase, 1850–1870," *California Law Review* (1984): 529–68; Fritz, *Federal Justice in California,* 225, points out that Chinese were less of a threat because they could not become naturalized citizens.

68. Stephen J. Field to John Norton Pomeroy, April 14, 1882, Field Collection, reprinted in Graham, *Everyman's Constitution,* 104–5. Ironically, Field continued by telling Pomeroy, "We are obliged to take care of the Africans; because we find them here, and they were brought here against their will by our fathers."

69. Some commentators suggest that Field's presidential ambitions influenced his decisions on Chinese cases; see Fritz, *Federal Justice in California,* 311, n. 73; Robert Green McCloskey, *American Conservatism in the Age of Enterprise, 1865–1910* (New York: Harper Torchbooks, 1951), 122–23; and Swisher, *Stephen J. Field: Craftsman of the Law,* 239.

70. *Chew Heong v. United States,* 112 U.S. 536 (1884)—the name was spelled differently in the circuit court case: *In re Cheen Heong,* 21 F. 791 (C.C.D. Cal., 1884). See Charles J. McClain, *In Search of Equality: The Chinese Struggle Against*

Discrimination in Nineteenth-Century America (Berkeley: University of California Press, 1994), 159–67, and Fritz, *Federal Justice in California*, 238–40.

71. *Chew Heong*, 112 U.S., at 562, 565, Field dissenting. Field also used the opportunity to strike out against Chinese immigrants and against the "unfairness" of the treaty with China (566–68).

72. *Chae Chan Ping v. United States*, 130 U.S. 581, 609 (1889); see McClain, *In Search of Equality*, 193–201, and Fritz, *Federal Justice in California*, 245–46.

73. *Fong Yue Ting v. United States*, 149 U.S. 698 (1893); see McClain, *In Search of Equality*, 210–13.

74. Field to Don Dickinson, June 17, 1893, Dickinson Papers.

75. A statement to this effect appears in the majority opinion, *Fong Yue Ting*, 149 U.S., at 728. When Justice Gray attempted to change the language, Field objected. It was important to him that the ramifications of the opinion in terms of lack of judicial process be spelled out (Stephen J. Field to Horace Gray, May 27, 1893, Horace Gray Papers, Library of Congress).

76. *Fong Yue Ting*, 149 U.S., at 754, Field dissenting; Earl Maltz, "The Federal Government and the Problem of Chinese Rights in the Era of the Fourteenth Amendment," *Harvard Journal of Law and Public Policy* 17 (Winter 1994): 223–52, makes the point that the status of the affected individuals is key in understanding the civil rights decisions of the late nineteenth century.

77. *United States v. Cruikshank*, 92 U.S. (2 Otto.) 542 (1876).

78. *United States v. Harris*, 106 U.S. (16 Otto.) 629 (1883).

79. *Baldwin v. Franks*, 120 U.S. 678 (1887); see Charles J. McClain, Jr., "The Chinese Struggle for Civil Rights in Nineteenth-Century America: The Unusual Case of *Baldwin v. Franks*," *Law and History Review* 3 (1985): 349–73.

80. See *Baldwin v. Franks*, 120 U.S., at 704, Field dissenting.

81. *Alta California*, March 10, 1880, 1–2, "Parrott's Case."

82. *In re Tiburcio Parrott*, 1 Fed. 481, 506 (C.C.D. Cal., 1880).

83. Ibid.

84. Ibid., 505–6.

85. *Alta California*, March 10, 1880, 1–2 (emphasis in original).

86. *Parrott*, 1 Fed., at 493, 498.

87. Ibid., 486–87. In this part of the opinion Hoffman was discussing the contract clause and the reserve power of the states, but his language could just as well have been applied to later liberty of contract arguments regarding the limits of the police power of the states.

88. See, for example, the *San Francisco Chronicle*, March 18, 1880, 1–3, "Coolie Labor," and March 22, 1880, 2–2. The *New York Herald*, which appears to be an Irish Democratic paper, also thought the outcome was proper (April 13, 1880, 6–5).

89. *Baker v. Portland*, 2 F. Cas. 472 (C.C.D. Ore., 1879), on rehearing 2 F. Cas. 475; see Ralph James Mooney, "Matthew Deady and the Federal Judicial Response to Racism in the Early West," *Oregon Law Review* 63 (1984): 591–95. The case did not actually overrule the state law, and Deady dismissed the suit on technical grounds.

90. Malcolm Clark, Jr., ed., *Pharisee Among Philistines: The Diary of Matthew Deady, 1871–1892* (Portland: Oregon Historical Society, 1975), 285 (entry August 27, 1879). Almost one month before the rehearing, Field sent a telegram to

Deady asking for a copy of the opinion (Field to Matthew Deady, July 31, 1879, Deady Collection). Another indication of approval was that Governor Perkins refused to appeal the case (*Alta California,* March 24, 1880, 1–3); for another example of approval, see *Washington Post,* March 23, 1880, 1–7, which called the case "a death blow to Kearnyism."

91. Samuel Carter III, *Cyrus Field: Man of Two Worlds* (New York: G. P. Putnam's Sons, 1968), 320.

92. *San Francisco Chronicle,* May 24, 1880, 3–4.

93. *San Francisco Examiner,* March 22, 1880, 2–3. George Hearst purchased the *Examiner* in 1880 (Williams, *Democratic Party and California Politics 1880–1896,* 25), but the paper did not change hands until October.

94. Even in the debate on ratification of the new constitution the articles on Chinese played only a minor part. Considerably more attention was paid to the provisions on corporations and taxation (Sandmeyer, *Anti-Chinese Movement in California,* 72). This is also a main theme in Swisher, *Motivation and Political Technique.*

95. *San Francisco Examiner,* October 2, 1879, 2–1; curiously, Field is left off a list of those villainous judges.

96. *Debates and Proceedings,* 1: 375–640.

97. Ibid., 376–77.

98. Ibid., 468, amendment by Ayers.

99. Ibid., 376. Section 8 similarly declared that the exercise of the police power of the state should never be abridged or construed as to permit corporations to conduct their business in such a manner as to infringe the equal rights of individuals or the general well-being of the state.

100. Ibid., 378. See also the comment of Mr. O'Donnell, "Shall the people control the corporations, or shall the corporations control the people" (453).

101. Ibid., 378.

102. Ibid., 480.

103. Ibid., 377. This was section 20 of the committee report. There were numerous amendments proposed, and debate on the provision occupied much of the evening session of November 26, 1878. See, for example, the remarks of Mr. Barbour and Mr. Estee, 455 and 511; see also Swisher, *Motivation and Political Technique,* 50–56. The new constitution eventually included an elected railroad commission with the authority to set rates (California Constitution, 1879, Art. 12, sec. 22; *Debates and Proceedings,* 3: 1518).

104. Ibid., 1: 489–96, speech of Edgerton.

105. Ibid., 494.

106. Ibid., 496.

107. Ibid., 471, 474.

108. Swisher, *Motivation and Political Technique,* 105–6, argues that the new constitution produced a rift in the Workingmen's party and ended Denis Kearney's leadership.

109. *Debates and Proceedings,* 3: 1517–18, the enrolled final reading of Art. 12.

110. Williams, *Democratic Party and California Politics, 1880–1896,* 206–7, points out that there was an element of myth in this issue.

111. Stuart Daggett, *Chapters in the History of the Southern Pacific* (New York:

Ronald Press Company, 1922), 380, citing *Congressional Record*, 45th Cong., 2d sess., March 12, 1878, 7: 1690.

112. Colton's Letters of November 16, 1877, November 23, 1877, published in the *San Francisco Chronicle*, December 23, 1883, 11.

113. 20 Stat. 56 (1878). The sinking fund scheme was employed because the Supreme Court invalidated an earlier attempt to withhold the full amount (16 Stat. 225 [1871]); *United States v. Union Pacific Railroad*, 91 U.S. 72 (1875).

114. *Nation*, October 30, 1879, 290; Colton's letters of April 20, 1877, November 15, 1877, February 23, 1878, March 16, 1878; published in the *San Francisco Chronicle*, December 23, 1883, 10, 11. Daggett, *Chapters in the History of the Southern Pacific*, 388, n. 29, citing the Huntington Manuscript, Bancroft Library, University of California at Berkeley, 24-25, 76-77.

115. *Sinking Fund Cases*, 99 U.S. 700 (Oct. term 1878). The Court delivered the opinion on October 20, 1879 (Fairman, *Reconstruction and Reunion*, 7: 607; Fairman implies that this was a collusive suit [612-15]).

116. *Sinking Fund Cases*, 99 U.S., at 759.

117. Ibid., at 725.

118. Ibid., at 747, Bradley dissenting; at 766, Field dissenting.

119. Ibid., at 746, Bradley dissenting; at 764, Field dissenting.

120. Ibid., at 737, Strong dissenting; at 762-64, Field dissenting. The exception for both Field and Strong was the federal government's power to enact bankruptcy laws, which Field believed added weight to his argument.

121. Ibid., at 764; see also 762, 63 (Field), 737 (Strong), 746 (Bradley).

122. Ibid., at 766-69.

123. Ibid., at 767. This idea was later developed into the corporate person doctrine (see chap. 8).

124. Ibid., at 768-69.

125. This statement is from the oral delivery as reported by the press. See Fairman, *Reconstruction and Reunion*, 7: 611; *San Francisco Chronicle*, October 21, 1879, 3-7; *San Francisco Examiner*, October 21, 1879, 2-4.

126. *San Francisco Evening Bulletin*, October 25, 1879 (quoting *New York Times*); Fairman, *Reconstruction and Reunion*, 7: 604-16.

127. Field to Matthew Deady, May 31, 1879, Deady Collection.

128. *Sinking Fund Cases*, 99 U.S., at 728.

129. *Alta California*, October 22, 1879, 2-1.

130. Davis, *History of Political Conventions in California*, 417 (resolutions 9 and 10); see also the Democratic convention of May 19, 1880, denouncing the doctrine of centralization (423).

131. *New York Sun*, October 23, 1879, 2-1; *New York Times*, October 23, 1879; *Chicago Tribune*, October 22, 1879; *San Francisco Evening Bulletin*, October 23, 1879, 3-6.

132. *San Francisco Examiner*, October 22, 1879, 2-3.

133. Field's campaign emphasized this position in the campaign pamphlet, "Sound in Doctrine, Brave in Deed," 6.

134. *San Francisco Evening Bulletin*, October 25, 1879.

135. *San Francisco Examiner*, October 21, 22, 23, 27, 28, 31, and November 4, 5, 8, 1879.

136. Ibid., October 27, 1879, 2–1.

137. Ibid., October 27, 1879, 2–1; October 22, 1879, 2–3; November 4, 1879, 2–3 (the case was *New York Central and Hudson River Railroad Co. v. Fraloff*, 100 U.S. 24, 32 (1879), Field dissenting.

138. See *Alta California* and *San Francisco Record-Union*. As might be expected, James O'Meara, an editor of the *Examiner*, believed the *Record-Union* was "the voice of the Central Pacific" (James O'Meara to Montgomery Blair, March 24, 1880, Tilden Papers).

139. *Washington Post*, May, 17, 1880, 1–3; *New York Sun*, October 23, 1879, 2–1; *San Francisco Chronicle*, May 17, 1880, 2–2.

140. James O'Meara to Montgomery Blair, March 24, 1880, Tilden Papers.

141. Perry Belmont to Thomas Francis Bayard, May 26, 1880, Bayard Collection.

142. Magrath, *Morrison R. Waite*, 258–60; Fairman, *Reconstruction and Reunion*, 7: 593–95, quoting Waite to Field, November 7 and 10, 1875, Waite Letterbooks; the case was *United States v. Union Pacific R.R. Co.*, 91 U.S. 72 (1875).

143. Clark, ed., *Pharisee Among Philistines*, 2: 416, (entry June 30, 1883).

144. Colton Letters, September 20, 1878; *San Francisco Chronicle*, April 18, 1885. Swisher, *Stephen J. Field: Craftsman of the Law*, 247, 240, n. 15, doubts the authenticity of this letter; Magrath, *Morrison R. Waite*, 231, does not.

145. This is documented in Magrath, *Morrison R. Waite*, 238–43, quoting an exchange of letters between Garfield and Whitlaw Reid. Although Rockefeller and Depew were naming a condition for their support of Republican hopeful James Garfield, their statement shows the extent to which railroad leaders favored Field's views.

146. See Field to Matthew Deady, July 20, 1891, Deady Collection; C. P. Huntington to Field, May 29, 1883, and Field to Huntington, May 31, 1883, Cyrus Field Papers; Field to John Norton Pomeroy, June 21, 1881, Field Collection (Field says he asked Lloyd Tevis to hire Pomeroy); James O'Meara to S. J. Tilden, June 5, 1880, Tilden Papers; Huntington to Colton, Colton Letters, November 10, 1875, December 23, 1875; *San Francisco Chronicle*, December 17, 1883, 2–3; *New York Herald*, August 23, 1880, 10–1.

147. The oldest of these clubs, the Pacific Club, was founded in 1852. For a glimpse of the lifestyle of San Francisco's social elite, see Julia Cooley Altrocchi, *The Spectacular San Franciscans* (New York: E. P. Dutton, 1949), 92–93, 157–257.

148. James O'Meara to Montgomery Blair, December 15, 1879, Tilden Papers.

149. *San Francisco Chronicle*, May 14, 1880, 3–5; *Atlanta Constitution*, May 12, 1880, 2–3.

150. Davis, *History of Political Conventions in California*, 422.

151. A list of the delegates is found in ibid. and in *Official Proceedings*, 52. The conclusion regarding delegate alignment is mine, pieced together from biographies and newspaper reports.

152. Davis, *History of Political Conventions in California*, 423–24, Resolution no. 9.

153. *Alta California*, June 17, 1880, 3–1; *San Francisco Evening Bulletin*, June 18, 1880, 1–1; *San Francisco Chronicle*, June 19, 1880, 2–5.

154. E. Casserly to Thomas Francis Bayard, May 22, 1880, Bayard Collection.

155. *New York Herald*, May 22, 1880, 4–2; *Atlanta Constitution*, May 23, 1880,

2-1; *Missouri Republican,* May 22, 1880, 1-3; *Chicago Tribune,* May 22, 1880, 6-4; *San Francisco Evening Bulletin,* May 20, 1880, 3-3; *New York Times,* May 20, 1880, 4-3.

156. *New Orleans Times-Picayune,* May 22, 1880, 1-4, May 23, 1880, 1-4, "Latest Telegrams," signed L. Q. W.; *Washington Post,* May 23, 1880, 1-5, "Political Points"; *Atlanta Constitution,* May 22, 1880, 1-7, "The Great Question," and June 16, 1880, 1-3 "Seeking a Wetnurse."

157. E. Casserly to Thomas Francis Bayard, May 29, 1880, Bayard Collection.

158. *Missouri Republican,* May 29, 1880, 2-3; *New Orleans Times-Picayune,* May 29, 1880, 1-6, June 5, 1880, 1-6, June 21, 1880, 1-2; *Washington Post,* April 12, 1880, 1-6, June 5, 1880, 2-4; *Deseret News,* June 16, 1880, 308-1.

159. Samuel J. Randall to Samuel Tilden, May 7, 1880, Tilden Papers; Charles N. Hersey to Manton Marble, June 6, 1880, Manton Marble Papers, Library of Congress.

160. *Missouri Republican,* May 23, 1880, 5-1; *Memphis Daily Appeal,* June 4, 1880, 2-1, June 13, 1880, 2-1; *New Orleans Times-Picayune,* June 1, 1880, 1-5; *San Francisco Examiner,* May 26, 1880, 2-4; *Deseret News,* May 19, 1880, 248-1; *Washington Post,* June 18, 1880, 1-1, 1-3; David Jordan, *Winfield Scott Hancock: A Soldier's Life* (Bloomington: Indiana University Press, 1988), 271.

161. See August Belmont to John Hunter, February 9, 1880, Bayard Collection, warning against collusion with Tilden's foes because Tilden was likely to support Bayard if he could not secure the nomination for himself.

162. Stephen Field to Burton Harrison, April 9, 1880, Harrison Family Collection, Library of Congress; Philip Roach to Manton Marble, June 7, 1880, Marble Papers.

163. See *Atlanta Constitution,* May 28, 1880, 1-8; *Philadelphia Inquirer,* June 10, 1880, 4-3; *Memphis Daily Appeal,* May 20, 1880, 1-3.

164. *New York Herald,* June 16, 1880; *San Francisco Evening Bulletin,* June 16, 1880; *New York Times,* June 18, 1880, 4-1; H. A. Tilden to W. M. Gwin, June 16, 1880, H. A. Tilden to editor of the *Sun,* June 17, 1880, Wm. M. Gwin to Henry A. Tilden, June 16, 1880, and lists of newspapers and letters, Tilden Papers.

165. *New York Tribune,* June 18, 1880, 2-1; *San Francisco Examiner,* June 18, 1880, 3-5.

166. *Cincinnati Commercial,* June 18, 1880, 6-4, June 20, 1880, 1-5.

167. *Cincinnati Commercial,* June 19, 1-1; June 20, 1-2, 1-5; June 22, 12-7, 1880 (the *Commercial's* owner was M. Halstead); *New York Tribune,* June 22, 1880, 1-2; *San Francisco Chronicle,* May 29, 1880, 3-3; *Cincinnati Enquirer,* June 19, 1880, 1-2; *Deseret News,* June 23, 1880, 325-2; *Atlanta Constitution,* June 17, 1880 1-1; *New York Tribune,* June 22, 1880, 1-1; William R. Barlow, "Cincinnati Hosts the Democrats," *Bulletin of the Cincinnati Historical Society* 22 (July 1964): 145-62. Kelly planned to dispute the credentials of the regular New York delegation.

168. *Memphis Daily Appeal,* June 20, 1880, 1-2; *Cincinnati Commercial,* June 20, 1880, 1-2, 1-4; *Cincinnati Enquirer,* June 21, 1-2, 9-1, June 22, 9-2, June 23, 1-1, 1880; *San Francisco Chronicle,* June 21, 1880, 3-3; *New Orleans Times-Picayune,* June 21, 1-6, June 22, 1-5, 4-2, 1880; *New York Sun,* June 21, 1880, 1-2; *Missouri Republican,* June 21, 1880, 1-3; *Atlanta Constitution,* June 19, 1880, 1-1.

169. Tilden's letter, dated June 18, 1880, circulated in the New York delegation and then was read to the convention on June 24, after the first ballot was taken (*New York Times,* June 21, 1880, 1–1; *Official Proceedings, Convention,* 103).

170. *Official Proceedings,* 25–49.

171. Ibid., 99.

172. Ibid., 69–70; *San Francisco Evening Bulletin,* June 24, 1880, 2–2; *San Francisco Chronicle,* June 24, 1880, 3–1.

173. *Official Proceedings,* 99 (first ballot); 114 (second ballot).

174. Fairman, *Reconstruction and Reunion,* 7: 485.

175. *Official Proceedings,* 99.

176. See Earl M. Maltz, *Civil Rights, the Constitution, and Congress, 1863–1869* (Lawrence: University Press of Kansas, 1990), 72–78, 100–106.

177. *New York Herald,* August 23, 1880, 10–1.

178. Field to "My Dear Brother Cyrus," August 8, 1880, Field to "My Dear Brother," August 26, 1880, Cyrus Field Papers. Field also displayed vindictiveness toward James O'Meara, an editor of the *San Francisco Examiner* and a Tilden supporter. See Clark, ed., *Pharisee Among Philistines,* 321; Field to Matthew Deady, October 23, November 29, December 22, 1880, Deady Collection.

179. Field to "My Dear Brother," August 29, 1880, Cyrus Field Papers; Field to Matthew Deady, June 10, 1880, Deady Collection.

180. See Williams, *Democratic Party and California Politics, 1880–1896,* 47–51, for more detail on Field's 1884 campaign.

8. Class Legislation

1. *San Mateo v. Southern Pacific Railroad Co.,* 13 Fed. 722, 736 (1882).

2. See Carl Brent Swisher, *Motivation and Political Technique in the California Constitutional Convention, 1878–1879* (New York: Da Capo Press, 1969), 80–81, 84.

3. Ibid., 66–77.

4. Ibid., 77–85; R. Hal Williams, *The Democratic Party and California Politics, 1880–1896* (Stanford, Calif: Stanford University Press, 1973), 32–33.

5. Williams, *Democratic Party and California Politics,* 33–34; *San Francisco and North Pacific Railroad Company v. State Board of Equalization,* 60 Cal. 12 (1882); *Central Pacific Railroad Company v. State Board of Equalization,* 60 Cal. 35 (1882).

6. See chap. 6, text accompanying notes 69–75. The railroad's request was based upon a different statute from the earlier case, however.

7. *San Mateo v. Southern Pacific Railroad Co.,* 13 Fed. 145 (1882); Act to Determine the Jurisdiction of Circuit Courts and to Regulate Removal of Causes from State Courts, 18 Stat. 470–71 (March 3, 1875); see Stanley Kutler, *Judicial Power and Reconstruction Politics* (Chicago: University of Chicago Press, 1968), 154–55.

8. *San Mateo,* 13 Fed., at 147–48.

9. Field to Matthew Deady, August 9, 1883, Deady Collection.

10. *San Mateo,* 13 Fed., at 150. There were actually two other issues in the *Railroad Tax Cases.* One was whether the tax law violated the due process clause of the Fourteenth Amendment. Railroad property was assessed by a State Board of Equali-

zation; the board's procedure did not provide for notice or for an opportunity to be heard. The other issue was based on an argument that the Southern Pacific Railroad operated as an agent of the U.S. government and was therefore exempt from taxation.

11. Field to John Norton Pomeroy, March 28, 1883, Field Collection; this is one of four letters from Field to Pomeroy reproduced in Howard J. Graham, *Everyman's Constitution* (Madison: State Historical Society of Wisconsin, 1968) 101-19.

12. *San Mateo,* 13 Fed., at 733.

13. Ibid., at 737-38; *Santa Clara,* 18 Fed., at 407.

14. *San Mateo,* 13 Fed., at 743-44; in *Paul v. Virginia,* 75 U.S. (8 Wall.) 168 (1868), Field ruled that corporations were not citizens entitled to privileges and immunities under the comity clause of Article 4, section 2. The term citizen, he explained, applies only to natural persons.

15. *San Mateo,* 13 Fed., at 744.

16. Williams, *Democratic Party and California Politics,* 73.

17. *Railway Company v. Whitton,* 80 U.S. (13 Wall.) 270 (1871).

18. *Dartmouth College v. Woodward,* 17 U.S. (4 Wheat.) 518 (1819).

19. *San Mateo,* 13 Fed., at 755.

20. *Providence Bank v. Billings,* 29 U.S. (4 Pet.) 514 (1830).

21. *Tomlinson v. Jessup,* 82 U.S. (15 Wall.) 454 (1872); see also *Minot v. Philadelphia, Wilmington, and Baltimore R. R.,* 85 U.S. (18 Wall.) 206 (1873) and *Trask v. Maguire,* 85 U.S. (18 Wall.) 391 (1873).

22. *San Mateo,* 13 Fed., at 754; *Santa Clara,* 18 Fed., at 405-17.

23. *Santa Clara,* 18 Fed., at 396.

24. *San Mateo,* 13 Fed., at 740.

25. Ibid., 741.

26. Williams, *Democratic Party and California Politics,* 32.

27. Ibid., 47, reports that twenty-two county organizations had adopted anti-Field resolutions.

28. Winfield J. Davis, *History of Political Conventions in California, 1849-1892* (Sacramento: California State Library, 1893), 458, 460.

29. Williams, *Democratic Party and California Politics,* 49.

30. Field to John Norton Pomeroy, July 28, 1884, Field Collection, printed in Graham, *Everyman's Constitution,* 109.

31. Field to J. DeBarth Shorb, December 14, 1884, Shorb Collection.

32. Field to Don Dickinson, November 22, 1893, Dickinson Papers. For details of Field's involvement in the patronage struggles, see Williams, *Democratic Party and California Politics,* 56-81.

33. Stephen J. Field to J. DeBarth Shorb, October 27, 1886, Short Collection.

34. Williams, *Democratic Party and California Politics,* 21, 58, citing from Field to George Ticknor Curtis, December 14, 1884, Grover Cleveland Papers, Library of Congress.

35. Williams, *Democratic Party and California Politics,* 32, citing *Los Angeles Times,* June 8, 1882; for a detailed description of the politics of settling the tax question, see Williams, *Democratic Party and California Politics,* 35-39.

36. *Santa Clara County v. Southern Pacific Railroad,* 118 U.S. 394, 396 (1886), from the reporter's statement of facts. The *San Mateo* case was settled and appeal

of the case to the Supreme Court was dismissed (*San Mateo County v. Southern Pacific Railroad,* 116 U.S. 138 [1885]). In the *Sinking Fund Case, Union Pacific Railroad v. United States,* 99 U.S. 700, 718–19 (1879), Waite had reasoned that government was "prohibited from depriving persons or corporations of property without due process of law." For all practical purposes this dicta had already recognized the corporate person.

37. *Home Insurance Company v. New York,* 134 U.S. 594 (1890); *Charlotte, Columbia, and Augusta Railroad Co. v. Gibbes,* 142 U.S. 386 (1892); *Horn Silver Mining Co. v. New York,* 143 U.S. 305 (1892). Field gave his enemies renewed cause for suspecting his motives when, just before resigning from the bench, he dissented from rulings that upheld California taxes on the franchise and property of the Central Pacific Railroad and Southern Pacific Railroad. These were not equal protection cases, however. Field claimed that the companies' franchises from the federal government made their property exempt from state taxation (*Central Pacific Railroad v. California,* 162 U.S. 91, 128 [1896], Field dissenting; *Southern Pacific Railroad v. California,* 162 U.S. 167, 168 [1896], Field dissenting; see also *Central Pacific Railroad v. Nevada,* 162 U.S. 512, 527 [1896], Field dissenting).

38. *Pembina Consolidated Silver Mining and Milling Co. v. Pennsylvania,* 125 U.S. 181 (1888).

39. *Minneapolis & St. Paul Railway v. Beckwith,* 129 U.S. 26, 30 (1889).

40. *Butchers' Union Co. v. Crescent City Co.,* 111 U.S. 746 (1884).

41. *Boyd v. Alabama,* 94 U.S. 645 (1877).

42. *Butchers' Union,* 111 U.S. at 750–51.

43. Ibid., at 755–57, Field concurring.

44. Ibid., at 764–66, Bradley concurring.

45. Ibid., at 755, Field concurring.

46. *Budd v. New York,* 143 U.S. 517, 550–51 (1892), Brewer dissenting.

47. *Illinois Central Railroad v. Illinois,* 146 U.S. 387, 452–55 (1892), and *Hart v. Burnett,* 15 Cal. 530 (1860). Field was so upset with the outcome that he told his friend Don Dickinson that it was of the utmost importance that Judge Blatchford's successor should be a person whose mind had not been warped by the great corporations (Field to Don Dickinson, June 20, 1893, Dickinson Papers).

48. See *Brown v. Maryland,* 25 U.S. (12 Wheat.) 419 (1827); *Willson v. Black-Bird Creek Marsh Co.,* 27 U.S. (2 Pet.) 244 (1829). Marshall was referring to the powers left to the states under the commerce clause doctrine. Howard Gillman, *The Constitution Besieged: The Rise and Damise of Lochner Era Police Powers Jurisprudence* (Durham, N. C.: Duke University Press, 1993) presents a different view of the development of police powers jurisprudence, linking it to a desire to preserve neutrality in government.

49. *Thurlow v. Commonwealth of Massachusetts,* 46 U.S. (5 How.) 504, 583 (1847).

50. *Butchers' Union,* 111 U.S., at 754.

51. See *Ex parte Bird,* 19 Cal. 130 (1861).

52. See *Boyde v. Alabama,* 94 U.S., at 645.

53. *Ex parte Jackson,* 96 U.S. 727 (1877).

54. *Crowley v. Christensen,* 137 U.S. 86, 91 (1890).

55. *Mugler v. Kansas,* 123 U.S. 623, 678 (1887), Field, separate opinion.

56. *Hager v. Reclamation District,* 111 U.S. 701, 704 (1884).

57. *Dent v. West Virginia,* 129 U.S. 114 (1884).

58. *Minnesota v. Barber,* 136 U.S. 313 (1880); *Powell v. Pennsylvania,* 127 U.S. 678, 695 (1888).

59. *In re Quong Woo,* 13 Fed. 229 (1882); *Barbier v. Connolly,* 113 U.S. 27 (1885); *Soon Hing v. Crowley,* 113 U.S. 703 (1885); see also *Yick Wo v. Hopkins,* 118 U.S. 356 (1886), in which Field agrees with a decision upholding licensing of laundries.

60. *Missouri Pacific Railway Company v. Mackey,* 127 U.S. 205, 210 (1888); see also *Minneapolis and St. Louis Railway Co. v. Herrick,* 127 U.S. 210 (1888); *Chicago & Milwaukee Railroad v. Ross,* 112 U.S. 377 (1884); *Baltimore and Ohio Railroad Co. v. Baugh,* 149 U.S. 368, 390 (1893), Field dissenting.

61. *Missouri Pacific Railway Co. v. Humes,* 115 U.S. 512 (1885); *Minneapolis & St. Louis Railway Co. v. Beckwith,* 129 U.S. 26 (1889). Dissenting in another case, he reasoned that a mechanics' lien should apply to an entire canal, not just to that portion upon which the contractor had worked (*South Fork Canal Co. v. Gordon,* 73 U.S. [6 Wall.] 561, 572 [1867]).

62. *Gulf, Colorado and Santa Fe Co. v. Ellis,* 165 U.S. 150 (1897).

63. *Chicago, Burlington and Quincy Railroad Co. v. Chicago,* 166 U.S. 226 (1897).

64. *Missouri Pacific Railroad Co. v. Nebraska,* 164 U.S. 403 (1896).

65. *Powell v. Pennsylvania,* 127 U.S. 678, 684 (1888).

66. Ibid., at 684.

67. Ibid., at 686.

68. Ibid., at 689, Field dissenting (emphasis added).

69. Ibid., at 694, Field dissenting.

70. Ibid., at 696, Field dissenting.

71. A change in the majority's attitude was evident even in subsequent cases that tested state laws prohibiting or limiting the sale of oleomargarine. A few years after *Powell,* it upheld a similar Massachusetts law (*Plumley v. Massachusetts,* 155 U.S. 461 [1894], Field dissenting). But then in May 1898, just a few months after Field had resigned from the Court, it ruled that, to the extent that it prevented importing oleomargarine from other states, Pennsylvania's prohibition was an unconstitutional invasion of Congress' power to regulate interstate commerce. Justice Rufus Peckham, who had joined the Court in December 1895, wrote the opinion in that case; Harlan and Gray dissented (*Schollenberger v. Pennsylvania,* 171 U.S. 1 [1898]).

72. *Allgeyer v. Louisiana,* 165 U.S. 578, 591 (1897).

73. The most prominent case is *In re Jacobs,* 98 N.Y. 98 (1885); a conventional account of the development of liberty of contract doctrine may be found in Roscoe Pound, "Liberty of Contract," *Yale Law Journal* 18 (1909): 454.

74. Richard C. McMurtrie, "A New Canon of Constitutional Interpretation," *American Law Register* 32 (January 1893): 4.

75. *Lochner v. New York,* 198 U.S. 45, 68 (1905), Harlan dissenting. I have written about *Lochner* in more detail in *Judicial Power and Reform Politics: The Anatomy of Lochner v. New York* (Lawrence: University Press of Kansas, 1990).

76. *Lochner,* 198 U.S., at 72–73, Harlan dissenting.

77. Ibid., at 57–58.

78. *Mugler v. Kansas,* 123 U.S., at 678.

79. *Spring Valley Water Works v. Schottler,* 110 U.S. 347, 352 (1884). For background and analysis of the protracted controversies surrounding *Spring Valley Water Works,* see Katha G. Hartley, "Spring Valley Water Works v. San Francisco: Defining Economic Rights in San Francisco," *Western Legal History* 3 (Summer/Fall 1990): 287–308.

80. *Spring Valley Water Works,* 110 U.S. 347, at 374, Field dissenting.

81. Ibid., at 364, Field dissenting.

82. Ibid., at 354; Field denied that a virtual monopoly existed (at 362–63).

83. Ibid., at 366, 383, Field dissenting.

84. Ibid., at 381, Field dissenting.

85. Field made this explicit in his dissent to *Ruggles v. Illinois,* 108 U.S. 526, 541, writing "I do not give any weight to *Munn v. Illinois.*"

86. The key case of this group is *Stone v. Farmers' Loan and Trust Company,* 116 U.S. 307 (1886).

87. *Stone v. Farmers' Loan and Trust Company,* 116 U.S., at 322, argument for appellee.

88. Ibid., at 331, 335.

89. Ibid., at 344, 346, Field dissenting.

90. Ibid., at 345, Field dissenting.

91. See Carl Brent Swisher, *Stephen J. Field, Craftsman of the Law* (Hamden, Conn.: Archon Books, 1963), 319; George C. Gorham, *Biographical Notice of Stephen J. Field* (Washington, D.C., n.d.), 107–8; Malcolm Clark Jr., ed, *Pharisee Among the Philistines: The Diary of Judge Matthew P. Deady* (Portland: Oregon Historical Society, 1975), 2; 536. For background on Fuller, see James W. Ely, Jr., *The Chief Justiceship of Melville W. Fuller, 1888–1910* (Columbia: University of South Carolina Press, 1995), 1–25; for a slightly different view of Fuller's appointment, see Richard C. Cortner, *The Iron Horse and the Constitution: The Railroads and the Transformation of the Fourteenth Amendment* (Westport, Conn: Greenwood Press, 1993), 100–102.

92. *Chicago, Milwaukee and St. Paul Railway Company v. Minnesota,* 134 U.S. 418 (1890); see James W. Ely, Jr., "The Railroad Question Revisited: *Chicago, Milwaukee & St. Paul Railway v. Minnesota* and the Constitutional Limits on State Regulations," *Great Plains Quarterly* 12 (Spring 1992): 121–34.

93. Cortner, *Iron Horse and the Constitution,* 102.

94. *Chicago & Northwestern Railway Co. v. Dey,* 35 F. 866, 879 (C.C.S.D. Iowa, 1888). Cortner, *Iron Horse and the Constitution,* 55–75, treats this case in detail.

95. *Chicago, Milwaukee and St. Paul Railway Company v. Minnesota,* 134 U.S., at 444, argument for plaintiff in error.

96. Ibid., at 458.

97. Ibid., at 461, Bradley dissenting.

98. Ibid., at 465, Bradley dissenting. This statement seems at odds with Bradley's earlier opinion that "if a State, by its laws, should authorize private property to be taken for public use without compensation, . . . I think it would be depriving a man of his property without due process of law" (*Davidson v. New Orleans,* 96 U.S. [6 Otto] 97, 107 [1877], Bradley concurring). Robert Lowery Clinton, *Marbury v. Madison and Judicial Review* (Lawrence: University Press of Kansas, 1989), 202, calls Bradley's *Davidson* concurrence the first clear intimation from the federal

bench of a willingness to enforce the compensation principle on the states by due process of law.

99. *Chicago, Milwaukee and St. Paul Railway Company v. Minnesota,* 134 U.S., at 466, Bradley dissenting.

100. Ibid., at 459, Miller concurring.

101. Ibid., at 465–66, Bradley dissenting.

102. *Budd v. New York,* 143 U.S. 517, 552 (1892), Brewer dissenting.

103. For this account I have paraphrased the work of Charles Evans Hughes, *The Supreme Court of the United States* (1928; rpt., New York: Columbia University Press, 1966), 75–76. The story also appears in Swisher, *Stephen Field,* 443–44. Charles Alan Wright, "Authenticity of 'A Dirtier Day's Work' Quote In Question," *Supreme Court Historical Society Quarterly* 13 (Winter 1990): 6–7, makes a convincing argument that this story is based upon hearsay and is inaccurate.

104. Field to Matthew Deady, June 10, 1892, and Joseph M. Dolph to Matthew Deady, December 6, 1892, Deady Collection.

105. Carl Brent Swisher, *Stephen J. Field: Craftsman of the Law* (1930; rpt., Hamden, Conn.: Archon Books, 1963), 111.

106. *Smyth v. Ames,* 169 U.S. 466, 547 (1898).

107. Ibid., at 526.

108. Paul Brest and Sanford Levinson, *Process of Constitutional Decision Making,* 2d ed. (Boston: Little Brown, 1983), 215, make the observation in roughly these words. They also note that *FPC v. Hope Natural Gas Co.,* 320 U.S. 591 (1944), expressly repudiated the rule of *Smyth v. Ames.*

109. *Smyth v. Ames,* 169 U.S., at 548.

110. For differing treatments of this era, see Howard Gillman, *The Constitution Besieged: The Rise and Demise of Lochner Era Police Powers Jurisprudence* (Durham, N.C.: Duke University Press, 1993), and Kens, *Judicial Power and Reform Politics.*

9. Stephen Field's Legacy

1. The speeches of the centennial celebration are published as an appendix to *United States Reports,* 134 U.S. 729, 744.

2. Ibid., 774–75.

3. *Barbier v. Connely,* 113 U.S. 27, 32 (1885).

4. *Pollock v. Farmers' Loan & Trust Co.,* 157 U.S. 429, 596 (1895), Field, separate opinion (emphasis added).

5. Ibid., at 607, Field, separate opinion.

6. *U.S. v. E. C. Knight,* 156 U.S. 1 (1895); *Interstate Commerce Commission v. Alabama,* 168 U.S. 144 (1897).

7. *In re Debs,* 158 U.S. 564 (1895).

8. Describing one of his fellow conservatives, Field said, "He has a great detestation for anything like communism or agrarianism of any kind" (Field to Matthew Deady, May 17, 1886, Deady Collection).

9. Howard J. Graham, *Everyman's Constitution* (Madison: State Historical Society of Wisconsin, 1968), 124–28.

10. Carl Brent Swisher, *American Constitutional Development* (Boston: Houghton Mifflin, 1943), 341.

11. Robert Green McCloskey, *American Conservatism in the Age of Enterprise, 1865–1910* (New York: Harper Torchbooks, 1951) 75, 103.

12. Charles W. McCurdy, "Justice Field and the Jurisprudence of Government-Business Relations: Some Parameters of Laissez-Faire Constitutionalism, 1863–1897," *Journal of American History* 61 (1975): 973.

13. Charles W. McCurdy, "The Roots of 'Liberty of Contract' Reconsidered: Major Premises in the Law of Employment, 1867–1937," *Yearbook of the Supreme Court Historical Society* (1984): 24.

14. Michael Les Benedict, "Laissez-Faire and Liberty: A Reevaluation of the Meaning and Origins of Laissez-Faire Constitutionalism," *Law and History Review* 3 (Fall 1985): 293; Howard Gillman, *The Constitution Besieged: The Rise and Demise of Lochner Era Police Powers Jurisprudence* (Durham, N. C.: Duke University Press, 1993); David M. Gold, *The Shaping of Nineteenth-Century Law: John Appleton and Responsible Individualism* (Westport, Conn.: Greenwood Press, 1990).

15. Gold, *Shaping of Nineteenth-Century Law,* 139.

16. James W. Ely, Jr.,*The Chief Justiceship of Melville W. Fuller, 1888–1910* (Columbia: University of South Carolina Press, 1995), 63.

17. Owen M. Fiss, *Troubled Beginnings of the Modern State, 1888–1910,* vol. 8, *Oliver Wendell Holmes Devise History of the Supreme Court of the United States* (New York: Macmillan, 1993), 81, discusses the *Income Tax Case.*

18. For treatment of Jacksonian Democracy, I have relied heavily on Harry L. Watson, *Liberty and Power: The Politics of Jacksonian America* (New York: Noonday Press, 1990), 149–50; Lawrence Frederick Kohl, *The Politics of Individualism: Parties and the American Character in the Jacksonian Era* (New York: Oxford University Press, 1989); Arthur M. Schlesinger, Jr., *The Age of Jackson* (Boston: Little, Brown, 1945); Marvin Meyers, *The Jacksonian Persuasion: Politics and Belief* (Stanford, Calif.: Stanford University Press, 1957), and Donald B. Cole, *The Presidency of Andrew Jackson* (Lawrence: University Press of Kansas, 1993).

19. Morton Keller, *Affairs of State: Public Life in Late Nineteenth Century America* (Cambridge, Mass.: The Belknap Press, 1977), 367.

20. McCurdy, "Roots of 'Liberty of Contract,' " 33.

21. See Robert J. Steinfeld, *The Invention of Free Labor: The Employment Relation in English and American Law and Culture, 1350–1870* (Chapel Hill: University of North Carolina Press, 1991); Jonathan A. Glickstein, *Concepts of Free Labor in Antebellum America* (New Haven: Yale University Press, 1991); Eric Foner, *Free Soil, Free Labor, Free Men: The Ideology of the Republican Party Before the Civil War* (New York: Oxford University Press, 1970). McCurdy, "Roots of 'Liberty of Contract,' " 27, also recognizes this meaning.

22. Steinfeld, *Invention of Free Labor,* 187, describes this evolution: "As the nineteenth century wore on, wage workers complained more and more bitterly that the power of property was making them slaves to their employers. And they could appeal to deeply entrenched American attitudes for support for their claims. But their argument was now more difficult and more contradictory."

23. Paul Kens, *Judicial Power and Reform Politics: The Anatomy of Lochner v. New York* (Lawrence: University Press of Kansas, 1990), 54–56, 74–78.

24. There are other theories about the roots of early twentieth-century constitutional doctrine. Some scholars see it as an outgrowth of British-American common law tradition (Edward Keynes, *Liberty, Property, and Privacy: Toward a Jurisprudence of Substantive Due Process* [University Park: Pennsylvania State University Press, 1996]). Others find in it an expression of social contract theory (Keynes, *Liberty, Property, and Privacy*; Fiss, *Troubled Beginnings of the Modern State, 1888–1910*). Some observers say the Court was merely filling a vacuum of power left because of Congress' inaction. Mary Cornelia Porter, "That Commerce Shall Be Free: A New look at the Old Laissez-Faire Court," *Supreme Court Review* (1976): 135–59, maintains that the Court actually tried to create a uniform national rule for economic regulation of certain types of businesses. Taking quite a different approach, other scholars maintain that, rather than laissez-faire policy, the legal theory of the era was merely an apology for greed (John P. Roche, "Entrepreneurial Liberty and the Fourteenth Amendment," *Labor History* 4 [Winter 1963]: 3–31).

25. Benedict, "Laissez-Faire and Liberty," 331.

26. Herbert Hovenkamp, *Enterprise and American Law, 1836–1937* (Cambridge: Harvard University Press, 1991), 96.

27. Benedict's careful observation illustrates the point: "Laissez-faire constitutionalism received wide support in late nineteenth-century America not because it was based on widely adhered-to economic principles, and certainly not because it protected entrenched economic privilege, but rather because it was congruent with *a well established and accepted principle* of American liberty" ("Laissez-Faire and Liberty," 298, emphasis added). Benedict is careful not to claim that laissez-faire constitutionalism was congruent with *the established and accepted* principle of American liberty.

28. Benedict, "Laissez-Faire and Liberty," 331, observes a symbiotic relationship between these traditions and laissez-faire theory.

29. For example, *Hodel v. Irving,* 481 U.S. 704 (1987); *First English Evangelical Lutheran Church of Glendale v. County of Los Angeles,* 482 U.S. 304 (1987); *Nollan v. California Coastal Commission,* 483 U.S. 825 (1987); *Lucas v. South Carolina Coastal Council,* 505 U.S. 1003 (1992); *Dolan v. City of Tigard,* 512 U.S. 374 (1994).

30. To the contrary, Howard Gillman's purpose in reevaluating the laissez-faire era seems to be to justify modern judicial activism. He argues that the Jacksonian-free-labor tradition's concept of the neutral state and distrust of special legislation gradually came into conflict with "the onslaught of corporate capitalism." The building tension eventually exploded in a "constitutional revolution of 1937," Gillman concludes. The new interpretation, which deemphasizes economic rights and stresses emphasizes personal liberties, brought modern legal doctrine into line with the realities of American society. Recognizing that "conservatives have used the lore of *Lochner* as a weapon in their struggle against the modern Court's use of fundamental rights as a trump on governmental power," Gillman wants to remove that weapon from their hands (*The Constitution Besieged,* 205).

31. Most accounts of the Terry incident present a partisan view. A relatively objective treatment is found in Swisher, *Stephen J. Field: Craftsman of the Law,* 321–61. Field's version is found in George C. Gorham, "The Story of the Attempted Assassination of Justice Field by a Former Associate on the State Supreme Bench," in

PR, 237–406. For versions more favorable to Terry, see A. Russell Buchanan, *David S. Terry of California: Dueling Judge* (San Marino, Calif.: Huntington Library, 1956), 191–231. I have consolidated these versions to write the account that follows and will make specific references only for quotes.

32. *Sharon v. Hill*, 26 F. 337, 348 (C.C.D. Cal., 1885).

33. *Stephen J. Field: His Character and Career as It Is Known in California* (1889?), 75. Pamphlet available at the Huntington Library.

34. Numerous letters discussing the case are collected in the Deady Collection.

35. For the state court case on appeal, see *Sharon v. Sharon*, 67 Cal. 185, 7 P. 456 (Cal., 1885); *Sharon v. Sharon*, 75 Cal. 1, 16 P. 345 (Cal., 1888); *Sharon v. Sharon*, 79 Cal. 633, 22 P. 26 (Cal., 1889).

36. *Sharon v. Hill*, 20 F. 1 (C.C.D. Cal., 1884); *Sharon v. Hill*, 22 F. 28 (C.C.D. Cal., 1884); *Sharon v. Hill*, 23 F. 353 (C.C.D. Cal., 1885); *Sharon v. Hill*, 26 F. 722 (C.C.D. Cal., 1885).

37. *Sharon v. Hill*, 26 F. 337, 361 (C.C.D. Cal., 1885).

38. *Sharon v. Terry*, 36 F. 337 (C.C. N.D. Cal., 1888).

39. Swisher, *Stephen J. Field: Craftsman of the Law*, 332–43.

40. Buchanan, *David S. Terry of California*, 219, 223–24, citing transcript of the record, *In re Neagle*. Buchanan also notes that the local sheriff swore he had examined Field's face and found no marks that indicated he had been struck.

41. Swisher, *Stephen J. Field: Craftsman of the Law*, 349, quoting from the testimony of G. I. Linderwood, transcript of *In re Neagle*, 123.

42. PR, 326.

43. After Terry's death, Sarah Althea lived with Mammy Pleasant for about two years. In 1892 she was committed to the state mental hospital and remained there until her death in 1937.

44. *In re Neagle*, 39 F. 833 (C.C. N.D. Cal., 1889), affirmed in *Cunningham v. Neagle*, 135 U.S. 1 (1890). Interestingly, the theory that freed Neagle ran contrary to the position Field had taken in Reconstruction cases such as *Tennessee v. Davis*, 100 U.S. 259 (1880).

45. Field to Don Dickinson, June 17, 1893, Dickinson Papers; he was probably referring to *Fong Yue Ting v. United States*, a case discussed in chapter 7. Although exclusion of Chinese immigrants was not by this time a subject that was likely to upset Field, he confided to Dickinson that "the decision has affected me very unpleasantly." Field emphasized the importance of the Reconstruction Amendments — "Every line of those Amendments has been obtained by bloody contest," he said. "I am not willing that any one of them should be given up: Nor am I willing to have it held that Congress has the power to suspend their guarantee and security with reference to any person who is a subject of a country at peace with us and who is a resident of our country." The Court's decision, he said, stood for "nothing else than that the Safeguards of the Constitution for life, liberty, and property can be suspended by Congress, with reference to any class, at its pleasure." The decision in this case was close. Fuller, Field, and Brewer dissented. Field says that Harlan was absent and was disposed to vote with his side. Even with Harlan's vote, however, the best Field could hope for with the existing makeup of the Court would be a 5–4 loss. Blatchford was in ill health and was struck with paralysis a few days after Field wrote this letter.

46. Field to Matthew Deady, July 18, 1883, Deady Collection. Field actually used the phrase "questions affecting mere property rights." I believe he used the word "mere" simply to distinguish constitutional from nonconstitutional issues. Throughout the rest of his life, he remained involved in the campaign to reorganize the federal judiciary. See letters from Stephen Field to William Evarts, July 28, 1890, January 6, 1891, William Maxwell Evarts Correspondence, Library of Congress.

47. Field to John Norton Pomeroy, July 28, 1884, Field Collection, printed in Graham, *Everyman's Constitution,* 108-9.

48. Field to Matthew Deady, May 15, 1884, Deady Collection. See letters from Stephen Field to William Evarts, July 28, 1890, January 6, 1891, Evarts Correspondence.

BIBLIOGRAPHY

Books, Articles, and Dissertations

Adams, Charles Francis, Jr. "Railroad Inflation," *North American Review* 108 (January 1869): 130-64.

——. *Railroads: Their Origin and Problems* New York: G. P. Putnam's Sons, 1886.

Altrocchi, Julia Cooley. *The Spectacular San Franciscans.* New York: E. P. Dutton, 1949.

Bakken, Gordon Morris. "California Constitutionalism: Politics, the Press and the Death of Fundamental Law," *Pacific Historian* 20 (1986): 5-17.

Bancroft, Hubert Howe. *The History of California.* Vol. 6, *1848-1859. The Works of Hubert Howe Bancroft.* Vol. 23. San Francisco: History Company, 1888.

——. *The History of California.* Vol. 7, *1860-1890. The Works of Hurbert Howe Bancroft.* Vol. 24. San Francisco: History Company, 1890.

Benedict, Michael Les. "Laissez-Faire and Liberty: A Reevaluation of the Meaning and Origin of Laissez-Faire Constitutionalism." *Law and History Review* 3 (Fall 1985): 243-331.

——. "Preserving Federalism: Reconstruction and the Waite Court." *Supreme Court Review* (1978): 39-53.

——. "Victorian Moralism and Civil Liberty in the Nineteenth-Century United States." In *The Constitution, Law, and American Life: Critical Aspects of the Nineteenth-Century Experience,* ed. Donald G. Nieman, 91-122. Athens: University of Georgia Press, 1992.

Berk, Gerald. *Alternative Tracks: The Constitution of American Industrial Order, 1865-1917.* Baltimore: Johns Hopkins University Press, 1994.

Berthold, Victor M. *The Pioneer Steamer California: 1848-1849.* Boston: Houghton Mifflin, 1932.

Bevans, Charles I., ed. *Treaties and Other International Agreements, 1776-1949.* Washington, D.C.: Department of State, 1972.

Buckanan, A. Russell. *David S. Terry of California.* San Marino, Calif.: Huntington Library, 1956.

Buck, Solon Justus. *The Granger Movement: A Study of Agricultural Organization and Its Political, Economic, and Social Manifestations, 1870-1880.* Lincoln, Nebr.: University of Nebraska Press, 1965.

Burchell, Robert A. "The Faded Dream: Inequality in Northern California in the 1860s and 1870s." *Journal of American Studies* 23 (August 1989): 215-34.

Camp, William Martin. *San Francisco: Port of Gold.* New York: Doubleday, 1947.

Carr, Ezra. *The Patrons of Husbandry on the Pacific Coast.* San Francisco: A. L. Bancroft, 1875.

Carter, Samuel III. *Cyrus Field: Man of Two Worlds*. New York: G. P. Putnam's Sons, 1968.

Caughey, John Walton. *Gold Is the Cornerstone*. Berkeley: University of California Press, 1948.

Chamberlain, Newell D. *The Call of Gold: True Tales on the Gold Road to Yosemite*. Mariposa, Calif.: The Gazette Press, 1936.

Chiu, Ping. *Chinese Labor in California*. Madison: State Historical Society of Wisconsin, 1963.

Clancy, Herbert J. *The Presidential Election of 1880*. Chicago: Loyola University Press, 1958.

Clark, Malcolm, Jr., ed. *Pharisee Among Philistines: The Diary of Matthew Deady, 1871-1892*. (Portland: Oregon Historical Society, 1975.

Cleland, Robert Glass, ed. *Apron Full of Gold: The Letters of Mary Jane Megquier from San Francisco, 1849-1856*. San Marino, Calif.: Huntington Library, 1949.

Clinton, Robert Lowery. *Marbury v. Madison and Judicial Review*. Lawrence: University Press of Kansas, 1989.

Cole, Donald B. *The Presidency of Andrew Jackson*. Lawrence: University Press of Kansas, 1993.

Cortner, Richard C. *The Iron Horse and the Constitution: Railroads and the Transformation of the Fourteenth Amendment*. Westport, Conn.: Greenwood Press, 1993.

Crampton, Charles Gregory. "The Opening of the Mariposa Mining Region, 1849-1859, with Particular Reference to the Mexican Land Grant of John Charles Frémont." Ph.D. diss., University of California, Berkeley, 1941.

Curtis, Michael Kent. *No State Shall Abridge: The Fourteenth Amendment and the Bill of Rights*. Durham, N. C.: Duke University Press, 1990.

Daggett, Stuart. *Chapters in the History of the Southern Pacific*. New York: Ronald Press, 1922.

Dalmatier, Royce D., Clarence F. McIntosh, and Earl G. Waters, eds. *The Rumble of California Politics, 1848-1970*. New York: John Wiley and Sons, 1970.

Davis, John P. *The Union Pacific Railway*. Chicago: S. C. Griggs, 1894.

Davis, Winfield J. *History of Political Conventions in California, 1849-1892*. Sacramento: California State Library, 1893.

Decker, Peter R. *Fortunes and Failures: White-Collar Mobility in Nineteenth-Century San Francisco*. Cambridge: Harvard University Press, 1978.

del Castillo, Richard Griswold. *The Treaty of Guadalupe Hidalgo: A Legacy of Conflict*. Norman: University of Oklahoma Press, 1990.

Desmond, Sister M. Benilda, O. P. "The History of the City of Marysville." Master's thesis, Catholic University of America, 1962.

Deverell, William. *Railroad Crossing: Californians and the Railroad, 1850-1910*. Berkeley: University of California Press, 1994.

Dingledine, Raymond L., Jr. "The Political Career of William Cabell Rives." Ph.D. diss, University of Virginia, 1947.

Dobie, Edith. *The Political Career of Stephen Mallory White*. Stanford University Publications, History, Economics, and Political Science. Vol 2, no. 1. Stanford, Calif.: Stanford University Press, 1927.

Ellis, W. T. *Memories of My Seventy-two Years in the Romantic County of Yuba, California.* Eugene: University of Oregon Press, 1939.

Ellison, Joseph. *California and the Nation, 1850-1869: A Study of the Relations of a Frontier Community with the Federal Government.* University of California Publications in History. Vol. 16. Berkeley: University of California Press, 1927.

Ellison, William Henry. *A Self-Governing Dominion: California, 1849-1860.* Berkeley: University of California Press, 1950.

———. "Memoirs of Hon. William M. Gwin." *California Historical Society Quarterly,* 4 parts, 19 (1940): 1-26, 157-84, 256-77, 344-46.

Ely, James, Jr. *Guardian of Every Other Right: A Constitutional History of Property Rights.* New York: Oxford University Press, 1992.

———. *The Chief Justiceship of Melville W. Fuller, 1888-1910.* Columbia: University of South Carolina Press, 1995.

———. "The Railroad Question Revisited: *Chicago, Milwaukee & St. Paul Railway v. Minnesota* and the Constitutional Limits on State Regulations." *Great Plains Quarterly* 12 (Spring 1992): 121-34.

Fairman, Charles. *Five Justices and the Electoral Commission of 1877.* In *Oliver Wendell Holmes Devise History of the Supreme Court of the United States.* Supplement to vol. 7. New York: Macmillan, 1988.

———. *Reconstruction and Reunion, 1864-88.* In *Oliver Wendell Holmes Devise History of the Supreme Court of the United States.* Vols. 6 and 7. New York: Macmillan, 1971.

———. "The So-Called Granger Cases: Lord Hale and Justice Bradley." *Stanford Law Review* 5 (1953): 587-678.

Feller, Daniel. *The Jacksonian Promise in America, 1815-1840.* Baltimore: Johns Hopkins University Press, 1995.

———. *The Public Lands in Jacksonian Politics.* Madison: University of Wisconsin Press, 1984.

Field, Henry M. *The Life of David Dudley Field.* New York: Charles Scribner's Sons, 1898.

———. *The Story of the Atlantic Telegraph.* New York: Charles Scribner's Sons, 1892.

Field, Stephen J. *Personal Reminiscences of Early Days in California.* 1877. Reprint. New York: Da Capo Press, 1968.

Fiss, Owen M. *Troubled Beginnings of the Modern State, 1888-1910. Vol. 8.* In *Oliver Wendell Holmes Devise History of the Supreme Court of the United States.* New York: Macmillan, 1993.

Flick, Alexander C. *Samuel Jones Tilden: A Study in Political Sagacity.* 1939. Reprint. New York: Kennikat Press, 1963.

Foner, Eric. *Politics and Ideology in the Age of the Civil War.* New York: Oxford University Press, 1980.

———. *Free Soil, Free Labor, Free Men: The Ideology of the Republican Party Before the Civil War.* New York: Oxford University Press, 1970.

———. *Reconstruction, 1763-1877: America's Unfinished Revolution.* New York: Harper and Row, 1988.

Frantz, Laurent B. "Congressional Power to Enforce the Fourteenth Amendment Against Private Acts." *Yale Law Review* 73 (1964): 1353-84.

Frémont, Jessie Benton. *Far West Sketches.* Boston: D. Lothrop, 1890.

Friedman, Jane M. *America's First Woman Lawyer: The Biography of Myra Bradwell.* Buffalo, N.Y.: Prometheus Books, 1993.

Fritz, Christian G. *Federal Justice in California: The Court of Ogden Hoffman, 1851-1891.* Lincoln: University of Nebraska Press, 1991.

———. "Politics and the Courts: The Struggle over Land in San Francisco, 1846–1866." *Santa Clara Law Review* 26 (1986): 127–64.

———. "Popular Sovereignty, Vigilantism, and the Constitutional Right of Revolution." *Pacific Historical Review* 63 (February 1994): 39–66.

Garrett, Lula May. "San Francisco in 1851 as Described by Eyewitnesses." *California Historical Society* 22 (September 1943): 253–80.

Gates, Paul W. *Land and Law in California: Essays on Land Policies.* Ames: Iowa State University Press, 1991.

Gates, Paul et al. *Four Persistent Issues: Essays on California's Land Ownership Concentration, Water Deficits, Sub-State Regionalism, and Congressional Leadership.* Institute of Governmental Studies. Berkeley: University of California, 1978.

George, Henry. *Our Land and Land Policy.* 1871. Reprint. New York: Doubleday and McClure, 1902.

———. "What the Railroad Will Bring Us." *Overland Monthly* 1 (October 1868): 297–306.

Gillman, Howard. *The Constitution Besieged: The Rise and Demise of Lochner Era Police Powers Jurisprudence.* Durham, N.C.: Duke University Press, 1993.

Glickstein, Jonathan A. *Concepts of Free Labor in Antebellum America.* New Haven: Yale University Press, 1991.

Gold, David M. *The Shaping of Nineteenth-Century Law: John Appleton and Responsible Individualism.* Westport, Conn.: Greenwood Press, 1990.

Gordon, John D. III. *Authorized by No Law: The San Francisco Committee of Vigilance of 1856 and the United States Circuit Court for the District of California.* San Francisco: Ninth Judicial Circuit Historical Society, 1987.

Gorham, George C. *Biographical Notice of Stephen J. Field.* Washington, D.C., n.d.

Graham, Howard J. *Everyman's Constitution.* Madison: State Historical Society of Wisconsin, 1968.

The Great Libel Case: Opdyke vs. Weed. New York: American News Company, 1865.

Grodinsky, Julius. *Transcontinental Railway Strategy, 1869-1893: A Study of Businessmen.* Philadelphia: University of Pennsylvania Press, 1962.

Grossman, Lewis. "John C. Frémont, Mariposa, and the Collision of Mexican and American Law." *Western Legal History* 6 (Winter/Spring 1993): 17–50.

Hartley, Katha G. "Spring Valley Water Works v. San Francisco: Defining Economic Rights in San Francisco." *Western Legal History* 3 (Summer/Fall 1990): 287–308.

Hittell, John S. *Resources of California.* San Francisco: A. Roman, 1863.

———. *The History of the City of San Francisco.* San Francisco: A. L. Bancroft, 1878.

Holliday, J. S. *The World Rushed In: The California Gold Rush Experience.* New York: Simon and Schuster, 1981.

Hovenkamp, Herbert. *Enterprise and American Law, 1836-1937.* Cambridge: Harvard University Press, 1991.

Howard, John Raymond. *Remembrance of Things Past.* New York: Thomas Y. Crowell, 1925.

Hughes, Charles Evans. *The Supreme Court of the United States.* 1928. Reprint. New York: Columbia University Press, 1966.

Hutchinson, W. H. "Southern Pacific: Myth and Reality." *California Historical Quarterly* 48 (December 1969): 325-34.

Hyman, Harold M. *A More Perfect Union: The Impact of the Civil War and Reconstruction on the Constitution.* New York: Alfred A. Knopf, 1973.

———. *Era of the Oath: Northern Loyalty Tests During the Civil War and Reconstruction.* Philadelphia: University of Pennsylvania Press, 1954.

Hyman, Harold M., and William M. Wiecek. *Equal Justice Under Law: Constitutional Development 1835-1875.* New York: Harper Torchbooks, 1982.

Irish, John P. "California and the Railroad." *Overland Monthly* 25 (1895): 675-81.

Johnson, David Allan. *Founding the Far West: California, Oregon, and Nevada, 1840-1890.* Berkeley: University of California Press, 1992.

Johnson, J. Edward. *History of Supreme Court Justices of California, 1850-1900.* 2 vols. San Francisco: Bender-Moss Company, 1963.

Jones, Alan. "Republicanism, Railroads, and Nineteenth-Century Midwestern Constitutionalism." In *Liberty, Property, and Government: Constitutional Interpretation Before the New Deal,* ed. Ellen Frankel Paul and Howard Dickman, 239-66. Albany: State University of New York Press, 1989.

Jordan, David M. *Winfield Scott Hancock: A Soldier's Life.* Bloomington: Indiana University Press, 1988.

Judson, Isabella Field, ed. *Cyrus W. Field: His Life and His Work.* New York: Harper and Brothers, 1896.

Julian, George W. *Speeches on Political Questions.* New York: Hurd and Houghton, 1872.

Keller, Morton. *Affairs of State: Public Life in Late Nineteenth Century America.* Cambridge, Mass.: Belknap Press, 1977.

Kelley, Robert. *Battling the Inland Sea: American Political Culture, Public Policy, and the Sacramento Valley, 1850-1986.* Berkeley: University of California Press, 1989.

Kembell, John Haskell. *The Panama Route, 1848-1869.* University of California Publications in History. Vol. 29. Berkeley: University of California Press, 1943.

Kens, Paul. *Judicial Power and Reform Politics: The Anatomy of Lochner v. New York.* Lawrence: University Press of Kansas, 1990.

———. "Liberty and the Public Ingredient of Private Property." *Review of Politics* (Winter 1993): 85-116.

Keynes, Edward. *Liberty, Property, and Privacy: Toward a Jurisprudence of Substantive Due Process.* University Park: Pennsylvania State University Press, 1996.

Klaus, Samuel, ed. *The Milligan Case.* New York: Alfred A. Knopf, 1929.

Kohl, Lawrence Frederick. *The Politics of Individualism: Parties and the American Character in the Jacksonian Era.* New York: Oxford University Press, 1989.

Kurland, Philip B., and Gerhard Casper, eds. *Landmark Briefs and Arguments of the Supreme Court of the United States: Constitutional Law.* Washington, D.C.: University Publications of America, 1975.

Kutler, Stanley I. *Judicial Power and Reconstruction Politics.* Chicago: University of Chicago Press, 1968.

Labbé, Ronald M. "New Light on the Slaughterhouse Monopoly Act of 1869." In *Louisiana's Legal Heritage,* ed. Edward F. Haas, 143–62. Pensacola, Fla.: Perdido Bay Press, 1983.

Levy, Jo Ann. *They Saw the Elephant: Women and the California Gold Rush.* Hamden, Conn.: Archon Books, 1990.

Lewis, Oscar. *Sea Routes to the Gold Fields: The Migration by Water to California in 1849–1852.* New York: Alfred A. Knopf, 1949.

———. *The Big Four.* New York: Alfred A. Knopf, 1938.

Lotchin, Roger W. *San Francisco, 1846–1856: From Hamlet to City.* New York: Oxford University Press, 1974.

Lynch, Jeremiah. *The Life of David C. Broderick: A Senator of the Fifties.* New York: Baker and Taylor, 1911.

Magrath, C. Peter. *Morrison R. Waite: The Triumph of Character.* New York: Macmillan, 1963.

Magruder, Allan B. "Removal of Suits from State to Federal Courts." *American Law Review* 13 (1879): 434–62.

Maltz, Earl M. *Civil Rights, the Constitution, and Congress, 1863–1869.* Lawrence, Kans.: University Press of Kansas, 1990.

———. "The Federal Government and the Problem of Chinese Rights in the Era of the Fourteenth Amendment." *Harvard Journal of Law and Public Policy* 17 (Winter 1994): 223–52.

Marks, Paula Mitchell. *Precious Dust: The American Gold Rush Era, 1848–1900.* New York: William Morrow, 1994.

Martin, Albro. *Railroads Triumphant: The Growth, Rejection, and Rebirth of a Vital American Force.* New York: Oxford University Press, 1992.

McAffee, Ward M. "Local Interests and Railroad Regulation in California During the Granger Decade." *Pacific Historical Review* 37 (February 1968): 51–66.

McClain, Charles J. *In Search of Equality: The Chinese Struggle Against Discrimination in Nineteenth-Century America.* Berkeley: University of California Press, 1994.

———. "The Chinese Struggle for Civil Rights in Nineteenth-Century America: The First Phase, 1850–1870." *Law and California Review* (1984): 529–68.

McClain, Charles J., and Laurene Wu McClain. "The Chinese Contribution to the Development of American Law." In *Entry Denied,* ed., Sucheng Chan, pp. 8–12. Philadelphia: Temple University Press, 1991.

McCloskey, Robert Green. *American Conservatism in the Age of Enterprise, 1865–1910.* New York: Harper Torchbooks, 1951.

McCurdy, Charles W. "Justice Field and the Jurisprudence of Government-Business Relations: Some Parameters of Laissez-Faire Constitutionalism, 1863–1897." *Journal of American History* 61 (March 1975): 970–1005.

———. "Stephen J. Field and the American Judicial Tradition." In *The Fields and the Law*, J. Bergan et al., 5–20. San Francisco: U.S. District Court for the Northern District of California Historical Society, 1986.

———. "Stephen J. Field and Public Land Law Development in California, 1850–1866: A Case Study of Judicial Resource Allocation in Nineteenth-Century America." *Law and Society* 10 (Winter 1976): 235–66.

———. "The Roots of 'Liberty of Contract' Reconsidered: Major Premises in the Law of Employment, 1867–1937." *Yearbook of the Supreme Court Historical Society* (1984): 20–33.

McGuire, James K., ed. *The Democratic Party of the State of New York*. 3 vols. New York: United States History Company, 1905.

McMurtrie, Richard C. "A New Canon of Constitutional Interpretation." *American Law Register* 32 (January 1893): 1–9.

Mendelson, Wallace. "A Missing Link in the Evolution of Due Process." *Vanderbilt Law Review* 10 (1956): 125–37.

Meyers, Marvin. *The Jacksonian Persuasion: Politics and Belief*. Stanford, Calif.: Stanford University Press, 1957.

Miller, George H. *The Railroads and the Granger Laws*. Madison: University of Wisconsin Press, 1971.

Miller, Stuart Creighton. *The Unwelcome Immigrant: The American Image of the Chinese, 1785–1882*. Berkeley: University of California Press, 1969.

Mooney, Ralph James. "Matthew Deady and the Federal Judicial Response to Racism in the Early West." *Oregon Law Review* 63 (1984): 561–648.

Morgan, H. Wayne. *From Hayes to McKinley: National Party Politics, 1877–1896*. Syracuse, N.Y.: Syracuse University Press, 1969.

Neely, Mark E., Jr. *The Fate of Liberty: Abraham Lincoln and Civil Liberties*. New York: Oxford University Press, 1991.

Nelson, William E. *The Fourteenth Amendment: From Political Principle to Judicial Doctrine*. Cambridge: Harvard University Press, 1988.

Nevins, Allan. *Frémont: Pathmarker of the West*. Lincoln: Bison Books, University of Nebraska Press, 1992.

Newmark, Harris. *Sixty Years in Southern California, 1853–1913*. New York: Knickerbocker Press, 1916.

Novak, William J. "Public Economy and the Well-Ordered Market: Law and Economic Regulation in Nineteenth-Century America." *Law and Social Inquiry* 18 (Winter 1993): 1–32.

———. The People's Welfare, Law and Regulation in Nineteenth-Century America. Chapel Hill: University of North Carolina Press, 1996.

O'Meara, James. *Broderick and Gwin*. San Francisco: Bacon, 1881.

Orsi, Richard J. "The *Octopus* Reconsidered: The Southern Pacific and Agricultural Modernization in California, 1865–1915." *California Historical Society Quarterly* 54 (1975): 197–220.

Palmer, Robert C. "The Parameters of Constitutional Reconstruction: Slaughter-House, Cruikshank, and the Fourteenth Amendment." *University of Illinois Law Review* (1984): 739–70.

Parke, Charles Ross. *Dreams to Dust: A Diary of the California Gold Rush*. Ed. James E. Davis. Lincoln: University of Nebraska Press, 1989.

Paul, Rodman W. *California Gold: The Beginning of Mining in the Far West.* Lincoln: University of Nebraska Press, 1947.

Pomeroy, John Norton. *Some Account of the Work of Stephen J. Field.* 1881. Reprint. Littleton, Colo.: Fred B. Rothman, 1986.

Porter, Mary Cornelia. "That Commerce Shall Be Free." *Supreme Court Review* (1976): 135–59.

Pound, Roscoe. "Liberty of Contract." *Yale Law Journal* 18 (1909): 454ff.

Przybyszewski, Linda C. A. "Judge Lorenzo Sawyer and the Chinese: Civil Rights Decisions in the Ninth Circuit." *Western Legal History* (Winter/Spring 1988): 23–56.

Ramey, Earl. "The Beginnings of Marysville." *California Historical Quarterly,* 3 parts, 14 (September 1935): 195–229; 14 (December 1935): 375–407; 15 (March 1936): 21–57.

Randall, J. G. *Constitutional Problems Under Lincoln.* Urbana: University of Illinois Press, 1951.

Reid, John Phillip. *In Defiance of the Law.* Chapel Hill: University of North Carolina Press, 1981.

———. *Law for the Elephant: Property and Social Behavior on the Overland Trail.* San Marino, Calif.: Huntington Library, 1980.

Riddleberger, Patrick W. *George Washington Julian: Radical Republican.* Indiana Historical Bureau, 1966.

Riggs, Robert E. "Substantive Due Process in 1791." *Wisconsin Law Review* (1990): 941–1003.

Robbins, Roy M. *Our Landed Heritage: The Public Domain, 1776–1970.* 2d ed. Lincoln: University of Nebraska Press, 1976.

Robinson, W. W. *Land in California.* Berkeley: University of California Press, 1948.

Roche, John P. "Entrepreneurial Liberty and the Fourteenth Amendment." *Labor History* 4 (Winter 1963): 3–31.

Rolle, Andrew. *John Charles Frémont.* Norman: University of Oklahoma Press, 1991.

Roosevelt, Theodore. "Judges and Progress." *Outlook,* January 6, 1912, 42.

Royce, Josiah. *Studies of Good and Evil.* 1889. Reprint. Hamden, Conn.: Archon Books, 1964.

Russ, Carolyn Hale, ed. *The Log of a Forty-Niner.* Boston: B. J. Brimmer, 1923.

Sandmeyer, Elmer Clarence. *The Anti-Chinese Movement in California.* Urbana; University of Illinois Press, 1939.

Saxton, Alexander. *The Indispensable Enemy: Labor and the Anti-Chinese Movement in California.* Berkeley: University of California Press, 1971.

Scheiber, Harry N. "Race, Radicalism, and Reform: Historical Perspective on the 1879 California Constitution." *Hastings Constitutional Law Quarterly* 17 (Fall 1989): 35–80.

Schlesinger, Arthur M., Jr. *The Age of Jackson.* Boston: Little, Brown, 1945.

Schmidt, Benno, Jr. "Juries, Jurisdiction, and Race Discrimination: The Lost Promise of Strauder v. West Virginia." *Texas Law Review* 61 (May 1983): 1401–99.

Schwartz, Bernard. *A History of the Supreme Court.* New York: Oxford University Press, 1993.

Sellers, Charles. *The Market Revolution: Jacksonian America, 1815-1846.* New York: Oxford University Press, 1991.

Selvin, Molly. *This Tender and Delicate Business: Public Trust Doctrine in American Law and Economic Policy, 1789-1920.* New York: Garland, 1987.

Senkewicz, Robert M., S.J. *Vigilantes in Gold Rush San Francisco.* Stanford, Calif.: Stanford University Press, 1985.

Shinn, Howard. *Mining Camps: A Study in American Frontier Government.* New York: Alfred A. Knopf, 1948.

Shutes, Milton H. *Lincoln and California.* Stanford, Calif.: Stanford University Press, 1943.

Silver, David M. *Lincoln's Supreme Court.* (Urbana: University of Illinois Press, 1956.

Sprague, A. P., ed. *Speeches, Arguments, and Miscellaneous Papers of David Dudley Field.* 3 vols. New York: D. Appleton, 1884.

Sproat, John G. *The Best Men.* New York: Oxford University Press, 1968.

Starr, Kevin. *Americans and the California Dream, 1850-1915.* New York: Oxford University Press, 1986.

Steinfeld, Robert J. *The Invention of Free Labor: The Employment Relation in English and American Law and Culture, 1350-1870.* Chapel Hill: University of North Carolina Press, 1991.

Stillman, J. D. B. "The Last Tie." *Overland Monthly* 3 (1869): 77-84.

Swisher, Carl Brent. *History of the Supreme Court of the United States: The Taney Period, 1836-1864.* Vol. 5. *Oliver Wendell Holmes Devise History of the Supreme Court.* New York: Macmillan, 1974.

————. *Motivation and Political Technique in the California Constitutional Convention, 1878-79.* New York: Da Capo Press, 1969.

————. *Stephen J. Field: Craftsman of the Law.* 1930. Reprint. Hamden, Conn.: Archon Books, 1963.

Thompson, Seymour D. "Abuses of the Writ of Habeas Corpus." *American Law Review* 18 (1884): 1-23.

Tsai, Shih-shan Henry. *The Chinese Experience in America.* Bloomington and Indianapolis: Indiana University Press, 1986.

Turner, William. *Documents in Relation to Charges Preferred by Stephen J. Field and Others Before the House of Assembly of the State of California Against Wm. R. Turner.* 2d ed. San Francisco: Whittin Towne and Company, 1856.

Twiss, Benjamin R. *Lawyers and the Constitution.* Princeton: Princeton University Press, 1942.

Umbeck, John R. *A Theory of Property Rights: With Application to the California Gold Rush.* Ames: Iowa State University Press, 1981.

van Ee, Daun. *David Dudley Field and the Reconstruction of the Law.* New York: Garland, 1986.

Watson, Harry L. *Liberty and Power: The Politics of Jacksonian America.* New York: Noonday Press, 1990.

Wiecek, William. *Liberty Under Law: The Supreme Court in American Life.* Baltimore: Johns Hopkins University Press, 1988.

————. "The Reconstruction of Federal Judicial Power, 1863-1875." *American Journal of Legal History* 13 (October 1969): 333-59.

Wilkins, James H., ed. *The Great Diamond Hoax and Other Stirring Incidents in the Life of Asbury Harpending*. Norman: University of Oklahoma Press, 1958.

Williams, David A. *David C. Broderick: A Political Portrait*. San Marino, Calif.: Huntington Library, 1969.

Williams, John Hoyt. *A Great and Shining Road: The Epic Story of the Transcontinental Railroad*. New York: Times Books, 1988.

Williams, R. Hal. *The Democratic Party and California Politics, 1880–1896*. Stanford, Calif.: Stanford University Press, 1973.

Wilson, Don W. *Governor Charles Robinson of Kansas*. Lawrence: University Press of Kansas, 1975.

Wiltsee, Ernest A. *Gold Rush Steamers of the Pacific*. 1938. Reprint. Lawrence, Mass.: Quarterman Publications, 1976.

Wingfield, Russell Stewart. *William Cabell Rives: A Biography*. Richmond, Va.: Richmond College Historical Papers, 1915.

Wright, Charles Alan. "Authenticity of 'A Dirtier Day's Work' Quote in Question." *Supreme Court Historical Society Quarterly* 13 (Winter 1990): 6–7.

Wunder, John R. "Anti-Chinese Violence in the American West, 1850–1910." In *Law for the Elephant, Law for the Beaver: Essays in Legal History of the North American West,* ed. John McLaren, Hamar Foster, and Chet Orloff, 212–36. Pasadena, Calif.: Ninth Judicial Circuit Historical Society, 1992.

Wyman, Mark. *Hard Rock Epic: Western Miners and the Industrial Revolution, 1860–1910*. Berkeley: University of California Press, 1979.

Wyman, Walker D., ed. *California Emigrant Letters*. New York: Bookman Associates, 1952.

Yen, Tzu-Kuei. "Chinese Workers and the First Transcontinental Railroad of the United States of America." Ph.D. diss., St. John's University, N.Y., 1976.

Pamphlets, Documents, Reports, and Records

Congressional Globe. 46 vols. Washington, D.C., 1834–1873.

Debates and Proceedings of the Constitutional Convention of the State of California. C. B. Willis and P. K. Stockton, official stenographers. 3 vols. Sacramento, 1880.

"The Gold Key Court or the Corruptions of a Majority of It." Pamphlet, Huntington Library, signed "Ex-Supreme Court Broker, n.d.

"Invalidity of the Queue Ordinance." Library of Congress, microfilm, call no. F870. C5U5, 1879.

Journals of the Legislature of the State of California and Its Second Session. Eugene Casserly, State Printer, 1851.

"Judge Field: Sound in Doctrine, Brave in Deed." Campaign pamphlet, Library of Congress call no. E664, f46J9.

Official Proceedings of the Democratic National Convention of 1880. Dayton, Ohio: Daily Journal Book and Job Rooms, 1882.

"A Possible Solution of the Chinese Problem: Views of Mr. Justice Field, from the *San Francisco Argonaut,* of August 9, 1879." Reading room, Library of Congress.

Statutes of California. 1850.

Stephen J. Field: His Character and Career as It Is Known in California. [1889?] Pamphlet, Huntington Library.

U.S. Statutes at Large.

U.S. Supreme Court Records and Briefs. Microfilm, Scholarly Resources, Wilmington, Del.

Archives

Thomas F. Bayard Collection. Library of Congress.

Salmon P. Chase. Papers. Historical Society of Pennsylvania. Philadelphia.

Grover Cleveland. Papers. Library of Congress. Portland.

Matthew Deady Collection. Oregon Historical Society.

Don Dickinson Papers. Papers. Library of Congress.

William Maxwell Evarts. Correspondence. Library of Congress.

Cyrus W. Field. Papers. New York Public Library, Special Collections.

Stephen J. Field Collection. Bancroft Library, University of California, Berkeley.

Field-Musgrave Collection. Perkins Library, Duke University, Durham, N.C.

Horace Gray. Papers. Library of Congress.

Harrison Family Collection. Library of Congress.

Theodore Hittle. Notes re *Personal Reminiscences of Early Days in California.* Sutro Branch, California State Library, San Francisco.

Abraham Lincoln. Papers. Library of Congress.

Manton Marble. Papers. Library of Congress.

J. DeBarth Shorb Collection. Huntington Library.

Samuel J. Tilden. Papers. New York Public Library, Special Collections.

Morrison R. Waite. Letterbooks. Library of Congress.

————. Papers. Library of Congress.

Newspapers and Magazines

Alta California (San Francisco)
Argonaut (San Francisco)
Atlanta Constitution
Chicago Tribune
Cincinnati Commercial
Cincinnati Enquirer
Deseret News (Salt Lake City)
Marysville Herald
Memphis Daily Appeal
Missouri Republican
Nation
New Orleans Times-Picayune
New York Herald
New York Sun
New York Times

New York Tribune
New York World
North American Review
Outlook
Overland Monthly
Philadelphia Inquirer
Richmond (Va.) *State*
Sacramento Daily Bee
Sacramento Union
San Francisco Chronicle
San Francisco Evening Bulletin
San Francisco Examiner
San Francisco Record-Union
Settlers' and Miners' Tribune (Sacramento)
St. Louis Globe Democrat
Washington Post

INDEX

Cases